WRITING
THE
AMISH

PENNSYLVANIA GERMAN HISTORY AND CULTURE SERIES,
NUMBER 5

Publications of the Pennsylvania German Society,
Volume 38 (2004)

Editor
Simon J. Bronner
The Pennsylvania State University, Harrisburg

EDITED BY DAVID L. WEAVER-ZERCHER

WRITING THE AMISH

THE WORLDS OF
JOHN A. HOSTETLER

THE PENNSYLVANIA STATE UNIVERSITY PRESS
UNIVERSITY PARK, PENNSYLVANIA

A KEYSTONE BOOK

A Keystone Book is so designated to distinguish it from the typical scholarly monograph that a university press publishes. It is a book intended to serve the citizens of Pennsylvania by educating them and others, in an entertaining way, about aspects of the history, culture, society, and environment of the state as part of the Middle Atlantic region.

Library of Congress Cataloging-in-Publication Data

Writing the Amish the worlds of John A. Hostetler / edited by David L. Weaver-Zercher.
p.   cm.—(Publications of the Pennsylvania German Society ; v. 38.
Pennsylvania German History and Culture series, number 5)
Includes bibliographical references and index.
ISBN 0-271-02686-3 (alk. paper)
1. Amish—United States-Historiography.
2. Hostetler, John Andrew, 1918– .
3. Historians—United States—Biography.
4. Ethnologists—United States—Biography.
5. Ethnology—United States.
6. Amish—United States—Social life and customs.
7. Amish—United States—Social conditions.
I. Weaver-Zercher, David, 1960– .
II. Publications of the Pennsylvania German Society (2001).
Pennsylvania German history and culture series ; no.5.

E184 .M45W75   2005
305.6'89773'0722—dc22
2005008352

The Pennsylvania State University Press
is a member of the Association of American University Presses.

It is the policy of The Pennsylvania State University Press
to use acid-free paper. Publications on uncoated stock
satisfy the minimum requirements of
American National Standard for Information Sciences—
Permanence of Paper for Printed Library Materials,
ANSI Z39.48–1992.

Contents

Illustrations

Foreword

Ann Hostetler

As an Amish-born scholar of the Amish people, John A. Hostetler embodied the tensions of relating to both the Amish and academic worlds. As his daughter, I was privileged to observe the many ways in which he sought to integrate his heritage and faith with his vocation as a "cultural worker." Paradoxically, my father's decision as a young adult not to join the Amish church enabled him to maintain close friendships among the Amish throughout his life. The Amish do not shun all who leave the community, only those who take the vows of church membership and then leave. Even though he traveled a wide social register, my father always kept in close contact with his family of origin and made sure that we, his children, felt connected to his brothers and sisters—through frequent visits and a decades-old family circle letter, which continues to this day.

When I was growing up I spent a week every summer on the farm of my father's Old Order Amish sister and her husband in Pennsylvania's Kishacoquillas (Big) Valley, my father's birthplace. During these weeks I encountered something of what my father valued so much in his culture of origin. Daily routines centered on the agricultural rhythms of small farm life. Water flowed from the mountain behind the house into the taps, so it was always plentiful, cold, and clear. My sisters and I washed dishes, tended the garden, helped with canning, and rode in the buggy to the store or the meat locker. We collected ladybugs from the garden and built matchbox houses for them; on rainy days we raced marbles on a handmade wooden marble roller or looked at slides of exotic places through a View-Master. When my grown cousins and their families would gather at my Old Order aunt and uncle's home, we would turn homemade ice cream with whatever fruit was in season—strawberries or peaches from the garden or market, blackberries and raspberries culled from the mountainside—and gather around the kitchen table expanded with a half-dozen extra boards. I didn't realize it then, but not everyone in the family would have been able to sit at this table.

Because of my grandfather's excommunication from the Amish church, followed by the decisions of some of his children not to join the Old Order Amish, my father's family spanned a spectrum of Amish, Mennonite, and "other" affiliations. His oldest sister was the only member of the family to remain Old Order; his oldest brother became a Mennonite in Iowa. His second sister married into the Old Order church, but she and her minister husband left with the split that became the Beachy Amish, which allowed black cars and electricity. My father's three other siblings represented conservative Mennonite and nondenominational affiliations. Within this spectrum it was clear to all of us that the Old Order way of life held something special for my father, and he found no better way to instruct us about it than to immerse us in that world—as beloved children and welcomed guests—so that we could experience it at its least problematic.

My father worked a great deal at home, although our mother clearly instructed my sisters and me to respect the closed door to his study. When it was open, we could knock and softly creep in to use paper, pens, markers, scissors, and stapler, as long as the tools were returned to their proper places. He also found more active ways to involve us. I remember collating, with my sister Mary, a seventy-one-page research report, which we laid out in stacks on the desks in a Penn State-Ogontz classroom. Although I remember this event with the same kind of affection with which I remember picking strawberries in my aunt's garden, my mother recently informed me that this was the summer my father's grant funds had run out, so the whole family had to pitch in and help. Although his own family had been painfully fragmented by his father's struggles with the Amish church, my father cherished and nurtured a holistic sense of family enterprise, a legacy from Amish culture that he particularly valued.

My mother, Beulah Stauffer Hostetler, met my father when she was an editor at the Mennonite Publishing House in Scottdale, Pennsylvania. They shared interests in writing, publishing, and religious and intellectual concerns. He consulted with her on all of his writing projects, and she was his most important confidante and critic. Always reading his work before it went to press, she helped him to accommodate his more strongly stated views to a wider reading public. After she entered a Ph.D. program in religious thought at the University of Pennsylvania during my high school years, my mother became less involved with my father's work, but our dinner table conversations, now seasoned with Troeltsch and Kierkegaard, grew more interesting. I saw my father take a renewed delight in these exchanges. No doubt the stimulation, if not the actual substance, of some of these conversations is reflected in his later revisions of *Amish Society* and other thinking about communal sectarian groups.

When I was somewhere between nine and twelve years old, my father would often take me along on his trips to Lancaster County, where he would visit Amish contacts and conduct clandestine reviews of tourist venues. I remember sitting in a docent lecture at the Amish Farm and House and hearing that Amish persons were only allowed to use green and blue as decorating colors because these were the colors of the earth and sky. I snickered at such absurdity; the overt use of nature symbolism seemed entirely foreign to my sense of Amish semiotics. Yet as I recalled my aunt's living room, I remembered that the window blinds were a dark forest green, and as I tried to recall the color of her walls, they became tinged, at least in my imagination, with a faint shade of blue. Through this experience I learned the power of interpretive paradigms and the ways in which they can color our perceptions, whether or not they are accurate.

In his work to articulate Amish culture and in his evaluation of the work of others, my father's first concern was accuracy of representation. He eschewed not only portrayals of the Amish that perpetuated literary stereotypes, but also any visual distortions of the Amish—from the sentimental and highly stylized to the caricatured and ridiculous. Refusing at first to use photographs in his books out of sensitivity to the Amish prohibition of photography, he commissioned a set of drawings for the first edition of *Amish Life*. When his publisher pushed harder for photographs, my father reluctantly agreed, trying to use pictures of those who had not yet joined the church. Later he broadened his selection of photographs—after all, there were thousands already in circulation—but he always sought to be respectful in his selections. I spent many hours with him at photographic exhibitions as he searched for pictures he thought would be illustrative, aesthetically pleasing, and acceptable to his Amish subjects.

My father's lifelong motivation was to portray the Amish as an American sectarian group deserving of respect rather than ridicule. In his own work he was concerned to find a hermeneutic within Amish culture, to elucidate the internal logic of the community. This concern served his Amish subjects well in *Wisconsin v. Yoder*, the 1972 Supreme Court case that exempted Amish children from mandatory high school attendance. While the Supreme Court does not actually "hear" expert testimony—only summaries of the case presented by lawyers for the opposing sides—my father's testimony in a lower court case was amply quoted by defense lawyer William B. Ball. I was there to hear it. In fact, our entire family accompanied my father to Washington, D.C., that eventful day. As a senior in high school, I found this trip tremendously exciting, enhanced by my mother's narrative of the importance of my father's contribution to this historic moment (he was the doer and she was the interpreter and evaluator as far as our understanding of my father's career was concerned). He showed us by example what he felt was important: in this case, the beauty of religious freedom and the power of the Supreme Court to uphold it. He deeply valued the opportunity for every member of our small family community to witness a moment in which this beauty and power was revealed.

My father's effort to balance objectivity and accuracy with a judicious activism was not always comfortable—for him or for others—as exemplified in the controversy over the filming of *Witness* in Lancaster County. But over the years the thousands of phone calls and letters my father received drew him into the role of cultural arbiter as well as scholar. For his family, these communications—from the Amish and Hutterites, from spiritual seekers and curious scholars, from lawyers, government officials, and the media—became part of the furniture of our daily life, but for him they represented the lifeblood of his work and calling. The enormous energy he put into relating to people and facilitating connections between and among them seems astounding to me now. Yet it came out of a sincere desire to integrate his life and work in a holistic way. In this sense he was as much an artist as an anthropologist, translating the integration of life and work, an Amish ideal, into the circumstances of his own rich and complex modern life, in which he served as ambassador among multiple worlds.

Preface and Acknowledgments

Attributions of scholarly preeminence rarely go uncontested. Still, it would be hard to counter the claim that, from the early 1960s to the late 1980s, John A. Hostetler (1918–2001) was the world's premier scholar of Amish life. His ascendance to that position came in 1963, when Johns Hopkins Press published the first edition of his magnum opus, *Amish Society*. Hostetler later enjoyed telling of the many rejection letters he received in the years prior to 1963, the exceedingly polite correspondence that outlined the risks of publishing books about small religious sects. In retrospect, of course, the Old Order Amish were not just any religious sect. Similarly, *Amish Society* was not just any book. Whereas previous works on Amish life had been sensationalized, reductively theological, or otherwise lacking in sociological depth, *Amish Society* proved to be intimately informed, intelligently analytical, and eminently readable. All this led one reviewer to deem *Amish Society* "far and away" the best book on the subject, one that towered over other offerings "like a skyscraper over a city of cabins." Although the reviewer's urban simile may have been misplaced for a book about the Amish, the gist of his assessment was apt. By 1993, *Amish Society* had reached its fourth edition and had sold over 100,000 copies.

The significance of Hostetler's work goes beyond mere sales figures, however, to the way he shaped both scholarly and public perceptions of the Amish. In that regard, his work cannot be separated from the mid-twentieth-century context in which it appeared, a context in which the Amish were quickly being transformed from a peculiar but little-known Pennsylvania German sect into a renowned cultural phenomenon, an American icon. The publicity-shy Amish did not seek this renown, and Hostetler, himself born and raised in an Amish home, sympathized with their desire to be left alone, away from the glare of flashbulbs and the glitz of tourist enterprises. Nonetheless, this cultural and consumerist embrace of the Amish paved the way for Hostetler's work, not only *Amish Society* and its corresponding scholarly publications, but also the many pieces he published for popular audiences, including his tourist-oriented *Amish Life*. Whatever the venue, Hostetler sought to use his social scientific expertise and his considerable knowledge of Amish life to paint authentic and respectful portraits of his Amish subjects—to *inscribe* onto readers' minds a narrative that commended the Amish, their style of living, and their place in American life. The result was a symbiotic, if somewhat accidental, relationship between the Amish and their leading mediator: even as the renown of the Amish helped to secure audiences for Hostetler's ethnographic work, Hostetler's success at "writing the Amish" served to bolster esteem for the sect in the American imagination.

To reduce Hostetler to a scholar of Amish life would both underestimate his historical contributions and his significance for continuing scholarly reflection. He was first and foremost a scholar, and his many other roles were augmented, if not enabled, by his status as a highly regarded university professor. At the same time, Hostetler determined that his responsibility to his Amish subjects went far beyond the production of evenhanded academic treatises and informed public lectures. First, Hostetler knew that, in America's marketplace of ideas, the academy was only one vendor. For that reason he remained closely attuned to popular presentations of Amish life, adding his own offerings to that eclectic mix even as he worked, sometimes surreptitiously, to censor other portrayals that he found problematic. Second, Hostetler knew that Amish society, though stable and strong, was nonetheless vulnerable to the decisions and activities of "the English" (non-Amish persons and entities), a vulnerability that, in many cases, was exacerbated by Amish tendencies toward reticence and nonresistance. Hostetler therefore frequently assumed the role of advocate for Amish people and culture, speaking to the powerful (including the United States Supreme Court) on behalf of Amish people and their interests. Of course, it was not possible for him to advocate on behalf of the Amish without also criticizing certain elements of the larger society in which the Amish lived. In this respect, Hostetler was also a cultural critic, censuring aspects of North American life that, in his view, were harmful to the Amish and, moreover, to English persons who embraced mainstream social practices unreflectively. Writer, lecturer, arbiter, advocate, and cultural critic—Hostetler assumed all of these roles with vigor, and he eventually came to see them all as one piece. It was his calling, he believed, to nurture a safer, more respectful environment for the Amish, an environment in which Amish culture could not only survive but also thrive.

This volume seeks both to recount and assess Hostetler's Amish-related work. It is not a comprehensive consideration of Hostetler's scholarship, which explored topics other than the Amish, let alone a comprehensive consideration of his life. Rather, this volume focuses specifically on aspects of Hostetler's life and career related to his work among the Amish. The first part of the book, entitled "Perspectives on John A. Hostetler," consists of four reflective essays in which Hostetler himself is the primary subject, the first one written by Hostetler at the close of his career, the other three written by others and published for the first time in this volume. The second part of the book, "Writings of John A. Hostetler," reprints in chronological order fourteen of Hostetler's many writings, all except one of them (a letter to Amish bishops, written in 1944) previously published between 1951 and 1989.

Our goal in assembling this volume is threefold. First, we hope that, by gathering Hostetler's writings, we will provide students of Amish-Mennonite life (and ethnographers more generally) with access to the Hostetler corpus and, correspondingly, with tools to evaluate his work, his intellectual evolution, and his significance as a scholar of Amish life. Second, we aim through this volume to contextualize Hostetler's work, both in the smaller streams of Amish-Mennonite history as well as in the broader social currents that shaped academic culture and North American society in the mid- to late-twentieth century. Third, we hope to advance a discussion on the nature of ethnographic representation, particularly as it pertains to the Old Order Amish. Given the renown of the Amish and the corresponding desire of English mediators to represent (and, in some instances, commodify) them, it is surprising how little scholarly reflection has been done on this topic. We hope that this book, which explores the complexity of the ethnographic task, will enhance this nascent discussion.

In ways both figurative and literal, this volume is an extension of Hostetler's work. In the more figurative sense, he demonstrated a keen interest in the way the Amish were portrayed in the cultural marketplace; indeed, his own autobiographical reflections testify to this concern as the impetus for his entry into Amish-themed representational work. More literally, this volume emerged from Hostetler's last scholarly undertaking, a book-length manuscript that combined autobiography with a few of his Amish-related writings. Hostetler undertook this project in the mid-1990s, but ill health forced him to abandon it before it was completed. Still, the manuscript was sufficiently developed that The Pennsylvania State University Press expressed interest in publishing it as part of its Pennsylvania German History and Culture Series, co-published with the Pennsylvania German Society. From 1999 to 2001, Hostetler (and after his death in 2001, his family) worked with editor Susan Fisher Miller to refine the manuscript, with much of their attention going to the redaction of Hostetler's autobiographical writing. In 2003, I was invited to edit the manuscript, a process that resulted in the addition of the three retrospective essays on Hostetler's work and a revised, expanded list of Hostetler's publications. The result is no doubt different from the manuscript Hostetler envisioned, and it is likely that he would disagree with some of its assertions. At the very least, the Amish-born Hostetler, ever sensitive to the perils of pride, would have been embarrassed by the first two sentences of this preface—the assertion that, for nearly three decades, he was the premier interpreter of Amish life. But clearly he was, which makes this volume, a coupling of his more influential writings with a critical assessment of his work, so important.

Like all scholarly undertakings, the production of this work was a shared endeavor, though given the way this particular volume emerged, it was more communal than most. As noted, Hostetler himself initiated the project, and he was assisted in various ways by Susan Fisher Miller as well as his family members, particularly his wife, Beulah Stauffer Hostetler. When the volume was reassigned to me in 2004, Fisher Miller and the Hostetler family continued to provide information, counsel, and feedback, even as they relinquished editorial control. I am indebted to their wisdom and their graciousness.

Others contributed to the project in various ways. Simon J. Bronner and Donald B. Kraybill were not looking for more work when I asked them to write retrospective essays for the volume, but they graciously consented, as did Ann Hostetler with respect to writing the foreword. The staff in the Special Collections Library at Penn State University (where most of Hostetler's papers are housed) demonstrated considerable patience and good humor in tracking down my requests for boxes and books; Jackie Esposito, in particular, went beyond the call of duty in assisting me there. Joe Springer at the Mennonite Historical Library in Goshen, Indiana, located resources for me, as did John Sharp and Dennis Stoesz at the Mennonite Church USA Archives, also in Goshen. Two other library staffs were of great help: Messiah College's Murray Library in Grantham, Pennsylvania (particularly Mike Brown, Beth Mark, Deb Roof, and Dee Porterfield), and the Lancaster Mennonite Historical Library in Lancaster, Pennsylvania (particularly Steve Ness, Brinton Rutherford, and Lloyd Zeager). Moreover, I continue to benefit from the helpfulness I received years ago from David Luthy at the Heritage Historical Library in Aylmer, Ontario. Others who tracked down information for me or otherwise assisted in this project include Josh Byler, Leonard Gross, Betty Hartzler, S. Duane Kauffman, Albert Keim, Sanford King, Elmer Miller, Levi Miller, Steven Nolt, Debbie Owen, Tammy Owens, Ron Pen, Stephen Scott, Lesley Spute, Diane Zimmerman Umble, G. C. Waldrep, Richard Weaver, Ruth Weaver, Valerie Weaver-Zercher, and Percy Yoder. Lynn Cockett and Bill White opened their home to me as I traveled to State College, and Julia Kasdorf provided me with hospitality while I was there. I am particularly indebted to Julia for sharing materials with me, and for freely offering her own ideas about John A. Hostetler and his work, ideas that have no doubt influenced mine.

Peter Potter, editor-in-chief at The Pennsylvania State University Press, demonstrated knowledge and professionalism every step of the way, not least in securing permission to reprint Hostetler's previously published writings. Simon J. Bronner, who serves as the series editor of the Pennsylvania German History and Culture Series, invited me to edit this volume and helped me to shape its contours. He, along with Peter Potter and Donald B. Kraybill, repeatedly offered counsel as I drafted and redrafted the volume's contents. Later, Tim Holsopple provided expert copyediting assistance. Ultimately, the responsibility for the volume's content falls upon me, but the decision-making and editing processes were nonetheless joint endeavors.

I would not have completed this project had Messiah College not awarded me a sabbatical for the 2003–4 school year, which I spent with my family in the hospitable embrace of the Hindman Settlement School in Hindman, Kentucky. Nor would I have completed the project had my wife, Valerie, not shielded me from our two young boys every morning so that I could write for a few hours. About two-thirds of the way through the project, three-year-old Samuel began writing his own "chapters" on our computer, sometimes telling me that, if I could wait for "just ten more minutes," he would then be able to play with me. I hope I didn't use that line on Samuel *too* often, but the evidence seems to indicate otherwise.

Finally, I am indebted to the work of John A. Hostetler. In the middle of my work on this project, I received a phone call from a scholar who wanted to do ethnographic work among the Amish and was having trouble gaining access to an Amish community. I begged off, telling her (honestly) that my work on the Amish hasn't been ethnographic and (a little less honestly, perhaps) that I didn't have many contacts in Amish communities. That one small event helped me to realize, at least in part, what a difficult task Hostetler faced in being a scholar, mediator, gatekeeper, and advocate for Amish life and culture. His scholarship set a high standard, establishing a legacy that makes this volume both possible and appropriate. At the same time, the complexity of his position and the delicacy of his task were considerable, even daunting. His mediating work was not for the faint of heart; it was, however, undertaken by a person who had

Amish interests at heart. I can only hope that this volume treats Hostetler with the same respect he afforded his Amish subjects.

David L. Weaver-Zercher
Hindman, Kentucky
2004

PART I

Perspectives on John A. Hostetler

The four essays in Part I provide retrospective analyses of John A. Hostetler's work as a scholar of Amish life. The first essay is autobiographical, written by Hostetler at the close of his scholarly career. The other three essays were written by active scholars specifically for this volume. Together they provide contextual assessments of Hostetler's work, as well as interpretive frameworks for reading Hostetler's writings in Part II of this volume.

Hostetler's essay, "An Amish Beginning," is a revision of a piece by the same title that appeared in *American Scholar* in 1992. After the original essay appeared, Hostetler began to assemble other materials for a book-length retrospective on his life. Most of those materials were additional autobiographical vignettes, the majority of which pertained to the first seventeen years of his life as an Amish boy, first in Pennsylvania and then in Iowa. Later, with the assistance of Susan Fisher Miller, these vignettes were adapted and incorporated into Hostetler's original *American Scholar* essay, producing a considerably longer and more personal account of his "Amish beginning." About two-thirds of the essay is now devoted to Hostetler's first seventeen years, with most of the essay's remainder devoted to his college education, his experiences as a World War II conscientious objector, and his graduate work at Pennsylvania State College and University. Readers looking for autobiographical reflections on Hostetler's mature scholarship, his role as a mediator between the Amish and the larger public, and his work as an advocate for Amish people and causes, will find few of those reflections here. At the same time, they will be introduced to various elements of Hostetler's early years that, according to him, shaped his commitments, his vocational choices, and his scholarship.

At its most basic level, "An Amish Beginning" constitutes Hostetler's answer to a question he was frequently asked: How did the Amish-born Hostetler become a university professor? But the essay served another purpose, providing Hostetler with the opportunity to do once again what he did throughout his career: educate his readers about Amish life. In this latter respect, two revisions to Hostetler's original "An Amish Beginning" essay are worth noting. First, the section describing his father's excommunication from the Peachey Amish Church is now considerably longer. Whereas the original essay offered only one paragraph of explanation, this revised version goes into some detail about four "happenings" that eventually led to disciplinary action against his father, Joseph Hostetler. Second, the revised essay includes a new section on Amish courtship practices in which Hostetler recounts *his own* experience with "bundling," a traditional courtship practice in which unmarried partners enjoy one another's company in bed. Interestingly, these two additional sections address the two features of Amish life that, during Hostetler's career, aroused the greatest degree of curiosity and, in some cases, disapprobation. It appears that, even at the end of his life, Hostetler was seeking to shape popular perceptions of these peculiar and often misunderstood aspects of Amish life.

The second essay in this section comes from Donald B. Kraybill, one of Hostetler's graduate students and himself a leading scholar of Amish life. Kraybill's personal retrospective offers insight into Hostetler's humble and quiet personality, which Kraybill connects to Hostetler's Amish upbringing and, just as significantly, to his effectiveness as a researcher in Amish communities. In addition to explaining the significance of Hostetler's scholarship, Kraybill outlines the sweeping transformations underway in both mainstream American society and Amish society during the decades Hostetler worked and wrote. Much of Hostetler's scholarship, Kraybill avers, is simply good ethnographic research, which Hostetler effectively tailored to various audiences. Still, says Kraybill, even though most of Hostetler's analytical categories were derivative, he nonetheless offered insights into Amish culture that were profoundly original and, moreover, unavailable to researchers whose fieldwork methods were less sensitive to the nuances of Amish life.

In the third essay of Part I, Simon J. Bronner examines Hostetler's scholarship through the lenses of Hostetler's academic disciplines.

Although Hostetler earned a Ph.D. in rural sociology, he would later range into the fields of folklife studies and, increasingly, anthropology, where he felt freer to produce values-conscious scholarship. Bronner pays particular attention to Hostetler's use of "folk society" as a way to articulate the distinctiveness of Amish life vis-à-vis mainstream American culture. As Bronner notes, Hostetler's presentation of Amish life is as much about middle-class America as it is about the Amish, and his writing about the Amish afforded him opportunities to critique certain aspects of mainstream American life. Bronner contextualizes Hostetler's work in three interconnected ways—by tracking contemporaneous currents in Hostetler's academic disciplines; by noting the emergence of a new, professional class in mid-twentieth-century America; and by limning the connections between Hostetler's sociological analyses and his worldview—and concludes his consideration of Hostetler's work by citing his legacy for the study of Anabaptist and communitarian groups. This legacy, Bronner suggests, was one of opening up the field of Anabaptist studies to interdisciplinary inquiry, a process that invited close examination of—and challenges to—his work as the field matured.

The final essay of Part I, by David L. Weaver-Zercher, focuses on Hostetler's religious background and the ongoing challenges he faced as a scholar, mediator, and advocate of Amish life. Weaver-Zercher recounts Hostetler's Amish boyhood, his decision to forgo baptism in the Amish church, his mid-century Mennonite Church context, his graduate education, and various aspects of his career as a man "betwixt and between" Amish culture and mainstream American life. Drawing on Hostetler's use of *calling* to explain his life trajectory, Weaver-Zercher argues that some aspects of Hostetler's work were disconcerting to him, an unease that was unavoidable given the complexity of his task, the multiplicity of his constituencies, and his own Amish sensibilities. At the same time, Hostetler's vocational, even spiritual, understanding of his Amish-related work provided him with important resources and personal meaning as he pursued his various tasks.

There are other lenses through which to examine Hostetler's Amish-related work. Even so, these four essays give careful attention to the most important elements of Hostetler's endeavor to write the Amish: his historical context, including his personal history; his chosen vocation as a scholar-mediator; his use of "folk" and "community" to explain Amish life; and his unparalleled advancement of the field of Amish studies. In that sense, these four essays provide vital perspectives for assessing Hostetler's work and its continuing significance for the study of Amish life.

Only four abbreviations appear in the footnotes and endnotes to the essays in Part I: "Hostetler Papers" is used to indicate the John A. Hostetler Papers in the Penn State University Archives, University Park, Pennsylvania; "KJV" is used to indicate the King James Version of the Bible; "JAH" is used to indicate John A. Hostetler in Hostetler's correspondence; and "Yoder Papers" is used to indicate the Joseph W. Yoder Papers in the L. A. Beeghly Library at Juniata College, Huntingdon, Pennsylvania.

1

AN AMISH BEGINNING[a]

John A. Hostetler, with Susan Fisher Miller

I grew up in a culture that emphasizes humility, simple living, and the fear of God. Discouraged or forbidden were various forms of self-advancement, higher education, the philosophical and speculative endeavors of life, as well as violence and the arts of war. Although the Amish retain a high percentage of their young people, a few choose not to become members of the church. Still fewer pursue academic professions, as I eventually did.

Some of my relatives before me did not remain Amish. For example, my father's brother Jake lived in Belleville, a small town near our farm in the Kishacoquillas Valley ("Big Valley") in central Pennsylvania. He was owner and manager of the village creamery. Jake owned a large black automobile. He brought important dignitaries to our farm. One day two visitors arrived. While my father was not about, they told my brother and me to stand by the hay wagon. We obeyed. A few days later we received, in the mail, a large photograph of my brother and me. We cherished it. Nobody wanted to burn it, though in Amish culture to pose for a "graven image" was deemed prideful and frowned upon. It lay around for a while and was finally tucked into the family Bible where it survived.

Our family paid return visits to Uncle Jake, his wife, Elsie, and their daughter, Frances. Jake's house was large and had beautiful furniture. He also had a radio. When the program *Amos and Andy* came on, everyone listened. Since our family had no radio (because it was worldly), I worried that Uncle Jake was in danger of going to hell. But I liked Uncle Jake because he talked to us as individuals and asked questions. Later I learned that he signed his name "J. A. Hostetler," and because my initials were the same as his, I wrote my name in the same manner.

---

a. All footnotes to this chapter are David L. Weaver-Zercher's editorial comments; Hostetler did not include notes himself.

FIG. 1.1 Four-year-old John A. Hostetler (right) and his brother, Jacob, in 1923. Reprinted by permission of the Penn State University Archives.

These early childhood excursions into the non-Amish world had lasting influences. I was attracted to the world beyond the confines of the Amish community. Uncle Jake was a model I admired.

CHURCH TROUBLE

When I was eleven years old, in 1930, my father was excommunicated from the Amish church.[b] Father and Mother had lived in the little Pennsylvania community all their lives. They had come from impeccably solid Amish stock of the one-suspender wearing variety (less conservative Amish groups allowed men to wear two suspenders). Father had just turned fifty. The farm he worked in the Big Valley between Jacks Mountain and Stone Mountain had been in the family line for generations, and we were surrounded by our grandparents, cousins, aunts, and uncles. But my father sold the farm and our family moved from Pennsylvania to Iowa.

Why did my family move to Iowa? What had Father done to estrange himself from his spiritual brothers and sisters? What had brought down the most dreaded edict, the "great ban" of spiritual exclusion and shunning?[c] As a young child I never quite knew. Preachers came to our home to talk privately. They stayed long into the evening. I listened from behind the stove as I sat on the wood box. Sometimes I would hesitate or sit on the steps after closing the door to go upstairs.

My father was not a morally bad person. He obeyed the rules of the church (the *Ordnung*) as he understood them. His grooming and hair length were more than adequate. So was the dress of my brother Jake and me. My sisters too were well within the order. Mother saw to it that their dresses were made from the patterns kept in the attic. We went to church regularly. But Father was dogged with one complaint after another from the bishop for exceeding the boundaries.

Father *was* an enterprising Amish man. Besides farming, he ran a threshing crew and a stone quarry. A Peerless steam engine served as the source of

b. More specifically, he was excommunicated from the Peachey Amish Church in the Big Valley, though the repercussions extended beyond that relatively small Amish community. For more on the Peachey Church, see Chapter 4.

c. In Old Order Amish churches, the *Bann* (excommunication) is typically followed by the *Meidung* (shunning). Shunning, or avoidance, takes various forms, though it usually involves the refusal to eat at the same table with the excommunicated church member and the cessation of other social and economic relations. In most cases, the excommunicant's spouse is expected to cease sharing a bed and sexual intimacies with the excommunicant.

power. He obtained a license by correspondence to operate the steam engine. The first electricity in Belleville was generated from a dynamo my father had installed in the large stone mill on our farm. The generator was run by a large waterwheel at the edge of a dam. He tried raising tobacco in the way Lancaster County Amish did. He built a large underground cave to store the many acres of potatoes we raised on our farm. He bought a machine that mixed molasses and corn products for the dairy herd. He planned and built a row of houses in the village of Belleville and installed underground water pipes from the mountain to farm homes in the Big Valley. He operated a sawmill in the wooded area of Stone Valley, about fourteen miles away and across two mountains, where he built a two-story "cottage" (as we called it) to house our family on work excursions there. In hunting season it became a lodge for businessmen from Philadelphia who were friends of Uncle Jake.

Father had troubles with the church leaders that seemed to start from many small incidents and ended in a grand finale. There was apparently not one single offense. The charges against him seemed to us children ambiguous. But against the background of his enterprising ways, the events that led to Father's expulsion and the decision to move to Iowa, as near as I can reconstruct, were as follows:

Happening #1

When my father was thirty-five years old, my parents made a journey to Indiana. They had taken grandmother Elizabeth Detweiler to visit her sister in Elkhart, while Mother and Father went on to Colorado Springs.[d] On the return trip my father stayed in Iowa for several days. While viewing the farms and countryside in Iowa he observed many broncos, young and partially tamed horses. Knowing that horses were much in demand in Pennsylvania, he set about to purchase a carload of wild Iowa horses. The officials of the railroad line agreed to hitch the freight car of horses at the rear of the passenger train. The horses were to be fed twice on the journey, first in Chicago and again upon arriving in Pennsylvania.

The Pennsylvania Railroad transferred the car to the short line, the Kishacoquillas Railroad, which brought the horses from Lewistown, Pennsylvania, to the heart of the Amish settlement in Belleville. The local Kishacoquillas Valley "K. V." train arrived on time, though from Father's viewpoint it ar-

---

d. The reference here is to Elizabeth Detweiler *Hostetler*, John Hostetler's maternal grandmother. John's mother, Nancy, was born Nancy D. Hostetler, and married Joseph H. Hostetler in 1905.

rived ahead of schedule. It was Sunday and Christmas morning. Amish carriages and sleds were wending their way to church as the beautiful snow was falling.

The railroad officials were baffled. Father could not be reached and there were orders to vacate the rail car. There were no stockyards at the station, so the train officials simply opened the gates at Coldwater Station near our farm—and the untamed horses ran over the Big Valley as the Amish gathered for their worship services!

The criticism against Father was, "That's one of his tricks." Feeding horses on Sunday was not wrong, but to unload a car of broncos and chase them from the station to the farm was borderline inappropriate, especially while others were on their way to church. The circumstances were awkward, unpredictable, and beyond the control of my father.

Happening #2

The wild Iowa horses were captured, stabled, named, clipped, and groomed. A special caretaker was hired to care for the horses. The next task was to tame the horses and break them for road and field work. Each morning after the stables were cleaned and bedded, my father and Bob Bratton, the teamster, would hitch up a wild bronco. Each was matched to a tame horse and hitched to a wagon. Practice rounds were held daily until all the horses were "road broke." Horses of similar size and color were matched together as a team.

There were two bay horses with blond manes that were especially attractive. My father determined that the two would be sold as a team in the upcoming sale. So that they would appear even more striking he purchased a new harness set for them. They were frequently seen in Belleville, for they were used for hauling grain to the flour mill.

Soon thereafter the Amish preachers came to talk to my father. A church member had complained that the brass buckles on the new harness were too fancy, too conspicuous, and "unnecessary." Would my father take off the large brass decorations? "Of course," he replied.

Happening #3

Having been a leading livestock farmer and a member of the Pennsylvania Dairyman's Association, my father built a new dairy barn according to the specifications of the Jamesway Corporation. The barn had round rather than straight rafters, and it had a curved hip roof. In it were new stalls with automatic drinking cups for each cow. The plan of the barn called for a cupola at the top with a weather vane that signaled the direction of the wind.

It was necessary to have ventilation, the preachers conceded, but it was un-necessary to have a fancy rooster as a weather vane.

The new barn was filled with purebred, registered shorthorn milking cows. Each was given a fancy name and records were strictly kept according to the Dairyman's Association's recommendations. The cows were groomed morn-ing and evening. A special sale day was arranged. The cows had been pho-tographed, and their pictures, names, and pedigrees were printed in a catalog that was distributed by the Association. This activity brought many distant visitors to our farm.

Again there were complaints. There was "too much fuss made" of the cows, and from the viewpoint of critical church members, just too much fraterniz-ing with the world. There was nothing wrong with purebred livestock, but to register them and then print their pictures was unnecessary. The sale date was announced and was held on schedule. This offense merited the "small" pun-ishment, confession of wrongdoing in church, and not the "great" punishment of exclusion.[e]

Happening #4

Mother's mother, Elizabeth (Detweiler) Hostetler, joined our residence after she no longer preferred to live alone. She lived in a special "grandma room," separate from, but on the back side of, our house. She ate at our dinner table whenever she wished.

Then the preachers came. "We heard that you mixed Grandmother's money in the bank with yours. Is it true?" they asked. My father was taken aback. "Come with me to the bank," he replied, "and we will ask the bank manager." "Oh, no," responded the bishop, "we wouldn't want to do that. We just wanted to tell you that the rumor is going around, and we wanted to know how you felt about it."

This experience upset the serenity of my father. Someone, he was certain, was instigating the rumor. The gossip was devastating, even though Father claimed the rumor was false. Father had been appointed executor of Grand-

e. In Amish churches, as in many Christian churches, discipline is meted out in varying degrees of sever-ity based on the seriousness of the transgression and the transgressor's perceived penitence. For Amish prac-tices in this regard, see Donald B. Kraybill, *The Riddle of Amish Culture*, rev. ed. (Baltimore: Johns Hopkins University Press, 2001), 131–41.

FIG. 1.2 Neighbors of the Hostetler family posing beside the Hostetlers' hip-roof barn, circa 1930. Reprinted by permission of the Penn State University Archives.

mother's estate. He offered to resign the position if the heirs would agree. The heirs, however, were divided; not all would accept his resignation.

My father determined the source of the rumor to have come from Ezra Renno, an uncle of the bishop and a man of sharp temperament who was heavy on *Ordnung*, the rules and discipline of the church. Father was advised to go and speak to him according to the commandment of Jesus to go and speak with a brother who offends you.[f] When Father went to see him, Ezra was indignant: "*Ummöglich*— impossible! I am an upright man, living in the truth." These were sharp words, and Father returned home defeated.

After repeated attempts at reconciliation, followed by exclusion from the church, my father had had enough.[g] He sold the Hostetler farm, and we boarded

f. Disciplinary practices in Amish-Mennonite life draw upon Jesus' instructions in Matt. 18:15–18, which outlines various steps for confronting sin within the church community. The first step is personal: "If thy brother trespass against thee, go and tell him his fault between him and thee alone" (Matt. 18:15, King James Version [KJV]).

g. Hostetler's account of his father's excommunication fails to note the lawsuit his father brought against his own brother-in-law. This event is recounted in Chapter 4. Other details pertaining to Joseph Hostetler's excommunication, though not the lawsuit, can be found in John A. Hostetler, "The Amish and the Law: A Religious Minority and Its Legal Encounters," *Washington and Lee Law Review* 41 (1984): 39–40. In this latter piece, included in this volume as Chapter 15, Joseph Hostetler is represented by the pseudonym "Henry Zook."

the Pennsylvania Railroad passenger train at Huntingdon, Pennsylvania, for our destination: Iowa City, Iowa. Mother was in tears and Father looked more serious than usual as we started the journey.

We were warned that in Iowa we would face hard work. The farm my father purchased near Kalona, Iowa, had been owned by a bachelor, Sam Manatt, who had allowed fencerows to grow into hedges and the garden and yards to grow up with weeds and brush. But we were exuberant about the adventure that lay ahead. In Kalona, the Amish church rules were less rigid than in Pennsylvania. We were permitted to wear two suspenders rather than one. Farming with tractors was allowed, so in Iowa we would plow with tractors (although not those with pneumatic tires).[h] There would be no stones to break the plow. The crops were to be planted in rich soil without costly fertilizer. Corn would be planted in rows that could be cultivated crossways. In Iowa people grew tall. My brother Jake and I believed we would grow taller than we would have in Pennsylvania.

And even though full reconciliation with the Amish church never became possible for my father in Iowa, as a family we continued regularly to attend the Amish services there.[i]

MY CALLING

I graduated from a country school, Snake Hollow Elementary School, in Washington County, Iowa, before Amish private schools were founded. I became friends of my "English" (non-Amish) playmates. My peers entered high school after graduation, but I willingly gave up all thoughts of doing so, for good Amish parents did not send their children to high school.

Secretly, though, a call to further my education overtook me, even though I knew I would have to wait until I was "of age" (meaning twenty-one) to pursue it. I was not looking for an escape of any kind, but I felt there was a destiny beyond my understanding. It would be revealed to me if I exercised patience, endurance, self-control, and peace of mind.

h. Although Old Order Amish churches have much in common, details of the *Ordnung* vary from community to community. Using tractors for field work would have been very unusual for Old Order Amish churches, signifying the relative liberality of the Old Order Amish in Kalona.

i. The Iowa Old Order Amish church initially accepted Joseph and Nancy Hostetler into membership, but when the leaders of their former church discovered this, the leaders threatened to break fellowship with the Iowa Amish unless they also excluded Joseph. The Iowa church heeded this threat, and Nancy chose to be excluded along with her husband. Still, the couple and their children continued to attend the local Amish church for six years (until 1936), when some of their children, led by John, began attending the nearby East Union Mennonite Church. Shortly thereafter, Joseph and Nancy also joined the Mennonite church.

FIG. 1.3 Students at Snake Hollow Elementary School in Washington County, Iowa, circa 1930; Hostetler stands directly in front of the teacher at right. Reprinted by permission of the Penn University State Archives.

I heard the call when I was disking or plowing during the week; the wide-open fields, the clear blue sky, and the expansive Iowa landscape may have had some influence on opening my mind to new horizons. But the call came to me especially on Sundays. The Sunday morning worship service was a time when my mind wandered and explored ideas without guilt. It was on Sunday afternoons that the sense of call was most urgent. Waiting, reading, resting, and wandering in the pasture and woodlands brought moments of inspiration.

When I was twelve years old I was allowed to attend vacation Bible school for one day at the East Union Mennonite Church, the church home of friends Duane and Dale Yoder. The teacher, Lina Ressler of Scottdale, Pennsylvania, a former missionary and writer known to children as "Aunt Lina," made the tabernacle real.[j] Her soft manner, deep personal interest, and prayers were touching. Bible school was such an enthralling experience for me that day that I thought I would like to attend all two weeks. Heaven would surely have to prevail over my parents! But there was no way I could persuade my parents to permit me to keep attending (I prepared the assignment for the next day anyway). This encounter made me want to be a Christian person, maybe a Mennonite, though I could not talk openly about it.

As I grew older, I tried self-education. I was interested in reading. The books available to me were extremely limited. Aside from the Bible, I read Dale Carnegie's *How to Win Friends and Influence People* and Daniel Kauffman's *Bible Doctrine*.[k] The Bible doctrine book was for me a gold mine. It explained the creation, the will of God, the fall of man, and the plan of salvation. I learned the reasons for honesty, sobriety, temperance, and why life insurance, divorce, attending movies, and worldly fashions were to be avoided. Later I purchased Kauffman's book *Helps for Ministers and Other Christian Workers*, which informed me how to organize a filing system and accumulate clippings on a wide range of topics.[l] As I developed a filing system, my interest in writing was sparked and my call to college was greatly strengthened. I exchanged letters with two pen pals through a Mennonite children's magazine called *Words of Cheer*. They

j. Lina Zook Ressler (1869–1948) was an "editor, city mission worker, teacher, missionary in India, wife and mother." She assisted her husband, Jacob, in editing *Words of Cheer*, the Mennonite children's periodical in which John Hostetler was first published. See the entry for "Ressler, Lina Zook" in the *Mennonite Encyclopedia* (Scottdale, Pa.: Herald Press, 1990), 5:767.

k. Daniel Kauffman, ed., *Bible Doctrine: A Treatise on the Great Doctrines of the Bible, Pertaining to God, Angels, Satan, the Church, and the Salvation, Duties and Destiny of Man* (Scottdale, Pa.: Mennonite Publishing House, 1914). Daniel Kauffman (1865–1944) was a prolific Mennonite writer and denominational leader. See the entry for "Kauffman, Daniel" in the *Mennonite Encyclopedia* (Scottdale, Pa.: Mennonite Publishing House, 1957), 3:156–57.

l. Daniel Kauffman, *Helps for Ministers and Other Christian Workers* (Scottdale, Pa.: Mennonite Publishing House, 1930).

informed me of their pets, family members, church, and travels. I was elated when, at age sixteen, the magazine published my first article, "Some Effects of Tobacco and Alcohol."[m]

Despite my vague calling, I knew the word *education* to be an ice-cold word to Amish people, one that signaled the way to waste and oblivion. The world into which I was born was not to be conquered by the intellect. Whatever there was to be conquered was done through diligence—faithfulness in doing what one knew and felt to be right. Too much thinking was a cop-out, an exercise in self-advancement.

Seeking education beyond eighth grade at Snake Hollow School did not appear to be a path I would follow. High school was a place in town for toughs and lazy people; going there meant going to town and learning the ways of the town. I was Amish, and going to high school was something no Amish person would do. (Besides, the most renowned Mennonite farmer in the area, Lewis Yoder, whose boys had invited me to Bible school, did not allow them to go to high school either.) My duty was to assist my father in the work of the farm.

A FARMER'S WORK

The diversity of tasks I performed on the farm between the ages of fifteen and twenty defies a job description. Father and I sawed and felled oak trees to make fence posts. We transported them a distance of eight miles on wagons or sleds with a team of horses. We removed the bark from the posts and let the posts harden for one year before putting up the fence. We hauled logs to the sawmill. From the lumber we made hog barns, turkey houses, and shelters for cattle. We repaired fences on days when it was too wet to plow or till the soil. I plowed new sod on land previously covered with timber. The stumps remained, and I plowed around them or tore up the roots when possible. When the plow was stuck in the stump, I unhitched it and pulled it out from the rear. I often worked fifteen-hour days. The work was difficult for me and left me very tired.

Aside from the major tasks of harvesting, corn husking, and haying, there were lesser tasks—some daily, some weekly, and some monthly. For instance, we ground corn and grain in a hammer mill and then mixed the feed with concentrate and minerals. We also shelled corn for the cattle. On some days we blasted stumps with dynamite and pulled them out with the tractor. In springtime we hauled manure with a team of horses (on a single day I hauled a record

m. John A. Hostetler, "Some Effects of Tobacco and Alcohol," *Words of Cheer*, 5 May 1935, 2.

thirty-two loads of manure to the fields). On rainy days, or during periods when work was sparse, I "tinkered" or made repairs around the farm. After spring rains, several of us would walk in the woods to collect mushrooms. I also made birdhouses in the woodworking shop.

Having heard the call to pursue education and to explore the world beyond the farm, I had little understanding during my youth that farming was an act of co-creation with God. I knew it was the work of God's stewards, but I did not view it as my life work. Working in the fields from morning until night— to raise more corn, to feed more hogs, and to buy more farmland—did not appeal to me.

COURTING

Despite questions about my future as an Amish farmer, my community's social milieu began to attract more of my attention. Like every culture, the Amish have customary ways to insure reproductive continuity from generation to generation. Mate selection, infant care, child rearing, and rewards for becoming an adult person all help to ensure that continuity.

To some extent, my gender identity was formed in the week-to-week cycles of Amish life, particularly Sunday church activities. Amish worship services are hosted by the various families of the community on a rotating basis. For males of the congregation, the barn of the host farm serves an almost ceremonial function. Family carriages stop in front of the barn and drop off the women, who proceed directly into the hosts' house. All the males, however, including the young boys, gather at the entrance to the barn. The men stand in a circle, exchanging handshakes as they arrive. Gentle but subdued talk—about the weather, about the health of ailing members of the community—travels between the adult men, but when there are no topics to talk about, the mumbled voices cease. Talk is revived as new arrivals join the circle. Even as a boy, my sense of belonging among the males in my extended family and community was reinforced by the ceremonial use of the barn on Sunday mornings.

But how does an Amish boy learn about courting and sexuality? My father told me nothing about anatomy except when we gutted a pig and made hams and sausage. My mother didn't either, but she did lay down an ultimatum: no girlfriend until I was twenty-one. That seemed unreasonable to me, but I understood her ultimatum as a form of protection: I was to keep my mind off the girls. Still, I learned a lot about courting well before I was twenty-one by watching my older brothers and sisters and by listening to my peers. Indeed, a sketchy though valuable source of courting and sexual knowledge came from the jokes exchanged among Amish boys at our Sunday afternoon gatherings.

As is true of many cultures, one of the keys to Amish courtship is being noticed by the opposite sex. A clean buggy, pulled by a spiffy horse with a shining harness, offered one avenue to make an impression. Before I had a buggy, I rode horseback, which had some advantages in navigating the Iowa mud. But there were obvious disadvantages. Amish girls seldom rode horses, and never to Sunday evening singings. When my father bought me a road horse and a used buggy I was proud (pride that had to be balanced by the ability to do hard work and conform in appropriate ways). Instead of going to Sunday services in the family carriage, I could now go in my own rig, taking one or two of my sisters along. I was now independent, coming and going by myself with my own horse and buggy, which had a storage battery with a bright headlight.

I soon sought to use my horse and buggy to my personal advantage. One Sunday morning on which we were to have Sunday school (among the Iowa Amish, Sunday school alternated with church services every other Sunday),[n] I carefully curried my horse, hitched him to the buggy, and tied him by the front lawn fence. As I looked at my rig from the porch, I wondered what more I could do to doll up my horse. I decided to cut some red roses, which I fastened to the bridle above the horse's ears and placed in the whipsocket.[o] But when my father saw what I had done, he tactfully suggested that I take the roses off. The implication was clear: this was not the Amish way. In any case, I now knew that flowers were not appropriate for going to church—but on a beautiful spring morning, when one is going to Sunday school and playing harmonica on the way, it had surely seemed worth trying!

During my years in Iowa, there were two different Amish youth groups in which I participated. The "kid crowd" was a Sunday institution among the boys who were not yet of courting age (that is, younger than age sixteen). We gathered at the home of whoever would have us for the noon meal, and in the afternoons we would go for walks, tell exaggerated stories, or discuss new types of farm machinery. Sometimes we persuaded other families to entertain us. Often it was not known where we would meet until Sunday school was over.

n. This is another indication of the progressiveness of the Amish in Kalona, Iowa. Most Old Order churches at that time (as well as today) would not have held Sunday school, which was viewed as a worldly practice.

o. The whipsocket is a small cavity on horseriding equipment into which a whip can be inserted when not in use.

The "crowd" (or "big crowd") was made up of all young people of courting age. Typically no "kids" were welcome at these gatherings. Gatherings of the crowd were usually planned well in advance, since preparations were necessary for the thirty to fifty persons who would meet at a home for the Sunday noon meal. The crowd devoted its Sunday afternoons to talking, and on Amish holidays there were ball games or, in wintertime, skating on nearby ponds or creeks. The backbone of the crowd consisted of the young couples that were going steady. Nonetheless, these Sunday afternoon events were for socializing, not for finding a date.

Every Amish adolescent cannot wait to attend the big crowd, and I was no exception. One rainy Sunday, right after Sunday school, my sister told me that I could come along to the crowd. Although I was not yet sixteen, the crowd was slated to gather at her friend Ada's house, and for that reason I too was invited. I was elated. On account of the muddy roads, I had ridden to church on horseback, and on the way to the crowd I galloped past many of the buggies, going lickety-split through the slop and water holes. In retrospect, I understand I was establishing an identity, but my sister was not happy. At the crowd she took me aside and told me in no uncertain terms that I had acted foolishly by splashing the dresses of the girls riding in buggies I had passed. Apparently I showed little remorse, for once we returned home, she also complained to my mother.

By the time I was seventeen, going to Sunday evening singings with the crowd was part of my routine. Although I was quite interested in girls, I lacked the courage to ask any of them for a date. The most that I could accomplish was to attend the singings with the other unattached boys as a nominal participant. We hung around mostly to look for excitement. On at least one occasion I ended up taking two girls back to their homes, girls who were close neighbors and whose brothers had not come to the singings. They had no other way to get back to their homes, and I could not politely refuse them. I recall the hour-long drive being sparse in conversation as the wind and rain dashed against the top of my one-seated buggy.

AN EXPERIENCE OF BUNDLING

To many outsiders, one of the most curious Amish courtship practices is bundling. Observed in only a few Amish communities today, bundling was a common practice in the past, and I participated in it myself—once. In 1936, when I was eighteen years old, my sister was married in Pennsylvania, and my family returned from Iowa for the wedding. After the wedding, some of us stayed in the Big Valley for a week before returning to Iowa. My cousin Ben,[p] who lived in the Valley, had a steady girlfriend, Ruthie, and he invited me to attend a Sunday evening singing with them. Since I was visiting from out of state, he decided to arrange a date for me. He planned to ask their friend Rachel, but thought he would first check with my sister to see if she approved. She nodded.

The singing itself and the visiting afterward went well. After the singing, the four of us climbed into a single-seated open buggy and drove off into the darkness. The horse followed country roads until we arrived at the farm where Rachel worked. The women went into the house and Ben and I tied up the horse under the barn's forebay. On this November night he threw a blanket over the horse and fastened it to the harness. We walked up to the porch and into the house.

Inside the girls had lit a lamp and were talking about the fine stitching on a new quilt. Ben and I removed our coats and hats and chatted with our dates about the recent wedding and the gifts the bride and groom had received. Soon Ruthie grabbed the kerosene lamp and headed for the stairway. The rest of us followed her, arriving in a bedroom that contained one bed, two chairs, and a dresser. Suddenly and without warning someone blew out the lamp. It was pitch dark; there was no moonlight and no shadows of any kind from the window. Ben and Ruthie must be on the bed, I thought, for I could hear the rustling of the straw tick. I started to feel my way around, remembering as best I could where the bed was. Without any instructions I realized that I was to lie on the bed with the others and, of course, I had to find Rachel in the dark. This was no game and no joke. The four of us laid on the bed, the women in the middle and my cousin and I on the outside. Ben and I had removed our coats, but we left our shoes and stockings on.

With absolutely no light, talking and touching were the only means of communication. We talked about work, visitors, and relatives, talking as a group and only rarely as couples. The talk was rather sparse, however. And though I lay near Rachel, I was terrified to touch her. I laid as still as possible, though I managed to bump an eyebrow against what must have been her cheekbone. I remained in that position for virtually the rest of the night, reluctant to move for fear I would lose the little contact I had with her.

Ben took the responsibility of keeping time. The conversation grew increasingly weary and repetitious. All of us were drowsy, but no one seemed to be afraid of falling asleep. Finally Ben declared it was four o'clock in the morning and thus time to move. With the aid of a flashlight we all made our way down-

---

p. All names in this account have been changed.

stairs. The three of us said goodbye to Rachel and got into the buggy. Ben drove to Ruthie's place and dropped her off, taking her to the door while I waited in the rig. He returned promptly, and we were home in bed before five.

On my return home I knew that I might not see Rachel again, although we did later exchange one greeting card. I also knew that in Iowa I would never experience bundling, for the Iowa Amish community did not condone or allow it.[q] I also suspected that, in Iowa, I would never date an Amish girl, for by this time I had made up my mind to join the Mennonite Church. What little I had learned about Amish courting would be of no help to me in the future.

STOMACH PAINS

When I was seventeen I began to feel nagging pains in my stomach. It was New Year's Day and terribly cold. My father and I were cutting down an oak tree with a crosscut pull saw. To clean up the pasture on New Year's Day seemed like a good way to start the year. I was old enough to assume the physical work of an adult. I was determined to keep up my end of the saw, and by noontime we had cut several trees. But I detected a dull ache in the pit of my stomach. It was not indigestion. It felt like hunger on a cold winter day. After lunch it persisted so that I could not help with the woodcutting.

The pain continued, though only off and on. On Sundays, and on those days when I did not exert myself, there was no pain. I knew if I told my family that I had belly pains only on the days I did heavy work that they would pass it off as a joke, but the pain persisted for several months. I thought I might have appendicitis, perhaps even cancer; my mother thought I had growing pains, which I preferred to believe. My father eventually took me to the doctor who said my appendix was not acutely inflamed—that is, not yet. He advised that I refrain from heavy work. I was not to lift feed bags, clean the turkey stalls, or haul grain for the threshing crew. Finally, the doctor advised that the appendix be taken out. He gave us a choice of having the operation at home or in the hospital. We chose the home operation. Dr. and Mrs. Frey came early on a Saturday morning with their satchels full of instruments, and Mrs. Frey took command of the kitchen and sterilized the instruments. The operation took place on the extension table in the living room. After recovery, I still felt the dull pain in my stomach. The operation made no difference.

q. Conservative Amish communities are more likely to condone bundling than more progressive Amish communities, which have often been influenced by outsiders' criticism that deems the practice immoral or otherwise uncouth. For more on bundling, see Chapter 4.

IMAGINING COLLEGE

At about the same time, I found myself wanting to go to college very badly. Without telling my parents I signed a contract with the American School of Correspondence to study the required high school subjects and pay tuition monthly. But mathematics and science courses were too difficult to integrate with the demands of farm work, and I was forced to drop the study. I paid a lawyer five dollars to terminate the contract. He informed the school that I had not reached legal age and did not have parental consent.

I then wrote a letter to Sanford Yoder, president of Goshen College, a four-year Mennonite college in northern Indiana, stating my interest in attending. Yoder, a Mennonite bishop who had lived in Kalona, Iowa, before becoming president of Goshen in 1923, responded with a very inviting letter. I purchased a small treasure chest with a lock and key to keep the letter from members of my family. Going to college was a subject I could not discuss with my parents. Whenever I was depressed, I opened the chest and read Yoder's letter again and again.

The solicitor for Goshen College, Chris Graber, stopped one day to talk to me. I was relieved that my parents were not at home when he came. I thanked him very much, but I knew there was no hope. I had earlier sounded out the matter with my parents and, in their opinion, there was no possibility that I could leave the farm. I was the youngest son, and father could not farm without me. Running away from home was unthinkable.

It was during this time that my father, always resourceful, signed a contract with Maple Crest Turkey Farms to secure ten thousand poults. We were to raise the birds and sell them back to the processing plant. My father designated me the "turkey man." The hired man would assist with the routine farm operations.

The turkey operation provided more than enough work to keep me busy. I took serious interest in raising turkeys and learning about their diseases and nutrition. I obtained books and magazines on raising turkeys. It was not long until I begged my father to let me attend a week's short course at the agricultural school in Ames, Iowa. The purpose was to learn how to diagnose diseases. Going to college was considered vain, but going to poultry school was "useful" for the farm economy and therefore less objectionable. I learned that the American Poultry Association regularly held a three-week school for culling poultry and for judging poultry shows. I acquired the textbook a year in advance and attended the course in Des Moines. I obtained a lifetime license for judging poultry shows. Caring for the turkeys was more interesting to me than plowing, disking, or planting crops.

In late adolescence, as I set my mind to the acceptable challenges of inno-

FIG. 1.4 Hostetler returned to Mifflin County in 1936 for his sister Sylvia's wedding, bringing this turkey as a wedding gift. Reprinted by permission of the Penn State University Archives.

vative farm work and raising turkeys, I was at the same time engaged in a struggle for spiritual meaning. In my reflective moments and on alternate Sundays
when there was no worship service, the call to pursue advanced formal education came on strong. It was further strengthened when I heard the Hesston
or Goshen College chorus sing at a nearby Mennonite church (Hesston was a
two-year Mennonite College in Hesston, Kansas). My mother heard them sing
as well. Her comment spoke volumes: "My, how pale those people look from
sitting indoors with their books."

Indeed, my non-Amish peers who went to college seemed impractical, even
to me. They were accumulating knowledge—in my view, more knowledge than
they could carry or practically put to use. I could not grasp it. Going to college year after year was like the farmer who sharpened his scythe every morning but never got around to cutting any grass. Heaping up masses of knowledge without putting it into practice would surely result in some kind of mental
paralysis. It was unnatural. How would I face the prospect?

In this respect I was fully conditioned by my Amish heritage. Amish leaders warned of the dangers of worldly learning, self-exaltation, pride of position, and the enjoyment of power. In their view, an educated person was one
who could see the validity of all points of view in an argument but identify
with none. An open-minded person was one whose mind was open at both ends.
I had absorbed something of these views from my community.

Yet the turkey enterprise did not answer my needs or my compelling call
to prepare for life. When my father purchased another farm across the road, I
had had enough. I announced at the family dinner table that I would not be a
farmer. "Don't buy a farm for me, for when I reach twenty-one I am going to
college." My forthright announcement was met with deadly silence, but my
calling was elsewhere. I felt there must be a higher purpose in life.

CHURCH MEMBERSHIP

In the midst of all this I declined voluntary adult baptism in the Amish church.
To be baptized in the Amish church meant a lifetime vow to uphold the discipline of the church. I truthfully could not make such a promise. What if some
day I would live in a place where there were no Amish people? Would I be
obliged to wear Amish trousers, hat, and suspenders and remain a farmer? If
I were to join another church, would I be excommunicated from the Amish
church and be shunned for the rest of my life? One of the Amish preachers
hinted that in such a case I would be in deep trouble. It would be best, he said,

not to make any vow rather than to make one and later break it. The Amish did, in fact, teach that baptism should be voluntary. The stress and trauma that plagued my father for several years back in Pennsylvania was a social sickness I wanted to avoid.

On the day that my peers—two boys and four girls—were meeting with the ministers upstairs in the Amish farm home for the first in a series of instruction classes, I drove my black pacer[r] to the East Union Mennonite Church. My absence at the Amish service would be conspicuous, I knew.

I preferred joining a Mennonite church to a more "worldly" church like a Methodist, Presbyterian, or Pentecostal church for, like the Amish, the Mennonites taught nonresistance and identified with the Anabaptist faith. I wanted to be a Christian person such as my parents, my grandparents, and the seven generations back to immigrant Jacob Hostetler who forbade his sons to shoot the Delaware Indians who, during the French and Indian War, attacked the Hostetler home, killing his wife and two other children.[s]

Driving my horse and buggy to the Mennonite church took great courage. Mennonites drove fancy, shining autos. The Mennonite boys were wearing flashy neckties, white shoes, and some even wore spats on their ankles. No one acted friendly toward me. In fact, not a single person spoke to me on my first visit. But I persisted in attending the Mennonite church regularly. Finally one member, our rural mail carrier, spoke to me.

My buggy was so conspicuous that I asked my father for a bicycle. He responded that if I waited a year he might buy me a car. One year later I was driving a two-tone Model A Ford, and I had many friends. But Mennonite boys were a world apart from the Amish. Their talk was about the latest model cars, tractors, and speed records. Some boasted about how many girls they could date in one year. I dated none.

LEAVING HOME

One autumn I learned of a six-week winter Bible term to be held at Goshen College. There were no entrance requirements. Although entering college at this point was impossible for me, going to school for Bible study during a time

---

r. A pacer is a horse whose predominant gait is the pace, a fast, two-beat gait in which the horse's legs move in lateral pairs.

s. For more on this event, see Richard K. MacMaster, *Land, Piety, Peoplehood: The Establishment of Mennonite Churches in America, 1683–1790* (Scottdale, Pa.: Herald Press, 1985), 126.

of sparse farm work seemed worth a try. So one evening, after the dishes were done, I approached my mother and father. "What's wrong with learning more about the Bible?" I asked. Mother was silent. Father, however, held out a glimmer of hope. He turned to Mother and said, "But Moses was a learned man."

Although attending the Goshen Bible term did not work out, I eventually found something that did. Without any high school credits, I was admitted to Hesston Junior College, fully aware of having turned my back on one of the most beautiful farms in Iowa. I found consolation in the Lord's command to Abram: "Leave your own country, your kinsmen, and your father's house, and go to a country that I will show you" (Gen. 12:1, New English Bible). During my first year at Hesston I enrolled in courses in civilization, psychology, Greek, salesmanship, typing, and public speaking. Even though I dropped out for three weeks during the first semester to help my father, my grades were above average. When possible I always took a course in public speaking to help me become more articulate. By working on Saturdays and serving as a janitor during the week, I managed to pay all my expenses for the first year.

In summer 1942, after a year of college, I sought employment to cover the next year's college expenses. A small group of boys hoped to make good money by working in Oregon's logging industry, and they asked me to join them. Our bed and board were provided by one of the owners of the logging company in the town of Sweet Home. We ate six o'clock breakfasts of cheese, potatoes, cooked cereal, and several different kinds of meat, then rode two hours on the back of a truck to the redwoods high in the mountains. I was a choke setter. I fastened the steel cables to the logs on a dragline, gave a signal to the man operating the dragnet, then quickly ran to a safe place. The logs were pulled through brush, rocks, and trees to a central loading zone. The hours were long and the work was rough and dangerous.

While in Oregon, my hopes for finishing college were dashed again, this time "for the duration." With the advent of World War II, I was ordered to appear before my local Iowa draft board on July 12, 1942, for induction into Civilian Public Service. I had applied for conscientious objector status and was instructed to join work camp No. 33 in Fort Collins, Colorado. I had learned the meaning of endurance on the farm, and now I was to learn its meaning in a work camp. I reasoned that the experience could be educational and broadening. There was no pay for conscientious objectors and no money from the government for living expenses. The Historic Peace Churches—the Mennonites, Amish, and Brethren—paid for the maintenance of the camps and gave each camper fifteen dollars per month for incidental expenses.

Of conscientious objectors to war there was a great variety. In addition to Amish and Mennonite boys, there were also political objectors, Jehovah's Witnesses, Assembly of God members, Friends, Christodelphians, and Methodists. Most were farm boys; all were willing and able workers. Through this experience my knowledge of religious groups and their beliefs was expanded. My first assignment was meat cutting. I was one of four cooks serving 150 campers. Evening courses were available in church history, psychology, rug making, woodworking, and first aid.

Thirty of us were selected for a special project in eastern Colorado, an arid and unproductive agricultural region. We constructed and lived in barracks thirty miles west of Sterling, Colorado. A single village store and post office constituted the village of Buckingham. We provided water facilities for range cattle. There were no wells or lakes. We dug wells from 60 to 340 feet deep and constructed large concrete cisterns for storing water. We also seeded dryland grass in the desert to keep the soil from blowing away. Rattlesnakes were rampant.

Living in Colorado's desert was confining and restrictive. I wanted to learn more about human nature and psychology, so I applied for a transfer to a mental hospital in New Jersey. At Marlboro State Hospital, a community of trained professionals cared for the sick, and conscientious objectors assisted them as orderlies. Although much of the work was routine (for instance, counting persons into and out of the dining hall), it was also possible to attend staff meetings where patients were being evaluated for discharge. Violent behavior on the ward was not uncommon. The schedule provided one day off per week. On these occasions I went to New York or Philadelphia to attend lectures and various cultural events. I attended New York's Riverside Church on several occasions to hear the controversial liberal theologian Harry Emerson Fosdick, who occasionally spoke favorably of conscientious objectors. And I learned *not* to visit Elizabeth Voth, a retired Mennonite missionary, at her home on Wednesdays because she spent the entire day on her knees praying. On entering the home, one was obliged to kneel with her for the rest of the day.

I began to write more articles for publication. My reading included philosophy, psychology, and religion. When I traveled by bus or rail, I often saw small blue pamphlets on magazine racks about superstition, witchcraft, and bundling among the Amish and Mennonites. I traced these pamphlets to their source, A. Monroe Aurand Jr., a publisher in Harrisburg, Pennsylvania, and I started a prolonged crusade to eliminate their distribution. I concluded that they sold well because nothing better was offered on the bookracks. Some years later, Al-

FIG. 1.5 One of Hostetler's Civilian Public Service assignments took him to the Marlboro State Hospital in Marlboro, New Jersey. Reprinted by permission of the Penn State University Archives.

fred Shoemaker of Franklin and Marshall College challenged me to write something more authentic. In response I wrote *Amish Life* in 1952, *Mennonite Life* in 1954, and eventually *Hutterite Life* in 1965.[t]

As the war grew more intense, conscientious objectors became more critical of the U.S. government and of the churches for cooperating with a government at war. Passive participation was not enough. Some socially active draftees began mental hospital reform. Others sought to enter foreign relief service. I began a modest enterprise of my own by visiting public libraries in large cities to examine their holdings on Christian pacifism. I offered free copies of selected books on pacifism, church history, and community life to libraries that did not have such volumes. I visited all thirty-six free Carnegie libraries in Philadelphia and many in New York and Newark. I purchased the books myself from meager savings and later persuaded the publishers to donate them.[u]

After a year of hospital work, I volunteered to become a caretaker in a "hu-

t. All three booklets were published by Herald Press in Scottdale, Pennsylvania. For more on Alfred Shoemaker, see Chapter 3.

u. Hostetler describes his library work in "Christian Books in Public Libraries," *Gospel Herald*, 18 May 1945, 124. There he identifies Guy Hershberger's *War, Peace, and Nonresistance* (Scottdale, Pa.: Herald Press, 1944) as one of the books he frequently donated.

man guinea pig" experiment for the study of atypical pneumonia. Conscientious objectors were given the opportunity to offer themselves as subjects in the study of typhus, malaria, jaundice, and nutrition. The pneumonia experiment was under the direction of Majors T. J. Abernethy and N. L. Cressy of the Army Medical Corps. The purpose of the experiment was to find out the cause, prevention, and treatment of atypical pneumonia and other types of colds. Experiments with animals, monkeys, rats, and rabbits had proved fruitless for establishing how the disease was transmitted. The experiment was conducted at Pinehurst, North Carolina, a golfing center where medical scientists leased a seventy-five-room residential hotel, the Holly Inn. Fifty volunteers and ten caretakers were required. For men who were digging postholes, and hoping to find work of greater humanitarian importance during the war, the opportunity was very attractive. Each of the men had an individual room, equipped with bath, telephone, writing desk, and furniture, along with opportunity for study and amusement. Regular hotel meals were served in the rooms. Books on a wide range of subjects were available from the Duke University library.

As caretakers, we served the fifty volunteers with food trays, laundry supplies, games, books, and magazines. Strict isolation was important. Books or objects could not be passed from one room to another without first exposing the object to fresh air and sunshine. Sixteen of the seventy-eight men contracted atypical pneumonia and a number of others developed colds. Half of the group had been exposed to the disease. Their throats had been sprayed with infectious material obtained from patients with atypical pneumonia. All of the men recovered completely, most of them within a week after exposure. The results, published in the *Journal of the American Medical Association*, proved that atypical pneumonia spread like an infection and could be transmitted.[v]

Once discharged from conscientious objector service, I completed my college work at Goshen College in one summer and two academic years. Although interested in history, I chose to major in Bible before switching to sociology. While an undergraduate, I served as assistant to Dean Harold S. Bender in the preparation of the four-volume *Mennonite Encyclopedia*. One of my assignments was to write articles on the Amish and related groups. This association acquainted me with the history and social dynamics of the various Mennonite groups.

v. See Commission on Acute Respiratory Diseases, "Transmission of Primary Atypical Pneumonia to Human Volunteers," *Journal of the American Medical Association* 127 (1945): 146–49.

FIG. 1.6 Hostetler participated in a "human guinea pig" experiment in Pinehurst, North Carolina, in 1945; here he stands (far right) with other project participants. Reprinted by permission of the Penn State University Archives.

My experiences in college and Civilian Public Service led me to apply to graduate school. I was attracted to the Pennsylvania State University for graduate study because it was near my native valley in central Pennsylvania. I was also attracted to the research and career of William Mather, a sociologist who prodded the social consciences of both the scientific community and the religious institutions. His observations were widely disseminated in the new media.[w]

My college transcript from Goshen was lacking in science courses, which meant that I could not be accepted into the Graduate School of Arts and Sciences without taking undergraduate courses to fill this deficiency. Professor Mather suggested that I apply to the School of Agriculture instead. Here I was accepted. First I was to register for a master's degree. I chose to do my thesis on "The Amish Family in Mifflin County." I lived in Big Valley during the

w. For more on Mather, and Hostetler's graduate education generally, see Chapters 3 and 4.

FIG. 1.7 In the summer of 1948, while an undergraduate at Goshen College, Hostetler worked on a peace advocacy team with John Howard Yoder (center) and Willard Hunsberger (right). Reprinted by permission of the Penn State University Archives.

summer and collected my data there. Married the previous summer, in June 1949, my wife Hazel (Schrock) and I rented a large empty farmhouse from Ben Glick for twelve dollars per month.

My master's oral examination committee consisted of Mather, sociologist Roy C. Buck, and Maurice Mook, an anthropologist. Mook gave me a difficult time in the oral exam by demanding a precise definition of assimilation. He insisted that I use precise terms, which he said were essential to the definition. Finally he phrased the definition himself: "Assimilation is culture change due to culture contact." What interested my committee most about my thesis was the decorative folk art I had found among Amish families.

Professor Mook's course "Folk Society" met every Monday night. There were ten of us, including Margaret Matson, Francis Ianni, Joe Bentivego, and others whom I have since forgotten. Mook told me ahead of time that I was to speak up in the class, for he wanted to learn all he could about the Amish people. He had us read Robert Redfield's article, "The Folk Society," which became a benchmark for comparing everything we discussed in class, including the Amish.[x]

x. Robert Redfield, "The Folk Society," *American Journal of Sociology* 52 (1947): 292–308.

FIGS. 1.8–9 Hostetler's most important graduate school mentors were sociologist William G. Mather (above) and anthropologist Maurice A. Mook (right). Reprinted by permission of the Penn State University Archives.

Did the Amish have art? Dance? What was their language? Were they self-sufficient? Did they use barter or money? Did they have a kinship system? And in all of these ways did they represent the opposite of industrial society? Other students discussed other folk societies. Yet it seemed that we discussed the Amish as if they were the most important topic in the course. The class even visited several Amish settlements—Kishacoquillas Valley, Half Moon Valley, Somerset County, and Juniata County, all in Pennsylvania, and Elkhart County in Indiana.

I began by writing articles for publication. My first book, *Annotated Bibliography on the Amish,* appeared in print while I was still a student.[y] I had submitted the manuscript to the publisher before I enrolled at Penn State. Mather suggested that I enter the book for the annual Chicago Folklore Prize offered by the University of Chicago. The prize was fifty dollars. I won.

Not all of my professors viewed the Amish as a fruitful field of study. Some years later, Roy Buck urged me to "get out of the Amish field" and perhaps get into a study of the granges in Pennsylvania, a movement that was dying, in my view. He told my wife Beulah[z] that I should get into something other than the Amish studies. She argued back that I should keep doing what I was doing well.

My professional interest in American community behavior, the Amish and related Anabaptist groups in particular, began with my professors who kept asking questions. They and the wide world are still asking questions, and I am still giving answers.

Over the past three centuries the Amish and other Anabaptist groups have been suspended between two opposing forces: the political forces that would eliminate ethnicity from the face of the earth and those human communities who regard ethnicity as a natural and necessary extension of the familial bonds that integrate human activities. Caught between these forces, the "plain people" have sometimes prospered and sometimes suffered for their faith. Those who would eliminate diversity argue that ethnicity is restrictive, narrow, corruptible, and fraught with nepotism and family jealousies. Totalitarian state systems often view ethnic communities as disruptive and evil. Such thinking,

---

y. John A. Hostetler, *Annotated Bibliography on the Amish: An Annotated Bibliography of Source Materials Pertaining to the Old Order Amish Mennonites* (Scottdale, Pa.: Mennonite Publishing House, 1951).

z. Hostetler's first wife, Hazel Schrock Hostetler, died in childbirth on 20 February 1951, along with their only child, Susan. John married Beulah Stauffer on 14 February 1953.

in effect, asks "queer people" to speak one language, obey all regulations, and get "cleaned up like the rest of us."

The role of the public school system is to facilitate uniformity and to provide preparation for those seeking to participate in mainstream American culture. For this reason, the word *education* as used in American society is regarded with suspicion by most Amish people. To them it signifies ego advancement, independence, and cutting the ties that bind one to the community of faith and work. For ethnic and religious groups who think of themselves as "strangers in the land," who conscientiously reject certain contemporary values, and who reject specific aspects of modern technology, the expanding role of public school is very threatening indeed.

For almost half a century the Amish had expressed their opposition to forced attendance to high school, a form of education they said would destroy their communities. Finally, in 1972, the Amish were exonerated from compulsory school attendance beyond the elementary grades. Even though I personally had felt compelled to exceed Amish constraints on education, I fully supported their cause in my testimony before the courts in *Wisconsin v. Yoder*, a case that was eventually decided by the U.S. Supreme Court.[aa] Today the Amish are quietly developing a school system that is integrated with their way of life. The Amish schools protect Amish youth from alienation inherent in the loss of community life and generally produce stable, dedicated adults who are productive members in both their faith community and in American society.

Faith communities in America function as mediating structures in the pluralistic makeup of our society. They check the excesses of heavy-handed bureaucracies. Healthy ethnic communities make members feel specifically bound and responsible to others. Even though sometimes limiting, such communities can be ennobling, supportive, therapeutic, and satisfying. These communities are an extension of familial love, informing us who we are, where we come from, and what is distinctive about us.

The Amish and others who settled in America generally found the essential conditions to form communities and to practice the free exercise of religion. They found for the most part a right that Supreme Court Justice Louis Brandeis called "the most comprehensive of rights and the right most valued

---

aa. For Hostetler's role in this case, see Albert N. Keim, *Compulsory Education and the Amish: The Right Not to Be Modern* (Boston: Beacon Press, 1975); and Lawrence Rosen, "The Anthropologist as Expert Witness," *American Anthropologist* 79 (1977): 555–78.

FIG. 1.10 In 1982, Hostetler and these Amish men participated in a religious freedom symposium marking the tenth anniversary of *Wisconsin v. Yoder*. Photograph by Richard Reinhold, reprinted by permission.

by civilized man," a right Americans should be proud to protect: the right to be left alone.

While testifying in *Wisconsin v. Yoder* I was cross-examined by John William Calhoun of the Wisconsin attorney general's office. Calhoun turned his swivel chair close to me, forefinger thrust out, and asked: "Now, Professor, don't you think that a person needs to have an education to get ahead in the world?" I pondered the question in the hushed courtroom and at length replied: "It all depends on which world."

2

THE REDEMPTIVE COMMUNITY:
AN ISLAND OF SANITY AND SILENCE

Donald B. Kraybill

Student rallies against the war in Vietnam punctuated life on the Temple University campus in the fall of 1970, when I matriculated in the graduate sociology program. I had applied to Temple because I wanted to study with John A. Hostetler, the leading scholar of Amish and Mennonite societies in North America. As his research assistant my first year, I was to manage his office while he was on leave for a year in Austria studying Hutterite history. He gave me some Hutterite demographic data to analyze, but advised me to focus on a social statistics course required of all doctoral students. In fact, he loaned me an old statistics book, which he said, with a grin, might be helpful. During my orientation, a letter arrived from the Lancaster Mennonite Information Center updating their plans to install a full-scale replica of the Hebrew tabernacle adjacent to the center to enhance their "ministry to tourists." "What will they do next?" Hostetler muttered. "Bring white elephants from Africa?" With that he was off to Austria, and I was left to steward his office and watch for signs of white elephants.

Although I had deliberately selected Temple in order to study with "John A.," the only course I took with him was an independent reading seminar in communal societies (I was enrolled in sociology and, although Hostetler had a joint appointment in sociology and anthropology, most of his teaching was in anthropology).[1] My major collaboration with Hostetler revolved around my dissertation. Upon his return from Austria, he applied for a grant to study socialization and cultural transmission among Mennonites, a grant that supported a three-year project on cultural transmission at Lancaster Mennonite High School and eventually resulted in my dissertation and several other publications.[2] Living in Lancaster but commuting to Temple for my courses, I became the de facto manager of the project. In addition to working with Hostetler, I had the good fortune of working closely with his longtime collaborator, anthropologist Gertrude Enders Huntington.

Pleased to have the support of Hostetler's grant for my research, I was surprised when he declined to chair my dissertation committee. He explained that he did not like university politics, committees, and bureaucracy. He proposed a chair who, he assured me, could steer the dissertation through the political maze with dispatch and told me that he (Hostetler) would gladly serve as a member of the committee. His disdain for bureaucracy and avoidance of university politics perhaps reflected his Amish upbringing as well as his somewhat shy and retiring personality. Despite having dozens of esteemed colleagues in professional circles, he was still a cultural outsider in spirit and temperament.

During my years at Temple (1970–75), Hostetler was completing his Hutterite research and writing *Hutterite Society*.[3] I was burdened with taking courses, managing the Mennonite school project, and writing my dissertation. We frequently reviewed the school project, but rarely discussed Amish studies. In fact, I recall few if any conversations about the 1972 Supreme Court decision on *Wisconsin v. Yoder* for which Hostetler served as consultant and expert witness. For the most part he worked on his scholarly projects with typical Amish humility—quietly and, apart from conversations with Huntington and a few other colleagues, privately. We did have occasional forays into conceptual issues, such as the time he arrived at the office enthused about an article on defensive structuring in the *American Journal of Sociology*.[4] We explored its analytical potential for better understanding the way in which sectarian communities structured their internal lives in response to larger social forces. He urged me to use defensive structuring theory for my dissertation, which I did, and I also used it later in *The Riddle of Amish Culture*.[5]

In the mid-1980s, my interest in Amish studies developed, and Hostetler and I collaborated on two short essays, one on Amish suicide and the other related to the *Witness* controversy.[6] Some years earlier, Hostetler had collected ethnographic data related to Amish suicides and death certificates from an Amish settlement. He had been intrigued by the possibility that marginal persons in Amish society—caught betwixt and between Amish values and American individualism—were more prone to suicide.[7] I analyzed the death certificate data and we combined the results into an article in 1986. Two years later we wrote an essay on the controversy surrounding the Paramount film *Witness*. Our renewed collaboration was facilitated by Hostetler's appointment as distinguished scholar-in-residence (1986–89) at Elizabethtown College in Pennsylvania, where I taught sociology. His appointment coincided with the initial development of the college's Young Center for Anabaptist and Pietist Studies.[8]

Hostetler's presence at Elizabethtown College made it convenient for me to consult with him during the research and writing of *Riddle*. He supported the project by introducing me to several Amish historians, who in turn opened doors for me into the Lancaster County Amish community. Hostetler also guided me to various print materials, including historical documents. Impressed by his quick responses to my requests for citations and documents, I asked for advice on organizing a filing system. "Just do whatever works for you," he advised.

The white elephants never came to Lancaster County, but the yellow bull-dozers did. When Hostetler came to Elizabethtown College in 1986, Lancaster County was swirling with controversy between land preservationists and proponents of development. Stirred by a state proposal to build a four-lane highway through choice Amish farmland, as well as other development projects that would ruin fertile soil and disturb the Amish community, Hostetler jumped into the fray. He wrote articles and organized conferences that promoted land preservation and stable communities, especially the Amish settlement of Lancaster County.[9]

Searching for a theme for the first Young Center conference in 1987, we discussed a variety of possibilities. Writing *Riddle* at the time, I was immersed in Peter Berger's work on modernization, so we titled the conference "Anabaptist Communities: Coping With Modernity." Hostetler found Berger's analysis of the impact of modernization an apt description of his own view of what he saw happening in Lancaster County. In Berger's words, "The forces of modernity have descended like a gigantic steel hammer upon all the old communal institutions—clan, village, tribe, region—distorting or greatly weakening them, if not destroying them altogether."[10] Hostetler felt the homelessness described by Berger and, despite understanding the stability of Amish life, feared it would eventually destroy his own beloved community. Although deeply troubled by the gigantic hammers smashing away at the communal bonds in Lancaster County, Hostetler himself had come back home—home to the passion for community that had driven him in the early 1950s, when he helped to energize the Mennonite Community Movement.[11] Indeed, his passion for community, nurtured by his Amish upbringing, was one of the themes that threaded its way throughout his long and productive career.[12]

THE CONTEXT OF HOSTETLER'S SCHOLARSHIP

Hostetler's work on Amish studies spanned nearly five decades (1948–96). He wrote his first two essays on Amish life in 1948 as a twenty-nine-year-old, seven more in 1949, and then published an award-winning bibliography of Amish studies in 1951.[13] His last essay, "The Amish as a Redemptive Community," which appeared in 1996, was first given as an address at the tricentennial conference on Amish beginnings in Alsace, France, in 1993.[14] Hostetler's prodigious output was shaped by influences under way in American society, the social sciences, and in the Amish community itself; the social transformations in these three arenas formed the lenses through which he viewed Amish life.

Writing in the preface to the first edition of *Amish Society* in 1963, he said, "We live in a world that is being transformed before our eyes by new inventions, new forms of communication, and new folkways." Moreover, he wondered if the costs of "industrializing, mechanizing, and urbanizing" the world were not sometimes "too great." Why introduce an automobile or tractor if human relationships "are cut into shreds"? "How much destruction of old values and alienation of parents from children, of neighbor from neighbor, of the spirit of man from the faith of his traditional culture, must there be?" he wondered.[15]

The transformations in American society that stirred these questions for Hostetler were many. His scholarship came of age during the post–World War II years that heralded the international dominance of American interests, the pursuit of prosperity, and the claims of progress, all of which were underscored by America's triumph in the war. In the 1950s, the engines of progress roared into high gear, producing greater industrial output, new applications of technology (including television, more highly mechanized farming, and commercial air travel), increased mobility via interstate highways, consolidated high schools, suburbanization, the growth of government, and increased bureaucratization— all driven by the incessant quest for progress. On a more particular note, the decline of small-scale family farms during this and subsequent decades influenced Hostetler's interpretations of Amish life.

The Soviet's success with Sputnik and the consequent race to the moon boosted America's commitment to science and its confidence in scientific solutions. In the social sciences, these events spurred the use of quantitative methods to gather empirical data through surveys. After World War II, sociology took a sharp positivist turn toward analyzing voluminous batches of data to test specific hypotheses with sophisticated statistical techniques, a procedure that, in Hostetler's mind, merely led to a fragmented understanding of human communities.[16] The gradual introduction of large mainframe computers in the 1960s facilitated the analysis of massive data sets, and by the early 1970s the doctoral program in sociology at Temple University required four courses in quantitative research methods and statistical techniques. All the required textbooks gave preponderant attention to hard-nosed empiricism committed to measuring and quantifying human behavior.[17] Graduate students interested in ethnographic research and humanistic interpretations of social life migrated to anthropology—where they found John Hostetler, who by this time had already deemed the qualitative methods of anthropology to be more holistic, integrative, and humane.

The growth and optimism of the 1950s turned sour in the 1960s, a souring that spawned a host of antiestablishment movements, including communal experiments and the back-to-nature quest. Suddenly the Amish were looking better. With high-speed highways and automobiles aplenty, the tourists were coming to see them—in droves. "Mix together the word Intercourse and Amish," said one Amish farmer, speaking of the Lancaster County village of Intercourse, "and you're bound to draw a lot of tourists."[18]

And there were plenty of Amish to see. Indeed, a major change in Amish life during Hostetler's career was its phenomenal growth. Between 1940 and 1990, the number of church districts in North America grew more than five-fold, from 154 to 784, reflecting a population increase from 25,000 to 128,000.[19] The growth of Amish society fueled the planting of new settlements, migration, diversity, and a growing number of divisions and affiliations.

The transformation of Amish society, however, spread beyond its sheer growth. During the 1950s and 1960s, the Amish faced severe conflicts with the state over education and Social Security. Many Amish parents in several states were arrested and imprisoned because they balked at sending their children to large consolidated public schools. This conflict abated, of course, after the Supreme Court decision in 1972. Arrests and conflict over participation in Social Security also declined after Congress exempted the Amish from the Social Security system in 1965.[20]

The big question hovering over the Amish during the formative years of Hostetler's research was simply this: Were they endangered by a rapidly modernizing, high-technology society? Even Hostetler sometimes made oblique references to "social scientists" who predicted the demise of the Amish.[21] On the other hand, would the American political system be able to tolerate, within its jurisdiction, a religious minority that refused to embrace the values of modernity? The fate of Amish life and the limits of democratic tolerance were both at stake in the interesting social experiment unfolding under Hostetler's microscope.

Beyond education and Social Security, other changes in American society also "stressed the Amish," as Hostetler put it in the preface of the first edition of *Amish Society*.[22] Changing patterns of farm technology meant that the Amish could no longer rely on horse-drawn equipment manufactured in American factories. In the 1970s and 1980s, rising land prices and encroaching urbanization were beginning to strangle family farming, the occupation that many, including Hostetler, considered the core of Amish culture. In short, in the early 1960s Hostetler noted that "the Amish . . . way of life is being changed by technology and the life ways of the urban world."[23]

In summary, Hostetler's interpretative perspectives can only be understood in the context of the transformations under way in American society, in the social sciences, and among the Amish themselves. All of these changes, as well as Hostetler's own work, contributed to the rehabilitation of the Amish in the American imagination during his career.[24] Labeled an "odd folk" with "quaint" hairstyles and "peculiar" dress by Aurand in the 1930s, by the 1980s the Amish had been transformed in the American mind into an esteemed people who came to exemplify the virtues of the American past.[25] Hostetler, writing in 1987, was very aware of this shift. He noted that a half-century earlier the Amish were considered "an obdurate sect living by oppressive customs," a "dying breed" that, like a "run-down clock," would soon be assimilated into modern life. However, "today," he continued, "they are esteemed . . . as islands of sanity in a culture obsessed with economic indicators and technology run rampant."[26]

CONCEPTUAL MODELS AND METHODS

Hostetler held a Ph.D. in rural sociology from Penn State University and, after 1965, held a joint appointment in sociology and anthropology at Temple University. Was he an anthropologist, a sociologist, or a rural sociologist? Such questions, in Hostetler's mind, were irrelevant ones that only served to further fragment our knowledge of the social world and human behavior. Nurtured by his formative years in a holistic community, Hostetler was searching for synoptic understandings of human experience that would most likely be found through interdisciplinary models grounded in holistic approaches.

He was attracted to anthropology, he said, because it does "a better job, focusing predominantly on the more incomprehensible, the nonverbal, and the holistic aspects of social and cultural behavior, or that which is immeasurable or ambiguous."[27] Rooted in anthropology, he drew insights from the European sociological masters such as Ferdinand Tönnies, Max Weber, and Ernst Troeltsch for the concepts of *Gemeinshaft* (community), *Wert-rational* (absolute values), and sectarian group theory, respectively. Moreover, tapping the resources of psychology, he also appreciated the importance of personality and the way culture shaped personality.[28] In the end, he sought to use the tools of the social sciences, in the broadest sense, to understand and interpret Amish life.

In many ways, Hostetler was a cultural sociologist ahead of his time, because that subfield of sociology only matured in the twilight of his career. Long considered the domain of anthropology, cultural studies gained prominence in the 1970s and later among qualitative sociologists, who stressed the centrality of culture for sociological analysis.[29] For Hostetler, culture was the preeminent interpretive category that opened insights into psychological, historical, social, and economic behavior. His was a holistic, integrative, and interdisciplinary approach that, in my judgment, modeled an excellent way of understanding the Amish as well as other human communities. In his words, "University professors have taught their students to think of the Amish as a cultural island, or as a traditional cultural system left over in the modern world, a type labeled as sect, folk, or *Gemeinschaft* society. The Amish may be viewed from any one of these theoretical perspectives, but such models leave out much." Later in the same essay, Hostetler expressed his reservations about conceptual frameworks: "[M]odels are incomplete and arbitrarily exclude things. What they exclude may be more important than what they include. They provide us with fragmented glimpses of the whole."[30]

Hostetler especially eschewed highly quantitative methods that relied on large surveys and statistical techniques to test hypotheses that only "yielded fragmented knowledge."[31] Reflecting his theoretical inclinations, Hostetler's research methods were most closely aligned with those of the anthropological tradition: participant observation, sustained fieldwork, document analysis, and face-to-face interviews. In many ways his fieldwork and participant observation in Amish society began as a child. His family's marginal status in the Amish community nurtured his sensitivities to social dynamics. The social-scientific tools he acquired in graduate school enabled him to reflect on and better understand his own experience as a product of Amish culture. He was, noted a close colleague, "more of a poet than a scientist in his study of social life," more intuitive than analytical.[32] He was guided not only by the tools of sociocultural analysis, but also by his own intuitive search for the grounds of unity in human community.

Perhaps more fundamentally, his methodological approach reflected the core values of Amish life itself, as well as the pragmatic constraints of gathering data in the context of a small society that had little interest in the world's scientific gymnastics. The emphasis on participant observation and face-to-face interviews was congruent with the fundamental values of the little community— symbolic practice rather than doctrine, oral communication rather than written,

FIG. 2.1 Hostetler's fieldwork was enabled by warm relationships with Amish people and a lifelong knowledge of Pennsylvania Dutch. Reprinted by permission of the Penn State University Archives.

and face-to-face visiting rather than the bureaucratic relationships emerging in the outside world. In addition, it simply would have been very difficult, if not impossible, to conduct large-scale surveys in a community that distrusted external intrusions.

Despite recognizing the limitations of conceptual models, Hostetler employed a number of them throughout his career—folk society, sectarian group theory, *Gemeinschaft*, high-low cultural context, commonwealth, charter, redemptive community—to understand and elucidate Amish society. Except for redemptive community, all of these models came from the traditional social science literature. High-low cultural context and commonwealth appear for the first time in the third edition of *Amish Society* (1980) but were not fully developed as interpretive schemes throughout the book. The two anthropological perspectives that permeated all editions of *Amish Society* and much of his other work were charter and folk society. Of these, charter was more fundamental to Hostetler's interpretation of Amish life.

Hostetler used Robert Redfield's folk society or "little community" as a conceptual frame for all four editions of *Amish Society*, but after introducing it early in these works, he did not use it much throughout them.[33] In the third edition of *Amish Society* (1980), Hostetler blends the components of *Gemeinschaft* societies and folk societies to generate four dimensions—distinctiveness, small scale, homogeneity, and self-sufficiency—that he considers descriptive of Amish communities. Sociologist Marc A. Olshan's severe critique of the ritualistic use of folk society to describe Amish life may have steered Hostetler away from it in his writings after 1981.[34] Olshan argued not only that the concept of folk society does not fit Amish realities but, more importantly, that the Amish make many choices, whereas folk societies are largely in the hands of fate. He also contended that, if collective choice and societal self-determination were considered, the Amish were more like a modern society than a folk society.

Whereas most of Hostetler's analytical categories are not sustained through the whole of *Amish Society*, the notion of charter is. Indeed, Hostetler invokes the idea of charter in many of his writings, often devoting a few pages to it in journal articles to introduce the core values of Amish culture.[35] In all editions of *Amish Society*, he uses charter as an interpretive category at the beginning of the book and concludes the last chapter(s) with a discussion of "the redefinition of the charter," or something to that effect. It is a sustaining concept that frames the entire corpus of his work.

What is charter? Hostetler borrows the concept from the anthropologist

Bronislaw Malinowski to describe "the fundamental values and common ends of the group, recognized by the people and accepted by them."[36] In the Amish case, charter encompasses *Gemeinde* (community), separation from the world, the vow of baptism, *Ordnung* (lifestyle regulations), exclusion, and closeness to nature. Key phrases that reflect the charter of the Amish worldview, according to Hostetler, include obedience and disobedience, separation from the world, humility, and pride. Charter, in the Hostetler usage, encompasses the root values that undergird and structure Amish culture.

In contrast to these models borrowed from the social sciences, "redemptive community" was likely Hostetler's own phrase, indebted perhaps to Sandra Cronk's analysis of "the rites of the redemptive process" among Old Order Amish and Mennonite communities.[37] Hostetler's use of redemptive community appears for the first time in the third edition of *Amish Society* (1980), and he expands on it throughout the remainder of his career. Unlike the other social-scientific models, redemptive community is an important shift in perspective because, in Hostetler's own words, the redemptive community is the "inside view," the Amish self-understanding of their life together. In some ways, redemptive community was Hostetler's term for the Amish charter because it named the values and common ends that the Amish themselves deemed fundamental to their way of life.[38]

As his scholarship matured, Hostetler became more interested in understanding Amish culture from within, using Amish categories of meaning rather than simply applying the standard social-scientific theories. Having developed his reputation as a social scientist and matured in his own self-understanding, he likely felt freer to follow his intuition beyond the constraints of the typical conceptual models.[39] Moreover, redemptive community suggested that religious meanings permeated all the crevices of Amish life. The redemptive community, in the Amish view, needs to separate from the rampant disobedience in the larger world in order to ensure eternal salvation.

Writing in 1988, Hostetler argued that "community building and community maintenance is part of the 'redemptive' process. 'Redemptive' in this context means being made whole."[40] Interestingly, his last published essay was titled, "The Amish as a Redemptive Community" (1996). Redemption—wholeness—was found through rites of obedience and community-building, underscoring some fundamental tenets of Anabaptist theology. So, starting with abstract models of social science early in his career, Hostetler later listened in new and attentive ways to how the Amish had constructed their own web of meaning and understood themselves within it. Having begun his career in the

1940s (pre-graduate school) writing on theological themes, he came full circle when he returned to a theological motif for the title of his final published essay in 1996.[41]

THE SIGNIFICANCE OF HOSTETLER'S SCHOLARSHIP

Although success is not a favorite Amish word, Hostetler's scholarship stood head and shoulders above other works on the Amish prior to and parallel with his. In a short bibliographical essay in *Amish Society* (1963), Hostetler notes that "a maze of books, pamphlets, and articles" on the Amish had appeared since 1894, including at least seventeen books.[42] None of them enjoyed the prominence or acclaim of *Amish Society* for a variety of reasons. The works of Walter M. Kollmorgen and George Calvin Bachman, which both appeared in 1942, and Elmer Lewis Smith's *The Amish Today*, which appeared in 1961, all focused primarily on the Amish of Lancaster County.[43] Kollmorgen's technical monograph, sketching the agricultural economy of the Amish, had a limited audience. Bachman, a Reformed pastor in Lancaster County, wrote perceptively about the Amish but lacked the tools of anthropology and sociology. Smith's *The Amish Today* came closest to tapping the resources of social science, but lacked the sophistication of analysis and organization for a successful book.

These publications fell below *Amish Society* for several additional reasons, most notably their superficial treatments of intricate cultural issues and their lack of endorsement by academic publishers. Hostetler's *Amish Society* carried a double legitimacy because Hostetler was an "Amish insider" and because the book had the blessing of a major scholarly press. Moreover, his perceptive analysis, grounded in social-scientific concepts, covered Amish communities in several states. In addition, his research and analysis of the communal Hutterites, who in contrast to the Amish used advanced technology, provided comparisons that sharpened Hostetler's interpretations of Amish society.

What were the factors that contributed to the success of Hostetler's scholarship? First and most importantly, it was reliable and authentic. Because of his upbringing among the Amish and his ongoing access to the community, he understood the nuances of Amish practices and perspectives in ways that would have required years of specialized fieldwork by an outsider. Despite his decision to forgo baptism in the Amish church, his relationships with Amish people allowed him to interpret them with a profound sense of respect and understanding—*Verstehen*, or sympathetic understanding, to use the language of Max Weber. His continuing respect for his birthright community garnered him access to the secrets of the "little community," adding legitimacy and accuracy to his interpretations. The intimacy that he enjoyed with extended family members and friends enabled him to write thick ethnographic descriptions of Amish culture. His work not only provided new descriptive data but also set a higher bar—a new standard for other scholars of Amish life.

Second, Hostetler understood the religious sentiments that lay beneath the surface of Amish culture. Unlike other investigators who artificially attached Bible verses to certain Amish practices, Hostetler grasped the nonverbal intuitions of the Amish spirit that shaped their worldview. He understood how religious perspectives, often not verbalized, filtered Amish views and motivated daily practice from dress to the selection of technology.

Perhaps the best example of this was his analysis of the role of silence and nonverbal behavior in Amish life. This theme emerged for the first time in the third edition of *Amish Society* (1980) and then continued throughout much of his later writing.[44] Based on Edward T. Hall's distinction between low-context and high-context cultures, Hostetler argued that, in the high-context culture of Amish society, silence and nonverbal behavior are key forms of communication.[45] This "silent discourse" on a "deeper level" explains the periods of silence in Amish prayers before and after meals, in worship services, on Sunday afternoons, in religious conversion, and in the face of interpersonal threats as well as suffering and disaster—to name but a few of the powerful ways in which the Amish use silence to build community, practice obedience, and respond to challenges.

I consider Hostetler's analysis of nonverbal behavior his most creative, original, and perceptive foray into Amish culture. Without a doubt, his solid scholarship has made a contribution to Amish studies that towers above all the other works in the field. Nevertheless, much of it is simply good scholarship, the kind that is expected from any mature ethnographer who gathers data carefully through field observations, interprets them with conceptual models, sets the story in historical context, and presents the findings in a readable fashion. Hostetler performs all of these functions in an admirable way, but his analysis of the silent discourse of Amish life rises above the typical standards, penetrating deep into Amish life to unmask hidden assumptions that guide everyday behavior. It is one thing to describe the dress or child rearing practices of the Amish, but quite another to elucidate the hidden, even unconscious, assumptions that shape a people's worldview and daily life.[46]

Finally, Hostetler's scholarship was significant because of the wide swath it cut and the powerful way it shaped public perceptions of the Amish. It is easy to focus on *Amish Society* as Hostetler's central contribution because it became the leading text for courses and reference on Amish matters for several decades, but it was only one of his many contributions. He also nourished the scholarship of Amish life with publications in academic journals, important monographs, and *Children in Amish Society*, which he coauthored with Gertrude Enders Huntington in 1971.[47]

Huntington was one of two women who helped to shape and refine Hostetler's scholarship. Hostetler gave Huntington's two-volume Yale dissertation on the Amish of Ohio special acclaim in a bibliographic essay in the first edition of *Amish Society,* calling it "genuinely insightful."[48] Without a doubt, "Trudy" Huntington was his closest and most influential colleague over the years, doing fieldwork for his research on the Hutterites and collaborating on a major study of Amish socialization that resulted in *Children in Amish Society.* She read numerous drafts of Hostetler's manuscripts, discussing and dissecting his arguments paragraph by paragraph, and sometimes word by word. Interestingly, their written correspondence is very limited, for they talked on the telephone once or twice a week over the many years of their collaboration.[49]

Another close colleague was Hostetler's spouse, Beulah Stauffer Hostetler. Especially in the first half of his career, she edited his manuscripts because, in her words, "John was not an editor."[50] The Hostetlers first collaborated in the production of *Amish Life* (1952), which Beulah designed in her work as a Herald Press editor.[51] A decade later, Johns Hopkins University Press gave her accolades for her editorial work on the first version of *Amish Society.* An artist, she drew sketches of Amish life for *Amish Society* (1963) and for an essay John wrote on Amish symbols.[52] Her doctoral dissertation, published as a book in 1987, used charter and defensive structuring theories, which reflected their collegial interests and professional partnership.[53]

Beyond his scholarly publications, Hostetler shaped the production of the documentary film, *The Amish: A People of Preservation*; provided expert testimony for the Supreme Court case *Wisconsin v. Yoder*; helped to initiate the National Committee for Amish Religious Freedom; supported Amish genealogical studies; and collaborated with genetic researchers at Johns Hopkins University.[54] Not content to communicate only to scholars, Hostetler worked hard to shape public perceptions of the Amish through popular booklets, most notably *Amish Life*, which in its various editions became the all-time best seller for Herald Press with sales exceeding 850,000 copies. All of these activities attest to the influence of Hostetler's scholarship that, in addition to advancing understanding of the Amish during his lifetime, also laid a foundation for other scholars to come.

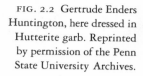

FIG. 2.2 Gertrude Enders Huntington, here dressed in Hutterite garb. Reprinted by permission of the Penn State University Archives.

EXTENDING HOSTETLER'S WORK

Dozens of scholars have built on Hostetler's work, using his arguments and themes as benchmarks for comparison, expansion, and in some cases critique. My work continues some of the central questions that captured his imagination: How are the Amish able to not only survive, but indeed thrive in the contemporary world? How do they produce integrated communities and social conditions that optimize human satisfaction and well-being? In some ways, Hostetler focused on the "fixed customs" of Amish life, to use his words in the first edition of *Amish Society*, although that description is not entirely fair because the last seven chapters deal with various types of social change.[55] Hostetler, however, tended to study internal changes, whereas I have been more interested in how interactions with the outside world shape not only Amish practices but also government policies toward and perceptions of ethnic minorities such as the Amish. In sum, my work explores the ways in which the Amish community *negotiates* with the outside world, impacting and changing all the parties at the cultural bargaining table.[56]

Other scholars have explored new areas of research by challenging, implicitly

FIG. 2.3 Participants in Johns Hopkins University's genetics research team, CIRCA 1967, included John A. Hostetler (left) and Beulah Stauffer Hostetler (third from left). Others, from left, were Hugh Gingerich, Bud Yoder, Ruth Ann Stauffer, Victor McKusick, and Freda Yoder. Reprinted by permission of the Penn State University Archives.

or explicitly, some of Hostetler's assertions. We have already noted the work of Marc Olshan, who pushed Hostetler in the early 1980s to rethink his assumptions about the folk society model. Other scholars, coming of age later than Hostetler (and, significantly, in the wake of significant socioeconomic changes in some Amish communities), have reviewed and revised his claim that agrarianism is part and parcel of Amish life. Whereas Hostetler identified agrarianism as an inextricable component of the Amish charter, further studies have noted the occupational shift away from farming to working in outside industries and especially the rapid growth of Amish-owned businesses, developments that, at least in the short term, have not spelled the demise of Amish society.[57] Still other scholars have extended Hostetler's discussion of Amish women (and gender issues more generally).[58] Scholars collaborating on a pathbreaking study of the Amish in Indiana have underscored anew the vast diversity of Amish life within numerous subgroups in the same state.[59]

However important the initiatives and insights garnered by a new generation of scholars, we all work in the shadow of Hostetler's contributions, turning frequently to his works for information and insight. Regardless of our conceptual models and research topics, we were taught by Hostetler to listen carefully and watch closely if we want to learn the secrets of the redemptive community. To a world of scholars who trade on sophisticated vocabulary and noisy arguments, he taught the importance of listening—listening even to the silence in order to hear the throb of the Amish heart. He also argued that the logic of Amish culture, however odd it might appear to outsiders, arises from an "island of sanity" surrounded by a larger culture "obsessed with economic indicators and technology run rampant."[60] These islands of silence and sanity, he reminds us, can become redemptive communities for those who willingly submit to their ways.

NOTES

1. Hostetler also directed Temple University's Center for Communal Studies, a project spurred by his interest in the Hutterites and utopian communal movements of the 1960s.

2. John A. Hostetler, Gertrude Enders Huntington, and Donald B. Kraybill, "Cultural Transmission and Instrumental Adaptation to Social Change: Lancaster Mennonite High School in Transition," Final Report to the U.S. Department of Health, Education, and Welfare, Office of Education, National Center for Educational Research and Development, 1974; Donald B. Kraybill, "Ethnic Socialization in a Mennonite High School" (Ph.D. diss., Temple University, 1975); Donald B. Kraybill, *Ethnic Education: The Impact of Mennonite Schooling* (San Francisco: R & E Research Associates, 1977); and Donald B. Kraybill, *Passing on the Faith: The Story of a Mennonite School* (Intercourse, Pa.: Good Books, 1991).

3. John A. Hostetler, *Hutterite Society* (Baltimore: Johns Hopkins University Press, 1974).

4. Bernard J. Siegel, "Defensive Structuring and Environmental Stress," *American Journal of Sociology* 76 (1970): 11–32.

5. Donald B. Kraybill, *The Riddle of Amish Culture* (Baltimore: Johns Hopkins University Press, 1989). Interestingly, Hostetler did not explicitly use the framework in *Hutterite Society* or in the third and fourth editions of *Amish Society* (Baltimore: Johns Hopkins University Press, 1980, 1993). However, his spouse devoted a chapter to defensive structuring in her study of the Franconia Conference of the Mennonite Church in eastern Pennsylvania. See Beulah Stauffer Hostetler, *American Mennonites and Protestant Movements: A Community Paradigm* (Scottdale, Pa.: Herald Press, 1987).

6. Donald B. Kraybill, John A. Hostetler, and David G. Shaw, "Suicide Patterns in a Religious Subculture: The Old Order Amish," *International Journal of Moral and Social Studies* 1 (1986): 249–63; and John A. Hostetler and Donald B. Kraybill, "Hollywood Markets the Amish," in *Image Ethics: The Moral Rights of Subjects in Photographs, Film, and Television*, eds. Larry Gross, John Stuart Katz, and Jay Ruby (New York: Oxford University Press, 1988), 220–35.

7. John A. Hostetler, "Persistence and Change Patterns in Amish Society," *Ethnology* 3 (1964): 191–92. This piece is reprinted in this volume as Chapter 11.

8. The new president of the college, Gerhard Spiegler, asked me in 1985 to prepare a proposal for an Anabaptist studies center. To initiate the center, Hostetler was appointed director

(1986–89) and distinguished scholar-in-residence. His spouse, Beulah Stauffer Hostetler, joined the faculty as assistant professor of sociology and religion, and as a research associate.

9. As director of the Young Center, Hostetler organized the first three conferences around preservationist themes: "Anabaptist Communities: Coping With Modernity," 1987; "Land, Ethics, and Community Values," 1988; and "Contemporary Issues in Lancaster County: Ecology, Land Use, and Health Care," 1989. In 1988, he submitted to the Pennsylvania Department of Transportation a fifty-page monograph entitled, "Land Use, Ethics, and Agriculture in Lancaster County," which included twelve excerpted essays from the likes of Warren Berger, Archibald MacLeish, Wendell Berry, and E. F. Schumacher (as well as his own passionate views on preserving land and community). The following year he presented a lecture, "Toward Responsible Growth and Stewardship of Lancaster County's Landscape," to the Lancaster Mennonite Historical Society, which was subsequently published in *Pennsylvania Mennonite Heritage* 12, no. 3 (1989): 2–10. The latter piece is reprinted in this volume as Chapter 18.

10. Peter L. Berger, *Facing Up To Modernity* (New York: Basic Books, 1977), 61. See also Peter L. Berger, Brigitte Berger, and Hansfried Kellner, *The Homeless Mind: Modernization and Consciousness* (New York: Vintage Books, 1974).

11. Hostetler's involvement in the Mennonite Community Movement is discussed in Chapter 4.

12. Hostetler's relationship to the Young Center culminated in an international conference organized by the center in 1993 on the tricentennial of Amish life (1693–1993). The gathering, which took place just prior to his seventy-fifth birthday, included the release of *The Amish and the State*, a Festschrift compiled in his honor. See Donald B. Kraybill, ed., *The Amish and the State*, 2d ed. (Baltimore: Johns Hopkins University Press, 2003).

13. John A. Hostetler, *Annotated Bibliography on the Amish* (Scottdale, Pa.: Mennonite Publishing House, 1951). The bibliography won the Chicago Folklore Prize in 1952.

14. John A. Hostetler, "The Amish as a Redemptive Community," in *The Amish: Origin and Characteristics, 1693–1993*, eds. Lydie Hege and Christoph Wiebe (Ingersheim, France: Association Française d'Historie Anabaptiste-Mennonite, 1996), 346–55.

15. Hostetler, *Amish Society* (1963), viii.

16. For discussions of the trend toward quantification, consult Ray P. Cuzzort and Edith W. King, *20th Century Social Thought*, 3d ed. (New York: Holt, Rinehart and Winston, 1980); Roscoe C. Hinkle Jr. and Gisela J. Hinkle, *The Development of Modern Sociology* (New York: Random House, 1954); and Paul F. Lazarsfeld, *Qualitative Analysis: Historical and Critical Essays* (Boston: Allyn and Bacon, 1972). For a recent discussion of the philosophical and methodological issues related to quantification in the social sciences, see Nicholas Rescher, *Objectivity: The Obligations of Impersonal Reason* (Notre Dame: University of Notre Dame Press, 1997).

17. Some of the required texts with a strong quantitative tilt included Hubert M. Blalock, *Social Statistics* (New York: McGraw-Hill, 1960); John H. Mueller, Karl F. Schuessler, and Herbert L. Costner, *Statistical Reasoning in Sociology* (New York: Houghton Mifflin, 1970); Karl F. Schuessler, *Analyzing Social Data* (Boston: Houghton Mifflin, 1971); and Gene F. Summers, ed., *Attitude Measurement* (Chicago: Rand McNally, 1970).

18. Amish farmer and historian Gideon Fisher, interview with author, 1988.

19. Hostetler, *Amish Society* (1993), 97.

20. Many of these conflicts are chronicled in Kraybill, ed., *The Amish and the State*.

21. See, for example, "Old World Extinction and New World Survival of the Amish: A Study of Group Maintenance and Dissolution," *Rural Sociology* 20 (1955): 212; "A New Look at the Old Order," *Rural Sociologist* 7 (1987): 280–81; and *Amish Society* (1993), 387. Hostetler him-

self seemed worried about the demise of Amish society in the face of modernization, but he never predicted it per se.

22. Hostetler, *Amish Society* (1963), viii.

23. Ibid., 3–4.

24. See David Weaver-Zercher, *The Amish in the American Imagination* (Baltimore: Johns Hopkins University Press, 2001) as well as Weaver-Zercher's comments in the preface to this book.

25. Ammon Monroe Aurand Jr., *Little Known Facts About the Amish and the Mennonites* (Harrisburg, Pa.: Aurand Press, 1938).

26. Hostetler, "A New Look at the Old Order," 280–81. In this article, reprinted in this volume as Chapter 17, the sixty-eight-year-old Hostetler reflects with unusual candor on his methodological approaches and current understanding of Amish society.

27. Ibid., 282.

28. His psychological interests appear in a section on the Amish personality for the first time in the third edition of *Amish Society* (1980), as well as in *Children in Amish Society*, coauthored with Gertrude Enders Huntington (New York: Holt, Rinehart and Winston, 1971).

29. A. L. Kroeber and Clyde Kluckhon review the long history of the concept of culture in anthropology in *Culture: A Critical Review of Concepts and Definitions* (New York: Vintage Books, 1952). The nascent emergence of culture in sociology was signaled by books such as those by Robert Wuthnow, *Cultural Analysis: The Work of Peter Berger, Mary Douglas, Michel Foucault, and Jürgen Habermas* (Boston: Routledge and Kegan Paul, 1984); and James Davison Hunter and Stephen C. Ainlay, eds., *Making Sense of Modern Times: Peter L. Berger and the Vision of Interpretive Sociology* (London and New York: Routledge and Kegan Paul, 1986). Since 1990 dozens of books on cultural sociology have appeared. See, for example, David Swartz, *Culture and Power: The Sociology of Pierre Bourdieu* (Chicago: University of Chicago Press, 1997). Cultural sociologists now have their own newsletter and subsection in the American Sociological Association.

30. Hostetler, "A New Look at the Old Order," 282.

31. Ibid.

32. Beulah Stauffer Hostetler, telephone conversation with author, 15 June 2004. She also noted that some reviewers of the first edition of *Amish Society* remarked about its "poetic qualities."

33. Robert Redfield, "The Folk Society," *American Journal of Sociology* 52 (1947): 292–308. Chapter 3 addresses in detail Hostetler's use of the folk society concept.

34. For two versions of Olshan's argument under the same title, see Marc A. Olshan, "Modernity, the Folk Society, and the Old Order Amish," in *Rural Sociology* 46 (1981): 297–309, and in *The Amish Struggle with Modernity*, ed. Donald B. Kraybill and Marc A. Olshan (Hanover: University Press of New England, 1994), 185–96. At the 1993 Amish tricentennial conference at Elizabethtown College, Olshan asked how a 1963 model (folk society as used in the first edition of *Amish Society* [1963]) could explain Amish realities in 1993.

35. According to Hostetler's spouse, his attendance at a Cornell University seminar in 1961 sparked his enthusiasm for the concept of charter (Beulah Stauffer Hostetler, telephone conversation with author, 15 June 2004). Much of his article, "Persistence and Change Patterns in Amish Society," was devoted to the Amish charter. This was preceded, of course, by his use of it in the first edition of *Amish Society* (1963).

36. Hostetler, *Amish Society* (1963), 47. See Bronislaw Malinowski, *A Scientific Theory of Culture, and Other Essays* (Chapel Hill, N.C.: University of North Carolina Press, 1944).

37. Sandra L. Cronk's "*Gelassenheit*: The Rites of the Redemptive Process in Old Order Amish and Old Order Mennonite Communities" (Ph.D. diss., University of Chicago Divinity School, 1977) is peppered with the phrase, "the redemptive process," but does not use "redemptive com-

munity." Nevertheless, she argues that the rites of *Gelassenheit* (surrender or yieldedness) are foundational to the community-building and redemptive process in Old Order communities. Hostetler begins to use the phrase "redemptive community" for the first time after the appearance of Cronk's dissertation in 1977. He mentions *Gelassenheit* one time in the third edition of *Amish Society* (1980, 298) but cites sources other than Cronk. Hostetler's spouse does not recall him "spending much time with Cronk's work" and was uncertain about the antecedents of "redemptive community" or his lack of interest in and use of *Gelassenheit* in later editions of *Amish Society* (Beulah Stauffer Hostetler, telephone conversation with author, 15 June 2004).

38. When Hostetler first used the term "redemptive community" in the third edition of *Amish Society* (1980), it constituted the first of six dimensions of the charter described in the book's fourth chapter, "The Amish Charter" (75–92).

39. "As he became more secure in his scholarship, he became less interested in theoretical models, more inclined to follow his intuition" (Beulah Stauffer Hostetler, telephone conversation with author, 15 June 2004).

40. Hostetler, "Land Use, Ethics, and Agriculture in Lancaster County," 4. The theme of redemptive community was also central in his "A New Look at the Old Order" essay in 1987.

41. An even better example of his use of theological language near the end of his career was his 1989 essay, "Toward Responsible Growth and Stewardship of Lancaster County's Landscape," regarding Lancaster County farmland and rural communities.

42. Hostetler, *Amish Society* (1963), 326.

43. Walter M. Kollmorgen, *Culture of a Contemporary Rural Community: The Old Order Amish of Lancaster County, Pennsylvania* (Washington, D.C.: U.S. Department of Agriculture, 1942); George Calvin Bachman, *The Old Order Amish of Lancaster County* (Norristown, Pa.: Pennsylvania German Society, 1942); and Elmer Lewis Smith, *The Amish Today: An Analysis of Their Beliefs, Behavior and Contemporary Problems* (Allentown, Pa.: Pennsylvania German Folklore Society, 1961).

44. Hostetler, *Amish Society* (1980), 374–76. Other examples include John A. Hostetler, "Silence and Survival Strategies among the New and Old Order Amish," in *Internal and External Perspectives on Amish and Mennonite Life*, ed. Werner Enninger (Essen, Ger.: Unipress, 1984), 81–91; and Hostetler, "A New Look at the Old Order," 287–89.

45. Edward T. Hall, *Beyond Culture* (New York: Doubleday, 1976).

46. Hostetler's analysis of the role of silence in Amish life is akin to what anthropologist Clifford Geertz called "thick description." Hostetler admired Geertz's work, which is summarized in a series of essays in Clifford Geertz, *The Interpretation of Cultures* (New York: Basic Books, 1973).

47. John A. Hostetler and Gertrude Enders Huntington, *Children in Amish Society: Socialization and Community Education* (New York: Holt, Rinehart and Winston, 1971).

48. Hostetler, *Amish Society* (1963), 327. Huntington's thousand-page dissertation, entitled "Dove at the Window: A Study of an Old Order Amish Community in Ohio," appeared in 1956.

49. Gertrude Enders Huntington, telephone conversation with David Weaver-Zercher, 18 June 2004.

50. Beulah Stauffer Hostetler, telephone conversation with author, 15 June 2004.

51. John and Beulah Hostetler were married the following year, in 1953. John's first wife, Hazel Schrock, died in childbirth in 1951 along with their only daughter.

52. John A. Hostetler, "The Amish Use of Symbols and Their Function in Bounding the Community," *Journal of the Royal Anthropological Institute* 94, no. 1 (1964): 11–22, reprinted in this volume as Chapter 10.

53. Beulah Stauffer Hostetler, *American Mennonite and Protestant Movements*.

54. See John A. Hostetler and Victor A. McKusick, "Genetic Studies of the Amish: A Summary and Bibliography," *Mennonite Quarterly Review* 39 (1965): 223–26.

55. Hostetler, *Amish Society* (1963), vii.

56. See particularly Kraybill, *The Riddle of Amish Culture*; and Kraybill and Olshan, eds., *The Amish Struggle with Modernity*.

57. Thomas J. Meyers, "Lunch Pails and Factories," in *The Amish Struggle with Modernity*; and Donald B. Kraybill and Steven M. Nolt, *Amish Enterprise: From Plows to Profits*, rev. ed. (Baltimore: Johns Hopkins University Press, 2004).

58. See especially Marc A. Olshan and Kimberly D. Schmidt, "Amish Women and the Feminist Conundrum," in *The Amish Struggle with Modernity*, 215–29. For popular considerations of Amish women, see Louise Stoltzfus, *Amish Women: Lives and Stories* (Intercourse, Pa.: Good Books, 1994); and Louise Stoltzfus, *Traces of Wisdom: Amish Women and the Pursuit of Life's Simple Pleasures* (New York: Hyperion, 1998). See also Chapter 3, which discusses Hostetler's analysis of gender in Amish life.

59. Several publications are forthcoming from this three-year study funded by the Lilly Endowment, Inc., including Thomas J. Meyers and Steven M. Nolt, *An Amish Patchwork: Indiana's Old Orders in the Modern World* (Bloomington: Indiana University Press/Quarry Books, 2005).

60. Hostetler, "A New Look at the Old Order," 280.

3

PLAIN FOLK AND FOLK SOCIETY:
JOHN A. HOSTETLER'S LEGACY OF THE LITTLE COMMUNITY

Simon J. Bronner

As he was about to turn seventy-three years old, John A. Hostetler returned to the county in Pennsylvania where he was born and addressed a local historical society audience on "What I Learned from My Heritage."[1] His choice of "heritage" was significant because, more than saying "what I learned from my past," he wanted to draw attention to the transmission of tradition from one generation to another within the context of community. In his view, his heritage was divided between two groups—the religious community in which he was raised and the academic one he adopted later in life. He derived fulfillment in both from the same virtue: in his words, a "viable community" insuring itself by "trust, by good faith and goodwill, and by mutual help." Both groups were also capable of inducing stress, whether exemplified by the excommunication of his father by the county's Peachey Amish church, or by dissatisfaction with the prevailing trends of his sociological "discipline." And both groups were relatively small communities struggling for sustainability, and redemption, in the realm of mass culture.

Always attuned to the basis of belief influencing social structure, Hostetler distinguished the Amish from academe as a split between a folk and scientific society, with the former an inward-looking group concerned for subjective faith and connection to the land and the latter an outward-looking network devoted to objectivity and transcendent use of the mind.[2] Both maintained differences with the imposing, worldly "world." One group was his "plain folk" or little community, while the other was his "colleagues" fitting into the "great" or elite "tradition." The former was distinguished by its traditional, communitarian character and its spiritual mission, and the latter by its intellectual, often individualistic purpose. Although both provided him with a sense of belonging, neither one in itself was totally satisfying.

In this essay, I interpret Hostetler's writing coming out of his attraction to the notion of the "little community." Drawn from theories of the "folk society" or "folk sociology," the idea of little community shaped Hostetler's outlook, distinguished his major scholarly contribution of *Amish Society*, and informed his various public campaigns throughout his life. For Hostetler, the idea was not only a tool to help elucidate the characteristics of Amish society, it was also a philosophy relevant to public policy and religious reform. The significance of Hostetler's use of the folk society concept, usually credited to Robert Redfield, is that Hostetler was the foremost, if not the first, social scientist to apply it to North America. Introduced with Latin American peasant societies in mind, the idea of the little community, or the small tradition, grew from attempts to describe "ideal types" of localized social structures dependent on, but distinct from, economic and socially dominant urban centers. For American studies, Hostetler's analysis was bold, considering that North America was thought to be lacking a peasant society, and by extension a common marginal class tradition rooted in the soil. Hostetler's contribution was to show what he called "social discourse" between the Amish and the world, an interrelationship of apparently conflicting worldviews. "Community" comes up repeatedly in his rhetoric, because he was convinced that viable communities offered a corrective to the dangers of individualism in modernizing commercial culture. Community-individual, folk-urban, sacred-secular, humility-pride, outsider-insider, love-alienation—Hostetler's categorizations are replete with polarizations he sought to resolve in local settings.

The constant backdrop for Hostetler's rhetorical oppositions was global modernization in the twentieth century and the resulting destruction of tradition. Apropos, "The World's War Against the Amish" was the provocative headline of one of his essays that emerged from the first edition of *Amish Society*, with the revealing subtitle, "Battling to Save a Way of Life, the 'Plain People' Are Losing." Its opening offers a theme that runs through much of his writing, that of a threatened traditional community in the larger world but not of it: "The outsider cannot help but be aware of the distinctiveness of the Amish people, nor fail to admire, in some respects at least, the qualities which set them apart from the modern industrial society surrounding them."[3] Sensitive to history, he understood the turbulent, war-torn mid-twentieth-century era he witnessed to be a pivotal moment of decision for the world. In this context, he wondered, could the viable community and spiritual core he linked to an earlier mode of living be restored? After arguing in the essay that the scales between the little community and world had decidedly tipped toward the world, he sought a balance between tradition and change, in his own life and for American society, that would reduce conflict and insure peace. His outline of strategies for preserving the Amish as a folk society was a reminder to the world of the function of community and tradition in its ethos. The idea of folk-ness in Hostetler's thought on the little community, I find, encapsulates his attachment to the Amish as a redemptive, ideal society for the world to draw upon for its own redemption. To elaborate the theme, I consider not only his social vision and sociological observation, but also the significance of his mes-sage from the mid-twentieth century to the beginning of a new millennium. To contextualize the message and relate it to his life script, I connect his ex-perience to other educated elites emerging in the mid-twentieth century who formed a "New Class" engaged in cultural critique based on a valuation of plain folk and folk society.

IN TWO SOCIETIES

The lines between Hostetler's memories of growing up Amish and his obser-vations as a sociologist were never as solid as he sometimes professed. After all, the virtues and stresses he observed in his own life he also drew in his mag-num opus, *Amish Society*. A distinguishing feature of later editions of the book was his claim of being able to gain "the view from the inside." But he was vague about what this perspective meant. He did not refer to his own experience as evidence, but he proposed that he had an advantage over other researchers who did not grow up Amish. After a reviewer of the first edition of *Amish Society* (1963) wrote that "the reader sometimes suspects that when Hostetler por-trays and analyzes the deviations of the Amish youth some of his own experi-ences may enter the text," Hostetler quickly dashed off a letter, insisting, "I steered away from doing any autobiographical treatments, for the simple rea-son that I still want to live with my relatives and maintain a reasonable happy relationship. All of the testimonials in the book actually were taken from inter-views with other people and did not happen to be Hostetler."[4]

Despite early decrees of maintaining a scientific distance from his personal experience, Hostetler later admitted to more of his memories informing his writing. In the third and fourth editions of *Amish Society* (1980, 1993) he ac-knowledged that "Mifflin County, Pennsylvania, where I lived as a member of an Amish family, and Washington and Johnson counties, Iowa, where I spent my youth until the age of twenty-two, taught me much about the depth and diversity of Amish culture." Again noting fulfillment and stress in his her-itage, he confessed, "I have experienced the ties of kinship and faith, but I have also seen the tragedies of division, exclusion, and fragmentation."[5] In fact, he originally submitted *Amish Society* to Johns Hopkins University Press with the subtitle "Fulfillment and Crisis in the Little Community" to draw attention to the forces working in a small, viable community, but he was encouraged to drop it in favor of the short title.[6]

The issue of Hostetler's objectivity as a social scientist was raised in the introduction to the first edition of *Amish Society* by eminent sociologist Charles Loomis, who had hired Hostetler to conduct interviews in Amish communities. Although Hostetler did not cite his memories of Amish life in the original text, Loomis highlighted Hostetler's Amish background and "Americanization": "The author himself is not only part of the Amish story, but part of the irrevocably changing America which comes in some measure even to 'separatists' such as the Amish."[7] Despite noting Hostetler's remaining family ties to the Amish, Loomis assured readers of Hostetler's "dedication to his science."[8] Although Loomis waxed poetic about Hostetler's narrative of Amish society being "*the* Amish story," the book was clearly also about American society.

In his original preface to *Amish Society*, Hostetler contrasted the Amish commitment to stability and tradition to the rapid change of modern American society. "We live in a world that is being transformed before our eyes by new inventions, new forms of communication, and new folkways," Hostetler wrote. This observation was the springboard to several provocative questions about whether this change truly represented progress, culminating with the pointed query, "How much destruction of old values, of alienation of parents from children, of neighbor from neighbor, of the spirit of man from the faith of his traditional culture, must there be?"[9] By the time he published his preface to the fourth and last edition in 1993, he changed the questions into assertions about the lessons of tradition and spirituality that could be gained from the Amish, and in his use of the pronoun "us" counted himself among the moderns: "American rural communities generally have been transformed into landscapes for development, investment, and commercial gain. Without preachment the Amish have taught *us* something of the human cost when old values are cast away, when parents are alienated from children, when neighbors are treated as strangers, and when man is separated from his spiritual tradition."[10] In *Amish Life*, Hostetler's short, popular treatment of Amish culture, he iterated a variant on the theme: "The Amish admiration for creation, their respect for nature and order, their practice of personal rather than impersonal relationships, have won the respect of many a visitor. In a world that has grown cold for lack of human contact, traditional communities like the Amish have important lessons to teach *us*."[11]

Hostetler's work, then, is as much about modern American society accelerating to the future as it is about the Amish and their traditions. His references are constantly in scaled, oppositional pairs—little and large community, group and nation, small and great tradition. He was predisposed to this polarization because of his absorption of the Anabaptist belief in two conflicting kingdoms. As explained by Hostetler's undergraduate mentor, Mennonite church historian Harold S. Bender, the New Testament vision of the church is characterized by a "singular duality" between the church and the "world": "The one is 'the dominion of darkness,' the kingdom of this world; the other is 'the kingdom of his beloved Son.' To enter the church is to be delivered from the one and transferred into the other." While the church may be in the world, it nonetheless represents a separate kingdom by being "distinct from the world, not of it," he writes. Bender's influential reading of the New Testament, especially for Mennonites, is that the "line of distinction between the two kingdoms is sharply drawn, the church and its members are separate from the world, yet operating redemptively in it." In language strikingly similar to Bender's summary of the Anabaptist creed, Hostetler observes in *Amish Society*, "The Old Order has maintained a dualistic conception of reality that approximates a fixed position; that is, sharp cultural definitions of church and 'world'. . . . The community (*Gemeinschaft*) is looked upon as a separate entity in but 'not of the World.'"[12] In his scholarship, Hostetler was drawn to the social duality of a little community that operates by its own norms in defiance of prevailing trends, but creates a relationship with a larger world and tries to redeem it.

Accordingly, Hostetler presents social science of the little community with a moral purpose of restoring identity through tradition, social interdependence, and spiritual values to modern society. His relational approach to the problem of Amish survival is to describe "the little community" remaining "around the edges of expanding civilizations."[13] In that location, it fulfills a function for the larger society, and may be dependent on it, but its viability is constantly threatened. The task that Hostetler took on was to show that the Amish are viable and that the world can help them remain so. As he developed his career, he not only admonished the world to allow the Amish to be different, he called on American society to be more similar to the Amish. He also had a message for the Amish: they could function better, reducing the harshness of their exclusionary practices and insuring the health of their members through scientific medicine. Out of his experience as participant-observer *in* two societies, he developed knowledge of each society's life as a cultural system. In his liminal location *between* two societies, he created what he thought was an objective vantage from which to interpret their relationship to each other. In that intermediary space he could become a mediator as well as interpreter. In the name of objectivity, even as it was colored by his Anabaptist background, he separated himself from romantics who overly idealized the Amish and from those who derided them for their anachronisms, from scientists who would turn the Amish into historic relics and from others who predicted their doom.[14]

BETWEEN TWO SOCIETIES

If Hostetler offered to uncover how Amish society works in relation to mass culture, what answers did he propose to his provocative questions about the recovery of American society's "values," "spirit," and "faith"? In his early editions of *Amish Society*, he professed to have "no ultimate answers."[15] In the third and fourth editions, however, he eliminated that disclaimer as he became thrust— or inserted himself—more and more into an intermediary role between the Amish and the "world." He frequently took the public role of mediator between the two, an advocate for the Amish in court, a watchdog against the wrong kind of writing on the Amish, and a vocal critic of modernizing society. The irony is that the task of mediation became critical because of a situation partially of his making—the popularization of the Amish.[16] Hostetler was instrumental in bringing the two societies together, and he simultaneously sought to separate them. That dynamic, that tension, was a drama based on his own life script.

Hostetler provided the prologue for his life script in two autobiographical articles, both published in 1992. In "An Amish Beginning," published in *American Scholar*, he does not, as we might expect, view the memory of his father's excommunication from the Amish church as the impetus for his leaving Amish culture. It was, he proclaims, the lure of higher education. If he sought a college education, he had to leave, because the Amish forbid, in Hostetler's words, "self-advancement, higher education, philosophical and speculative endeavors of life." He describes the move to academic life in almost mystical terms, an inevitable pilgrimage of one who is "inwardly compelled" by a higher power. As he writes, "I was not looking for an escape of just any kind, but I felt there was destiny beyond my understanding. It would be revealed to me if I exercised patience, endurance, self-control, and peace of mind." Indeed, he refers in religious rhetoric to his "call": "I felt compelled to obey the call, though I did not know where it would take me."[17]

If Hostetler's *American Scholar* essay emphasizes the cultivation of the mind, "What I Learned from My Heritage" underscores the uplifting of the spirit through the building of community. He elaborates in the heritage essay on the virtues of the Amish "redemptive" community he left. According to Hostetler, the redemptive community is "a place where people are made whole." This notion of social purity built on trust means that members of the community see themselves as "recipients of an undeserved gift." They show their gratitude by proving themselves worthy, faithful, grateful, and humble. They reciprocate by offering to God in return a community permeated with the attributes of the divine: walking in righteousness, sacrificial suffering, obedience, submission, humility, and nonresistance.[18] As a result, harmony within the church-community is a major and constant concern, and the relationship of church and community is inseparable. In contrast to modern society in the period of industrialization and urbanization, according to Hostetler, "They asked, in their time, not 'What will this new invention do for me as an individual,' but 'What is best for the welfare of our community?'" The various answers given by different communities in a region means that divisions will be created in response to the world. The implication is that community wholeness is disrupted by the world, and the fragmented communities must then self-consciously commit to maintain themselves by "protecting the church-community from pernicious threats."[19]

Hostetler reflects that he learned to value the small scale of the local culture he later viewed as an authentic or folk experience. He appreciated the social interconnection of life in a landed community, contrasting it to the artificial world of mass culture that, in his view, manipulated people with "what advertisers and profitable corporations would have us value and desire." The destruction of farming and the natural landscape is a symptom of modernization undermining the redemptive function of community, Hostetler opines. If one accepts that nature is the manifestation of the divine, or a gift from God, then destroying it and threatening the little community that plowed it as a "pure offering to God" betrays God's trust.[20] These ideas, presented in 1992, were hardly new thoughts to him. Thirty-five years earlier, Hostetler had editorialized that the Amish "may be counted among the best—old-fashioned, one must say—farmers of the nation," asserting that their success in tilling the soil stemmed from the faith that undergirded their lives.[21]

Given Hostetler's interest in, or calling to, writing the Amish as a redemptive community, he sought to find an academic home for his passion. As with so many of his issues of identity, he moved about and grew attachments but never fully settled in. As with his search for a folk community where people are made whole, he wanted in his academic quest to understand people as a whole, and he often viewed disciplines as fragmenting the total picture of society. In "What I Learned from My Heritage," for example, he does not identify himself as a sociologist, although he is often categorized as one. "Sociology provided fragments of knowledge," he sighed, and overall, he complained,

"Science has advanced our knowledge of the human community by fragmenting it." Again using a missionary rhetoric of spreading the idea of community,
he refers to his academic coming-of-age as a "journey" for finding meaning.
"My journey," he writes, "took me from community awareness to history, to
sociology, to anthropology."[22]

Hostetler was drawn to anthropology, he said, because it offered synthesis,
dealt in wholes, and rationalized what seemed to moderns to be bizarre. He reveals, "When I learned what culture was, it was a surprise to discover that every
society has a culture, a total life-way. That culture is logical and consistent
from the point of view of the individual in his culture made sense."[23] Still, anthropology often insisted on understanding the culture by being foreign to it,
and Hostetler railed against social scientists who in his view misunderstood
the Amish because they had not lived among them.

The rising interdisciplinary field of folklife studies was attractive to Hostetler
because it encouraged the insider's perspective and the study of "total culture"
of a people, particularly among the Pennsylvania Germans. Hostetler contributed materials on Amish expressive culture such as clothing, songs, and speech,
which were of great interest to folklorists. Hostetler joined zealous adherents
of the folklife approach, such as Don Yoder and Alfred Shoemaker, at several
major folklife conferences.[24] Hostetler published several times in the journal
Pennsylvania Folklife, but, as if to distinguish himself from Yoder and Shoemaker, he appended the descriptor "A Sociologist's Analysis" to his essay on
Amish family life to underscore social rather than expressive goals.[25] He shared
with Yoder and Shoemaker a precarious balance of helping the "public" gain
proper appreciation of Amish tradition while being careful to not dilute the
scholarly interpretation or fostering a tourist gaze.[26] Still, he did not identify
himself as a folklorist, although he later taught courses on folk society and
Amish folk culture. Maurice Mook, an important mentor to Hostetler, kept
pushing him to delve further into folklore and folklife studies.[27] It may very
well be that Hostetler was attracted to the term "folk society" because it represented to him a disciplinary and epistemological synthesis, combining the
cultural expressiveness and signal of tradition in folklife with the concern for
social process and community in society.

CAMPAIGNS AND PASSIVE RESISTANCE

As an undergraduate, Hostetler embarked on a curricular journey, searching
for a disciplinary identity as he took courses in history and majored in Bible

before switching to sociology. War loomed over his studies, and his formal education was interrupted when he was inducted into Civilian Public Service as a conscientious objector. In his reminiscences, he saw this service as more than putting in time; he viewed it as "passive resistance" to the government's waging of war. Showing his belief in reading as an awakening power, he began to donate copies of books on pacifism, church history, and community life to libraries during wartime.[28]

Attending Mennonite-affiliated Goshen College after the war, he came under the influence of Harold S. Bender, often given credit for spurring Anabaptist studies and church history in America.[29] Given to instilling "a sense of mission" and "a sense of stewardship of life and talents" in Mennonite education, Bender tapped Hostetler to assist him with the editing of the monumental four-volume *Mennonite Encyclopedia*.[30] Bender asked him to contribute entries on the Old Order Amish and related groups, including profiles of Hostetler's boyhood communities in Belleville and Mifflin County, Pennsylvania. The assignment forced him to think about representing the Amish to a public audience. Although his entries were informational rather than interpretative, he already began to formulate a campaign against misrepresentations of the Amish. He resented the prevalent journalistic images of the Amish as relics of a bygone era or a backward people hanging on to bizarre customs and beliefs.

Hostetler's first assault was on A. Monroe Aurand Jr.'s popular pamphlets on the Amish, especially his publications on bundling that Hostetler labeled reprehensibly "obscene."[31] For Hostetler, they were crass commercial exploitations of the Amish as well as compilations of titillating misinformation, resulting in an image of the Amish as cultural oddities, if not sexual amusements for the world. He also was concerned about the perception that Aurand's publications were scholarly studies, because the rhetoric of analysis—such as "a study of," "sociology," and "folklore"—appeared in some titles.[32] He would not have the Amish laughed at by the public; the Amish, in his view, needed to be taken seriously for the improvement of modern society. Hostetler embarked on what he called "a prolonged crusade" to eliminate the distribution of Aurand's pamphlets. His outrage also spurred him to compile an annotated bibliography in 1951 with pointed comments on the existing scholarship regarding the Amish.[33] He dismissed Aurand, for example, by remarking on his *Little Known Facts About the Amish and the Mennonites*, "Some writers still delight in playing up the seemingly odd or curious incidentals of the Amish way of life. Many of the statements of this writer if not contrary to fact are actually misconstrued or out of proportion to the total picture."[34]

Hostetler saved his most heated and righteous indignation for Elmer Lewis

Smith's popular pamphlet on Amish bundling published in 1961, expressing special disappointment because he thought Smith, as an academic, should know better.[35] Smith was a professional sociologist, but Hostetler felt that he did not uphold the ethics of the social science community and indeed was guilty of "exploitation of Amish knowledge."[36] "You have performed a very great disservice to your profession as a social scientist and to the Amish people in issuing *Bundling Among the Amish*," Hostetler bluntly wrote to Smith. Taking the identity of an Amish man, he complained, "This publication will do great harm to *my* people."[37] He followed by urging the publisher, "I can only hope that you will choose the greater act of morality in taking these books away from an already misguided public."[38] "Whether the facts are true or not is quite beside the point," Hostetler then wrote the president of the Pennsylvania German Society, "the way in which he has handled them is in very poor taste and adds nothing to our understanding of the Amish people."[39]

Poring over the outsider Smith's writing on the Amish gave Hostetler a chance to clarify the insider's perspective he brought to the subject. In a review of Smith's larger, more scholarly study, *The Amish People* (1958), Hostetler wrote, "The attempt on the part of the author to fit Bible verses to Amish practices seems forced and unjustified in several instances: Quotations are given which the Amish do not or have not used to support their traditions."[40] In unpublished notes on the book, Hostetler asserted, "Quoting Biblical passages in support of traditions is done by the Amish leaders but frequently this is not done until some 'outgrouper' makes the observation."[41] For Hostetler, the significant guiding principle for the Amish was their reliance on tradition to perform the social function of holding the community together. As he wrote, "The observer expects to find a 'rationale' in the ingroup structure and if he fails to find it he frequently reads values into the data." Rather, "Amish life is largely one that is sanctioned by tradition and is not so existentially and rationally perpetuated in their natural habitat."[42] An example Hostetler cited was Smith's explanation of Amish women wearing white garments only once during their lifetimes, at their weddings. Whereas Smith connected the custom to a passage in Rev. 19:7–9, Hostetler claimed it derived from a precedent in their European cultural experience, when garments were spun with flax.[43]

Hostetler's opinion on the importance of social and cultural practice to the viability of community is reflected in his rhetoric of "life" drawn from the discourse of folk "life" as a living tradition bound by community.[44] Countering the modernist view that the Amish blindly *follow* tradition, and therefore lack a democratic sense of freedom, Hostetler strived to show that the Amish freely *choose* their lifeway and perform traditions out of a commitment to a redemp-

FIG. 3.1 Hostetler's publications often included images of barn raisings, which he used to underscore the characteristic of mutual aid in the "little community." Photograph by Karl G. Rath, Pennsylvania Historical and Museum Commission.

tive community. Acknowledging the significance of the biblical injunction to live in a redemptive community, he nevertheless emphasized the power of a heritage "shaped by the faith and struggle of their European past."[45] Underscoring the social functions of traditions in the present day, he avowed that their society persists, even grows, in the face of a threatening world, because "work, family, mutual aid, religion, and social affirmation, for example, are integrated into a satisfying web of life."[46] For Hostetler, the key was having the sense of the whole operating as a social system.

ENGAGEMENT OF THE NEW CLASS

Hostetler drew on the sociologists at the Pennsylvania State College (later University and known widely as Penn State), as well as Michigan State sociologist Charles Loomis, for a perspective on the functional operation of social systems as viable units. Before coming under their influence, Goshen College's historically minded Harold Bender had a hand in shaping Hostetler's attention to precedent and faith. Bender, an advocate of "social ministry" for the reconstruction of human society, encouraged Hostetler to continue his education toward social ends, and Hostetler responded by choosing a secular institution—Penn State.[47] There he gained scientific credentials while maintaining his sense of religious mission. As Hostetler explains in "An Amish Beginning," Penn State was attractive because it was near his Amish boyhood home in Mifflin County and he could work with like-minded sociologist William Mather on the faculty. Hostetler appreciated the way Mather "prodded the social conscience of both the scientific community and the religious institutions."[48] Mather, who like Hostetler had grown up on a farm, allowed that social science scholars could be informed by their religious convictions and could apply their work to the reform of the church. Among Hostetler's papers is a copy of Mather's address "The Mission of the Rural Church," and Hostetler highlighted the section on "Reverence for the Land." Hostetler was struck with Mather's observation that "One of the most basic changes in agricultural rural communities has been the growing commercialization of agriculture. . . . The farm becomes a business enterprise, and often the farmer operates it on a short-range policy of overworking the soil for immediate profit to the ruin of its value for future generations." Mather followed this observation with a biblical reminder: "When God planted the garden eastward in Eden, he said to Adam whom He put in charge, 'replenish the earth.' That means to fill it up again, not to empty it out."[49] Another of Mather's statements that resonated with Hostetler was the concluding observation that "when people move in little more than a generation from the small, snug isolation of the old rural neighborhood into such a great and confusing world as our modern one, they have great enlargements of soul to make."[50]

In Mather's critique of commercialization and mass culture is a sign of the emergence of the "New Class" in the mid-twentieth century to which Hostetler formed a philosophical tie.[51] Following World War II, the role of colleges in preparing youth for professional careers expanded, and the rising institutions offered unprecedented promises of advancement to many aspirants to the middle class. During this period, the expansion and democratization of education were at the center of debates about civil rights and the disruption of cultural and political control by elites. Social movements to recognize ethnic, religious, and racial pluralism in America took shape during the 1950s, often fermented by educated "public intellectuals" who hoped to break up the hegemony of a Brahmin old guard in business and ivory towers.[52] The economy was expanding and diversifying from its former industrial base into service and information sectors, including the growth of government service. At that time, many new members of the middle class used education to form professional intellectual identities—such as professors, journalists, attorneys, social workers, and therapists—that challenged the old power of business, family privilege, and inheritance. Some observers discuss this period as a period of bifurcation in the middle class, in which this professional class entered into an adversarial relationship with business.[53]

Many members of the new professional class came from tradition-oriented backgrounds such as farming and immigrant communities, and like Mather appeared distrustful of urban growth and commercialization even as they felt swept up by them. They often formed new interdisciplinary academic movements challenging conventional European-centered, classical disciplinary boundaries, or they challenged elitist conventions by seeking out vernacular and ethnic subjects close to home as relevant to America's problems and worthy of cultural study. Moreover, they often chose these vernacular subjects based on their own backgrounds, and legitimated their own participation in society as a result, even as they experienced psychological conflict between their former, traditional identities at society's margins and their newfound identification with elites at the center. One ploy was to claim to be modern by combining scientific advancement with spiritual awareness of community, a rhetoric that implied a critique of dominant commercial and old education forces, as well as the empowerment of local, often marginalized communities. Indeed, an interpretation of American society as ethnically plural (and the approach of social studies as "pluralism-in-microcosm") served the class's ideological concerns for reorienting social power.[54] Notably during the 1950s, Richard Dorson made a splash by underscoring as America's master narrative the ethnically diverse, living folk traditions of the Upper Peninsula of Michigan, rather than the homogeneous model of old New England. Similarly, Charles Loomis, who came to be a strong influence on Hostetler, called for a fuller accounting of America's diverse identities for the purpose of understanding "persistence and change" in American society.[55] Loomis sounded the keynote of "improvement" in New Class interests, appealing in A Strategy for Rural Change to "those who have professional responsibility for changing or improving life": the teacher, minister, and social worker, among others.[56] Because acting in community was considered a lost social skill in an individualistic modern society, studies of "community-in-microcosm" served to provide models of successful social integration, while "pluralism in microcosm" emphasized the tolerance for communities within national political systems.

Concerned for the access to power to instill change and advance socially, New Class members commonly created distance from their vernacular subjects even as they offered a defense of their subjects' traditional values. New Class members often displayed a status anxiety because they held intellectual authority but lacked economic or political clout, partially, they felt, because of their traditional background and fresh arrival in the middle class. One rhetorical strategy that reduced the anxiety was to make claims to scientific expertise and claim authority of information in the new economy based on education. The stance of objectivity and professionalism was essential to this claim of authority, even if they advocated for a social vision that incorporated traditional values into a new social order.[57] They often appealed to the broad "public" in writings that manifested revisionist understandings of American diversity, and they took on roles as public intellectuals mediating between their heritage and improving life as professionals.[58]

Hostetler's telling statement of New Class interest is found in "Toward a New Interpretation of Sectarian Life in America," published shortly after he arrived at Penn State. Exhibiting his own brand of status anxiety as an "educated sectarian," Hostetler wrote, "Like other 'Dutchmen' the sectarian who has taken the trouble to get an education has not returned to the community to serve his people."[59] He complained that outsiders have not helped the public gain an informed understanding of sectarian life, and in focusing on what is odd and titillating about the Amish, have reinforced the elitist and exploitative attitude of mass culture toward sectarian groups. Probably referring to writer Joseph W. Yoder, Hostetler was also critical of educated sectarians who exhibited tendencies to romanticize the groups from which they came.[60] He explained the modern alternative he favors: "In this day of scientific achievement and inquiry there must be a new approach to the study of the sectarian society combining the features of unbiased and intellectual honesty in comprehending the entire culture."[61]

As a New Class member rising from traditional culture, Hostetler was unwilling, however, to give up "tradition" totally for the sake of scientific achievement. In "Tradition and Our Scholars," written for a Mennonite audience in 1957, he noted that it had become more acceptable for Mennonites to pursue Mennonite topics in higher education rather than to exchange "their Mennonite tradition for another one."[62] At the same time, he said, "tradition is usually regarded as something to be freed from," an allusion perhaps to a common compensatory practice for members of the New Class.[63] Hostetler, however, called for tradition to be used as a guide for application toward problems of social equality, and he asserted that the Christian scholar was in a position to lead through humility, by which he meant acknowledging the role of the little community and seeking ways to reform the world by showing what was good in tradition. Social science scholarship in the past, he complained, tended to undermine religion and become prophets of doom. "As a result," he wrote, "modern civilization finds itself cut off from any deep faith, and modern man is more uncertain, more undecided, and doubts whether life has a point."[64] Hostetler therefore called on Christian scholars of the new generation to be leaders in advancing "objective" knowledge that would show the "good in tradition" and help modern society foster a "living belief." Thus he expressed the dilemma of the New Class in a Mennonite context: reforming the state while being a part of it; retaining the heritage, tradition, and spirituality of the little community while participating in mass culture; and using education and knowledge as a key to advancement and change while not sacrificing the stability and security of the small group.[65]

Hostetler's revisionist interpretation of American society during the 1950s and 1960s, in keeping with New Class objectives of gaining authority through information to effect social change, is set in the frame of new professionals such as himself using their traditional backgrounds but adopting the modern stance of science to achieve reform. In *Amish Society*, Hostetler identified social involvement as a virtue of tradition apparently sacrificed in the rush toward modernization. He elaborated on the authoritarian, bureaucratic, and hierarchical models of corporate America that contributed to a sense of individual alienation rather than social integration. In the original preface to *Amish Society*, he therefore emphasized the book's consideration of "change within a small society that is surrounded by a dominant one."[66] "The effort here," he wrote, "is to understand custom on the one hand and change on the other"—a summary of balance in a society between the forces of tradition and modernity. The community of tradition was "integrated," whereas the community of modernity was one of "conflict and stress."[67] He offered a New Class metaphor of a therapeutic physician examining a patient, and implied therefore that a prescription for social health could be applied: "A patient who allows himself to be thoroughly examined by a skilled physician undertakes the risks of discovering his strengths and weaknesses. In the same way a society which falls into the scrutiny of scientific investigation is liable to have its internal strengths and weaknesses exposed."[68] But he was vague—intentionally and cleverly so I think—about whether the society in question was the Amish or America. The answer is undoubtedly both.

More evidence of Hostetler's New Class interests is found in a list of books he requisitioned when he accepted a sociology post at Penn State-Ogontz in 1962. The first texts on his list were *Social Theory and Social Structure* (1957) by Robert K. Merton, *Sociology Today* (1959) by Robert K. Merton and others, and *Sociological Imagination* (1959) by C. Wright Mills.[69] Merton's functionalist approach was surely appealing to Hostetler. It is Merton who proposed the idea of customs serving manifest and latent functions; the manifest was a conscious motivation, such as holding a wedding ceremony to unite two people, whereas latent functions were social consequences typically outside of participants' awareness. In the case of the wedding, the latent function was to transmit the values of the society at a time when the community was drawn together and thereby stabilize it. The social scientist's role, Merton argued, was to point out the latent functions that may not be recognizable by a society, and to find applications in new settings.

Especially pertinent to New Class ideology is Merton's chapter on the "Role of the Intellectual in Public Bureaucracy," such as the university or government. As opposed to technicians who implement policy, Merton argued, intellectuals seek to modify economic and political structure.[70] The irony, and anxiety, of the postwar period was that many intellectuals found themselves as the new arrivals within bureaucracies of universities and governments. They sought social as well as scientific innovation while realizing they were representatives of the urban industrialized structure. Hostetler understood the irony when he wrote to a Penn State colleague, "It appears that we are located in a somewhat bureaucratic woods with the trees being so close that we cannot see each other."[71] Later equating bureaucratization with an anti-diversity ideology and urban living, Hostetler editorialized, "Today some of our bureaucratic elements who view the ethnic communities from the windows of our skyscrapers see diversity in language, dress, and morality as an unmanageable problem. They ask: 'Would it not be more civilized if all those queer people out there spoke one language, obeyed all our regulations, and got 'cleaned up' like the rest of us?'"[72] The traditional idea of effecting a face-to-face interchange, characteristic of community, was undermined by the bureaucracy, so Hostetler suggested. Accordingly, Hostetler taught in his American society classes C. Wright Mills's idea of an emerging power elite in modernizing societies, militaristic and corporate in its power base, that commands the resources of bureaucratic organizations, marginalizes traditional groups, and thus undermines cultural democracy. The works of Mills, calling for a socially responsible intellectual, and Merton, a son of immigrant parents who developed ideas of a successfully integrated community that Hostetler adapted, are often cited in New Class analyses.[73]

Significantly, Hostetler's New Class brand of social observation finds sectarian or traditional communities operating for cultural—indeed human and spiritual—benefit, and therefore holding a legitimate place within American democratic society. In *Amish Life*, he felt compelled to ask, "What contribution have the Amish made to society?" His answer there was that "their neighborliness, self-control, good will, and thrift contribute immeasurably to the foundations of our civilization."[74] In "Toward a New Interpretation of Sectarian Life in America," Hostetler refers to the redemptive quality of Amish society by asserting, "it is often those 'remnants' who have held to religious ideals, those primary groups who have perpetuated community solidarity, that societies have looked to in reconstructing their civilization."[75] The problem, he iterates, is in being objective and scientific in narrating remnant groups like the Amish. Enlarging the scope of his Amish studies to a view of "community in microcosm," Hostetler concludes, "Although this discussion has been focused on the Mennonites and Amish because of my personal acquaintance and study in this field, yet there are doubtless other minority cultures making a unique contribution to the larger society if we can acquire the techniques of discovering those values."[76] Other minority cultures gained notice through the 1950s and 1960s as evidence of America's cultural democracy, but, to his credit, Hostetler came to influence a host of considerations of the Amish as America's exemplary communitarian, tradition-centered group. It is even ironic that, rather than being countercultural or separatist, the Amish in some narratives became America's contemporary ancestors because of their preindustrial farming practices and community emphasis.[77] In such accounts, according to

David Weaver-Zercher, the Amish "exemplified a degree of 'togetherness' that middle-class Americans wished for themselves."[78]

In his campaigns against the commercialization and distortion of the Amish, and in promoting an understanding of the Amish in terms of social processes, Hostetler arguably performed New Class functions and exhibited New Class status anxieties. In one significant regard, however, Hostetler differs from many figures given to analysis in the emerging New Class; coming from an Amish-Mennonite background, he was skeptical of government attending to the interests of marginalized communities and checking the corrupting forces of commercial culture. He apparently did not long for a return of federal New Deal programs empowering and employing cultural workers in a revitalization of a "democratic Left," as activist Michael Harrington espoused.[79] In the concluding section of the first edition of *Amish Society* (1963), he related an exemplary story ridiculing government officials for advising the Amish during World War II to scrap their horses so they could produce more farm products. He pointed out that the Amish use of horses was already giving the country the highest possible output. More than twenty years later, he more caustically referred to "large-scale, alienating bureaucracies of public life," and commented, "The growing antibureaucratic mood in industrializing societies is not without foundation. Too many megastructures result in widespread alienation." That is not to say he would not call upon government to enact protective measures, as he showed in his advocacy for Amish farmland preservation and for exemption of the Amish from compulsory school laws. Yet he frequently stated that the key to Amish survival was others respecting their "fundamental right to be left alone."[80]

Hostetler also departed from the common assumption that the New Class was a highly secularized group. Still, Mather and Hostetler fit into the idea propounded by Peter L. Berger that, in their positions of intellectual authority, New Class members can have religious functions of explaining suffering and evil, and thereby call for a spiritual as well as political melioration of society.[81] Often they do so by focusing intellectual endeavors on troubling or provocative social processes rather than elitist texts, thus raising questions of how mass society operates, or should operate. Mather's introduction to *Amish Life* underscored Hostetler's success in presenting Amish "Biblical values and sociological values basic to their way of life," which, in Hostetler's rendering, offered "the modern hurried, worried world" a host of valuable lessons.[82] For Hostetler, the manifestation of the connection between religious and social values was his concern for Amish society as a little community relative to "expanding civilization," and his sensitivity as a New Class member to social stratification and fragmentation. Hostetler's use of polarizations such as rural-urban and folk-scientific is another indication, because it invites a resolution allowing for a combination of tradition and modernity, spiritual and material.

PLAIN FOLK AND THE STABLE COMMUNITY

Hostetler's "folk" stood in opposition to city and technological life, and intervention seemed necessary to prevent the wholesome folk from abandoning their moral, honest rural life. In his view, the social unit most at risk, and most capable of perpetuating tradition, was community. Addressing the assumption that parents can preserve the religious values of their children, even if the values are contrary to their social environment, he observed, "The really powerful traditions are a product of community rather than family," and "the family cannot long maintain any tradition different from its supporting community."[83] Hostetler bemoaned most of all the loss of attendant values—"neighborliness, personal interest, mutual aid of goods-in-kind"—and he called for regaining community by cultivating informal face-to-face associations instead of continuing to build bureaucratic organizations.

Using "folk" to conflate informal face-to-face association with transmission of tradition from one generation to another, Hostetler offered another jeremiad against a lost sense of community in "Folk Art and Culture" for *Christian Living*, a Mennonite family magazine. Noting the rapidly vanishing folk arts in modern America, he preached, "The regrettable tendencies among the arts today are symbolic of the general frustration of mankind as a result of our machine age."[84] The metaphor of the machine age undermining social and religious life continues in his jeremiad as he bemoans the effects on creative imagination wrought by "hurry-up living and assembly-line production." Once again Hostetler sees the maintenance of the little community as a key to realizing art and tradition as "things of the spirit," contending that *folk* art "can flourish best in stable communities where needs are met co-operatively by ingenuity, by interdependence." Using the rhetoric of wholeness, Hostetler writes that the folk artist "is an integrated whole personality" who "prefers to live in functional completeness," a role he contrasts to the scientist who performs a specialized function and "lives out of context with the rest of society."[85] Admitting that the clock could not be turned back on this modernization, he calls for incorporating values of folkness in "building a truly modern community." Hostetler's modernism is thus distinguished from a corporate-capitalist modernity, which he implies is psychologically detrimental to its participants. He writes, "if there were greater promotion of creative art in industry and among rural folk it is probable that few mental hospitals would need to be built each year." Rather than turn to government to conserve America's traditional arts as occurred during the New Deal, Hostetler calls for colleges, church groups, and community organizations to utilize authorities "who have a fair grasp of *rural* folk art and folk culture" to help disseminate traditional techniques from one locale to another.[86]

In his jeremiads, Hostetler presumes a devolutionary slide of tradition in modern society. Even among the tradition-oriented "plain people" he finds rapidly increasing assimilation to the machine age. His designation of the Old Order Amish as not just plain people, but "plain folk," signals their resistance to the self-fulfilling prophecies of the "modern scientific world."[87] In his address "Pennsylvania's Plain Folk" at a conference devoted to reasserting rural life in an industrial age, Hostetler observed that, in defiance of evolutionary expectations, the Amish "not only retain the older traits in their entirety, but modify them in the direction of more conservatism."[88] The example he gives is of the prescribed length of haircuts, which was intentionally longer in 1950 than it was in 1900. He further elaborated this theme in "The Amish Use of Symbols and Their Function in Bounding the Community," published in 1963. Here his essential insight is that symbolism in modern industrial society differs from that of a folk culture, for "in a simple society symbolism has its origin in informal associations rather than in formal processes."[89] He thus sets up another contrast between the Amish, in which symbolism is determined by custom and conformity, and "our progressive civilization," which derives symbols from "speculation, from formal and rational procedures, from scientific pursuits, from economic competition, and from the signs of material achievement."[90] His study focused on dress, normally associated with fashion and ostentation in modern society, but which among plain folk epitomized trustworthiness and religious piety.

Hostetler asks, if modernization inevitably sweeps across the land, why, then, have the Amish persisted, even grown, in numbers? In answer to this question, he identifies the provision of security; that is, by centering their society on mutual aid and a sense of social fellowship, the Amish "provide for the elementary needs of the individual from the cradle to the grave."[91] In creating distinct symbols of plainness, in contrast to the patterns of industrial society, the Amish derive psychological and spiritual support. The implication is that modern urban society instills status anxiety because of constant contact with strangers and uncertainty of identity in an individualistic, success-oriented world. He subtly also criticizes modern religion in his assertion that the Amish in contemporary life are fulfilling the function of Christianity, which "in its earlier stages utilized effectively the representations of the fish, the dove, the lamb, and many other symbols."[92]

THE LITTLE COMMUNITY AND FOLK SOCIETY

Hostetler conceptualized the Amish as a little community in his first anthropology seminar, entitled "Folk Society," taught by Maurice Mook at Penn State in 1949. The new course revolved around a groundbreaking essay, Robert Redfield's "The Folk Society," published two years earlier in the *American Journal of Sociology*. Folk societies, Redfield proposed, have certain features in common that enable scholars to define them as a type in contrast to the society of the modern city. The features of the folk society are that it is small, isolated, homogeneous, and nonliterate, with a strong sense of group solidarity. Underscoring the familiarity of folk with one another, Redfield postulated that "members of the folk society have lived in long and intimate association with one another."[93] Further, the folk society tends to have little division of labor, be economically self-sufficient, and conform to a behavioral norm. "Custom" is important for fixing the rights and duties of individuals, and the sacred prevails over the secular. Redfield's application of the concept was in Mexico and the Yucatan peninsula, of special relevance to the role of peasant societies in conjunction with "expanding civilizations," although he invited broad comparisons of other "folk*like*" communities.[94]

The folk society concept immediately aroused discussion and debate, probably because it invited commentary on the perceived displacement of traditional communities by urbanization, industrialization, and bureaucratization during and after World War II. Whereas prewar anthropologists had primarily sought out "primitive" or tribal groups in remote locations, the folk society concept suggested conceiving of cultural islands closer to home and to modernity.[95] Folk society featured an integral, if unequal, relationship between modern, dominant civilization and the little community, not one apart from it. One notable commentator suggested that Redfield acted more in the spirit of a social philosopher than a social scientist, for he attributed a moral order to traditional communities and implied that technology and urbanization were naturally corrupting.[96] Folk society had a connection to New Class ideology because the model setting urban and folk as dominant and subordinate patterns, respectively, called upon the objective scientist to show how the positive values of the folk society could be incorporated into growing urban life, and how the folk culture could be preserved as a natural, self-sufficient system.[97] The timing of the proposal to expand "folk sociology" in the postwar period was not mere coincidence, as Redfield himself observed the same year he published "The Folk Society": "There never was a time when social science was more needed than it is today. The extreme peril in which we live arises from the small political and social wisdom we have in the face of our immensely dangerous material strength. We should have more control over the physical world, yes, surely; but it is far more necessary that we learn to control the relations among men."[98]

Hostetler remembered the discussions of folk society in Mook's seminar as being among the liveliest of his academic career. The concept raised hard questions not just on how to explain new patterns of social systems, but also how to preserve tradition-centered societies and apply their lessons to modern life. A number of groups came under scrutiny in the class, but as Hostetler recalls, "we discussed the Amish as if they were the most important topic in the course."[99] When Mook eventually proposed the course as a permanent fixture in the curriculum, the catalog description read, "comparative study of several folk societies with emphasis upon Pennsylvania Amish."[100] In *Amish Society*, Hostetler embraced the folk society model, delineating its main features as "distinctiveness," "smallness," "homogeneity," and "self-sufficiency." He understood, however, that the Amish did not neatly fit into the ideal type of Redfield's folk societies in Latin America, acknowledging that they did not meet the criteria of being "age-old" and "completely geographically isolated" as were peasant and tribal societies.[101] Hostetler thus preferred Redfield's use of "little community" as a rural subculture with folk society features within a modern state.[102] Emphasizing the social "contract" among the community's members, Hostetler offered a defining characteristic of the society as possessing a strong sense of "we-ness," in its double meaning of togetherness and smallness.[103] The "folk" or "little community," Hostetler pronounced in his introduction, was the critical "bench mark" for understanding the Amish.[104]

What exactly is the understanding of the Amish from the perspective of the folk or little community? Asserting that traditional small communities are "disappearing from the modern world"—a process that leads to the homogenization of mass culture—Hostetler observes that the Amish look upon strong community identification, or tradition, as necessary for personal and social fulfillment, and contrasts this positive valuation of tradition with a post-industrial worldview that considers tradition an obstacle to the democratic ideal of progress. In using the rhetoric of the little community, Hostetler makes the Amish exemplify the idea of preindustrial community in America, conceived as a matter of an orientation toward tradition and social interdependence. In so doing, he departs from the previous analytical strategy of making the Amish culturally odd or socially unique in the American cultural landscape. Once left out of narratives of the American experience, the Amish in Hostetler's depiction become part of the saga of escape from religious persecution and building a new, redemptive society in the New World.

In emphasizing the social structure of the Amish as fitting into an ideal type, Hostetler also diverges from the religious interpretation that the persistence of the Amish comes from unusual biblical devotion. Pointing out that other biblically devoted groups have embraced more change than the Amish, Hostetler finds that positing literal application of the Bible by the Amish is insufficient to explain "plain" customs. A historical explanation based upon their adherence to European foundations does not satisfy him either, because it does not account for contemporary social adaptations and divisions. For Hostetler, the little community best explained the cohesiveness of the Amish, as well as some of their conflicts, because it suggested that the maintenance of tradition is a function of community. Accordingly, Hostetler argued, the Amish make decisions about handling change and conflict by considering their effect on little community features of mutual aid, social interdependence, and group solidarity. They positively value their smallness and plainness, because such attributes provide benefits of security, stability, and redemption. As Hostetler points out to "the English," this choice is not irrational, inflexible, or anachronistic, for it results in a sense of belonging and purpose that modern society could stand to restore. He shakes the presumption that progress in the form of rapid change is a natural evolution. According to Hostetler, a group can decide, as the Amish had, to hold social relations above all else. Not without conflict, Amish society in Hostetler's social functional interpretation can embrace apparently exclusionary practices as a way to reduce conflict and ensure solidarity.

Hostetler certainly appreciated the glowing reviews that *Amish Society* generated, such as the one by Pennsylvania German scholar John Joseph Stoudt, who wrote, "Of all the recent books about the Amish, John Hostetler's *Amish Society* is far and away the best, towering above these other works like a skyscraper over a city of cabins."[105] Still, he anxiously awaited the response to his use of folk society from social science circles. The responses were mixed. For instance, a reviewer for the *American Journal of Sociology* accepted Hostetler's explanation of how the Amish maintained "remarkable continuity" despite threats to their way of life, but he faulted Hostetler for exaggerating the group's stability by excluding from analysis Amish who left the fold.[106] Hostetler read with special interest the review by his teacher of Folk Society, Maurice Mook. While praising Hostetler's use of Redfield's little (folk) community as a "fresh and original" feature of the book, Mook also chided his student for not discussing the analysis extensively. "Most of the nuances of Redfield's analysis are lacking," Mook wrote, "and no account is taken of the various criticisms of Redfield's formulation."[107] Mook insisted, for example, that as a concept it needed more connection of the social structure to expressive culture, namely folklore.[108] Hostetler apparently took the jabs well, noting that other reviewers thought he overemphasized the sociological analysis. Still, in the third and fourth editions of the book, Hostetler modified the section on "folk society" and elaborated on the little community as a "little commonwealth," noting that members claim to be ruled by the law of love and redemption. By using "commonwealth," Hostetler sought to adapt Redfield's concept more to the American scene in which a group is located in a "part of a national domain that geographically and socially is sufficiently unified to have a true consciousness of its unity."[109]

Whether in response to the anthropological Mook or not, Hostetler subsequently expanded in later editions of *Amish Society* (1980, 1993) the idea of the Amish "charter." In the first edition (1963), he succinctly defined charter as "the fundamental values and common ends of the group, recognized by the people and accepted by them."[110] Charter encapsulated for Hostetler the way that distinctive, "otherworldly" moral principles are communicated and understood by the group. In later editions, Hostetler elaborated the role of myth and folklore in conveying these moral principles and supporting the social structure. Taken from the functionalist anthropology of Bronislaw Malinowski, the idea of charter related to the little community by positing that myth and folklore are not just reflections of a society's values, but also serve the social function of maintaining it, providing precedent for present-day behavior. As expressive traditions, myth and folklore institutionalize the behavior of a society by enforcing its norms. In the last edition, Hostetler explained his adaptation of a concept Malinowski meant for primitive, isolated society to a traditional group such as the Amish in modern society: "Acting as a charter, myth endows the society's values with prestige and supernatural force. It is not only a conservative force, perpetuating the status quo with powerful integrative functions as indicated by Malinowski, but it is also a language of social discourse which provides the members with purpose."[111]

The charter need not be reduced to writing to be effective, Hostetler pointed out, and in the Amish case includes social understandings of the church as a redemptive community, followed by separation from the world, the vow of baptism, *Ordnung* (unwritten regulation of what is appropriately "plain" and sinfully of the world), excommunication and social avoidance, and closeness to nature. While many societies have these charters, the Amish use theirs, Hostetler argued, as a hedge against social change and a mechanism to maintain cultural continuity in the little community. Again, traditions become functions of the social impulse to form a little community, which presumes that members of the group consent to its customs, particularly as crises arise in regard to adapting to change. There is a risk, therefore, that the community cannot reach consensus. Then disagreement over traditions could result in division into other little communities in which members are in accord with one another over decisions about adaptations. "In times of social conflict and change," Hostetler emphasized, "myth provides a language of argument using signs and symbols to establish meaningful distinctions from those of other groups."[112] As Donald B. Kraybill argues in Chapter 2, using charter became increasingly significant in Hostetler's later interpretations of the Amish to show how traditions could become instruments of division as well as cohesion, thus contributing to the dynamic nature of Amish society. While the folk society was a "type" or structure, charter constituted the process by which its separateness, stability, and change are sustained.

THE LEGACY OF AMISH SOCIETY

Besides sparking scholarly interest in the Amish and forcing their consideration in a pluralistic narrative of America, *Amish Society* inspired a host of works on other religious groups struggling to maintain distinct communities within national and mass cultures. Perhaps Hostetler hoped for more studies applying the little community idea to ethnic and minority groups generally, but his greatest impact was on the interpretation of Anabaptist groups. Calvin Redekop's *Mennonite Society* (1989) emphasized the rhetoric of community, asserting that "the Mennonites are a social group united by the religious faith cohering in the religious community, a community which has a unique cast and which provides a 'boundary' mechanism for identity."[113] Carl Bowman followed with *Brethren Society* (1995), which offered a more historical than ethnographic approach to a religious group's dynamics. Whereas Hostetler explained the Amish commitment to smallness and plainness, Bowman narrated the Brethren's move beyond plainness, with the critical implication that the group lost some of its core values as a result. Borrowing some of Hostetler's rhetoric,

Bowman promised that "special attention will be paid to the competing moral commitments that produced tension, cultural conflict, and adaptation along the way. Change will be traced in true ethnographic fashion, with some of the finer threads of Brethren culture being laid bare from the Brethren's own point of view."[114]

Hostetler had himself added an Anabaptist group to the list of those receiving analysis as a little community with the publication of *Hutterite Society* (1974), although unlike the communitarian Amish who held property individually, the communalistic Hutterites held property as a community. He modified some of the generalizations he made in *Amish Society* as a result, because he found that the Hutterites did not follow the "normal pattern of tradition-directed societies with respect to social change."[115] The Hutterites did not modify their social structure as their population expanded, and they thrived as a little community even though they accepted mechanization. Hostetler stuck to his social-functional explanation used in *Amish Society* by pointing out that the innovations did not alter "basic social patterns." Instead, change was accepted that would maintain "a smoothly functioning colony" and retain their religious values.[116] As with the Amish, Hostetler warned that "a small society that comes under the scrutiny of scientific investigation exposes itself to the risks of disclosure—of its weaknesses and its strengths," and, also as with the Amish, Hostetler found "communities of people who live a satisfying, stable, and rewarding life."[117]

The image of rewarding communitarian life in Hostetler's scholarship was shaken, however, when in the late 1980s he became embroiled in a bitter controversy regarding the attempts of a twentieth-century group called the "Society of Brothers," or *Bruderhof*, to join the Hutterites. Including them in the continuous line from the Amish and Hutterites to the present, Hostetler at first appeared supportive and adopted the phrase "intentional community" for what he called their "pioneering effort to find new ways of living based on love and self-giving."[118] Their effort, he implied, held the promise of applying the lessons of the folk society to new communal organizations, and the group consulted Hostetler as it emerged in the 1950s from its persecuted origins in Nazi Germany. A series of unions, conflicts, and eventually acrimonious expulsions occurred between the Hutterites and the Society from World War II to the 1970s. A reconciliation occurred in 1974, which Hostetler called "a great spiritual culmination," and he wrote a flattering foreword to one of the Society's publications in 1988.[119] But he had a change of heart after learning of "cultic behavior" such as imprisonment for dissidents, severe interrogations of children, and beatings for members who wished to leave the community. He adjusted his thinking about the Society as a modern-day continuation of the Anabaptist little community by drawing a contrast between its totalitarian and cultish "closed society" and the openness of the sectarian Amish and Hutterites. Stating a sociological principle that "a good indicator of the maturity of a community is how it treats those persons who leave," he found that closed communities, unlike little communities (in their best sense), treat former members as "enemies, traitors and failures." Putting aside his social scientist role, he objected to the cultish behavior as running counter to the Anabaptist tradition, and he appealed to the Society "to not 'call down fire from heaven' against those who wish not to 'unite' with them."[120] Invoking the memory of his Amish childhood, he could not reconcile the "self-annihilating" tactics of the Society with the mutual trust he experienced as an Amish youth. In this instance, he was clearly unnerved by the way that the lessons of the Christian folk society had been applied.[121]

Hostetler could point out, however, that other intentional communities drew more benevolently on his idea of a folk society to promote a communitarian ethic organized around mutual aid.[122] In *Intentional Community and the Folk Society* (1971), for example, a leader of the village of Yellow Springs, Ohio, opens with rhetoric drawn from Hostetler: "Intentional communities and communes have been undertaken primarily to develop alternative better ways of life in contrast to those dominant in the world, hopefully a way of brotherhood, cooperation, justice and life fulfilment." Like the Amish, folk societies "have values that people of the urban middle class and intellectuals have lost and cannot well regain on their own," the writer editorialized.[123] Such communities struggle to be "viable society," several writers avowed, but they agreed with Hostetler that mutual aid as a social ethic could be a powerful tool for broader social reconstruction.

Donald B. Kraybill's landmark work, *The Riddle of Amish Culture* (1989), owes considerably to Hostetler's sociological analysis and call for application, but dealt more with Amish expansion and modernization rather than threatened survival and conservatism.[124] More ethnographically localized in Lancaster County, Pennsylvania, than Hostetler's sociological generalizations from several Amish communities, Kraybill viewed the Amish as less of a cultural island and more of a dynamic group in cultural interchange as a result of booming tourism, selective adoptions of technology, expanding Amish commercial enterprise, and increased Amish mobility. In his acknowledgments, Kraybill credited his teacher Hostetler with "unwavering support" of his project. For his part, Hostetler cited his student's delineation of Amish cultural "riddles"— that is, accommodations to modern society in apparent contradiction to Amish moral principles—in his 1987 essay, "A New Look at the Old Order," com-

menting that Kraybill's categorization nicely expressed the gap between outsiders' and insiders' worldviews: "To the outsider such concessions may appear
to be contradictory. To the participant in Amish life they are natural and necessary. They hold in restraint the adverse influences of modernization on their
personal lives, their families, and communities."[125]

Kraybill, too, shared with Hostetler the goal of urging "the cultural mainstream" to learn from the Amish story, especially in alternative ways of organizing social life. A Hostetlerian social-functional analysis of change is still
apparent in the first edition of *Riddle*, although in the second edition Kraybill
moved further away from the Redfieldian folk-urban polarization by interpreting customs in light of "social and cultural capital" and by casting core
values in terms of cultural personality. The legacy of the little community remains in Kraybill's attention to the Amish as a tradition-directed, communitarian society in contrast to the future-oriented, individualistic "modern society."[126] Kraybill, like Hostetler before him, sought reconnection of the two to
form a "middle ground, a social order that anchors the individual in a larger
body and at the same time applauds choice and creative expression."[127] Kraybill hoped that the solution to his common riddle would end the adversarial
relationship between individual and community, folk and modern, suggested
by both Redfield and Hostetler.

Kraybill, like Hostetler, emphasized the bedrock of the cohesive family in
Amish society, and the submissive roles of women within the family and society. Understanding the pressures unraveling families and the influence of feminism on women's roles in mainstream culture, both authors addressed traditional gender roles in Amish society with an eye toward "the world." Kraybill
defended the Amish approach by observing "high levels of social and personal
satisfaction" among Amish women, further noting the contrast with women
in modern society, who are often "burdened by conflicting role expectations
and professional pressures to excel" and who thus "may experience greater anxiety over their roles than many Amish women."[128]

This statement echoed views expressed by Hostetler. In 1963, for instance,
Hostetler described the cooperative, closed system of the family as one in which
"an Amish woman knows what is expected of her in the home, and her attitude is normally one of willing submission."[129] The system is effective in providing security and belonging, Hostetler reasoned, because gender roles are
sharply defined and the Amish woman's place is clearly in the home, where
she recognizes the status of the man as leader. Hostetler would later expand
Amish Society's consideration of women's roles, crediting collaborator Gertrude
Huntington for helping him to see woman's status in a more nuanced way,

from the "inside" of an Amish woman's experience. He tried to explain that the chartered concept of "submission" for the woman did not mean her oppression. He wrote, for example, "The wife has an immortal soul and is an individual in her own right. . . . Important family decisions typically are joint decisions. The Amish wife participates actively in any decisions to move to a different locality, which was not true of what was called the 'corporation wife.'"[130]

If Hostetler was trying to show that the Amish woman was empowered, many feminist scholars were not so convinced, expressing concerns that the Amish system of patriarchy as described by Hostetler could appear to be an admirable model of tradition for modern society or a gloss over abuse within Amish life. In Anabaptist studies and women's studies, there was also a concern that the main accounts of Amish society were from a male perspective and therefore showed bias in underscoring men's leadership and activities. The studies by male ethnographers and historians, some critics contended, did not properly account for women's critical functions in sustaining the little community. Margaret Reynolds, for example, complained that Hostetler, as well as Kraybill and Redekop after him, were tied into the patriarchy they described, leading them to overstate the harmony of family structure in plain sects. They did not fully assess the inequality of women's roles or appreciate women's voices in their narratives, she argued.[131] She was one of the vocal participants in the first academic conference on women of Anabaptist traditions in 1995 with the challenging title of "The Quiet in the Land?" Hostetler's assumptions about women's roles in plain sects were evidently points of departure for presenters' uncovering "the quiet and not-so-quiet histories of women" and for making connections with women's studies in the United States and Canada.[132]

Criticism also came from sociologist Marc Olshan, who underscored the lasting effect of Hostetler's use of folk society by claiming in 1981 that it had become "an unthinking ritual . . . performed by social scientists."[133] Olshan resisted the ritual, claiming that uncritical acceptance of the concept inhibited rather than encouraged understanding of the Amish. Hostetler was not taken aback by the critique; even he questioned whether using folk society gave an adequate appraisal of group dynamics and social change. He therefore tended in later editions of Amish Society to emphasize functionalist ideas of charter and redemptive community, which he thought were more flexible as analytical tools, particularly with respect to cultural contradictions or paradoxes.[134] Olshan saw the implication in the folk society model that the Amish may be wrongly viewed as antimodern or premodern, whereas he sympathetically considered them to be making a choice as part of contemporary society to value tradition and community and be separate from "the world." Pointing to technology,

Amish aid programs, and transportation, Olshan argued that the Amish "have demonstrated a remarkable sensitivity to and control over the process of change," and they therefore represent the "very essence of self-conscious choice" characteristic of the contemporary United States and uncharacteristic of a Redfieldian folk society.[135]

Hostetler, as his own severe critic, seemed to argue against himself, or in agreement with Olshan, when he claimed in the fourth edition of *Amish Society* (1993) that "Amish communities are not relics of a bygone era. Rather they are demonstrations of a different form of modernity."[136] Moreover, even as he defended early editions of *Amish Society* as embodying "the perspectives of the times in which they were written," he observed that the "present revitalization of ethnic and religious groups calls for a reevaluation of traditional social theories."[137] Still, he insisted that the culture clash between "civilized ways" and the Amish was as apparent as it was several decades before, and the lessons of community and the quality of human experience he drew were still relevant. He stuck with a description of Redfieldian folk society, if not to understand the Amish totally, at least to illuminate the "tradition-directed character of Amish society."[138] The relation of tradition as a guide for living to the function of community was paramount. Yet the use of "folk" by that time, especially by American folklorists and interactionist sociologists, had taken on a different analytical meaning.

THE CHANGING FOLK MODEL

Although Hostetler's concern for the place of community in modern life resounded through late-twentieth-century discourse, the rhetorical strategy of polarizing folk and urban societies for the purpose of cultural analysis became less common. A strong current of criticism arose with respect to the evolutionary presumption that urban cultures are modern developments that are lacking in tradition.[139] Partly in response to the perceived romanticization of rural and plain folk, a movement arose to describe urban folklife and appreciate the fostering of traditions within urban, industrial, and technological environments. Rather than viewing urban tradition as a new development evolving *from* rural folklife, as Redfield argued, the revisionist scholars looked for historical examples *of* endemic urban folk and folklife.[140]

As Maurice Mook implied in his reviews of *Amish Society*, problems arose from a rigid structural definition of societies and the desire to create comparative categories for them; scholars increasingly called for considerations of changeful process, including the "dynamics," "performance," and "artistic communication" of individuals in unique situations and contexts, rather than static quality of small groups and their expressions.[141] The functional notion of traditions maintaining community came under criticism as a form of explanation, because the function could be shown to be a consequence of actions rather than a cause of them.[142] Whereas Hostetler asked how rooted folk societies operate and change, a rising number of folk studies queried the individual's formation of identity and construction of social reality.[143] Inspired by the social interactionist theories of sociologist Erving Goffman, among others, the new folk studies suggested community as situated variously (in socially constructed areas such as private and public, "backstage" and "frontstage") and often imagined by individuals.[144] The symbolic interactionist approach pertaining to formations of identity, Hostetler observed, took its cue from the individualistic nature of modern society rather than the lessons he wanted to generalize for the study of groupness from the communitarian, landed Amish.[145]

Perhaps the most radical change was the revised, some say distinctly American, conception of "folk." When Hostetler suggested "plain folk" and "folk society" applied to America, he conformed to the European thinking of folk as a noun representing a lower or marginalized portion of modern society along the lines of a peasant society.[146] In the view of folk as a portion, the lives of the folk follow tradition and are old-fashioned; they are connected to one another by characteristics of *"distinctiveness, smallness of scale, homogeneous culture patterns, and the strain toward self-sufficiency."*[147] In summary, terming folk as a portion is a dependent rather than independent strategy, because it was defined in opposition to a dominant urban society.[148] Arguably, Hostetler thought of folk as a stratum of society, because he thought of himself as Amish man and university professor in different strata, or, following my interpretation, caught *between* strata of folk and modern. In the spirit of the democratizing (some say fragmenting) 1960s, folk increasingly became referred to as an adjective describing a process of oral transmission involving all people rather than a noun for a rustic or exotic group. The social context for performances of folkness became expanded for an individualistic, mobile nation. Alan Dundes codified a definition of folk as *"any group of people whatsoever* who share at least one common factor."[149] A folk group could consist of two persons by this definition and be fleeting in duration; its expressive lore did not need a long lineage to qualify as folk art. The theoretical implication was that folk material was constantly renewed and introduced, rather than stable through time. The essential characteristic is that people possess traditions that contribute to a sense of group identity. The implication is a rather democratic or individualistic notion that all people participate in culture as folk; folk is not limited to a stratum or location of society.[150]

Hostetler responded to these symbolic interactionist trends in the third and fourth editions of *Amish Society* (1980, 1993). He inserted a discussion of the Amish as a high-context culture in the sense that "awareness of situations, experience, activity, and one's social standing is keenly developed."[151] Although continuing his pattern of creating definitions dependent on opposition with "bureaucratized segments of culture," he moved his analysis more toward consideration of communication in a social system and differences in performances of values within various situations, such as the school, home, and public settings.[152] Emphasizing a behavioral component to his analysis of the individual volition of Amish individuals, Hostetler formed a gerund, "contexting," to describe the choices that they make in daily life. He elaborated on this process in a chapter entitled "Backstage Amish Life" (formerly titled "Tension and Crisis in the Community"), which used Goffmanian rhetoric of backstage and frontstage, private and public space, and constructions of reality.[153] Challenging the static view of the Amish community, he approached youth "hops" and "reunions" among the Amish as situated performances, customs apparently undermining the ordered values of the society. After all, these customs contained expressive displays of dancing and excessive drinking, which he recognized as performances of individualism, in his words "limited self-determination."[154] He explained how these apparently subversive displays actually function to strengthen the redemptive community rather than weaken it, because they serve as an escape valve for youth in anticipation of adulthood when socially chartered expectations take precedence.

Hostetler also gave a nod to the idea of culture as symbolic communication in a section on "The Silent Discourse," which was added to the third edition of *Amish Society* (1980). He found that Amish sparseness of words is an indication that religious experience is communicated in conduct rather than in spoken words or written records. Hostetler observed that "by screening the flow of information that comes into the community, and by developing a sensitivity to signs and symbols, the society expresses its traditions in life."[155] Whereas moderns perceive silence as a form of introspection, for the Amish it is an active force, "a way of living and forgiving, a way of embracing the community with charity and the offender with affection," Hostetler pointed out.[156] In a nuanced analysis, Hostetler showed that the Amish in the late twentieth century have exhibited diversity in their approaches to the silent way as more Amish families abandon farm work and form larger settlements. Rather than seeing an opposition between self and society, however, Hostetler suggested a "dialectic" between "the impulse of community self-realization and the desire for individual fulfilment."[157] Here is where he interpreted the individual formations of identity, as well as the differentiation of what he calls (in a postmodern mode) "Amishness."[158]

Although Hostetler professed that folk society was useful to explain the significance of tradition to a group, its shortcoming for him was that it failed to explain the fullness and intentionality of the community's experience. The folk for him do not merely follow tradition, they choose it. The idea of the little community still held force for him as a lesson for the world, and the explanation for its viability is that it is sustained by familial love. His legacy is inscribed in the appeal for cultural diversity and heritage conservation, especially for varieties of ethnic identities, which "as peoplehood and as an extension of familial love, informs us who we are, where we came from, and what is special about us."[159] That diversity he sought to portray was for him ultimately the emotional, unscientific meaning of being "distinctly human."[160] He wanted the study of culture not to just be analytically *effective*, but humanly *affective*.

Even late in life, Hostetler was still driven by a prophetic mission. "The loss of community and the trusting relationships nurtured in family, neighborhoods, church, voluntary associations, and cultural pluralisms threaten the health of the wider democratic society," he warned in 1985.[161] Sensing the erosion of New Class activism in the self-absorbed generation of the 1980s, he reissued a call for "mediating structures" to check the excesses of government and expand familial love to wider, more distantly related human groups.[162] According to Hostetler, those communities that could bring those goals about were ethnic and religious because they make members bound and responsible to others. Still advocating for "we-ness" in its multiple meanings of "little" and communitarian, he left a message for both Amish and moderns to "know ourselves" historically, spiritually, and culturally.[163] That is what he learned from his heritage, what was the whole of his experience, and what he would have his readers realize from his narrative of the Amish.

NOTES

1. John A. Hostetler, "What I Learned from My Heritage," *Mennonite Family History* 11 (1992): 106–10. The address was to the Mifflin County Mennonite Historical Society.

2. See John A. Hostetler, "Folk and Scientific Medicine in Amish Society," *Human Organization* 22 (1963/1964): 269–75.

3. John A. Hostetler, "The World's War Against the Amish," *Johns Hopkins Magazine*, February 1964, 5.

4. Paul M. Harrison, review of *Amish Society* (1963), by John A. Hostetler, *Journal of Bible and Religion* 33 (1964): 283–84. Letter from John A. Hostetler (hereafter cited as JAH in Hostetler correspondence) to Paul M. Harrison, 14 September 1964, John A. Hostetler Papers, Penn State University Archives (hereafter cited as Hostetler Papers), Box AL03.01.

5. John A. Hostetler, *Amish Society*, 4th ed. (Baltimore: Johns Hopkins University Press, 1993), x.

6. JAH to Jack G. Goellner, 13 May 1963, Hostetler Papers, Box AL03.01.

7. Charles Loomis, introduction to *Amish Society* (1963), by John A. Hostetler (Baltimore: Johns Hopkins University Press, 1963), xvii.

8. Ibid., xviii.

9. Hostetler, *Amish Society* (1963), viii-ix.

10. Hostetler, *Amish Society* (1993), ix. Emphasis added.

11. John A. Hostetler, *Amish Life* (Scottdale, Pa.: Herald Press, 1983), 46. Emphasis added.

12. Harold S. Bender, *These Are My People: The Nature of the Church and Its Discipleship According to the New Testament* (Scottdale, Pa.: Herald Press, 1962), 112; Hostetler, *Amish Society* (1963), 316.

13. Hostetler, *Amish Society* (1963), 21.

14. See John A. Hostetler, "Our Tradition and Our Scholars," *Gospel Herald*, 8 January 1957, 25–26, 45.

15. Hostetler, *Amish Society* (1963), ix.

16. In a 2001 *Mennonite Quarterly Review* tribute to Hostetler, Donald B. Kraybill estimated that 850,000 copies of Hostetler's *Amish Life* (1952) and *The Amish* (1995) had been sold (see Kraybill, "In Memoriam: John A. Hostetler, 1918–2001," *Mennonite Quarterly Review* 75 [2001]: 403). *Amish Society* went into four editions (1963, 1968, 1980, and 1993) and was widely adopted as a required text in college courses. Nonetheless, Jack G. Goellner, editorial director at Johns Hopkins University Press, wrote Hostetler on 18 June 1969, gleefully informing him, "I think we shall almost certainly put *Amish Society* into paperback next Spring and bait the Turnpike watering spots for those tourists from Dubuque who come 'mit scheckels even'" (Hostetler Papers, Box AL03.01). Johns Hopkins University Press appealed directly to tourists in the *New York Times Book Review*, blaring the message, "If Amish country is your destination for summer travel, let the third edition of this best selling book show you Amish life as few outsiders have ever seen it" (8 June 1980, 47). At the time of Hostetler's death in 2001, *Amish Society*, *The Amish*, *Amish Roots*, and *Amish Life* were still in print and continued to sell well. Sales of *Amish Society* went past the 100,000 mark in 1993. For more on Hostetler's role as a mediator of the Amish, see Chapter 4.

17. John A. Hostetler, "An Amish Beginning," *American Scholar* 61 (1992): 553. A revision and expansion of this essay is included in this volume as Chapter 1.

18. Hostetler, "What I Learned from My Heritage," 107.

19. Ibid.

20. Ibid, 106–10.

21. John A. Hostetler and Maurice A. Mook, "The Amish and Their Land," *Landscape* 6 (1957): 29.

22. Hostetler, "What I Learned from My Heritage," 109.

23. Ibid., 110. Hostetler had previously announced his move away from sociology toward an anthropological home in "A New Look at the Old Order," *Rural Sociologist* 7 (1987): 278–92, reprinted in this volume as Chapter 17.

24. See Simon J. Bronner, *Following Tradition: Folklore in the Discourse of American Culture* (Logan: Utah State University Press, 1998), 266–312; and Don Yoder, *Discovering American Folklife: Essays on Folk Culture and the Pennsylvania Dutch* (Harrisburg, Pa.: Stackpole, 2001). Hostetler's paper "Toward a New Interpretation of Sectarian Life in America" (reprinted in this volume as Chapter 6) was originally presented at the 1951 Pennsylvania Folk Culture Seminar, then published in the Pennsylvania Dutch Folklore Center's organ, the *Pennsylvania Dutchman* 3, no. 4 (1951): 1–2, 7. Hostetler's work in folk medical systems later attracted the attention of folklorist Wayland Hand, director of the Center for the Study of Comparative Folklore and Mythology at the University of California at Los Angeles. Hand and Yoder invited Hostetler to participate in the UCLA Conference on American Folk Medicine in 1973; see John A. Hostetler, "Folk Medicine and Sympathy Healing Among the Amish," in *American Folk Medicine*, ed. Wayland D. Hand (Berkeley and Los Angeles: University of California Press, 1976), 249–58, reprinted in this volume as Chapter 14.

25. John A. Hostetler, "Amish Family Life: A Sociologist's Analysis," *Pennsylvania Folklife* 12, no. 3 (1961): 28–39.

26. See David Weaver-Zercher, *The Amish in the American Imagination* (Baltimore: Johns Hopkins University Press, 2001), 114–21. Working with Don Yoder and J. William Frey, Alfred Shoemaker established the Pennsylvania Dutch Folklore Center at Franklin and Marshall College in 1949 and founded the first department of folklore in the United States at the college at the same time. Later, they formed the Pennsylvania Folklife Society, which concentrated on Pennsylvania German topics and took a "total-culture" approach that Hostetler also favored. Yet Shoemaker encountered controversy over the presentation of the Amish at the Pennsylvania Dutch Harvest Frolic, held in Lancaster, Pennsylvania, in 1961. Shoemaker also produced tourist guides with caricatures of Amish figures on the cover that dismayed the Amish and disturbed some scholars. Maurice Mook sent Hostetler a clipping on 24 September 1961, entitled "Dr. Shoemaker's Pennsy Dutch Frolic Almost 'Hexerei'd By the Stolid Amish," which documented the prohibition placed by Amish bishops on their flocks from participating in the Harvest Frolic. Shoemaker denied that there was anything "theatrical" in his representation of the Amish, but the paper described the event as a "king-sized Chautauqua." Mook wrote Hostetler, "There are, as usual, lots of complaints, yet people flock to it and A.L.S. cleans up. His national publicity this year was terrific. He is quite a promoter all right" (Hostetler Papers, Box AL06.18). For more discussion of Shoemaker and the festival, see Bronner, *Following Tradition*, 266–312; and Don Yoder, "The Pennsylvania German Connection," *F&M Today*, November 1983, 8–12.

27. John A. Hostetler, "Maurice A. Mook (1904–1973): An Appreciation," *Pennsylvania Folklife* 26, no. 2 (1976/1977): 34–37.

28. Hostetler, "An Amish Beginning," 558; see also John A. Hostetler, "Christian Books in Public Libraries," *Gospel Herald*, 18 May 1945, 124; and "The Christian Challenge of Peace," *Gospel Herald*, 31 August 1945, 412.

29. See Albert N. Keim, *Harold S. Bender, 1897–1962* (Scottdale, Pa.: Herald Press, 1998).

30. Hostetler, "An Amish Beginning," 559.

31. He was responding to the popularity of pamphlets such as A. Monroe Aurand Jr., *Bundling Prohibited! Pennsylvania History, Folk-Lore and Sociology* (Harrisburg, Pa.: Aurand Press, 1929); and *Little Known Facts About the Amish and the Mennonites: A Study of the Social Customs and Habits of Pennsylvania's "Plain People"* (Harrisburg, Pa.: Aurand Press, 1938).

32. Ibid.

33. John A. Hostetler, *Annotated Bibliography on the Amish* (Scottdale, Pa.: Mennonite Publishing House, 1951). The book won the Chicago Folklore Prize for that year.

34. Ibid., 3.

35. Elmer L. Smith, *Bundling Among the Amish* (Akron, Pa.: Applied Arts, 1961).

36. JAH to Grant Stoltzfus, 9 February 1962, Hostetler Papers, Box AL06.09.

37. JAH to Elmer L. Smith, 3 November 1961, Hostetler Papers, Box AL06.09. Emphasis added.

38. JAH to Melvin Horst, 4 November 1961, Hostetler Papers, Box AL06.09.

39. JAH to Preston Barba, 4 November 1961, Hostetler Papers, Box AL06.09.

40. John A. Hostetler, review of *The Amish People*, by Elmer Lewis Smith, *Gospel Herald*, 13 May 1958, 455.

41. John A. Hostetler, unpublished review of *The Amish People*, by Elmer Lewis Smith, Hostetler Papers, Box AL.06.09. This review was intended for the *Pennsylvania Magazine of History and Biography*.

42. Ibid.

43. Hostetler, review of *The Amish People*, 455.

44. See Bronner, *Following Tradition*, 266–312.

45. Hostetler, *Amish Life*, 3.

46. Ibid., 45.

47. A revealing statement is Bender's *The Anabaptist Vision* (Scottdale, Pa.: Herald Press, 1944), which points out that while the Anabaptist vision does not give a detailed blueprint for the reconstruction of human society, it calls for believers to practice what Jesus taught (35–36). See also Bender's chapter "The Holy Community," in *These Are My People*, 42–66.

48. Hostetler, "An Amish Beginning," 560.

49. William G. Mather, "The Mission of the Rural Church," 3, Address to the National Planning Conference for Northern Baptist Churches in Town and Country, Green Lake, Wisconsin, 1948, Hostetler Papers, Box AL05.24.

50. Ibid., 4.

51. See B. Bruce-Briggs, ed., *The New Class?* (New York: McGraw-Hill, 1979).

52. See Russell Jacoby, *The Last Intellectuals: American Culture in the Age of Academe* (New York: Basic Books, 1987); Thomas Bender, *Intellect and Public Life: Essays on the Social History of Academic Intellectuals in the United States* (Baltimore: Johns Hopkins University Press, 1993); Richard Posner, *Public Intellectuals: A Study of Decline* (Cambridge: Harvard University Press, 2001); Helen Small, ed., *The Public Intellectual* (Oxford, U.K.: Blackwell, 2002); and Arthur M. Melzer, Jerry Weinberger, and M. Richard Zinman, eds., *The Public Intellectual: Between Philosophy and Politics* (Lanham, Md.: Rowman and Littlefield, 2003).

53. See Jay Mechling, "Richard M. Dorson and the Emergence of the New Class in American Folk Studies," *Journal of Folklore Research* 26 (1989): 11–26.

54. Ibid., 25.

55. Richard M. Dorson, *Bloodstoppers and Bearwalkers: Folk Traditions of the Upper Peninsula* (Cambridge: Harvard University Press, 1952); and Charles P. Loomis, *Social Systems: Essays on Their Persistence and Change* (Princeton, N.J.: D. Van Nostrand, 1960).

56. Charles P. Loomis and J. Allen Beegle, *A Strategy for Rural Change* (New York: Schenkman, 1975).

57. Mechling, "Richard M. Dorson and the Emergence of the New Class," 25.

58. Two frequently cited texts of this appeal are Robert Redfield, *The Social Uses of Social Science*, ed. Margaret Park Redfield (Chicago: University of Chicago Press, 1963) and Robert Merton, *Social Theory and Social Structure*, enl. ed. (New York: Free Press, 1968).

59. Hostetler, "Toward a New Interpretation," 1.

60. Joseph W. Yoder (1872–1956) was the author of the popular memoirs *Rosanna of the Amish* (1940) and *Rosanna's Boys* (1948). He fits the description of an Amish man who in his later years (sixty-eight when he published *Rosanna of the Amish*) writes nostalgically of his background. He also published the controversial *Amish Traditions* in 1950, which criticized Amish bishops for perpetuating divisions within the Amish church and blindly obeying the *Ordnung*. See John A. Hostetler, "Joseph W. Yoder (1872–1956)," *Mennonite Historical Bulletin* 18, no. 1 (1957): 1–2. For a biography and literary criticism of Yoder, see Julia Kasdorf, *Fixing Tradition: Joseph W. Yoder, Amish American* (Telford, Pa.: Pandora Press U.S., 2002).

61. Hostetler, "Toward a New Interpretation," 1.

62. Hostetler, "Tradition and Our Scholars," 26.

63. Ibid., 25.

64. Ibid., 26.

65. Compare Hostetler's dilemma, for example, to the goals to increase a sense of social integration within modern mass society by Robert N. Bellah, et al., *Habits of the Heart: Individualism and Commitment in American Life*, updated ed. (Berkeley and Los Angeles: University of California Press, 1996); Robert D. Putnam, *Bowling Alone: The Collapse and Revival of American Community* (New York: Touchstone, 2001); and Robert Perrucci and Earl Wyson, *The New Class Society: Goodbye American Dream?* 2d ed. (Lanham, Md.: Rowman and Littlefield, 2003).

66. Hostetler, *Amish Society* (1963), viii.

67. Ibid.

68. Ibid., ix.

69. John A. Hostetler, "Book Order List in the Areas of Sociology and Cultural Anthropology for Ogontz Campus," submitted to the Penn State-Ogontz librarian, 15 June 1962, Hostetler Papers, Box AL04.01.

70. Merton, *Social Theory and Social Structure*, 213.

71. JAH to Paul M. Harrison, 14 September 1964, Hostetler Papers, Box AL03.01.

72. John A. Hostetler, "The Plain People: Historical and Modern Perspectives," in *America and the Germans: An Assessment of a Three-Hundred Year History*, vol. 1, *Immigration, Language, Ethnicity*, ed. Frank Trommler and Joseph McVeigh (Philadelphia: University of Pennsylvania Press, 1985), 115.

73. Bruce-Briggs, ed., *The New Class?*; and Mechling, "Richard M. Dorson and the Emergence of the New Class."

74. Hostetler, *Amish Life* (1974), 36–37.

75. Hostetler, "Toward a New Interpretation," 7.

76. Ibid.

77. See Fred B. Kniffen, "Milestones and Stumbling Blocks," *Pioneer America* 7 (1975): 1–8; and Randy-Michael Testa, *After the Fire: The Destruction of the Lancaster County Amish* (Hanover: University Press of New England, 1992). In the former essay, Kniffen states that the Amish "live as we did" (6). In the latter, the author is confronted by an Amish man who asks, "Why should our way of life concern you?" He replies, "Because if your way of life falters, we all fall down. We need you to point out how far we have strayed" (181). Hostetler wrote the foreword to Testa's book, and while emphasizing the Lancaster County Amish as a faith community, he nonetheless underscored the need to preserve Amish society because "at stake is a national treasure" (ix). For historical background on the shift from master narratives of the Amish as countercultural to providing therapeutic functions of a premodern American heritage, see Weaver-Zercher, *The Amish in the American Imagination*, 67–81.

78. Weaver-Zercher, *The Amish in the American Imagination*, 99.

79. See Michael Harrington, "The New Class and the Left," in *The New Class?*, 123–38. For other perspectives on the linkage between New Deal cultural projects and leftist reform projects of the 1950s, see Michael Denning, *The Cultural Front* (London: Verso, 1997); and Jerrold Hirsch, *Portrait of America: A Cultural History of the Federal Writers' Project* (Chapel Hill: University of North Carolina Press, 2003).

80. Hostetler, *Amish Society* (1963), 323; Hostetler, "The Plain People," 114–15.

81. Peter L. Berger, "The Worldview of the New Class: Secularity and Its Discontents," in *The New Class?*, 51.

82. William G. Mather, introduction to *Amish Life* (1974), 3; Hostetler, *Amish Life* (1974), 37.

83. John A. Hostetler, "Tradition and Your Community," *Christian Living*, March 1957, 4.

84. John A. Hostetler, "Folk Art and Culture," *Christian Living*, November 1954, 4–5.

85. Ibid.

86. Ibid., 5. Emphasis added.

87. John A. Hostetler, "Pennsylvania's Plain Folk," in *New Aims in Rural Life: Proceedings of the Thirty-Fourth Conference of the American Country Life Association*, ed. Paul C. Johnson (Chicago: Prairie Farmer Publishing Company for the American Country Life Association, 1955), 20–26.

88. Ibid., 20–21.

89. John A. Hostetler, "The Amish Use of Symbols and Their Function in Bounding the Community," *Journal of the Royal Anthropological Institute* 94, no. 1 (1964): 19.

90. Ibid.

91. Ibid., 12.

92. Ibid.

93. Robert Redfield, "The Folk Society," *American Journal of Sociology* 52 (1947): 300.

94. See Robert Redfield, *The Folk Culture of Yucatan* (Chicago: University of Chicago Press, 1941); *The Little Community* (Chicago: University of Chicago Press, 1950); and "The Natural History of the Folk Society," *Social Forces* 31 (1953): 224–28.

95. See John A. Hostetler, "The Amish: A Cultural Island," in *Readings in Sociology*, 3d ed., ed. Edgar A. Schuler (New York: Thomas Y. Crowell, 1967), 89–105.

96. Fred W. Voget, "The Folk Society—An Anthropological Application," *Social Forces* 33 (1954): 105–13.

97. See Howard W. Odum and Alvin Boskoff, "Structure, Function, and Folk Society," *American Sociological Review* 14 (1949): 749–58; Howard W. Odum, *Understanding Society: The Principles of Dynamic Sociology* (New York: Macmillan, 1947); Horace Miner, "The Folk-Urban Continuum," *American Sociological Review* 17 (1952): 529–37; Redfield, "The Natural History of the Folk Society"; and Sidney W. Mintz, "The Folk-Urban Continuum and the Rural Proletarian Community," *American Journal of Sociology* 59 (1953): 136–43.

98. Redfield, *Social Uses of Social Science*, 197. See also Howard W. Odum, "Folk Sociology as a Field for the Study of Society," *Social Forces* 31 (1953): 193–223.

99. Hostetler, "An Amish Beginning," 561.

100. Hostetler also taught the course at Penn State-Ogontz during the 1960s. William Mather wrote Hostetler on 7 December 1962 and suggested that he teach Folk Society, explaining, "This would shortly be very popular with students and would fit your background very well. . . . Write Mook for text suggestions, but the best authority I know is John A. Hostetler." Hostetler Papers, Box AL05.24.

101. Hostetler, *Amish Society* (1963), 21.

102. Ibid., 9. See Redfield, *Little Community.*

103. In *Amish Society* (1963), Hostetler offers a definition of folk society as "*Gemeinschaft*-like, where there is a strong sense of 'we-ness'" (6). *Gemeinschaft* (which he translates as "natural groupings") is a term he derived from the writing of Ferdinand Tönnies. Hostetler explains, "He designated as *Gemeinschaft* the 'social order which being based upon consensus of wills rests on harmony and is developed and enabled by folkways, mores and religion'; he designated as *Gesellschaft* 'the order which being based upon a union of rational wills rests on convention and agreement, is safeguarded by political legislation, and finds its ideological justification in public opinion'" (4–5). Hostetler's source for Tönnies's work was his mentor Charles P. Loomis's translation of *Gemeinschaft und Gesellschaft*; see Ferdinand Tönnies, *Fundamental Concepts of Sociology (Gemeinschaft und Gesellschaft)*, trans. Charles P. Loomis (New York: American Book Company, 1940).

104. Hostetler, *Amish Society* (1963), 6.

105. John Joseph Stoudt, review of *Amish Society* (1963), by John A. Hostetler, *Pennsylvania Magazine of History and Biography* 88 (1964): 238.

106. Joseph W. Eaton, review of *Amish Society* (1963), by John A. Hostetler, *American Journal of Sociology* 70 (1965): 738–39.

107. Maurice A. Mook, review of *Amish Society* (1963), by John A. Hostetler, *Journal of American Folklore* 78 (1965): 165.

108. Maurice A. Mook, review of *Amish Society* (1968), rev. ed., by John A. Hostetler, *Journal of American Folklore* 82 (1968): 88.

109. John A. Hostetler, *Amish Society*, 3d ed. (Baltimore: Johns Hopkins University Press, 1980), 5.

110. Hostetler, *Amish Society* (1963), 47.

111. Hostetler, *Amish Society* (1993), 23. Hostetler cited Bronislaw Malinowski's essays in *Magic, Science, and Religion* (New York: Anchor, 1954) and in *A Scientific Theory of Culture* (Chapel Hill: University of North Carolina Press, 1944) for the functionalist concept of charter. See also Ivan Strenski, ed., *Malinowski and the Work of Myth* (Princeton: Princeton University Press, 1992); and Bronislaw Malinowski, "The Role of Myth in Life," in *Sacred Narrative: Readings in the Theory of Myth*, ed. Alan Dundes (Berkeley and Los Angeles: University of California Press, 1984), 193–206. In Chapter 2 of this volume, Donald B. Kraybill argues that Hostetler's turn from an emphasis on the folk society to charter was prompted by the critiques of Marc Olshan. See Marc A. Olshan, "Modernity, the Folk Society, and the Old Order Amish," *Rural Sociology* 46 (1981): 297–309; and "Modernity, the Folk Society, and the Old Order Amish," in *The Amish Struggle with Modernity*, ed. Donald B. Kraybill and Marc A. Olshan (Hanover: University Press of New England, 1994), 185–96.

112. Hostetler, *Amish Society* (1993), 23. For elaboration on the "anti-charterist" critique in favor of structural and symbolic interpretations, see James F. Weiner, "Myth and Metaphor," in *Companion Encyclopedia of Anthropology*, ed. Tim Ingold (London: Routledge, 1994), 592–95; and Alan Dundes's headnote to Malinowski, "The Role of Myth in Life," 193–95.

113. Calvin Redekop, *Mennonite Society* (Baltimore: Johns Hopkins University Press, 1989), 89.

114. Carl F. Bowman, *Brethren Society: The Cultural Transformation of a "Peculiar People"* (Baltimore: Johns Hopkins University Press, 1995), 19–20.

115. John A. Hostetler, *Hutterite Society* (1974; reprint, Baltimore: Johns Hopkins University Press, 1997), 296.

116. Ibid., 298–300.

117. Ibid., xviii.

118. John A. Hostetler, "Expelled Bruderhofers Members Speak Out," Peregrine Foundation Web site, 2001, http://www.perefound.org/em-s_sp.html.

119. Hostetler, *Hutterite Society*, 279–83; John A. Hostetler, foreword to *Community for Life*, by Ulrich Eggers (Scottdale, Pa.: Herald Press, 1988), 7–10.

120. Hostetler, "Expelled Bruderhofers."

121. See John W. Friesen and Virginia Lyons Friesen, *The Palgrave Companion to North American Utopias* (New York: Palgrave Macmillan, 2004), 200–201; and John A. Hostetler, "The Society of Brothers who Call Themselves Hutterites: Some Personal Concerns," *KIT Newsletter*, November 1993, 8–9. See also Julius H. Rubin, *The Other Side of Joy: Religious Melancholy among the Bruderhof* (New York: Oxford University Press, 2000).

122. See John A. Hostetler, *Communitarian Societies* (New York: Holt, Rinehart and Winston, 1974); and William M. Kephart, *Extraordinary Groups: The Sociology of Unconventional Life-Styles* (New York: St. Martin's Press, 1976).

123. Griscom Morgan, "Intentional Community and the Folk Society: Reconstruction Through Mutual Aid," in *Intentional Community and the Folk Society*, ed. Community Service Staff (1971; reprint, Yellow Springs, Ohio: Community Service, 1991), 1.

124. See Donald B. Kraybill, *The Riddle of Amish Culture* (Baltimore: Johns Hopkins University Press, 1989). The revised edition was published in 2001.

125. Hostetler, "A New Look at the Old Order," 290–91.

126. Kraybill, *Riddle of Amish Culture* (1989), 42–43, 260. For background on Kraybill's concept of "social capital," see Michael Woolcock, "Social Capital and Economic Development: Toward a Theoretical Synthesis and Policy Framework," *Theory and Society* 27 (1998): 151–208; Alejandro Portes, "Social Capital: Its Origins and Applications in Modern Sociology," *Annual Review of Sociology* 22 (1998): 1–24; Ronald S. Burt, "The Contingent Value of Social Capital," *Administrative Science Quarterly* 42 (1997): 339–65; and Putnam, *Bowling Alone*, 15–28.

127. Kraybill, *Riddle of Amish Culture* (1989), 260.

128. Kraybill, *Riddle of Amish Culture* (2001), 87.

129. Hostetler, *Amish Society* (1963), 151.

130. Hostetler, *Amish Society* (1993), 150. Hostetler footnoted his statement by stating, "An observation made by Gertrude E. Huntington in 'The Amish Family,' in *Ethnic Families in America*, ed. Charles H. Mindel and Robert W. Habenstein (New York: Elsevier Scientific Publishing Co., 1976), p. 307. I am indebted to Gertrude E. Huntington for assistance in clarifying the nature of family structure and roles in Amish society."

131. Margaret C. Reynolds, "Transmission of Tradition in the Old Order River Brethren: Gender Roles and Symbolic Behavior in a Plain Sect" (Ph.D. diss., Pennsylvania State University, 1996), 42. See also Margaret C. Reynolds, *Plain Women: Gender and Ritual in the Old Order River Brethren* (University Park: Penn State University Press, 2000).

132. Kimberly D. Schmidt, Diane Zimmerman Umble, and Steven D. Reschly, acknowledgments in *Strangers at Home: Amish and Mennonite Women in History*, ed. Kimberly D. Schmidt, Diane Zimmerman Umble, and Steven D. Reschly (Baltimore: Johns Hopkins University Press, 2002), xi.

133. Olshan, "Modernity, the Folk Society, and the Old Order Amish," 185.

134. Hostetler, "A New Look at the Old Order."

135. Olshan, "Modernity, the Folk Society, and the Old Order Amish," 194–95.

136. Hostetler, *Amish Society* (1993), ix.

137. Ibid., viii–ix.

138. Ibid., 9.

139. See George M. Foster, "What is Folk Culture?" *American Anthropologist* 55 (1953): 159–73.

140. See Américo Paredes and Ellen Stekert, eds., *The Urban Experience and Folk Tradition* (Austin: University of Texas Press, 1971); Richard M. Dorson, *Land of the Millrats* (Cambridge: Harvard University Press, 1981); Barbara Kirshenblatt-Gimblett, "The Future of Folklore Studies in America: The Urban Frontier," *Folklore Forum* 16 (1983): 175–234; and Hermann Bausinger, *Folk Culture in a World of Technology*, trans. Elke Dettmer (1961; reprint, Bloomington: Indiana University Press, 1990). For examples of urban folk studies, see Amanda Dargan and Steven Zeitlin, *City Play* (New Brunswick: Rutgers University Press, 1990); Jerome Mintz, *Hasidic People: A Place in the New World* (Cambridge: Harvard University Press, 1992); and Eleanor Wachs, *Crime-Victim Stories: New York City's Urban Folklore* (Bloomington: Indiana University Press, 1988).

141. See Sidney W. Mintz, "On Redfield and Foster," *American Anthropologist* 56 (1954): 87–92; Roger D. Abrahams, "Personal Power and Social Restraint in the Definition of Folklore," in *Toward New Perspectives in Folklore*, ed. Américo Paredes and Richard Bauman (Austin: University of Texas Press, 1972), 16–30; Dan Ben-Amos, "Toward a Definition of Folklore in Context," in *Toward New Perspectives in Folklore*, 3–15; and Deborah A. Kapchan, "Performance," in *Eight Words for the Study of Expressive Culture*, ed. Burt Feintuch (Urbana: University of Illinois Press, 2003), 121–45.

142. See Elliott Oring, "Three Functions of Folklore: Traditional Functionalism as Explanation in Folkloristics," *Journal of American Folklore* 89 (1976): 67–80.

143. See Elliott Oring, "The Arts, Artifacts, and Artifices of Identity," *Journal of American Folklore* 107 (1994): 211–47; Roger D. Abrahams, "Identity," in *Eight Words for the Study of Expressive Culture*, 198–222; and Dorothy Noyes, "Group," in *Eight Words for the Study of Expressive Culture*, 7–41.

144. See Charles Lemert and Ann Branaman, eds., *The Goffman Reader* (Oxford, England: Blackwell, 1997); Victoria E. Bonnell and Lynn Hunt, eds., *Beyond the Cultural Turn: New Directions in the Study of Society and Culture* (Berkeley and Los Angeles: University of California Press, 1999); Howard S. Becker and Michal M. McCall, eds., *Symbolic Interaction and Cultural Studies* (Chicago: University of Chicago Press, 1990); and Kent L. Sandstrom, Daniel D. Martin, and Gary Alan Fine, *Symbols, Selves, and Social Reality: A Symbolic Interactionist Approach to Social Psychology and Sociology* (Los Angeles: Roxbury, 2003).

145. Hostetler, "A New Look at the Old Order," 282.

146. Alan Dundes, *Interpreting Folklore* (Bloomington: Indiana University Press, 1980), 2. See also Alan Dundes, "The American Concept of Folklore," *Journal of the Folklore Institute* 3 (1966): 226–49; and Bronner, *Following Tradition,* 73–140.

147. Hostetler, *Amish Society* (1980), 10. Emphasis in original. For a discussion of the influence of the folk society concept on definitions of folk, see Elliott Oring, "On the Concepts of Folklore," in *Folk Groups and Folklore Genres*, ed. Elliott Oring (Logan: Utah State University Press, 1986), 11–14.

148. Dundes, *Interpreting Folklore,* 2.

149. Alan Dundes, "What is Folklore?" in *The Study of Folklore*, ed. Alan Dundes (Englewood Cliffs, N.J.: Prentice-Hall, 1965), 1–3. Emphasis in original.

150. See Bronner, *Following Tradition,* 41–43. Indicative of the trend away from the folk society model is the dropping in 2003 of the university-wide anthropology course "The Folk Society," introduced by Maurice Mook in 1949 at University Park and taught by Hostetler at Penn

State-Ogontz during the 1960s. The prevalent "folk" courses in the curriculum now revolve around "American Folklore," emphasizing the expressive culture of individuals acting in groups.

151. Hostetler, *Amish Society* (1980), 18. Hostetler's use of the communicative models of high-context and low-context come from Edward T. Hall, *Beyond Culture* (Garden City, N.Y.: Doubleday, 1976).

152. Ibid.

153. Ibid., 333–50.

154. Ibid., 349.

155. Ibid., 374.

156. Ibid., 375.

157. Ibid., 374.

158. Ibid., 383.

159. Hostetler, "The Plain People," 107.

160. Ibid., 115.

161. Ibid., 114.

162. Ibid. His criticism of the late twentieth-century era characterized by the "isolated 'I,'" as he puts it, is found in Hostetler, "What I Learned from My Heritage," 109–10.

163. Hostetler, "What I Learned from My Heritage," 110.

4

AN UNEASY CALLING: JOHN A. HOSTETLER
AND THE WORK OF CULTURAL MEDIATION[1]

David L. Weaver-Zercher

In the fall of 1949, thirty-year-old John A. Hostetler published a review of a century-old book in the *Budget*, a weekly newspaper oriented to an Amish readership. The book, a pseudonymous memoir about a boy named "Hostetler," tells the story of an Amish teenager who, under the influence of revivalist preaching, becomes converted, joins the Methodist Church, and then launches his own preaching career.[2] Reflecting on that narrative for his Amish readers, John Hostetler—who, like the Hostetler in the memoir, had chosen to forgo Amish church membership for a more world-embracing form of Christianity—noted that "going from Amish to Methodism is a pretty big jump," one he would certainly not advise. For although "some persons who leave the Amish faith find peace in other denominations," many feel "out of place all their days." Moreover, while the nineteenth-century Amish convert "seems to have done much good in the Methodist church," we must nonetheless ponder "what good may have resulted if he would have stayed in the Amish church and witnessed there."[3]

Hostetler wrote this review just a little more than a decade after he had declined Amish baptism in favor of becoming Mennonite and, more generally, in favor of a future in which higher education was both valued and encouraged. Given this context, it is intriguing to consider his suggestion that his nineteenth-century predecessor might have accomplished more good had he stayed and worked within the bounds of the Amish church. Even more intriguing is the question of which category Hostetler saw himself occupying. Was he an erstwhile Amish boy who now felt out of place in the world of "the English"?[4] Or was he one who had somehow found peace in his non-Amish context?

The answer, of course, is not to be found in the alternatives Hostetler set forth in his review. From his subsequent recollections, it is clear that he found more satisfaction as an educated Mennonite than he believed he ever would have experienced had he remained Amish. It is no less evident, however, that Hostetler often felt out of place in an English world that, at many turns, operated from moral and sociological assumptions markedly different from those of the Amish community in which he was raised. An examination of Hostetler's life provides a fascinating study of a man betwixt and between—a person who left his socially integrated birth community for participation in other worlds, but a person who, in a certain sense, never really left.[5]

It is important to explain here what it means to say that Hostetler "left his birth community" but "never really left." Hostetler was "born Amish," that is, his parents were Old Order Amish church members, and for seventeen years he participated in the lives of his parents' churches, first in Pennsylvania, then in Iowa. After that period, for reasons explored later in this essay, he opted to forgo Amish baptism and the corresponding vow to uphold the Amish *Ordnung*. From the standpoint of church membership, then, Hostetler never became Amish.[6] In other respects, however, the Amish-born Hostetler remained Amish long after he became Mennonite—in terms of his cultural sensibilities, his theological leanings, and his genealogical self-consciousness. These latter considerations led a mature Hostetler to claim, at least on some occasions, that he was *still Amish*, an assertion he made decades after he had opted to become Mennonite. Nonetheless, Hostetler's abiding Amishness was always tempered (and complicated) by his non-Amishness. In many ways he became a thoroughly modern man, pursuing roles and activities forbidden in Amish life and addressing problems in ways that revealed he no longer viewed the world through Amish eyes.

Being betwixt and between is not particularly unusual. Most twenty-first-century Americans find themselves embedded in multiple communities, stretched by competing commitments, and nagged by feelings of identity fragmentation. Nonetheless, Hostetler's situation was unique. First, the social chasm between some of his primary communities—for instance, his rural Pennsylvania birth community and his Temple University academic community—yawned incredibly wide, much wider than the communal divides most Americans traverse. Second, and central to this essay's consideration, Hostetler devoted much of his professional life to mediating between the unworldly Amish and the worldly world, endeavoring on the one hand to help the larger world appreciate the integrity of Amish life, endeavoring on the other to help the Amish navigate the threatening world in which they lived.[7]

As a rule, being a mediator is not easy, and Hostetler's experience proved to be no exception. It was, of course, his choice to assume that role (more precisely, a *series* of choices). At the same time, Hostetler sometimes conceded that the work of mediating between the Amish and the larger world was thrust upon him by forces beyond his control. Late in his life he would sometimes invoke the language of "calling" to describe his experiences and his choices, particularly with respect to those pivotal moments that thrust him into new situations as an Amish boy and an English academic. A careful consideration of Hostetler's life reveals that his sense of calling evolved over time—he was called first to the world of advanced education, then to the task of mediating information about the Amish, then finally to the work of advocating for the Amish in an unfriendly world.[8] In the end, he was able to review his life and understand it as a whole, woven together by his preparation and commitment to protect and sustain Amish society.[9]

Which returns us to his query about his nineteenth-century predecessor and the possibility of doing good. For Hostetler, doing good *on behalf of the Amish* was never far from his mind. What precisely that entailed took different turns during his career, for not only did Amish communities across North America confront new challenges during these decades, Hostetler himself encountered new resources for defining the good. Generally speaking, however, the chief good Hostetler sought to achieve throughout his career was nothing less than safeguarding the vitality of Amish society. Much of that endeavor was performed with his pen, in writings both sociological and theological, both popular and scholarly. But other facets of Hostetler's full and varied career—working with the National Committee on Amish Religious Freedom, testifying in court cases involving Amish defendants, joining with medical professionals to diagnose Amish genetic maladies, campaigning to preserve Lancaster County farmland, even his numerous attempts to censure (and in some cases censor) representations of the Amish he found problematic—can be read as means toward his ultimate end: helping the Amish survive.

This essay explores Hostetler's mediating work among the Old Order Amish. In particular, it offers a biographical framework for understanding Hostetler and his work, beginning with his Amish boyhood (and his decision to forgo Amish church membership) and highlighting various aspects of his career as a mediator of Amish life. It was an uneasy calling for this ex-Amish Amish man, for Hostetler's goal of supporting and sustaining Amish life often influenced the means he felt compelled to employ, sometimes placing him in uncomfortable situations as a scholar-mediator of Amish life. Along with navigating his own betwixt-and-betweenness, Hostetler could not possibly avoid the problem of multiple constituencies and the dilemmas that trying to simultaneously satisfy them entailed. In other words, given what he hoped to accomplish, Hostetler needed to be attentive to diverse groups with divergent expectations and moral codes: the North American academic community, a growing consumer market populated by Amish-hungry readers, his Mennonite Church colleagues, and the Amish people (including relatives) he sought to represent. To be sure, the predicaments Hostetler faced are not unique among ethnographers who, even in the most uncomplicated of contexts, struggle to communicate the distance between their subjects and their audiences. Still, it is helpful to note from the start that Hostetler's situatedness, framed by his Amish family history and his nation's burgeoning commercial market in all things Amish, saddled him with an exceedingly complex ethnographic task. In that sense, his life provides a useful window through which to explore the challenging work of cultural mediation.

BORN AMISH

An almost certain corrective for the misperception that North American Amish life is monolithic would be a weekend excursion through Pennsylvania's Kishacoquillas ("Big") Valley in central Mifflin County. There, framed by Stone Mountain to the north and Jacks Mountain to the south, a patient Amish-watcher would encounter "yellow-toppers," "white-toppers," and "black-toppers," the informal names for local Amish groups driving buggies with tops colored according to their churches' respective *Ordnungs*. A closer look would reveal Amish men wearing different sorts of suspenders ("one-strappers" and "two-strappers") and Amish women donning bonnets or head coverings of various shapes and sizes. The names of the various Amish affiliations are harder to remember, in part because the names change over time, in part because the groups are called different names by different people; for example, the Byler Church, also called *die Alt Gmay* (the Old Church); the Peachey Church, later called the Renno Church; the Nebraska Church, also called the Old School; and the Zook Church, now known as the Beachy Amish. At least ten different Amish and Mennonite groups or affiliations, from the most conservative to quite progressive, bespeckle the Kishacoquillas Valley, and their combined numbers total between four and five thousand people.[10] And while the differences between many of these groups may appear to the outsider quite trivial, they nonetheless signify fissures that continue to run deep decades after their initial eruptions.

Hostetler was born in the Kishacoquillas Valley in 1918 to a family associated with the Peachey Church. At that time, the Peachey Church, formerly known as the Upper District, was fifty years removed from an 1863 schism

FIG. 4.1 The Kishacoquillas Valley, from the top of Jacks Mountain looking toward Stone Mountain, circa 1950. Photograph by R. S. Beese, reprinted by permission of the Penn State University Archives.

with the Valley's Middle District.[11] As with many church divisions in Amish history, the factors instigating the 1863 divide were numerous and complex; in fact, the schism itself was almost twenty years in the making until it finally and irretrievably occurred.[12] In 1911, seven years before Hostetler was born, the Peachey Church experienced a further division, this time over the practice of *Meidung*, or shunning. More specifically, one of the two Peachey Church bishops, John P. Zook, opposed the "strong *Meidung*" in which excommunicated members of the church would be socially shunned even if they took up fellowship with another Amish or Mennonite church. In opposition to Bishop Zook stood the other Peachey bishop, David C. Peachey, who sought to uphold the strict ban. The Zook-Peachey division resulted in two predictably named Amish churches—the Zook Church and the Peachey Church—but even then the division had not completely played itself out. In 1919, when two members of the Peachey Church were placed under the strict ban, forty more Peachey members left the Peachey fold for the more lenient Zook Church.[13]

Remaining in the attenuated Peachey Church through this 1919 fracture was the Hostetler family: parents Joseph and Nancy and their six children (a seventh child would be born in 1921).[14] But their decision to stay Peachey in

1919 would prove, in retrospect, only to delay for ten years the family's break from the church, a break that was fueled by Joseph's proclivity to push boundaries, particularly those related to moneymaking. Years later, a former Peachey church member would write to John Hostetler, telling him "I know nothing [about your family] except what was told me," namely, that the Hostetlers "were renegades and misfits."[15] From a conservative Amish standpoint, those descriptors appear quite apt, especially for the enterprising Joseph, who was formally and finally excommunicated from the Peachey Church in 1929. According to John's autobiographical essay in the *American Scholar*, published in 1992, Joseph Hostetler "was dogged with one complaint after another from the bishop," complaints that mostly pertained to economic innovations such as registering purebred milking cows and building houses in the town of Belleville.[16] Later in the 1990s, in the process of recording more autobiographical reflections, John added further details about his father's conflict with the Peachey Church leadership, which "seemed to start from many small incidents and end in a grand finale."[17] Dubbing them as "Happenings," the now nearly eighty-year-old son underscored three interconnected realities: his father's entrepreneurialism; a community that considered his father short on humility; and the unseemly activities of a few petty, if not vengeful, church members who wanted the maverick reined in. The son's account concludes with an austere sentence that, perhaps strategically, conceals more than it reveals: "After repeated attempts at reconciliation, followed by exclusion, my father had had enough."[18]

Although this later account sheds more light on Joseph Hostetler's church troubles than did John's 1992 essay, both accounts fail to mention a particularly noteworthy "happening": a lawsuit Joseph filed against his brother-in-law Levi Hostetler in the Mifflin County Court of Common Pleas in the fall of 1929.[19] The conflict revolved around Joseph's handling of his mother-in-law's money, which had become a source of gossip in the community. In an effort to stop the rumors, Joseph filed a $10,000 lawsuit against Levi for "maliciously intending to deprive the said plaintiff of his good name, fame, credit and esteem." What exactly had Levi done in this regard? According to the claim, Levi had called Joseph a "crook" in front of two other men, and had further said that Joseph was "dishonest, untrustful, and used forcible methods in getting [his mother-in-law] Lizzie Hostetler's signature on a paper which would help him financially." That an Amish church member would file such a lawsuit is both surprising and telling. Having lost confidence in his church community to respect his person and restore his name, he decided instead to cast his lot with the state. One need not know too much Amish history to recognize that such a decision, unless fully and irrefutably recanted, would decimate Joseph's standing in his church. Less than a year later, the Hostetler family, led by their excommunicated and excluded father, moved to Iowa.

Joseph and Nancy Hostetler envisioned Iowa as a place of new beginnings, a place where they could restore their family name and renew their Amish membership in a different and geographically distant Amish community. What they did not anticipate was the long reach of the Mifflin County Amish leadership. When Joseph Hostetler sought membership in an Amish church near Kalona, Iowa, he was refused on account of the Iowa church's desire to maintain good relations with the Mifflin County church, which threatened to break fellowship with the Iowa church if it embraced Joseph Hostetler. More than thirty years later, in 1961, the elder Hostetler remained incensed by the actions of the Mifflin County Amish leadership, complaining to a still-Amish grandson that, "since they started on us," the Mifflin County bishops have never hesitated to "stick their nose in where they have no business." Specifically, the Big Valley preachers "had the Iowa Preachers [try to]. . . keep the Meidung."[20] Although the Big Valley preachers failed in this regard—that is, they failed to convince the Iowa Amish community to shun Joseph Hostetler entirely—they did succeed in having the Iowa churches bar Hostetler from church membership. Not exactly pariahs, as they would have been in Big Valley, the Hostetlers were never fully embraced by Iowa's Amish community. Joseph and Nancy continued to attend Kalona's Amish church for a number of years, but they eventually became Mennonite, as did most of their children.[21]

Although John Hostetler never experienced the *Meidung* as his father did (because John never joined the Amish church, he could not be excommunicated or shunned), he nonetheless gave significant thought to Amish-style discipline. First, his father's experience made him cautious about making a baptismal vow he could not keep, a caution that contributed to his decision to refuse Amish baptism.[22] Even after he made that decision (about 1936) and became a full-fledged Mennonite, he continued to reflect on Amish disciplinary practices and their effects upon those who were disciplined, most notably his father. Hostetler's reflections came to a head in 1944 when, at age twenty-five, he took it upon himself to write and circulate a letter to Amish bishops that challenged the practice of "strict shunning." Drawing on John Horsch's recently published *Mennonites in Europe*, Hostetler argued that Menno Simons and other early Anabaptists never condoned the coercive shunning practices that, in his estimation, now characterized many North American Amish churches.[23] Granted, he wrote, the "right use" of shunning (that is, shunning enacted upon transgressors who were clearly "out of fellowship with God") was

FIG. 4.2 Joseph Hostetler (left, with bear skin), with John A. Hostetler and Lee Kanagy (right, with fox skin), in Alberta's Peace River Valley, 1947. Reprinted by permission of the Penn State University Archives.

biblically justified, but "my own experiences and contacts with your folks have convinced me that shunning has been converted into a weapon of force to use for holding church members." Moreover, he said, it is too often being used "as a weapon of prejudice against those who leave your branch of the Amish denomination and join themselves with other Christian believers."[24] Even at this juncture, eight years after turning Mennonite, Hostetler continued to have many contacts in the Amish world, and his letter may have been prompted by various experiences and observations. Clearly, however, his father's ordeal, now fifteen years and counting, was its primary impetus. Why, he wondered, should his God-fearing, church-serving father be treated like a transgressor after all these years? Hostetler ultimately sent his letter to scores of Amish bishops in at least four states, though he targeted one in particular. In the course of sharing a draft of the letter with his parents, he mentioned the current Peachey bishop by name, asking "who besides John Renno in the Valley should have it?"[25]

It is difficult to gauge Hostetler's level of optimism in his anti-shunning missive: did he really think that the tradition-sensitive Amish world would listen to the Mennonite son of a disgruntled ex-member?[26] Optimism aside, he continued, at least for a time, to demonstrate a marked antipathy toward the practice of strong *Meidung*. In a 1951 letter to Joseph W. Yoder, another Pennsylvania Amish-boy-turned-English-man, he offered feedback on Yoder's newest book, a stinging critique of Amish practices entitled *Amish Traditions*.[27] Hostetler's response to Yoder's book was affirming, particularly with respect to Yoder's condemnation of the strong *Meidung*. "Has John Renno slapped you under the ban yet?" he teased his older friend, then continued: "I wish [Renno] would read your book, and if he ever does he will suffer from an acute case of schizophrenia or cerebral hemorrhage. The only other alternative I can see is for him to repent from his position, which I frankly think is impossible without losing face." Moving specifically to the book's consideration of strong *Meidung*, the now thirty-two-year-old Hostetler observed in summary fashion that Yoder had "stated the case against the strict Meidung beautifully." Comparing the strong *Meidung* to what he perceived as Roman Catholic imperiousness, Hostetler opined that he knew "of no power which equals this formal control outside of nunnery or monastery."[28]

Hostetler wrote his letter to Yoder in 1951, just one year prior to the release of his popular tourist booklet, *Amish Life*. In other words, even as Hostetler was commending Yoder for his critique of Amish disciplinary practices, he was preparing his own portrayal of Amish life that, by almost any measure, was as affirming of the Amish as Yoder's portrayal was disparaging of them. This, however, should not be counted as intellectual inconsistency or disingenuousness, for it is clear, even in his letter to Yoder, that Hostetler had a high regard for Amish life and culture. The real tragedy of strong *Meidung*, he told Yoder, was that "it is running a good name into the ground."[29] In other words, if the Amish would somehow wake up to their mistaken and cruel practice of strong *Meidung*, they would improve their community life and enhance their witness to the world. Of course, enhancing this reticent witness would soon become Hostetler's foremost concern.

BEING MENNONITE

Both theologically and geographically, Hostetler's incipient steps away from the Amish fold constituted a relatively short journey—though it certainly did not feel that way to him. Like many who leave their Amish community for the world, Hostetler's denominational destination was the Mennonite Church, in his case the East Union Mennonite Church near Kalona, Iowa. In the years preceding his decision to forgo Amish baptism, Hostetler had attended the East Union Church on various occasions, sometimes at the behest of Mennonite friends, and he would later recall that he encountered something there that fed his soul in ways the Amish church did not.[30] Still, his decision to refuse Amish baptism at age seventeen was not an easy one—his struggle (replete with stomach pains, anxious thoughts, and bouts of depression) calls to mind the extended conversion dramas of seventeenth-century Puritans.[31] Even after making the break, the decision felt hard to him, for rather than experiencing the exhilaration of newfound religious freedom, Hostetler felt awkward and out of place. Not insignificantly, his late-in-life recollections of those first visits to East Union Church were mostly negative, underscoring more than anything the seeming shallowness of his new Mennonite peers who wore "flashy neckties," talked about "the latest model cars," and bragged about "how many girls they could date in one year."[32]

The worldliness Hostetler perceived among Iowa's Mennonites was likely more profound than he would have perceived in Pennsylvania, for Midwestern Mennonites tended to be less strict, particularly with respect to dress, than Mennonites in the East.[33] Regardless of geography, however, Hostetler's relatively short ecclesiastical jump from the Amish to the Mennonites would prove over time to be a profound sociological leap, vaulting him from a traditional, agrarian society to one that was fast embracing the accoutrements of twentieth-century American mass culture. Few aspects of traditional, North American Mennonitism did not experience stress during the 1930s and 1940s (Hostetler's first years as a Mennonite), the result being a denomination in 1950 that was much less rural, much less socially integrated, and much less plain than it had been in 1920. These changes would only gain velocity in the 1950s and 1960s, as Mennonites continued to abandon their farms for the suburbs and, not coincidentally, the activities, occupations, and entertainments of America's middle class. Although the changes in this regard should not be overstated (even today, North American Mennonites exhibit some sociological distinctiveness vis-à-vis the larger society), Hostetler's decision to become Mennonite in the late 1930s meant hopping aboard a moving denominational train at the very time its passengers were casting off their most conspicuous traits—plain dress, agrarianism, and close-knit, separatist communities—traits that the Old Order Amish assiduously retained.[34]

Like other Mennonites during these years, Hostetler worked hard to make sense of these changes.[35] In the early 1940s, while performing Civilian Public Service in lieu of entering the military, Hostetler devoted significant energy to thinking about nonconformity. Of particular interest to him was the problem of plain dress, and his files bulge with long, fervent letters debating the issue with family and friends. His arguments, almost all of which oppose plain dress, parallel his argument against the strong *Meidung*: rather than attracting people to the Christian life, they created a barrier to it. "I am perfectly willing to do anything the Lord wants me to do," he told his closest friend, "but by wearing the plain coat I would necessarily be limiting myself to that group of people." No, he continued, "give me that [necktie] and I will wear it rather than isolate . . . myself from . . . the world."[36] His opposition to plain dress, he asserted in another letter, should not be interpreted as opposition to the principle of Christian nonconformity. Rather, his objection was to the specific application of this principle. "I have not yet seen a piece of clothing which made me believe that the man who wore it belonged to Christ," he told his sister Barbara. "We can be hot for God without wearing peculiar clothing."[37]

Hostetler's identification of the true Christian faith with a passionate, intensely personal commitment to God—being "hot for God"—was hardly novel in the mid-twentieth-century Mennonite Church, where evangelical understandings of the Christian life were both widespread and ascendant. But for him, as well as for other Mennonites emerging from an Amish past, defining the faith in this way carried with it an implicit critique of Amish religious life, which, in their view, placed too much emphasis on formal tradition and too little on personal commitment to spiritual principles. The critique was not a new one in Mennonite circles. In the late nineteenth century, Missouri Mennonite leader Daniel Kauffman publicly criticized Amish formalism, alleging that the Amish clung to "old customs" at the expense of "Gospel principles."[38] The danger in this, Kauffman warned, was that it set up Amish people for a devastating fall, for once they realized their religious traditions had no scriptural basis, they would quickly "break loose" from all regulations and be "delivered, body and soul, to the world." In other words, although Mennonites may appear "worldly" to their Amish neighbors, it was really the tradition-bound Amish who were most in danger of falling prey to godlessness. Whether Kauffman had anything more than anecdotal evidence to support his theory of spiritual devastation is doubtful. The point remains, however, that views like his enjoyed wide currency among Mennonites in both the nineteenth and twentieth centuries.[39]

Given his participation in this milieu, it is hardly surprising that Hostetler manifested a Kauffmanesque view of Amish spirituality at this point in his life. Writing for a Mennonite Church periodical in 1954, Hostetler recounted for his readers a revival movement that was making inroads among Amish communities, particularly in the Midwest.[40] The movement, fueled by itinerant revivalists and newsletters advocating evangelical understandings of conversion and holiness, would eventually lead some in the Old Order to leave the Amish church for more evangelically oriented Anabaptist fellowships.[41] In 1954, however, the movement was just commencing, and Hostetler wrote enthusiastically about its promise. Observing that the revival was responding, at least in part, to "the presence of degenerate spiritual life in Amish communities," Hostetler proceeded to compare it to events in the nineteenth-century Mennonite Church, when "men of vision and of courage" challenged traditionalists who opposed Sunday schools and English language use in worship. These innovators, who were "moved by the Spirit of God," eventually overcame the opposition and pushed the Mennonite Church forward, saving it from almost certain demise. This same process, Hostetler averred, was now being repeated in Amish churches, where men of God were challenging their tradition-bound brothers and sisters to move beyond formalistic Christianity. "Traditions can be a fine thing," Hostetler concluded, "but when a tradition blocks the direct teaching of Christ and the Spirit of God, that tradition needs to be broken."[42]

Hostetler published this article (boldly entitled "God Visits the Amish") in 1954, almost twenty years after he had refused Amish baptism. It would not be many more years, however, until Hostetler would come to embrace a much less sanguine view of revivalist activity among the Old Order Amish. Part of this transformation can be traced to Hostetler's maturing sociological sensibilities, which will be considered later in this chapter. But Hostetler's growing institutional involvements in the Mennonite Church were also important to his reassessment. Most significant in this regard was his participation in the Mennonite rural life movement (or "community life movement"), which emerged in the 1940s in response to concerns among Mennonites that the erosion of their denomination's rural base threatened its very survival. J. Winfield Fretz, the movement's chief architect, linked that threat to an even more ominous one, asserting that Mennonites' drift to the city was bad not only for Mennonites, but for the nation as a whole, because rural communities best fostered the values of "neighborliness, honesty, [and] self-reliance."[43] In this and other ways, Fretz and his fellow Mennonite rural life advocates echoed the well-traveled assertions of non-Mennonite intellectuals like Arthur Morgan and Baker Brownell who, in the 1940s and 1950s, advocated the "small community" as an antidote to America's ills.[44] The difference, of course, was that Fretz and his Mennonite followers focused on their own religious denomination as evidence of both the value and the erosion of rural communities. In 1945, Fretz and others founded the Mennonite Community Association with the expressed objective of stemming that erosion, and Hostetler soon

lent his considerable energies to the association's work. In 1950, one year after receiving his bachelor's degree in sociology from Goshen College, the thirty-
one-year-old Hostetler joined the editorial board of the association's journal,
Mennonite Community, a role he would fill in various capacities for almost a
decade.[45]

The Mennonite rural life movement would prove to be fleeting, a casualty
of the very social forces it sought to attenuate. For our purposes, however, it is
significant to note that the movement provided Hostetler with ideological resources to assess and, in some cases, to discard assumptions he held as a younger
Mennonite, assumptions that sometimes marked his early writings about
Amish life. Hostetler's changing perspectives can be seen by comparing his
treatment of tradition in "God Visits the Amish" (1954) with that in a second
Christian Living article, "Tradition and Your Community" (1957), published
three years later. Hostetler's assessment of tradition in 1957 is decidedly more
positive than it was in 1954. Although he continues to make a distinction between tradition and "our deeper spiritual values," his latter article constitutes
a stern warning to Mennonite readers that discarding time-honored traditions
places their future in peril. For although "maintaining tradition is for most of
us not sufficient motivation for a way of life," it nonetheless "gives meaning
to the more abstract values" Mennonites claim to possess and, moreover, provides the glue to hold their otherwise precarious communities together. "We
[Mennonites] may well ask ourselves," Hostetler concludes, "whether in discarding traditions we have not also thrown away many of the finer disciplines
of community life."[46]

In addition to demonstrating Hostetler's growing respect for tradition, "Tradition and Your Community" manifests another significant aspect of Hostetler's
expanding corpus of writing: his determination to utilize the Amish as an exemplary corrective to non-Amish life, particularly Mennonite life. The article's subtitle, "A Study in Survival Based on the Amish," underscores Hostetler's
approach in this regard, and the article itself proceeds to contrast the continuing vitality of the Amish in North America with their counterparts' demise
in early twentieth-century Europe. According to Hostetler, Amish survival in
North America has a decisive explanation: it owes to their formation of socially "concentrated communities." These communities, writes Hostetler, serve
as powerful engines for transmitting traditions that, coming full circle, bind
community members together. Of course, biological families have traditions
too, but families, says Hostetler, are not strong enough to maintain their traditional practices when they come under stress. "Mennonite families who move
to the city soon lose their . . . Christian Mennonite principles." In contrast, he

says, "the Amish have been able to retain their way of life through maintaining a sense of community."[47]

Hostetler's utilization of the Amish as a corrective to non-Amish life did not begin with this 1957 *Christian Living* article. As early as 1951, when he published "Toward a New Interpretation of Sectarian Life in America" in the *Pennsylvania Dutchman*, Hostetler demonstrated a readiness to use his knowledge of Amish life for emendatory purposes.[48] What is different in 1957 is the place of Mennonites in his argument. Whereas in 1951 he talked about the distinctive traits of Pennsylvania Dutch "sectarians," a category into which he lumped both Mennonites and Amish, his 1957 piece contrasted the Amish to Mennonites at almost every turn. Part of this can be traced, of course, to the respective articles' audiences; whereas his 1951 *Pennsylvania Dutchman* article was oriented to Pennsylvania Germans of various church backgrounds, his 1957 *Christian Living* piece was written specifically for Mennonites. But in addition to having a different audience, the latter article was written by an author whose sociological analysis of Amish-Mennonite life had become much more sophisticated in the intervening years. Moreover, these six or seven years had provided Hostetler with abundant evidence that the Mennonite train he boarded in 1936 was increasingly aligned with mainstream, middle-class American life and increasingly removed from Old Order life. If Hostetler's writings are any indication, he was not enthusiastic about this expanding chasm, and in certain respects his exhortative writings can be read as his effort to stem the divide. Even so, Hostetler was himself experiencing a growing distance from Old Order Amish life, not least because of scholarly pursuits that, as any Amish bishop could have told him, insisted that he view the world through very non-Amish eyes.

BECOMING A SCHOLAR

Late in life, Hostetler would trace his decision to leave the Amish Church to his desire for (indeed, his *calling* to pursue) advanced education.[49] Although his father's unsavory experiences in the Amish church also played a role, Hostetler's autobiographical reflections describe an intellectually inclined teenager who enjoyed reading and thinking more than plowing, planting, and milking. His earnest but somewhat awkward attempt to combine intellectual pursuits with Amish life—training to become a poultry judge—proved unsatisfying, and he soon decided on a more radical solution to his dilemma: declining membership in the Amish church. The decision was not an easy one, in part because Hostetler had imbibed heavily the educational views so prominent in his home community. According to his recollections later in life, Amish leaders frequently warned of education's tendency to foster "self-exaltation, pride of position, and the enjoyment of power." His mother added her own sort of warning, observing that visiting students from a Mennonite college appeared pale "from sitting indoors with their books." In this environment Hostetler could not help but feel conflicted about pursuing more education. "My non-Amish peers who went to college seemed impractical, even to me," he wrote in the mid-1990s. "They were accumulating knowledge—in my view, more knowledge than they could carry."[50]

Given Hostetler's level of skepticism toward impractical learning, it is rather remarkable that he pursued not only a bachelor's degree, but eventually a master's degree, a doctorate, and a university professorship. That Hostetler would choose this strikingly un-Amish vocational path attests in no small part to the influence of Harold S. Bender, the larger-than-life Mennonite churchman who, from 1924 to 1962, taught and administered at Goshen College. Bender, whose training in biblical studies was gradually eclipsed by his interest in Anabaptist-Mennonite history, provided a model of scholarship that addressed some of Hostetler's concerns about impracticality. For Bender, the study of Anabaptist history was not merely for the joy of learning or for advancing disciplinary discussions; rather, such study served a larger purpose of shaping Mennonite church life in the present.[51] When Hostetler finally matriculated at Goshen in early 1947 (after one year of study at Hesston Junior College and a four-year stint in Civilian Public Service), Bender quickly spotted the twenty-eight-year-old's scholarly precocity.[52] Already the editor of *Mennonite Quarterly Review* and recently tabbed as editor of the multivolume *Mennonite Encyclopedia*, the over-committed Bender happily set Hostetler to work identifying potential encyclopedia entries.[53] Even more significant to Hostetler's emerging vocational identity was Bender's invitation to write articles on Old Order Amish topics, including the primary Old Order Amish entry that appeared in the encyclopedia's fourth and final volume. This final volume would not appear until 1959, twelve years after Hostetler first assisted Bender in his work. Still, it is not too much to claim that, as early as 1947, Bender set Hostetler on a trajectory that would eventuate in his role as the nation's leading interpreter of Amish life.

Hostetler's training in rural sociology at Pennsylvania State College would only enhance that trajectory.[54] Starting in the fall of 1949, Hostetler spent four years at Penn State, where he studied with sociologist William G. Mather and anthropologist Maurice A. Mook. Mather was Hostetler's primary advisor, but

Mook played a larger role in helping their student develop theoretical frameworks that would later inform his work.[55] Years later, Hostetler would contrast anthropology as he discovered it under Mook to mid-twentieth-century American sociology, noting that whereas sociology "tended to skirt values and to fragment human groups," anthropology "put into holistic perspective the entire range of elements in a functioning human community."[56] This bleak evaluation of sociology can hardly be pinned on Mather, whose scholarship was deeply values-conscious. Nevertheless, even as Hostetler published occasional articles in journals of rural sociology, his disciplinary identity would increasingly tend toward anthropology, a field of study that, in his words, "aims to describe in the broadest sense what it means to be human."[57]

In addition to helping Hostetler assemble theoretical tools for interpreting Amish life, Hostetler's graduate school mentors provided their protégé with something else he lacked in 1949: the sense that the Amish were a worthy subject for rigorous academic study, even for (and perhaps *especially for*) a person with Amish roots. That Mook's class on folk societies kept returning to the topic of Amish life—with Hostetler granted expert status—made a lasting impression on the budding scholar, as did the fact that Mook, already an established scholar, now began to orient his research in the direction of Amish culture. Given the proximity of the Mifflin County Amish community to State College, it is possible that Mook's research would have moved in this direction without Hostetler's presence. Clearly, however, the student was influencing the professor as much as the professor was informing the student. One Penn State professor went so far as to accuse Mook of taking advantage of Hostetler's expertise, an accusation born in response to Mook's frequent public lecturing on Amish-related topics.[58] Hostetler did not seem to mind, however, in part because Mook had nourished in him the confidence to study the Amish academically.[59] Moreover, Mook's post-graduate school correspondence with Hostetler reflects the same opinion that Mather frequently verbalized, namely, that Hostetler was *the* leading authority on Amish life, one who needed to write a book on the Amish sooner rather than later.[60]

Still another factor contributed to Hostetler's emerging identity as a scholar of Amish life: his 1953 marriage to Beulah Stauffer, an editor at the Mennonite Publishing House in nearby Scottdale. Hostetler's marriage to Stauffer was his second marriage, his first one ending tragically in February 1951 when his first wife, Hazel, died in childbirth along with their only child.[61] Hostetler's Amish-related work was already under way when he married Hazel Schrock in 1949, and he may have continued on that path had they spent their entire lives together. Still, Hazel had her sights set on the mission field, and it is very possible that mission or relief work would have been the couple's vocational future.[62] Beulah Stauffer, on the other hand, mirrored John's proclivities as a scholar and provided various sorts of support and intellectual exchange as he pursued his academic work. In 1952, after Hazel's death but before John and Beulah's 1953 wedding, the couple worked together on *Amish Life*, a popular, tourist-oriented booklet that John wrote and Beulah designed for Herald Press.[63] A few years later, when one of John's graduate school professors urged him to reorient his research, Beulah responded that John should continue to do what he did best: research and write about Amish life. In these ways and others, Beulah helped to nurture and advance her husband's emerging identity as a scholar of Amish life.[64]

Hostetler's burgeoning identity as an interpreter of Amish life can be seen in his publication record, which, beginning in 1949, shifts appreciably from theologically oriented writings on the Christian life to articles on Amish-related topics. By the end of 1951, halfway through his four-year graduate program (and midway between Hazel's death and his marriage to Beulah), Hostetler had already published a score of articles on Amish history and culture and was now hard at work on *Amish Life*.[65] And lest he be accused of being too close to his subject matter, he embraced and asserted the notion that his sociological training had given him adequate distance to be suitably objective. In an article published in the *Pennsylvania Dutchman* in 1951, Hostetler made a strong case for persons like himself being positioned in precisely the right place for interpreting Amish and Mennonite life. On the one hand, Hostetler argued, mainstream social scientists had not been good interpreters of sectarian life, for they typically "lacked insight or were only superficially interested in the subject." On the other hand, untrained sectarian interpreters had themselves exhibited inappropriate biases, "idoliz[ing]" their religious background "with a sort of 'divine' halo." The goal, he asserted, was to obtain an intimate but "objective" understanding of sectarian life, an understanding that could be accomplished "only within . . . that branch of knowledge which studies social phenomena scientifically."[66]

As noted above, Hostetler would soon qualify his enthusiasm for social scientific study, concluding that sociology's bent toward quantitative objectivity resulted in corpse-cold scholarship with little relevance to life. Early in his career, however, Hostetler's assumption of a disciplined objectivity provided him with something he needed both psychologically and vocationally: a sense of scholarly distance from his Amish past. Just as importantly, his exposure to sociological theory enabled him to evaluate various aspects of Amish life through a different set of lenses. For instance, although Hostetler continued throughout life to be troubled by shunning's personal effects, he increasingly understood the purpose it served in maintaining Amish communities. Similarly, Hostetler's sociological insights curbed the evangelical leanings that, as late as 1954, had colored his assessment of Amish religious life. "I am more convinced than ever," he wrote to an Old Order friend in 1964, "that maintaining a proper Christian community (as opposed to individual salvation) is the Gospel in its love dimensions." Hostetler's comment in this regard was not without a context; rather, it came in response to the emergence of "Send the Light Crusade," a group of ex-Amish persons who sought to convert their Amish acquaintances to more evangelical, heartfelt forms of Christianity. This group claimed to liberate Amish people from spiritual darkness, Hostetler complained, but what it really did was destroy Amish culture. Hostetler was not entirely opposed to Amish renewal movements, he told his friend, as long as their renewal practices fit "within the tradition." "[H]ad there been such a renewal group in my own experience when I was a boy, I may *still be more Amish than I am now*," he said.[67]

The construction of Hostetler's observation—"I may still be more Amish than I am now"—provides a poignant summary of Hostetler's sense of himself at midlife. When he wrote this sentence in 1964, he was forty-five years old and nearly thirty years removed from his decision to forgo Amish baptismal instruction. Educated, suburban, and professional, he was by almost every measure a thoroughly modern man. Yet in his mind he was still Amish (though, of course, not as Amish as he *could* be). His sociological training may have altered his views of Amish life, but it did not purge him of his Amishness entirely. For that reason, he saw himself uniquely equipped to fill a mediating role that no one else could. In many respects, he was right.

A MAN IN THE MIDDLE

If Harold Bender, Maurice Mook, William Mather, and Beulah Stauffer provided Hostetler with the positive impetus to become a scholar-mediator of Amish life, Harrisburg publisher A. Monroe Aurand Jr. supplied the negative one. From the late 1920s to 1949, Aurand wrote and self-published more than twenty-five monographs on Pennsylvania German life, with topics ranging from cooking and child rearing to religion and humor.[68] Few topics, however, interested Aurand as much as bundling, a courtship custom in which courting men and women lay in bed fully clothed—or, depending on the story at hand, not so fully clothed. According to Aurand, the Pennsylvania Dutch were America's most enthusiastic bundlers, and among the "Dutch" themselves, none bundled more fervently than the Old Order Amish.[69] Aurand's pamphlets provided just enough detail to fuel the imagination, which was more than enough detail for Hostetler to brand these portrayals "foul, filthy, and obscene."[70] In the late 1940s, Hostetler launched a short-lived effort to block their distribution, though he quickly came to the conclusion that the best defense against Aurand-like portrayals of the Amish was a good offense: offering something better. By 1952, Hostetler's thirty-two-page booklet *Amish Life* was providing stiff competition to Aurand's booklets in bookstores and tourist venues alike, eventually selling close to a million copies.

Hostetler later wrote that Alfred Shoemaker, the entrepreneurial director of Lancaster's Pennsylvania Dutch Folklore Center, first suggested to him that he produce a popular work to counter Aurand.[71] While that may be true, Hostetler's Mennonite academic contemporaries also encouraged him.[72] Relatively uninterested heretofore in mainstream cultural productions, mid-century Mennonites demonstrated a growing sensitivity to the way they (and, by association, their Amish cousins) were being perceived and portrayed by others.[73] In 1945, for instance, Elizabeth Horsch Bender published a review in *Mennonite Quarterly Review* that evaluated three Amish-themed novels—even though the newest of these novels was by then fully five years old.[74] Along with this heightened sensitivity came the resolve to shape these portrayals and perceptions, a resolve expressed most baldly in a piece published in 1951 by Mennonite Grant Stoltzfus, entitled "Memorandum to Persons Interested in Disseminating Information about the Mennonites and the Amish and Their Way of Life." Stoltzfus, much like his friend Hostetler, found the current market offerings on Mennonite and Amish life "tawdry," but the blame, he said, fell not on the businesses that sold them. "Can we blame these businesses for handling [this literature]," he asked rhetorically, "until we take some positive steps to provide something better?"[75] Although it is not exactly clear whom Stoltzfus meant by "we," his clarion call was fulfilled the following year, when Hostetler's *Amish Life* hit the bookstands. In a review published shortly thereafter in the Mennonite Church weekly, Stoltzfus praised Hostetler's work as "long overdue" and noted that "many will rejoice that at last something like this has appeared."[76]

In addition to the rising status-consciousness of mid-century Mennonites, a second historical process helped to thrust Hostetler into the role of public mediator: the rising renown of the Amish, accompanied and fueled by a growing consumer market in Amish-themed products, including tourism. This market-related renown, while modest by late twentieth-century standards, was rooted in a host of factors unrelated to the Amish themselves, factors ranging from the popularization of photojournalism to the democratization of travel and tourism.[77] But even as the market's catalyzing forces were multiple and complex, so too were the problems it presented to those who were not enamored of its emergence. In the end, Hostetler, along with his Mennonite publishing colleagues (and, on another level, some of his Pennsylvania German acquaintances) decided that to participate in the Amish culture market was preferable to letting it run its course without their contributions. Some Mennonites even perceived happy side effects to this sort of participation, not the least of which were the dollars it would generate for Mennonite publishing efforts.[78]

Like any author, Hostetler was not unconcerned about the sales of *Amish Life*, and he earnestly negotiated with Herald Press to receive an appropriate royalty.[79] But to see him as somehow *motivated* by anticipated royalties would clearly be wrong. All told, the royalties Hostetler received in his career, most of which were generated by *Amish Life* and *Amish Society* in their various renditions, totaled about $150,000—not an insignificant amount, but hardly something around which to orient a career.[80] Later in his career, when Hostetler publicly criticized Paramount Pictures for producing *Witness* (an act he claimed was rooted in Hollywood's lust for money), he found himself facing counter accusations that he was himself profiting off the Amish.[81] On one level, these accusations contained some truth: Hostetler *had* made money from his Amish-related writing and, perhaps more significantly, had advanced his standing in the academy by his Amish-related work. Still, a few thousand dollars per year and esteem from his colleagues were hardly the motivating factors for Hostetler to do his work. To return to his language of calling, Hostetler's work of mediating information about Amish life to a curious public was responding to a call far more profound than the siren song of money and academic prestige.

But what exactly was the concern that drove his representational work? Most fundamentally, it was an abiding desire to paint an ethnographic portrait of Amish that was faithful to reality, respectful of the Amish, and mindful of his various audiences. To be sure, Hostetler was not entirely unique in this regard; many other interpreters of Amish life, before and after him, voiced similar complaints that others' portrayals of the Amish were inaccurate, insensitive, or both. But Hostetler, unlike most other mediators, was more than a sympathetic observer who sought to get things right. He was an Amish-born mediator who still considered himself Amish, at least in some respects. And although his early reflections indicate that he was not wholly enamored with Amish life, the passing years seem only to have heightened his regard for the people who, unlike him, chose to resist the world and remain fully Amish. Granted, it was

LITTLE KNOWN FACTS ABOUT

BUNDLING

IN THE NEW WORLD

THE OLD-FASHIONED CENTER-BOARD
The Pennsylvania Germans invented all kinds of ways and means to get the courting couples together — and all kinds of knick-knacks to keep them apart when they got together! Girls were safer in the old days, in bed with their beaux, than they are today roaming the world over in search of adventure!

By A. MONROE AURAND, Jr.

Member:
Pennsylvania German Folklore Society, &c.

Copyright by THE AURAND PRESS, LANCASTER, PENNA.

FIGS. 4.3–4 In response to A. Monroe Aurand Jr.'s bundling-heavy publications, Hostetler wrote *Amish Life*, using his lone childhood photograph on the cover. Reprinted by permission of Gerald Lestz (Aurand Press) and Herald Press.

Amish Life

By John A. Hostetler

not the path for him. In a letter written late in life, he confessed to another mediator of Amish life that his early fieldwork forays into Mifflin County were exceedingly stressful, that "sleeping under the heavy covers put me back under the culture strain," and that "one day with the Amish . . . took me two days to recover."[82] No, the one-hundred-percent Amish life was not for him, but unlike some who abjure the religion of their childhoods, his axes to grind with the life left behind were relatively few. To the contrary, Hostetler reserved his complaints almost solely for mediators who, from his perspective, underscored the wrong things and told stories out of turn, representational transgressions that, in his opinion, reflected poorly on the Amish and, more ominously, jeopardized their future.

It is important to note here that Hostetler himself was not averse to writing honestly about Amish life, even if that meant exposing its less sanguine aspects. In one early essay, for instance, Hostetler tells of a prominent Amish minister who hanged himself, an event he associates with the stress of maintaining the *Ordnung*.[83] The same article gives voice to Amish teenagers who are devastated by their churches' prohibition of advanced education; it provides accounts of Amish parents whose disciplinary practices tend toward violence; and it describes the adolescent practice of "running wild" that is tolerated, if not encouraged, in the larger Amish settlements. The candidness of this article was not an anomaly in Hostetler's work, for accounts such as these appear in all four editions of his *Amish Society*.[84] Significantly, however, Hostetler reserved the exploration of these "backstage" elements of Amish life—spiteful disciplinary practices, alcohol abuse, and petty lawbreaking—for his more scholarly writings, where he could contextualize their existence and temper his readers' reactions.[85] While not entirely ignoring these issues in his popular publications, he consistently refused to entertain casual audiences with sensational details that, to his chagrin, some other authors seemed happy to provide.

Hostetler's approach in this regard is best illustrated by his treatment of bundling. Whereas some popular mediators of Amish life devoted significant attention to this practice, spicing their offerings with salacious anecdotes, Hostetler addressed bundling only in passing, even in his scholarly work. In fact, it is arguable that Hostetler actually *downplayed* its prominence in North American Amish life.[86] In any case, Hostetler's voluminous writings shared precious few details about the practice, and he was incensed by those who opted instead to satisfy their readers' prurient interests. A decade after he sought to suppress A. Monroe Aurand's bundling-heavy offerings, Hostetler mounted another campaign against a bundling book, this one written by Elmer Lewis Smith.[87] In a torrent of letters to colleagues and acquaintances, Hostetler branded Smith's *Bundling Among the Amish* "injudicious," "in very poor taste," and "obscene."[88] Interestingly, Hostetler did not question the veracity of Smith's material. In fact, he complained to Smith's publisher that the book's material "is no discovery to those of us who know the Amish."[89] But the question for Hostetler was not one of truth versus fiction; it was one of style, audience, and appropriateness. "The material might have been published in a professional journal," he told one colleague, "but to issue it in style and content to an obscene audience [*sic*] is quite another matter."[90]

Perhaps more to the point, Hostetler was concerned about the potential effects of such writings. Hostetler believed that Smith-like portrayals of the Amish, which emphasized moral failings and libidinal oddities, did a terrible disservice to real-life Amish people. He told Smith in a pointed letter that publications like his portend "great harm to *my* people."[91] This five-word phrase, brief though it is, goes to the heart of both Hostetler's self-identity and his vocational identity. The Amish, he believed, were *his* people, a reference to his continuing sense of Amishness, both culturally and genealogically. But the phrase also reflects an ethnographic sensibility—an accurate one—that he, much more than Smith, knew and understood Amish life.[92] Moreover, while recognizing that Smith and others could rightfully publish their own portrayals, he nonetheless believed that they, like he, should be ever mindful of undermining public esteem for the Amish. From a twenty-first-century vantage point, it is hard to imagine the Old Order Amish in need of more public esteem. In 1960, however, this esteem was considerably less pronounced.[93] Moreover, the question of long-term Amish survival in North America, both in Hostetler's mind and in the minds of most sociologists, was still an open one. As a social scientist, Hostetler was well aware of social forces over which he had little power. Nurturing public esteem for the Amish, however, was an achievable goal. Early in his career, he decided to do what he could in that regard.

In defending the Amish against what he considered untoward, invasive representations, Hostetler often used tactics that were less academic than political; in addition to writing occasional reviews for scholarly publications, he sometimes orchestrated campaigns. In some cases, as with Smith's bundling booklet and two Amish-themed novels written in the 1970s, these campaigns consisted mostly of letter writing and behind-the-scenes maneuvering.[94] In 1984, however, Hostetler's efforts to derail a popular representation of the Amish—the feature film *Witness*—were much more public, entailing op-ed pieces in newspapers and pleas to the general public to write letters of opposition.[95] Even when his campaign to stop the movie failed, Hostetler continued his anti-*Wit-*

ness efforts, criticizing the movie in a *People* magazine interview and later in a volume devoted to media ethics.[96] In all these venues, Hostetler traced his opposition to numerous factors, including inaccuracies relative to Amish life and the disruptions real-life Amish people experienced during the movie's Lancaster County filming. But the main reason for Hostetler's opposition to *Witness* was his desire to secure the long-term health and vitality of Amish culture. His most vigorous critique of the movie pointed to its potential negative effects on Amish life, including the possibility that *Witness* would serve to double Lancaster County's annual tourist influx.[97] While it is arguable that, in the case of *Witness*, Hostetler overestimated the negative effects of a popular portrayal of the Amish, it is important to note that no one acts in retrospect. From his perspective—a perspective that knew not only Amish people, but also the challenges they faced in maintaining their culture in late twentieth-century America—popular portrayals such as *Witness* would certainly not benefit the Amish, and might in fact harm them.[98]

In addition to his concern about *Witness*'s deleterious effects on Amish life, Hostetler expressed a second basic concern about the movie, one that referred to its Hollywoodesque features, indeed, to the very fact that it was a Hollywood film with Amish characters. Here we see most vividly Hostetler's continuing Amishness, for he not only provided reasons why the Amish themselves would not make such a movie, he also argued that, given the dominant Amish perspective on Hollywood filmmaking, *no one* should make a movie like *Witness*. The film's fundamental transgression, Hostetler complained, was "violat[ing] Amish integrity" by intruding into "their religious space and symbols."[99] Not that *Witness* held a monopoly in that regard; given the Amish perspective on both photography and worldly entertainments, Hostetler asserted, any attempt to make a "Hollywood film" would be necessarily out of bounds.[100] Clearly Paramount Pictures (and probably most media outlets) and the film's director (and probably most artists) disagreed with the notion that subjects' moral sensitivities should be given veto power over mediators' representational endeavors. For Hostetler, however, being sensitive to Amish concerns was part and parcel of being a mediator of Amish life. Why should Hollywood think otherwise—unless, of course, they were driven by the allure of box office receipts?[101]

Hostetler's concern with the style in which the Amish were mediated was not limited to *Witness*, however, or even to Hollywood. His bewilderment with some of Lancaster County's Amish-themed tourist venues was as much about their style of presentation as it was about the content of their messages. Reflecting Marshall McLuhan's view that the medium is the message, Hostetler demonstrated a low regard for tourist entrepreneurs who, in his estimation, represented the Amish in ways that lacked requisite humility and restraint. This attitude, it seems, contributed to Hostetler's estrangement from Merle Good, a Mennonite entrepreneur who founded and operated People's Place, a leading Lancaster County tourist enterprise.[102] On one level, Good and Hostetler had much in common, each working hard to offer informed, sensitive interpretations of Amish-Mennonite life. Moreover, both men demonstrated a zealousness to tell progressive Mennonites and the larger American public that the Old Order Amish had much to teach them. Perhaps some of their conflict can be traced to competition for the same audience, but a more fundamental source was their different styles, approaches, and contexts for mediating Amish-Mennonite life. Hostetler was an Amish-born academic whose work was scholarly, whose salary was secure, and whose esteem was considerable in both the Amish and the academic communities. Good was a Mennonite-born entrepreneur who lacked Hostetler's academic credentials and his Amish connections, and whose presentation of Amish life needed to be closely attuned to consumer desires. For his part, Good was quite willing to question the assumption that social scientists offered uniquely valuable insights for understanding Amish-Mennonite life.[103] For his part, Hostetler disdained Good's tenaciously entrepreneurial approach to representing Amish culture. In a diary-like reflection late in life, Hostetler recounted a visit to People's Place in which he suffered a profound sense of embarrassment when he saw his name cited prominently in the venue's polished displays.[104] Hardly the most glitzy tourist outlet in Lancaster County, and widely praised as being both informative in content and sensitive in style, People's Place was nonetheless more extravagant and less nuanced than Hostetler's books and journal articles. Moreover, the entrepreneurial Good was not at all shy about promoting himself and his various media ventures. In Hostetler's eyes, Good's approach smacked of *Hochmut*, of pride.[105]

This is not to say that Hostetler refused to promote his own Amish-related ventures.[106] Nor did Hostetler choose only words to communicate his messages about Amish life. Nonetheless, what finally distinguished Hostetler from Good and a host of other mediators (at least as far as he could tell) was the abiding discomfort he felt with the whole process of representation, including his own representational work. In the same piece in which he recounted his visit to People's Place, Hostetler also confessed to uneasiness with publishing *Amish Life* and *Amish Society*. "I tried hard to be restrained [and] authentic," he wrote with respect to *Amish Society*, but when the book finally appeared after fourteen years of work, he felt mostly "embarrassed," especially by the favorable reviews it generated. Worse yet, he recalled, he soon found himself "pressed" by media outlets to "give talks, make appearances, and help make a documentary film," all of which he eventually did.[107] It was all rather disconcerting to an Amish boy turned scholar-mediator whose role as the leading authority on Amish life depended on self-assertion, at least to some degree. The academy, replete with its vitas, faculty ranks, and other forms of latent competition, was un-Amish enough, but the Amish culture market was even worse—it demanded representational approaches that stretched Hostetler to his ethical limits, approaches that made his calling to represent the Amish a distinctly uneasy one. This may have been the biggest challenge Hostetler faced as a mediator of Amish life. It was not, however, the only one.

THE CHALLENGES OF MEDIATION: THE AMISH, THE ENGLISH, AND THE MARKET

The challenges that all scholars face are only compounded for ethnographers, for in addition to meeting the academy's expectations, they also must tend to their subjects. In Hostetler's case, tending to his subjects entailed a unique set of complexities. On the one hand, the Old Order Amish were fast becoming a consumer phenomenon, a process that generally increased Amish people's wariness of those who sought to portray them. At the same time, some of Hostetler's subjects consisted of family members, friends, and longtime acquaintances. To be sure, these birthright connections provided him with a degree of cultural access that most ethnographers can only dream of. Still, the task of reporting ethnographic findings is delicate enough without having to worry about the reactions of one's biological aunts, uncles, siblings, and cousins.

From the beginning of his ethnographic work among the Amish, Hostetler knew what all ethnographers know: offending his hosts would spell the end of his work. In 1951, when Joseph W. Yoder published his book-length critique of Amish life, *Amish Traditions*, Yoder solicited his younger colleague to write a review, knowing that Hostetler was himself less than enamored with some aspects of Amish life. By this time, however, Hostetler had already begun his master's thesis on Amish family life, a thesis that necessitated doing fieldwork in his Mifflin County birth community. Hostetler declined Yoder's request, explaining to him that, "until I get my Ph.D. and the data I want from Amish homes, I must keep my mouth shut."[108] Hostetler, of course, did not conclude his data gathering in 1951; rather, he continued to do ethnographic work among the Amish for the next four decades. For this reason, he continued to work hard to foster and maintain good relations with Amish people, even ones he did not know personally. In 1957, for instance, when two Amish educators took exception to Hostetler's criticism of Amish teacher training practices, Hostetler responded to their letters quickly, appreciatively, and with no defensiveness.[109] In fact, his responses to the men focused mostly on their respective invitations to visit their schools. "Your letter is so genuine that I hesitate to comment further," he concluded in one of his letters, "but [I] will live in the expectation of meeting you."[110]

Hostetler's deference to his subjects demonstrates an ongoing concern about access, but it also reflects his commitment to taking his subjects seriously. Finally, of course, ethnographers must themselves choose which stories to tell, and Hostetler was no exception in this regard. Still, he took pains to run much of his written work past select Amish persons before seeing it into print. For instance, in 1970, one year prior to the publication of *Children in Amish Society*, Hostetler sent a draft manuscript to an Amish acquaintance, Joseph Stoll, soliciting from him "comments for improvement."[111] A few years later, Hostetler asked Stoll's brother-in-law, David Luthy, to review a "delicate" chapter he had drafted for the third edition of *Amish Society*. Luthy's input, Hostetler wrote, was to go beyond mere fact-checking to reading the chapter with Amish eyes. He said Luthy should feel free to examine the chapter for "bias" and, with respect to another chapter, "take out what might be objectionable" to Amish readers.[112]

Again, much of Hostetler's concern about offending his Amish subjects can be traced to professional considerations (such as access) and ethical constraints (such as granting Amish people some say over his representational practices). But in addition to these concerns, Hostetler had more personal reasons for eschewing the publication of objectionable material. More than simply writing about his community of origin, Hostetler was writing about family members, many of whom remained firmly embedded in the Amish world. Although some of his Amish relatives were quietly supportive of his work, others were skeptical, in part because they considered erudition suspect, more specifically because Hostetler's writings were, in their opinion, of little use to his Amish subjects. "We don't need more books because we know more than we are able to practice," was the way Hostetler paraphrased some family members' reactions to his writings.[113] Ultimately, Hostetler did not agree with their assessment that his work had little value. Nonetheless, he always remained sensitive to his family members' views, a sensitivity that only strengthened his resolve to produce scholarship that went beyond proliferating knowledge to effecting good for Amish people and their communities.[114]

Hostetler's concerns about the effects of his work on Amish life shaped his gatekeeping activities as well, both with respect to the general public and with respect to fellow scholars. Hostetler was not the only gateway into Amish culture in the 1960s, 1970s, and 1980s, but his renown as a scholar made him the logical choice for many who wished to gain access. One of the ironies of his representational work, especially in light of his pleas to leave the Amish alone, was the way in which it inspired some readers to seek them out. That was never the *intent* of Hostetler's writing; nevertheless, his files teem with letters requesting contact information for an Amish homestay or, in many cases, for the purpose of converting. Some of the letters he received demonstrate very little forethought ("I am interested in joining the Amish Church . . . [although] at this time I know nothing about it"), whereas others reflect a more serious wrestling with the realities of Amish life.[115] In any case, letters such as these numbered in the hundreds, perhaps thousands, each one placing Hostetler in the unenviable position of deciding whether to encourage or discourage the letter writer, and ultimately whether to provide the writer access to Amish people or communities. A person with fewer Amish-like sensibilities would have generated a form letter to skirt this dilemma. Instead, Hostetler chose to respond personally, addressing the specific questions embedded in each letter.

Hostetler's responses varied from person to person, and they also varied over time. Sometimes he was markedly dissuasive, especially when the inquirer demonstrated little knowledge of Amish life. "The Amish are not what you describe them to be," he told one man who claimed to be enamored of their "natural way of life" but not their religious commitments. Even in this case, however, Hostetler encouraged the writer to read *Amish Society* and then get back in touch, at which point "I will be glad to correspond with you about specific persons you might like to talk to."[116] Significantly, this particular interchange dates to 1967, relatively early in Hostetler's role as a public gatekeeper. Over time, Hostetler grew much less inclined to countenance such inquiries, largely because of the burden these seekers were placing upon their Amish hosts. Moreover, he increasingly involved Amish persons in the gatekeeping process. In 1975, for instance, Hostetler wrote to an Amish friend to complain that the large number of inquiries he was receiving was becoming unmanageable. He asked his friend for advice, noting that one of the Amish man's brethren had recently instructed Hostetler "to tone it down," that is, to refrain from forwarding on to their community so many letters. In response, Hostetler's Amish friend acknowledged that the whole issue was a very difficult one, that the best Hostetler could do was "spread [the seekers] around, especially the ones you think are serious." The man also suggested that he and Hostetler get together sometime to develop guidelines for vetting the requests.[117] There is no evidence the men ever did so, but it is clear that Hostetler's gatekeeping became increasingly fastidious as the years went by. At the close of his career, he often quoted an Amish-written piece that encouraged seekers to find spiritual resources closer to home. "If you admire our faith, strengthen yours," wrote the pseudonymous Uncle Amos. "If you admire our sense of commitment, deepen yours."[118]

Scholars, like the broader public, also placed Hostetler in the unenviable position of granting or refusing access to the Amish. In these cases Hostetler's sense of whether a scholar's work would benefit the Amish played the leading role in determining his response. For example, Hostetler enthusiastically abetted the work of Johns Hopkins University medical personnel, whose genetic research in Amish communities (aided by Beulah Hostetler's tireless genealogical work) helped to diagnose maladies specific to some Amish populations. Requests from other scholars were more ambiguous, however, in their potential to accrue benefits to real-life Amish people or to bring harm to them. In some of these cases, Hostetler seems to have imposed artificially high, self-referential standards for sanctioning their work. For instance, in an evaluation letter he sent in 1983 to the National Endowment for the Humanities regarding a proposed Amish-themed documentary, Hostetler concluded that, "unless the applicant has had an anthropological relationship with the native culture for two decades, or has grown up in the culture . . . , I would not favor the proposed project."[119] Five years later, however, Hostetler granted quick and intimate access to a researcher who had little previous contact with Amish culture. Granted, the second researcher, Randy-Michael Testa, was proposing only to do dissertation research on Amish educational practices, not produce a documentary film. Moreover, the manner in which Testa approached Hostetler— an eloquent letter, filled with deferential language, winsome academic connections, and references to his faith—should not be discounted in helping to win Hostetler's support.[120] Still, Hostetler's decision rested at least as much on his sense that Testa's ideological sensibilities paralleled his own with respect to what was good for the Amish. When four years later Hostetler contributed the foreword to Testa's *After the Fire: The Destruction of the Lancaster County Amish* (1992), he devoted special attention to an anecdote Testa recounted in his initial letter of inquiry, an anecdote that went to the heart of Hostetler's now self-conscious calling: the protection of Amish culture from forces that sought to destroy it.[121]

Hostetler's attentiveness to ends—that is, to the anticipated results of his representational efforts—also shaped the contours of his own work, particularly as it pertained to photography. Hostetler was well aware of the Amish

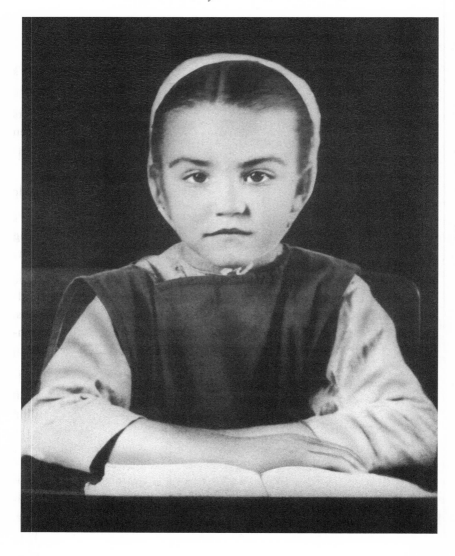

FIGS. 4.5–6 In the 1952 edition of *Amish Life*, John A. Hostetler restricted his use of photos to unbaptized Amish children (opposite), complementing them with ink drawings of Amish adults. Drawing by Ann Killins, reprinted by permission of Herald Press.

taboo against photographs and, at least in the context of the *Witness* debate, he complained about outsiders who violated that taboo.[122] At the same time, he himself included photographs of Amish persons in his books and, in one case, lent his services to the production of an Amish-themed documentary. At various points in his career, Hostetler sought to come to terms with his noncompliance with this taboo, noting in one instance that his book's illustrations derived from already extant photographs taken by persons who had nurtured "neighborly relations with Amish people over a period of many years."[123] Later in his life, he tried once again to explain his middle-of-the-road approach, observing that posed pictures constitute to Amish persons the "most objectionable" violation of this taboo, whereas unobtrusively secured photographs often do not concern the Amish subjects all.[124] Hostetler's thinking on this issue can hardly be reduced to a crass justification of media-savvy methods. Rather, he had discussed the issue with numerous Amish persons, trying hard to decipher a consistent and useful Amish perspective.[125] What he discovered, in fact, were a *variety* of Amish perspectives. In some cases, Amish people found the production of Amish-themed photographs by out-

siders wholly unjustifiable. Others, however, told Hostetler they could abide
the practice as long as photographers demonstrated sufficient courtesy, asking permission before taking their pictures and keeping disruptions to a minimum. Still others contended that permission-seekers placed them in an existential quandary, and that they preferred to keep their consciences unsullied
by simply not being asked.[126]

In light of this ambiguity, and for a variety of other reasons—encouragement
from market-conscious publishers, the reality that hundreds of Amish-themed
photographs were already circulating, and the commonsense notion that good
photographs were educationally useful—Hostetler liberalized his use of photographs over time.[127] For instance, when producing the first edition of *Amish
Life* in 1952, Hostetler and his publisher limited photographic usage to unbaptized Amish persons (that is, Amish children) and a few long-range shots
in which individual subjects cannot be identified.[128] Moreover, the first editions of both *Amish Life* and *Amish Society* included a number of ink drawings
that served to reduce the need for photographs. Subsequent editions of these
works, however, move in similar iconographic directions, shedding their drawings while adding more photos, including close-ups of Amish adults. In the
midst of all this, Hostetler expressed occasional reservations about his use of
photographs, though he ultimately overcame many of them, or at least found
ways around them. In 1967, between the first and second editions of *Amish
Society*, William Lindholm, the chairman of the newly established National
Committee for Amish Religious Freedom, asked Hostetler where he could get
"a few good shots" of Amish life to accompany news releases about Amish legal difficulties. Hostetler responded that he could easily secure photographs
for Lindholm, but he preferred not to get involved. "I have 'transgressed' on
this point about all I can manage," he confessed to his English friend. That
Hostetler placed quotation marks around the word *transgressed* hints at his uncertainty on the issue. Was it *really* a transgression to take photographs of Amish
life? Was it a transgression to *reprint* photos that already existed? Hostetler was
not entirely sure how to answer these questions, but it is clear that the whole
thing made him uncomfortable. In this particular case, he finally chose an equiv-
ocating response, refusing to secure the pictures himself but informing Lindholm that "news services such as World Wide" would be a good place for Lindholm to find some himself.[129]

Perhaps more than anything, Hostetler's participation in the production of
an Amish-themed documentary film reveals Hostetler's thinking about the appropriateness of photographic and cinematic representations of Amish life. The
film, *The Amish: A People of Preservation* (1975), was a cooperative effort between

Hostetler (who conceived the idea), Mennonite storyteller John Ruth, and cameraman Burton Buller, and it was soon picked up for distribution by Encyclopedia Britannica and excerpted on CBS's *60 Minutes*.[130] From the beginning, the filmmakers admitted to their production techniques, which involved clandestine filming using long-range camera lenses hidden in various places. This, they believed, not only provided a heightened degree of authenticity, it also conformed to the sometimes expressed Amish opinion that they would rather not know if their images were being captured on film.[131] Of course, the issue of clandestine filming quickly raised questions among scholars, one of whom wrote that "such methods" were ethically problematic, much akin to folklorists hiding tape recorders under their coats. Still, the reviewer continued, "the same scholars [who would criticize clandestine approaches] would not ignore the advantages of documenting an event in its natural context."[132]

Hostetler was well aware of the ethical issues involved, and he also knew that his involvement in the project could undermine his good standing with his Amish subjects. Still, he decided to forge ahead, for two reasons. First, Hostetler recognized that, like it or not, other documentary films were being made and marketed. Correspondingly, and perhaps more fundamentally, Hostetler believed that the Amish themselves would benefit from the existence of his documentary alternative. In a meeting with a small group of Lancaster County Amish leaders, Hostetler outlined these reasons and, for all practical purposes, was granted a green light to proceed.[133] Later, in an effort to head off potential criticism from other influential Amish persons, Hostetler wrote a long letter explaining his position. Television executives had been pressuring him to do this for years, he explained to his Amish contacts, but only now did he decide to become involved. The film "won't stop the tourist trade," he admitted, but it will provide "informative answers to sincerely interested people." More specifically, *A People of Preservation* might diminish the influence of another film circulating in tourist venues, a film Hostetler deemed "one of the most disgusting I have seen."[134] All said, the genre may have been different, but the problem, the rationale, and even Hostetler's acerbic language of "disgust," were not at all new: twenty-five years later, it was A. Monroe Aurand Jr. and *Amish Life* all over again.

Even so, the genre *did* make it different, or at least made Hostetler's representational dilemma more poignant. Words were one thing for this Amish-boy-turned-scholar, but film was something else, particularly in light of the Amish taboo against photography. But what was he to do? In an early-career letter to an Amish friend, Hostetler complained that even the Mennonite Publishing House tended too much toward "Madison Avenue" in its marketing approach. Would it not be better, Hostetler continued, to use "face-to-face" methods rather than "worldly psychology" to attract customers?[135] This, it seems, was Hostetler the Amish man talking. Still, Hostetler the modern knew that the market was a force, and he was ultimately unwilling to let it run its course without his contributions. He may not have liked becoming a player in this representational market (as we have noted, he sometimes used the language of being "pressed" to produce his representations), but the alternative he envisioned, an Amish culture market without his imprint, seemed even less attractive.[136] Therefore, in this particular case, he determined that the end of bolstering Amish culture justified his means.

In the final analysis, Hostetler's work on *A People of Preservation* reveals not only his representational dilemma, but also the particular way he navigated his life as an Amish-modern. In a certain respect, Hostetler's very decision to participate in an Amish-themed documentary film project demonstrated his lingering Amishness, in the sense that he was establishing a representational *Ordnung* for himself that was ultimately concerned with the *effect* on Amish community life. The *means* of sustaining Amish community life, whether plowing with horses (in the Amish case) or filming Amish persons (in Hostetler's case) were not wholly irrelevant, but in the end it was the community's life and health that mattered. In that respect, Hostetler's Amishness served him well in navigating the dilemma of cinematic representations of Amish life. Still, we would be remiss not to note that a personal *Ordnung*, in which one's own conception of right and wrong is the final arbiter, is a *modern* ethical orientation, not an Amish one. As noted above, Hostetler was careful to consult with Amish leaders before undertaking the documentary project, and he worked hard to be sensitive to their concerns. At the same time, he was not asking their permission to undertake the project, nor was he subject to the disciplinary actions of a particular Amish community.[137] In sum, Hostetler's representational *Ordnung*, which took into account Amish wishes, Mennonite sensibilities, academic expectations, and market realities, was a complex and ultimately *personal* ethical formulation. In that regard, Hostetler the Amish man was also very modern.

ADVOCATING FOR THE AMISH

If circumstances in the larger culture influenced Hostetler's representational work, so too did they shape his role as a public advocate. As the Amish culture market was expanding in the second half of the twentieth century, so was the reach of the state, particularly with respect to bureaucratic regulations. Moreover, socioeconomic changes continued to imperil rural life in general and the family farm in particular. Although Hostetler sometimes referred to the Amish as a "cultural island," he knew better than most that Amish culture was not an island unto itself, that the desires and decisions of the larger society exacted tangible effects upon Amish life. Although the Amish were not defenseless in the face of these challenges, they were nonetheless reticent to advocate for themselves and, in many cases, quite willing to trust in God (and their own instincts) to deliver them from their difficulties. It was in this context that Hostetler emerged as their leading public advocate.

Hostetler's emergence in this regard cannot be separated from his role as scholar and writer. Hostetler's ethnographic work nurtured in him a respect for Amish life that reverberated through his writings. As a result, many Amish persons came to see him as a friend of the Amish people, one who knew their foibles but opted to accentuate the positive. In addition, Hostetler demonstrated in various ways, not least through his work with Johns Hopkins medical researchers, that he was genuinely concerned about the health and well-being of Amish people and their culture. Not coincidentally, many Amish people welcomed him to their communities time and again, talking with him in ways that they would not talk with other outsiders. It was this long-standing, affectionate relationship that most impressed a colleague who, in 1993, feted Hostetler for his work. "The most enduring tribute" to Hostetler, said Donald B. Kraybill, lies in the "warm welcome" he enjoys among the Amish after decades of probing their lives.[138]

The esteem Hostetler had for Amish culture, and the respect Amish persons had for him, created a climate in which he could effectively function as their advocate. Most noteworthy in this regard was Hostetler's legal advocacy in the face of schooling regulations that, by the mid-1960s, had plagued Amish communities for almost fifty years. During these years, Amish noncompliance with schooling laws, particularly those pertaining to age-based compulsory attendance, had resulted in legal judgments ranging from fines to jail sentences to state-sanctioned removals of Amish children from their homes.[139] To many Americans, the stubbornness of the Amish in this regard owed to either foolishness or greed. Who could possibly find fault with a high school education—except, of course, people who valued ignorance or the economic fruits of their children's labor? To the Amish, however, a high school education and, just as important, the context in which it was provided, undermined their ability to socialize their offspring. To them, it was a question of maintaining their children's commitment to Amish ways. And given that the Amish church rarely gains converts from the outside world, it was to them ultimately a question of survival.

Hostetler agreed with that assessment. Consequently, he devoted considerable energy to convincing both the public and the courts that certain laws violated Amish religious freedom. In addition to publishing pieces for popular and scholarly consumption, Hostetler joined forces with other professionals to found the National Committee for Amish Religious Freedom (NCARF), an organization designed to fund and coordinate the legal defenses of Amish persons found in violation of laws that impinged on Amish life.[140] Hostetler's role in all of this was twofold, reflecting once again his position as a man in the middle. On the one hand, Hostetler was charged with persuading Amish persons to participate in legal challenges; on the other, he was expected to provide expert testimony for legal proceedings. The latter of these two tasks received more public acclaim, but the former task was more delicate and, in many ways, peculiarly fitted to Hostetler's gifts. To be sure, he did not convince every Amish person that legal challenges were practically useful and religiously justifiable, but he convinced some.[141] Moreover, he convinced the right people to persist long enough in one particular battle for it to proceed to the U.S. Supreme Court. In 1972, the Court handed down its *Wisconsin v. Yoder* decision, which ruled that Amish parents could rightfully withhold their children from high school. The case continues to serve as a benchmark for religious liberty cases involving religious minorities.[142]

More than other life experiences, Hostetler's role in *Wisconsin* shaped his sense of calling as a protector of Amish culture. Other scholars may have been able to offer helpful testimony, but Hostetler was the logical, and undoubtedly the best, choice to testify on the nature of Amish life. William B. Ball, the constitutional lawyer who argued *Wisconsin* before the Supreme Court, lauded Hostetler's contributions, as did a writer in the *American Anthropologist*, who concluded that Hostetler's testimony was likely "indispensable" to the case's outcome.[143] Hostetler reserved his involvement in *Wisconsin* for the final few paragraphs of his autobiographical essay in the *American Scholar*. There he quotes his pithy reply to the prosecution's query about the ability of Amish children to make their way in the world without a high school education ("It all depends on which world," Hostetler quotes himself as saying).[144] While Hostetler was sometimes embarrassed by his involvement in the Amish culture market, there is no indication that he ever felt embarrassed by his contribution to *Wisconsin*. To the contrary, in addition to helping to confirm his calling, *Wisconsin* provided Hostetler with resources by which to interpret other aspects of his work that he found discomfiting.

FIG. 4.7 Attorney William B. Ball (left), John A. Hostetler, and Rev. William C. Lindholm (right), chairman of the National Committee for Amish Religious Freedom, gather in 1993. Photograph by Terry Way, reprinted by permission.

On a more concrete level, *Wisconsin* boosted Hostetler's resolve to undertake other forms of advocacy, not only in the courts, but also against *Witness*. As noted above, Hostetler's anti-*Witness* campaign in 1984 replicated in some ways his earlier attempts to censor textual representations of the Amish. In other ways, however, this campaign paralleled more closely his work with *Wisconsin* thirteen years earlier, for it not only battled a powerful, well-financed opponent, but it demanded, in Hostetler's view, the support of relevant Amish leaders, the assistance of well-connected English friends, and the currency of public disapprobation toward outsiders' treatment of the Amish. Significantly, even Hostetler's philosophical arguments against *Witness* took on *Wisconsin*-like overtones, suggesting in some instances that the filmmakers were violating the Amish people's religious liberty.[145] This rights-based argument, of course, would have held no sway in court, but it did find resonance in the courtroom of public opinion, generating similar responses from like-minded critics. In the end, Hostetler and his allies did little to slow *Witness*'s advance, and like other campaigns against controversial films, their work may actually have benefited the movie by increasing publicity for it.[146] But the cause was not entirely lost. Shortly after filming ended, the Pennsylvania Department of Commerce pledged to Amish leaders that it would no longer promote the Amish "as subjects for feature films."[147] Even this victory, however, was hollow, for the department later asserted that it would offer support to filmmakers of Amish-themed movies, even if it would not "promote" the Amish as subjects.[148]

Much of Hostetler's work as an advocate for his Amish subjects gave him energy. In the case of *Witness*, however, it brought him pain, for the process generated a significant degree of counter-criticism directed at him and, in some cases, toward his Amish subjects. A number of critics, led by the film's director Peter Weir, accused Hostetler of being hypermoralistic, hypocritical, or both, caustically noting that Hostetler's books contained photographs "stolen off the Amish" and, more generally, that Hostetler had made his living "off the Amish."[149] Hostetler's claim that *Witness*'s sex and violence violated the "integrity" of the Amish struck some of their neighbors as odd, and he consequently received letters from persons eager to recount the sordid activities of Amish people they knew.[150] A more trenchant criticism came from one of Hostetler's fellow mediators, who raised the question of whether Hostetler, in speaking against *Witness*, was completely forthcoming in his claim that he was speaking *on behalf of* the Amish.[151] These criticisms, leveled at Hostetler when he was in his mid-sixties, caught him off guard. He was not a stranger to controversy, particularly with respect to censuring others' portrayals of Amish life. But never had *his* authority as a scholar-mediator of Amish life been so publicly and pointedly disputed. Even worse, his integrity as an ethnographer—and his beneficence toward his Amish subjects—was now being questioned, at least by some. For a person who had endeavored for thirty-some years to represent the Amish with clarity and sensitivity, encountering such charges was devastating and, in a manner reminiscent of his father, he considered filing a lawsuit against Weir for defamation of character.[152] In the end, however, he chose a different path, opting to take comfort in the many expressions of appreciation he received for his Amish-related work, including his opposition to *Witness*.

What shall we make of Hostetler's advocacy work, particularly as it pertains to *Witness*? There is some evidence that Hostetler, in claiming to be a spokesperson for the Amish, both underreported his involvement in shaping Amish peoples' views and overstated the unanimity with which Amish persons regarded the film. Even three years later, when Hostetler published a retrospective analysis on the controversy, he frequently invoked monolithic language as he summarized "*the* Amish position" on *Witness* and, correspondingly, understated his agency in catalyzing the conflict.[153] Whether Hostetler did this self-consciously is difficult to assess. In any case, his anti-*Witness* advocacy work manifested a politically useful "strategic essentialism" that rendered his subjects more univocal than they were in reality.[154] It is important to point out—and critique—Hostetler's essentialist rendering of his Amish subjects. At the same time, it is important to acknowledge that Hostetler understood two basic truths about Amish life. First, he knew that Amish life, much more than most American subcultures, functioned on the principle of unity; that is, even though Amish people often held different opinions about what was right or appropriate, Amish communities did not give heed to each individual's opinion. Second, Hostetler knew that the Amish, while neither powerless nor inarticulate, nonetheless tended toward reticence and nonresistance. Given this reality, and given too that he viewed *Witness* as a real threat to Amish life, Hostetler felt more than justified in speaking boldly on behalf of the Amish in strategic fashion. He may not have told the story in all its complexity, but what Amish person does? Indeed, what *advocate* does? For Amish and advocates alike, the end takes priority, and achieving that end will sometimes mean fashioning a social reality that is more unified in theory than it is in actuality. Ironically, even as an advocate, Hostetler's Amishness served him well.

CONCLUSION: ANTHROPOLOGY AS WITNESS

We return once again to Hostetler's query about his nineteenth-century predecessor, the youthful Amish man who chose a Methodist future over the Amish *Ordnung*: might this Methodist convert have accomplished more good by staying in the Amish church and witnessing there? John Hostetler raised this question in 1949, when he was thirty years old. Chances are, by 1959, he would have found the question odd, perhaps even irreverent. As late as 1954, when Hostetler published "God Visits the Amish," he held the opinion that the Old Order Amish would benefit from a strong, evangelical witness from without, one that would temper their traditions and infuse them with a much-needed dose of God's Spirit. Even then, however, the seeds of a drastically different perspective were beginning to sprout in his work, a perspective that soon turned his notion of *witness* upside down. In sum, Hostetler came to believe that it was not the Amish who needed the world's witness, it was the world that needed an Amish witness.[155]

Long before Hostetler embraced his vocation as a mediator of Amish life, cultural observers had noted ways in which the Amish provided a prophetic corrective to the larger society.[156] In that sense, the Amish themselves, quiet as they were, had become witnesses to a different, perhaps even better, way of life. Even so, mid-twentieth-century perceptions of the Amish were mixed, as

were predictions about their ability to survive in an increasingly technological society. It was in this context that Hostetler came of age as a scholar, and
he quickly assumed the role of amplifying their witness by publishing informed,
respectful accounts of Amish life. In time his amplifying work would assume
other forms, including testifying before public officials and bearing witness
against a Hollywood film (ironically entitled *Witness*). These roles, some of
which Hostetler claimed were pressed upon him by forces beyond his control,
brought him vocational meaning, personal satisfaction, and significant renown.
At the same time, they brought him considerable pain, for they saddled him
with complex representational dilemmas, jeopardized relationships with Amish
family and friends, and, at least in the case of *Witness*, made him a target of
public criticism. More fundamentally, Hostetler's decision to lead a life of mediation between the Amish and the larger world meant embracing the suffering that comes when a culture you love is threatened by forces beyond its control, and beyond your control as well.

Hostetler's experience in this regard can hardly be counted unique. In her
book *The Vulnerable Observer: Anthropology That Breaks Your Heart*, Ruth Behar
recounts trying to explain to her aunt what anthropology really is. When her
aunt offers her own, antiseptic definition ("the study of people and their customs"), Behar fashions a different definition she would like to set forth, if only
she had the courage: "Anthropology," Behar writes, "is the most fascinating,
bizarre, disturbing, and necessary form of witnessing left to us at the end of
the twentieth century."[157] It is, she writes, a vulnerable undertaking, for it requires sensitivity to at least two worlds that almost always work from different assumptions. Herein lies the temptation of ethnographers to "go native,"
to abandon their former worlds for something fresh and enchanting. But then,
says Behar, those other worlds come calling, ordering the anthropologist to
write an insightful essay or give an inspiring talk.[158] Of course, all anthropologists know what they are getting into when they choose their vocation. But
do they *really*? The fact is, says Behar, there is no way to *really* know until one
does the work, not just the ethnographic research but the witnessing as well,
all the time ruing the fact that one's ethnographic terrain is shifting, changing, and passing away. Here Behar cites a letter she received from a fellow anthropologist who noted the grief anthropologists suffer, "not because we lose
our subject matter (we don't), but because we fear the total loss of that rooted
and continuous and meaningful life which we had sought outside our own."[159]
Summarizing her own views in this regard, Behar notes that anthropologists,
almost to a person, leave behind trails of "longings, desires, and unfulfilled ex-

pectations in those upon whom we descend." About that vulnerability, she writes, "we are still barely able to speak."[160]

That Hostetler was not unique in feeling the anthropologist's vulnerability does not make his situation any less poignant. The challenges to and the transformations of Amish culture he witnessed during his forty-year career—the explosion of Amish-themed tourism, the expanding reach of the state, the stress of farmland development, and the waning of Amish agrarianism, to name just a few—were enough to make any anthropologist tremble, if not weep. Of course, Hostetler was more than an anthropologist of Amish life. He was an Amish-born modern who, in his fieldwork, his writing, and even his spiritual longings, returned to his birth culture dozens of times every day. He did not regret his adolescent decision to pursue a different future. He did, however, regret that the non-Amish worlds he chose to inhabit lacked the connectedness, the community, and the integrity his Amish world retained. Above all else, he yearned for that world to survive, and so he worked toward that end, seeking to secure for himself a rooted and meaningful life, hoping to secure for his people a future that he himself forsook.[161]

NOTES

1. My thanks to the following people who read and responded to this chapter in an earlier stage: Simon Bronner, Ronald Burwell, Ann Hostetler, Beulah Hostetler, Laura Hostetler, Mary Hostetler, Gertrude Huntington, Douglas Jacobsen, Julia Kasdorf, S. Duane Kauffman, Albert Keim, David Luthy, Elmer Miller, Levi Miller, Steven Nolt, Calvin Redekop, Pauline Stevick, G. C. Waldrep, and Ruth Weaver.

2. The book, which occupies the realm of creative nonfiction, was entitled, *Hostetler, or, the Mennonite Boy Converted: A True Narrative* (New York: Carlton and Porter, 1848). In it, the author ("A Methodist Preacher") conflates the terms *Amish* and *Mennonite*, with *Amish* probably being the protagonist's specific religious identity.

3. John A. Hostetler, review of *Hostetler, or, the Mennonite Boy Converted: A True Narrative*, by "A Methodist Preacher," in *Budget*, 6 October 1949, 5.

4. The Old Order Amish often call non-Amish persons "the English," a reference to outsiders' inability to speak Pennsylvania Dutch.

5. My reference to "betwixt and between" is indebted to anthropologist Victor Turner's famous essay, "Betwixt and Between: The Liminal Period in *Rites de Passage*," reprinted in his book *The Forest of Symbols: Aspects of Ndembu Ritual* (Ithaca: Cornell University Press, 1967), 93–111. Although it would be a stretch to say that Hostetler's career as an Amish scholar was a rite of passage, he does seem to be occupying a liminal state in which he is both Amish and modern, or perhaps more accurately, not-Amish-not-modern.

6. In Amish churches, excommunication (the *Bann*) and shunning (the *Meidung*) occur only with respect to Amish persons who vow to keep the *Ordnung* but then break that vow. That John

Hostetler never made that vow meant that he was never placed under the *Bann*, a fact that was crucial to his later ability to do fieldwork among Amish people and communities.

7. As Simon Bronner notes in Chapter 3, interpreting their traditionally inclined birth communities was a common vocational practice among mid-century New Class intellectuals. The practice remains common in religious studies, with much of the better scholarship performed by persons who, in various ways, live with one foot (but only one foot) in their childhood religious communities. See, for instance, Grant Wacker, *Heaven Below: Early Pentecostals and American Culture* (Cambridge: Harvard University Press, 2001), x.

8. Although this chapter addresses separately Hostetler's work as a mediator of information about the Amish and his work as an advocate on their behalf, the line between representation (speaking *about* one's subjects) and advocacy (speaking *for* one's subjects) is fuzzy and sometimes nonexistent. Generally speaking, however, Hostetler's work in mediating information about Amish life preceded chronologically and theoretically his most vigorous advocacy work, and this essay therefore treats those tasks in that order. For the relationship between representation and advocacy, see Linda Alcoff, "The Problem of Speaking for Others," in *Feminist Nightmares: Women at Odds: Feminism and the Problem of Sisterhood*, ed. Susan Ostrov Weisser and Jennifer Fleischner (New York: New York University Press, 1994), 288–89.

9. Hostetler's autobiographically oriented manuscript that served as the impetus for this volume carried the tentative title, "My Calling." He had previously used the term *call* in a 1992 autobiographical essay to explain his desire as an Amish teenager to pursue the forbidden fruit of higher education. See John A. Hostetler, "An Amish Beginning," *American Scholar* 61 (1992): 555.

10. "Our Heritage," in *Juniata River Valley: Official Visitor's Guide to Mifflin and Juniata Counties 2004* (Lewistown, Pa.: Juniata River Valley Visitors Bureau, 2004), 5–10.

11. Earlier in the nineteenth century, the Amish churches in the Big Valley were divided into three administrative units: the Upper, Middle, and Lower Districts. The Lower District, which became the Byler Church, had broken fellowship with the other two districts in 1846. See S. Duane Kauffman, *Mifflin County Amish and Mennonite Story, 1791–1991* (Belleville, Pa.: Mifflin County Mennonite Historical Society, 1991), 118.

12. Ibid., 119–20. The catalyst for the dispute was a disagreement over the proper mode of baptism: should it be administered outdoors, with the water poured over the head of the candidate kneeling in a stream, or should it be administered indoors?

13. Ibid., 305–7.

14. Farming a tract of land one mile south of Belleville at the Coldwater Station, Joseph and Nancy's roots ran deep into the Big Valley's Amish-Mennonite history. Nancy Hostetler was herself born a Hostetler; her marriage in 1905 to a distant cousin would hardly have been deemed remarkable.

15. John R. Renno to John A. Hostetler (JAH), 14 February 1977, John A. Hostetler Papers, Penn State University Archives (hereafter cited as Hostetler Papers), Box AL04.03. Renno was himself excommunicated from the Peachey Church in the 1950s, placed under the ban by his father, Bishop John B. Renno.

16. Hostetler, "An Amish Beginning," 553.

17. Those reflections appear in a revised essay, also titled "An Amish Beginning," which is included in this volume as Chapter 1. Susan Fisher Miller inserted these reflections into the original essay in conversation with Hostetler and his family. See the preface to this volume for further discussion of the revision process.

18. Ibid.

19. A copy of the lawsuit, *Joseph H. Hostetler vs. Levi Hostetler*, filed 7 September 1929, can be found in the Hostetler Papers, Box AL05.07. According to John Hostetler's wife, Beulah, John may not have known about his father's lawsuit until after he had written his original *American Scholar* essay in 1992, but he did know about it in advance of the revision. Beulah Stauffer Hostetler, telephone conversation with author, 28 May 2004.

20. Joseph H. Hostetler to David and Katie Detweiler, 26 September 1961, Hostetler Papers, Box AL05.07. David Detweiler was the son of Joseph's oldest daughter, Lizzie, who was twenty-one years old and a church member when her father was excommunicated. In the letter, Joseph criticizes his daughter and son-in-law for supporting the Peachey/Renno Church leadership in their exclusion of him.

21. Shortly after John Hostetler refused baptism in the Iowa Amish church and began attending a local Mennonite church, the Mennonite ministers visited Joseph and Nancy and invited them to attend as well. They did and, like their son, soon joined the East Union Mennonite Church. They continued to dress Amish throughout their lives. Beulah Stauffer Hostetler, telephone conversation with author, 28 May 2004.

22. Hostetler, "An Amish Beginning" (*American Scholar* version), 555.

23. John Horsch, *Mennonites in Europe* (Scottdale, Pa.: Mennonite Publishing House, 1942).

24. JAH to "Dear Brethren" [*sic*], [July 1944], Hostetler Papers, Box AL05.05. This undated letter is reprinted in this volume as Chapter 5.

25. JAH to Joseph and Nancy Hostetler, 4 July 1944, Hostetler Papers, Box AL05.05.

26. He later acknowledged that his letter received "an Amish burial" in that it was entirely and utterly ignored. See Julia Kasdorf, *Fixing Tradition: Joseph W. Yoder, Amish American* (Telford, Pa.: Pandora Press U.S., 2002), 175.

27. Joseph W. Yoder, *Amish Traditions: Dedicated to the Welfare of the Amish People Everywhere to Lighten Their Burdens and to All People Searching for the Truth* (Huntingdon, Pa.: Yoder Publishing, 1950). Yoder was author of two popular treatments of Amish life, *Rosanna of the Amish* (Huntingdon, Pa.: Yoder Publishing, 1940); and *Rosanna's Boys* (Huntingdon, Pa.: Yoder Publishing, 1948). For a thorough consideration of Yoder, see Kasdorf, *Fixing Tradition*.

28. JAH to Joseph W. Yoder, 2 February 1951, Joseph W. Yoder Papers, L. A. Beeghly Library, Juniata College, Huntingdon, Pennsylvania (hereafter cited as "Yoder Papers").

29. Ibid.

30. See John A. Hostetler, "A Century of Life Together," *Christian Living*, March 1986, 12. In addition to attending one day of Bible school at age thirteen, Hostetler attended chorus programs presented by students from Mennonite colleges.

31. Hostetler, "An Amish Beginning" (*American Scholar* version), 554.

32. Ibid., 556.

33. "Mennonites" in this paragraph and the paragraphs that follow refers to Old Mennonites, also called the Mennonite Church, at that time the largest Mennonite denomination in North America and, like the Amish, comprised mostly of persons of South German and Swiss origin.

34. See David Weaver-Zercher, *The Amish in the American Imagination* (Baltimore: Johns Hopkins University Press, 2001), 126–27. My claim that mid-twentieth-century Mennonites were abandoning these Amish-like traits would not apply to certain other groups that went by the name Mennonite, for example, the various Old Order Mennonite groups.

35. In 1944, the Mennonite Church General Conference passed a resolution calling for "a comprehensive treatment and exposition of the doctrine of nonconformity," the result being John C. Wenger's *Separated Unto God: A Plea for Christian Simplicity of Life and for a Scriptural Nonconformity to the World* (Scottdale, Pa.: Mennonite Publishing House, 1951).

36. JAH to Lee Kanagy, 25 October 1943, Hostetler Papers, Box AL05.06.

37. JAH to Barbara Hostetler, 26 October 1943, Hostetler Papers, Box AL05.06.

38. Daniel Kauffman, "Our Iowa Field," *Herald of Truth*, 15 July 1896, 209. A bishop in the Mennonite Church's Iowa-Missouri district, Kauffman later served as editor of the denomination's *Gospel Herald* from 1908 to 1943.

39. For further evidence, see Weaver-Zercher, *The Amish in the American Imagination*, 124–27, 137–41.

40. John A. Hostetler, "God Visits the Amish," *Christian Living*, March 1954, 6–7, 40–41.

41. See Steve Nolt, "The Amish 'Mission Movement' and the Reformulation of Amish Identity in the Twentieth Century," *Mennonite Quarterly Review* 75 (2001): 7–36.

42. All quotations in this paragraph are from Hostetler, "God Visits the Amish," 6, 40–41. The Mennonite audience to which Hostetler was writing would largely have embraced his assumptions about the less than satisfactory state of Amish religious life.

43. J. Winfield Fretz, "Community," in *Mennonite Encyclopedia* (Scottdale, Pa.: Mennonite Publishing House, 1955), 1:657.

44. Arthur Morgan, *The Small Community: Foundation of Democratic Life* (New York: Harper and Brothers, 1942); and Baker Brownell, *The Human Community* (New York: Harper and Brothers, 1950).

45. Hostetler sat on the editorial committee of *Mennonite Community* for three years (1950, 1952, and 1953). When *Christian Living* succeeded *Mennonite Community* in 1954, Hostetler served as the new periodical's Community Life editor for five years, until 1959.

46. All quotations in this paragraph are from John A. Hostetler, "Tradition and Your Community," *Christian Living*, March 1957, 4–6, 28. See also John A. Hostetler, "Our Tradition and Our Scholars," *Gospel Herald*, 8 January 1957, 25–26, 45. According to the *Gospel Herald* piece, Jesus Christ "would not have us fight tradition" (26).

47. Hostetler, "Tradition and Your Community," 5–6.

48. John A. Hostetler, "Toward a New Interpretation of Sectarian Life in America," *Pennsylvania Dutchman* 3, no. 4 (1951): 1–2, 7, reprinted in this volume as Chapter 6.

49. See especially the section entitled "My Calling" in Hostetler's revised essay, "An Amish Beginning," included in this volume as Chapter 1.

50. All quotations in this paragraph are from the revised version of Hostetler's "An Amish Beginning," included in this volume as Chapter 1.

51. For Bender's strategic use of history, see Rodney James Sawatsky, "History and Ideology: American Mennonite Identity Definition Through History" (Ph.D. diss., Princeton University, 1977), 189–203, 261–97.

52. According to Bender's biographer, Albert Keim, Bender identified Hostetler as one of the two best students he taught during his lengthy career, the other being theologian John Howard Yoder. Albert N. Keim, e-mail message to author, 3 June 2004.

53. See Albert N. Keim, *Harold S. Bender, 1897–1962* (Scottdale, Pa.: Herald Press, 1998), 439.

54. When Hostetler matriculated in 1949, the institution was Pennsylvania State *College*. By the time he received his Ph.D. in 1953, it had become Pennsylvania State *University*.

55. It was in one of Mook's courses that Hostetler encountered Robert Redfield's influential article on "the folk society," which Hostetler would use to interpret Amish life. For a consideration, see Chapter 3.

56. Quotation from John A. Hostetler's unpublished essay, "Maurice A. Mook, Anthropologist," photocopy. The essay was a three-page chapter of an unpublished manuscript, at one

point entitled "My Calling: An Amish Scholar in Two Worlds." This was one of a number of unpublished short essays Hostetler wrote in the 1990s that discussed persons who influenced his life.

57. John A. Hostetler, "What I Learned from My Heritage," *Mennonite Family History* 11 (1992): 110. This article contains Hostetler's most negative critique of mid-century American sociology.

58. Hostetler, "Maurice A. Mook, Anthropologist." The professor who made this remark to Hostetler was sociologist Roy C. Buck.

59. Hostetler later wrote that it was through Mook that he "came to appreciate the Amish as an unique cultural development." John A. Hostetler, "Maurice A. Mook (1904–1973): An Appreciation," *Pennsylvania Folklife* 26, no. 2 (1976–77): 35.

60. See William G. Mather to JAH, 7 December 1962, Hostetler Papers, Box AL05.24; and Maurice A. Mook to JAH, 6 February 1962, Hostetler Papers, Box AL06.18.

61. For Hostetler's moving account of Hazel's death, see John A. Hostetler, "Book Review Column," *Budget*, 8 March 1951, 2.

62. See Hazel Schrock Hostetler's obituary, which appeared in the *Budget*, 8 March 1951, 6. The obituary notes that, "a few days before her departure, [Hazel] with her husband offered themselves for foreign service in the near future, but this was not to be so."

63. John A. Hostetler, *Amish Life* (Scottdale, Pa.: Herald Press, 1952). Herald Press was the book publishing arm of the Mennonite Publishing House. John and Beulah's correspondence in the latter half of 1952 reveals their growing fondness for one another, and eventually becomes an endearing mix of business and pleasure. Their correspondence can be found in the Hostetler Papers, Box AL05.07.

64. Beulah would continue to help John with his work throughout his career, particularly in the form of editing his prose. For a further discussion of her contributions to his work, see Chapter 2.

65. One of his publications during these years was his *Annotated Bibliography on the Amish* (Scottdale, Pa.: Mennonite Publishing House, 1951), which was awarded the Chicago Folklore Prize in 1952.

66. Hostetler, "Toward a New Interpretation," 1, 7.

67. JAH to Joseph Stoll, 20 May 1964, Hostetler Papers, Box AL04.04. Emphasis added. For further evidence of Hostetler's antipathy toward evangelical proselytizing, see JAH to P. J. Boyd, 14 May 1968, Hostetler Papers, Box AL04.05. Hostetler's antipathy toward these proselytizing endeavors is part of a long tradition of antagonism between anthropologists and missionaries.

68. See Barbara E. Deibler, "The Bookish Aurands," *Pennsylania Portfolio* 6, no. 2 (1988/1989): 27–31; and Barbara E. Deibler, "The Aurands in Print," *Pennsylvania Portfolio* 7, no. 1 (1989): 21–25.

69. Aurand published six different books on bundling, including *America's Greatest Indoor Sport: Two-in-a-Bed, or The Super-Specialist's Handbook on Bundling with the Pennsylvania Dutch* (Harrisburg, Pa.: Aurand Press, 1930). Aurand described bundling as a way to accommodate the Pennsylvania Dutch libido, a practice he said was legitimated by the use of bundling bags that encased the women's bodies and thereby discouraged intercourse. Aurand's works sent mixed messages, however, about the degree of continence maintained in these close encounters.

70. JAH to Paul Erb, 28 July 1953, in book editors' files at the Mennonite Publishing House, Scottdale, Pennsylvania.

71. Hostetler, "An Amish Beginning" (*American Scholar* version), 558.

72. In some unpublished autobiographical reflections Hostetler wrote in the 1990s, he recalled that the encouragement to write *Amish Life* came from Mennonites Guy Hershberger and Melvin Gingerich, and does not mention Shoemaker's name. Hostetler Papers, Box AL06.16.

73. While the term "status anxiety" often carries pejorative connotations, it is nonetheless true that these assimilating Mennonites were much more concerned with outsiders' perceptions of them (that is, their cultural status) than were the Old Order Anabaptist groups. In that sense, they reflected the anxieties of the New Class. See B. Bruce-Briggs, ed., *The New Class?* (New Brunswick, N.J.: Transaction Books, 1987).

74. Elizabeth Horsch Bender, "Three Amish Novels," *Mennonite Quarterly Review* 19 (1945): 273–84. The three novels Bender reviewed were Helen R. Martin, *Sabina: A Story of the Amish* (New York: Century Co., 1905), Ruth Lininger Dobson, *Straw in the Wind* (New York: Dodd, Mead and Company, 1937), and Joseph W. Yoder, *Rosanna of the Amish* (Huntingdon, Pa.: Yoder Publishing, 1940).

75. Grant M. Stoltzfus, "Memorandum to Persons Interested in Disseminating Information," *Pennsylvania Dutchman* 3, no. 1 (1951): 7.

76. Grant M. Stoltzfus, review of *Amish Life*, by John A. Hostetler, in *Gospel Herald*, 11 November 1952, 1118.

77. John A. Jakle, *The Tourist: Travel in Twentieth-Century North America* (Lincoln: University of Nebraska Press, 1985); and Michael L. Carlebach, *American Photojournalism Comes of Age* (Washington, D.C.: Smithsonian Institution Press, 1997).

78. Some Mennonites further predicted that works like *Amish Life* would secure "an opening" for Mennonites to sell other forms of Christian literature to non-Mennonite readers. See Stoltzfus, review of *Amish Life*, 1119.

79. See, for example, JAH to A. J. Metzler, 15 October 1952, Hostetler Papers, Box AM02.24, in which Hostetler quotes D. Kilham Roberts, *Authors', Playwrights' and Artists' Handbook* (London: Tom Lane, 1934) on royalty rates.

80. According to a spreadsheet Hostetler compiled in the early 1990s, he had received by then approximately $67,000 in royalties from Herald Press, approximately $52,000 from Johns Hopkins University Press, and approximately $20,000 from Holt, Rinehart and Winston. Given the income Hostetler generated from other sources (for example, lectures and other publishers), my $150,000 estimate is probably conservative. Moreover, this amount does not account for inflation, meaning that the $150,000 amount would be much higher in current dollars. Still, I stand by my point that Hostetler was not motivated to do his writing by the royalties he received. Records in Hostetler Papers, Box AM02.24.

81. Hostetler's involvement in the *Witness* dispute will be explored later in this essay.

82. JAH to Julia Kasdorf, 27 March 1997, Hostetler Papers, Box AM02.06. Kasdorf's medium for interpreting Amish life was poetry; see especially *Sleeping Preacher* (Pittsburgh: University of Pittsburgh Press, 1991).

83. John A. Hostetler, "Persistence and Change Patterns in Amish Society," *Ethnology* 3 (1964): 185–98, reprinted in this volume as Chapter 11. The quotation is from page 192 in the original.

84. See, for example, Hostetler's description of "rowdyism" and criminal activity in his first edition of *Amish Society* (Baltimore: Johns Hopkins University Press, 1963), 265–70.

85. In his third edition of *Amish Society* (Baltimore: Johns Hopkins University Press, 1980), Hostetler devotes a full chapter to "Backstage Amish Life" (333–50).

86. For instance, Hostetler's first edition of *Amish Society* (1963) devotes only one paragraph to the practice, calling it "the old way of spending time together" and focusing on internal Amish

debates about its appropriateness. Other than noting that the participants "lie on the bed without undressing," Hostetler offers no discussion of what bundling entails and no commentary on its sexual or asexual nature (160). Interestingly, Hostetler's revised version of "An Amish Beginning" includes a description of *his* one bundling experience, a double-dating encounter that appears more nerve-racking than it was sexually charged. Whether Hostetler wanted his readers to extrapolate from the asexuality of his experience is impossible to say.

87. Elmer Lewis Smith, *Bundling Among the Amish* (Akron, Pa.: Applied Arts, 1961).

88. JAH to Preston A. Barba, 4 November 1961; JAH to Grant Stoltzfus, 3 November 1961; and JAH to Omer Lapp, 4 November 1961, Hostetler Papers, Box AL05.04.

89. JAH to Melvin Horst, 4 November 1961, Hostetler Papers, Box AL05.04.

90. JAH to Omer Lapp, 4 November 1961, Hostetler Papers, Box AL05.04.

91. JAH to Elmer L. Smith, 3 November 1961, Hostetler Papers, Box AL05.04. Emphasis added.

92. It is not unusual for ethnographers and anthropologists to talk about their subjects with the personal pronoun "my." While this term indicates a sense of proprietorship, the line between appropriateness in this regard and inappropriateness is difficult to fathom. I contend in this essay that Hostetler's sense of proprietorship, revealed most poignantly in his condemnation of other representations of Amish life, was largely benevolent, though not above critique (for instance, see my discussion of *Witness* below).

93. Public esteem for the Amish had been rising since the 1930s, and Hostetler himself noted this growing esteem in his 1955 article, "Why Is Everybody Interested in the Pennsylvania Dutch?" *Christian Living*, August 1955, 6–9, 38, reprinted in this volume as Chapter 9. Still, the Amish had not yet achieved the iconic status they enjoy today. Moreover, English people in Amish regions often expressed a profound dislike for Amish people and their practices. Localized prejudice toward the Amish continues today, though it is probably less severe than it was in the 1950s.

94. The two novels, *Jonathan* and *Amish Soldier*, had the added dimension of being published by Herald Press, the Mennonite Church press that published *Amish Life*. See David L. Weaver-Zercher, "A Novel Conversion: The Fleeting Life of *Amish Soldier*," *Mennonite Quarterly Review* 72 (1998): 141–59.

95. For instance, "Marketing the Amish Soul," *Gospel Herald*, 26 June 1984, 452–53, reprinted in this volume as Chapter 16, which provided the phone number to the Pennsylvania governor's office.

96. Dawn Clayton, "John Hostetler Bears Witness to Amish Culture and Calls the Movie *Witness* 'A Mockery,'" *People*, 11 March 1985, 63–64; and John A. Hostetler and Donald B. Kraybill, "Hollywood Markets the Amish," in *Image Ethics: The Moral Rights of Subjects in Photographs, Film, and Television*, ed. Larry Gross, John Stuart Katz, and Jay Ruby (New York: Oxford University Press, 1988), 220–35.

97. Hostetler and Kraybill, "Hollywood Markets the Amish," 225.

98. I have argued elsewhere (*The Amish in the American Imagination*, 152–80) that *Witness* served as something of a scapegoat for Hostetler, for the real stressors to the Amish way of life (for example, rising farmland prices) lay elsewhere. I have also argued that, in a way Hostetler did not seem to recognize, *Witness* actually paralleled his work of augmenting public esteem for the Amish. At the same time, by 1985, Hostetler probably did not think the Amish needed more public esteem; what they needed was protection. In that regard, I do not want to dismiss his concern that *Witness* would bring more harm than good to the Amish, particularly in the way it would advance their already significant renown. Although Lancaster County tourism did

not increase significantly because of *Witness*, it is likely that the film boosted interest in the Amish generally, perhaps contributing to tourism growth in other Amish settlements.

99. John A. Hostetler, "'Witness' Violated Amish Integrity," *Harrisburg Patriot News,* 6 March 1985, A10.

100. See Hostetler, "Marketing the Amish Soul," 452.

101. Hostetler showed little sympathy for director Peter Weir's argument that making a film on the Amish had artistic merit. Rather, he viewed *Witness* as "shallow entertainment" aimed at "pecuniary gain." Ibid., 453.

102. There were other, more personal factors, including Hostetler's view that Good did not fairly treat writers who published with Good's publishing company, a view that was not unique to Hostetler. For information about Good, see Phil Johnson Ruth, "Merle Good and Phyllis Pellman Good: 'Sort of a Business, Sort of the Church, Sort of the Arts,'" in *Entrepreneurs in the Faith Community: Profiles of Mennonites in Business,* ed. Calvin W. Redekop and Benjamin W. Redekop (Scottdale, Pa.: Herald Press, 1996), 217–39.

103. See Merle Good, "Are Sociologists Equipped?" *Festival Quarterly* 21, no. 1 (1994): 5–6.

104. John A. Hostetler, "Answer to Merle Good," Hostetler Papers, Box AL06.16.

105. Given Good's approaches to representing Amish life, it is not surprising that he, unlike Hostetler, was supportive of *Witness*. For their clash over *Witness*, see Weaver-Zercher, *The Amish in the American Imagination*, 166–72.

106. In March 1955, five weeks after the debut of the Amish-themed Broadway musical *Plain and Fancy*, Hostetler took a business trip to New York City to promote *Amish Life* in various venues. See "Contacts in New York," Hostetler Papers, Box AL04.02.

107. Hostetler, "Answer to Merle Good." See also JAH to Judith Molinaro, 16 February 1985, Hostetler Papers, Box AL06.16. Writing during the *Witness* controversy, Hostetler tells Molinaro that he had been "pushed to write books about the Amish," but he would not be "pushed" into supporting *Witness* in any way.

108. JAH to Joseph W. Yoder, 2 February 1951, Yoder Papers. It should also be noted Hostetler was not wholly enamored with Yoder's work, so he was probably glad to have this reason to refuse his request.

109. The complaints were directed at Hostetler's "Yoder School," *Christian Living*, September 1958, 3–7.

110. JAH to Christian G. Esh, 2 October 1958, Hostetler Papers, Box AM02.15.

111. JAH to Joseph Stoll, 30 March 1970, Hostetler Papers, Box AL04.04.

112. JAH to David Luthy, 16 May 1978, Hostetler Papers, Box AM02.24.

113. Hostetler, "Answer to Merle Good."

114. Perhaps the clearest example of this was Hostetler's publication, with Gertrude Enders Huntington, *Children in Amish Society* (New York: Holt, Rinehart and Winston, 1971), a project that was undertaken to support Amish objections to age-compulsory education.

115. Mrs. M. Genest to JAH, 28 February 1957, Hostetler Papers, Box AL05.21. For a more thoughtful letter, see Anthony Karl Walker to JAH, 14 October 1994, Hostetler Papers, Box AM02.06.

116. JAH to John Beauchamp, 12 October 1967, Hostetler Papers, Box AL05.21.

117. JAH to David Wagler, 8 May 1975; and David Wagler to JAH, 15 May 1975, Hostetler Papers, Box AL04.02.

118. Hostetler took this quotation from Uncle Amos's column in *Small Farmer's Journal* 17, no. 3 (1993): 43–44. Ironically, Uncle Amos was himself a college-educated convert to the Amish faith who, in a 1993 letter, told Hostetler that reading *Amish Society* provided "a big stimulus"

to his spiritual pilgrimage. See Uncle Amos's letter to JAH, 28 October 1993, Hostetler Papers, Box AMo2.07.

119. The proposal was submitted by Victoria Larimore, who eventually received funding from the Ohio Humanities Council for making *The Amish: Not to Be Modern*. Copies of Larimore's grant application and Hostetler's letter (dated 10 May 1983) are in the Heritage Historical Library, Aylmer, Ontario.

120. Testa's letter cited his Harvard connections to theologian Harvey Cox and educator Robert Coles; see Randy-Michael Testa to JAH, [April 1988], Hostetler Papers, Box ALo2.18.

121. The story pertained to Testa's attempt to protect a plain family traveling on a busy highway. See Randy-Michael Testa, *After the Fire: The Destruction of the Lancaster County Amish* (Hanover: University Press of New England, 1992), xiii–ix.

122. Hostetler, "Marketing the Amish Soul," 452–53.

123. Hostetler, *Amish Society* (1980), 312.

124. John A. Hostetler, "On Taking Photographs," photocopy. Hostetler prepared this 700–word reflection in the late 1980s or early 1990s.

125. For a response to one of Hostetler's inquiries, see Eli E. Gingerich to JAH, 6 May 1986, Hostetler Papers, Box ALo5.15.

126. Ibid.

127. For Johns Hopkins University Press's desire for photographs, see John Gallman to JAH, 9 May 1963, Hostetler Papers, Box ALo3.01.

128. Beulah Stauffer Hostetler, telephone conversation with author, 28 May 2004.

129. William C. Lindholm to JAH, [February 1967]; and JAH to William C. Lindholm, 21 February 1967, Hostetler Papers, Box ALo6.01.

130. John Ruth, e-mail message to author, 21 June 2004. According to Ruth, Hostetler's role was threefold: conceiving the idea, consulting on the script, and lending his endorsement regarding the film's authenticity. Ruth also said that Hostetler "certainly considered it his brainchild, a supplement to his writing about the Amish."

131. See "John Ruth on Filming the Amish," *Festival Quarterly* 4, no. 3 (1977): 16–17, 24.

132. Simon J. Bronner, review of *The Amish: A People of Preservation*, in *Journal of American Folklore* 92 (1979): 121–23. Ruth himself noted in a post-release interview that the filming process put him "on shaky ethical ground." See "John Ruth on Filming the Amish," 16–17.

133. John Ruth, e-mail message to author, 21 June 2004.

134. JAH to David Wagler and David Luthy, 14 April 1975, Hostetler Papers, Box ALo4.02. The film Hostetler dubbed "disgusting" was *The Gentle People*. He does not offer any reasons for his negative assessment.

135. JAH to David Wagler, 18 October 1963, Hostetler Papers, Box ALo4.02.

136. In response to an Amish nephew who questioned his involvement in the film, Hostetler outlined his dilemma ("for over twenty years I have been confronted with requests to help make a film") and defended the film (it is "very informative, sympathetic, and deeply moving"). At the same time, Hostetler downplayed his role in initiating the film ("I was asked to see it and was given the opportunity to check it for accuracy") and explained that his consulting work was "considered part of my job" as a university professor. The answer satisfied his nephew, who wrote that Hostetler's explanation gave him "a different picture" from what he had read in the newspaper. JAH to Joseph B. Detweiler, 17 July 1978; and Joseph B. Detweiler to JAH, 21 July 1978, Hostetler Papers, Box ALo5.07.

137. According to Beulah Hostetler, John's wife, her husband "knew better than to ask permission," since the Amish leaders would not have granted it explicitly. Still, they informed

Hostetler that, if he felt a film must be made, they would not stand in his way. Beulah Stauffer Hostetler, telephone conversation with author, 28 May 2004.

138. Donald B. Kraybill, "A Tribute to John A. Hostetler," presented 23 July 1993, Elizabethtown College, Elizabethtown, Pennsylvania.

139. See Thomas J. Meyers, "Education and Schooling," in *The Amish and the State*, rev. ed., ed. Donald B. Kraybill (Baltimore: Johns Hopkins University Press, 2003), 87–106.

140. For an example of Hostetler's public relations efforts, see John A. Hostetler, "The Amish Way of Life is at Stake," *Liberty*, May/June 1966, 12–13, reprinted in this volume as Chapter 12. For the NCARF, see William C. Lindholm, "The National Committee for Amish Religious Freedom," in Kraybill, ed., *The Amish and the State*, 109–23.

141. For Amish resistance to joining in legal battles, see Dan Bontrager to the NCARF, 14 May 1969, Hostetler Papers, Box AL06.22.

142. For a retrospective, see Albert N. Keim, *Compulsory Education and the Amish: The Right Not to be Modern* (Boston: Beacon Press, 1975).

143. Lawrence Rosen, "The Anthropologist as Expert Witness," *American Anthropologist* 79 (1977): 564.

144. Hostetler, "An Amish Beginning" (*American Scholar* version), 561. According to the court transcript, Hostetler's actual words were: "It depends which world." See Rosen, "The Anthropologist as Expert Witness," 562.

145. Hostetler, "Marketing the Amish Soul," 453.

146. The director at Johns Hopkins University Press admitted to Hostetler that he and his wife attended the movie, "something we almost surely wouldn't have done without knowing about the fuss." J. G. Goellner to JAH, 11 March 1985, Hostetler Papers, Box AL06.16.

147. James O. Pickard to A. S. Kinsinger, 11 September 1984, Hostetler Papers, Box AL06.16.

148. "State of Pennsylvania Agrees to Discourage Movies Depicting Amish," *Gospel Herald*, 5 February 1985, 96.

149. Quotations by Weir, recorded in "'Witness' Filming Ends Here Amid New Dispute about Accuracy, Amish Privacy," *Lancaster New Era*, 30 June 1984, 4. For similar kinds of criticism, see Shelby E. Chunko, "Amish Will Survive," letter to the editor, *Lancaster Intelligencer Journal*, 30 June 1984, 10; and Linda Miller Espinoza, "Furor Unjustified," letter to the editor, *Lancaster New Era*, 9 February 1985, 8.

150. For instance, Ike Stoltzfus to JAH, 30 June 1984, Hostetler Papers, Box AL06.16. This theme also became prominent in letters published in Lancaster County newspapers, for instance, "Amish Not Perfect," letter to the editor, *Lancaster New Era*, 13 February 1985, 10.

151. Merle Good, "Reflections on *Witness* Controversy," *Gospel Herald*, 5 March 1985, 163. For a similar criticism, see Winston Weaver to JAH, 12 March 1985, Hostetler Papers, Box AL06.16.

152. Citing the 30 June 1984 *New Era* article in which Weir attacked Hostetler, attorney William B. Ball (with whom Hostetler had worked on the *Wisconsin* case) wrote to Weir: "It is our opinion that statements contained therein are both false and defamatory, justifying appropriate legal action." A copy of the undated letter, copied to the *New Era*'s editor, can be found in Hostetler Papers, Box AL06.16.

153. Hostetler and Kraybill, "Hollywood Markets the Amish," 225, emphasis added; see also Weaver-Zercher, *The Amish in the American Imagination*, 172–80.

154. For "strategic essentialism," see Gayatri Chakravorty Spivak, "Subaltern Studies: Deconstructing Historiography," in *The Spivak Reader: Selected Works of Gayatri Chakrovorty Spivak*,

ed. Donna Landry and Gerald MacLean (New York: Routledge, 1996), 203–35. Hostetler employed this strategy in another way: in response to a letter-writer who noted the diversity of Amish feelings about the movie, Hostetler contrasted "loyalty-loose Amish" to "a central core of the culture," suggesting that Amish persons who had little problem with the movie were not committed Amish members. JAH to Winston Weaver, 19 March 1985, Hostetler Papers, Box AL06.16.

155. By the end of his career, Hostetler was happy to note that other observers (for example, Wendell Berry) were coming to this conclusion, and he frequently referred to the Amish as a "redemptive community." See John A. Hostetler, "A New Look at the Old Order," *Rural Sociologist* 7 (1987): 278–92, reprinted in this volume as Chapter 17.

156. See, for example, W. H. Richardson, "A Day with the Pennsylvania Amish," *Outlook*, 1 April 1899, 781–86.

157. Ruth Behar, *The Vulnerable Observer: Anthropology That Breaks Your Heart* (Boston: Beacon Press, 1996), 5.

158. Ibid.

159. Ibid., 83.

160. Ibid., 25.

161. Hostetler's late-in-life focus on Lancaster County farmland preservation manifested his desire to secure a future for the Amish as he knew them, which meant of course an agrarian future. See John A. Hostetler, "Toward Responsible Growth and Stewardship of Lancaster County's Landscape," *Pennsylvania Mennonite Heritage* 12, no. 3 (1989): 2–10, reprinted in this volume as Chapter 18. For Hostetler's work on farmland preservation, see Chapter 2.

PART II

Writings of John A. Hostetler

The following writings represent the thinking and Amish-related scholarship of John A. Hostetler. All but one of the pieces—the first entry, a letter Hostetler wrote and circulated to Old Order Amish bishops in 1944—were previously published in books, journals, or periodicals. Assembled here in chronological order, they illustrate Hostetler's sustained and wide-ranging interest in Amish culture. Moreover, they provide a trajectory of Hostetler's career as a scholar of Amish life, demonstrating changes as well as constants in his intellectual life.

The bibliography at the end of this volume attests to Hostetler's productivity as a writer. The arithmetic of that productivity—twenty-five books and monographs and over two hundred chapters and articles— tells only half the story, for in addition to publishing voluminously, Hostetler wrote on a broad array of topics and published in a wide variety of venues. Although much of his writing dealt with Amish life, he also wrote about Mennonites, Hutterites, and a variety of sociological topics that emerged from his study of Anabaptist groups and rural life more generally. From a disciplinary standpoint, most of his scholarly writing can be classified as sociology or anthropology, but he occasionally ventured into history and even more often into theology. Hostetler's earliest writings were almost all theologically and devotionally oriented. The disciplinary focus of his writing changed in the course of his graduate work in rural sociology in the 1950s, and most of his scholarly writing in the 1960s and 1970s reflects that shift toward social scientific approaches. Still, Hostetler never lost his willingness to reflect theologically, a willingness exemplified by this part's last entry, a biblically infused article about the stewardship of Lancaster County farmland published in 1989.

Hostetler's topical range correlated to his desire to reach different audiences. On the one hand, Hostetler sought to converse with other scholars, publishing his findings in specialized journals such as *Ethnology*, *Population Studies*, and *Rural Sociology*. On the other, Hostetler sought to communicate his academically informed ideas to the general public, an orientation that resulted in the publication of numerous popular booklets and periodical articles. In many cases, these popular pieces appeared in church-related periodicals, particularly ones connected to the Mennonite Church (for example, *Christian Living* and *Gospel Herald*). In that sense, the vast majority of Hostetler's writings can be placed into one of three categories according to audience: writings intended for scholars of sociology and anthropology; those intended for the general North American public; and those intended for North American Mennonites. To be sure, Hostetler wrote occasional articles for still other audiences (for example, his coauthored genetic studies of the Amish were published in medical journals), but those exceptions were relatively few.

Given Hostetler's prolificacy and the breadth of his published work, selecting representative works for inclusion in this volume constituted a formidable challenge. Why these particular pieces? It should again be noted that this volume does not seek to consider the full scope of Hostetler's life; in fact, it does not even seek to assess the scope of his scholarly interests. Rather, this book chronicles and appraises Hostetler's career as a *scholar-mediator of Amish life*. That means the first criterion for inclusion, and the only unassailable one, pertained to Amish subject matter; that is, was a particular piece of writing about Amish life or somehow pertinent to Amish life? A second criterion was the significance of the work's content in the corpus of Hostetler's writings and, more generally, in terms of its cultural impact; generally speaking, we sought to include pieces that reflected his most substantive contributions to the study and understanding of the Amish. A third criterion was our desire to reflect both the range and the evolution of Hostetler's thinking about Amish life. Hostetler published on a range of Amish topics— clothing, medicine, education, language, and social change, just to name a few—and, as good scholars are inclined to do, he sometimes changed his mind. By including a range of articles, assembled in chronological order and contextualized with headnotes, we hope to highlight the breadth and dynamism of Hostetler's scholarship. Finally, we sought to represent via these writings the various dimensions of Hostetler's work as a scholar-mediator; that is, we sought to include not only articles written for fellow scholars, but also publicly oriented scholarship that more readily reflects his ideological concerns.

Of course, space considerations ultimately limited what could be included, and astute readers will notice that the following selections do not include excerpts from *Amish Society*. This, too, was a considered decision. Not only does *Amish Society* remain easily accessible to those who wish to buy or borrow it, many of Hostetler's lesser-known works reveal details and transitions in his thinking that cannot be located in *Amish Society*. Moreover, many of *Amish Society*'s most significant contributions (for example, the notion of an Amish charter that appeared in all four editions of *Amish Society*, and Hostetler's treatment of silence, which appears in the third and fourth editions) can be found in works that *are* included in this volume. In any case, these selections provide a useful and illumining survey of Hostetler's work; readers who wish to explore his work in more depth are encouraged to consult the bibliography at the end of this volume.

A few comments are in order about the editing of Hostetler's previously published writings. For the most part, the following pieces appear as they did in their original contexts, though some minor changes have been made. Specifically, misspelled words and typographical errors have been corrected, and hyphenation and spelling practices have been updated to contemporary standards. The spellings of proper names, unless clearly misspelled, have not been altered, nor have British word-spellings been altered in the selection from the *Journal of the Royal Anthropological Institute*. Other forms of punctuation (for example, the use of commas and semicolons) have not been altered unless, by the judgment of the editor, the punctuation practice in the original is confusing. Similarly, citation styles have not been altered, although in some cases citation details have been modified to correct misinformation and to make citations within each article stylistically consistent. A few of the following writings have been excerpted from longer chapters or articles, with deleted sections indicated by ellipses on a separate line of text. Gender-exclusive language has been maintained for reasons of historical veracity.

The editing standards applied to this part's one unpublished piece, Hostetler's 1944 letter to Amish bishops, were different from those applied to his previously published works. See the headnote to the 1944 letter (Chapter 5) for an explanation of the editing standards applied to it.

The headnotes that introduce each piece were written by David L. Weaver-Zercher. Weaver-Zercher's editorial notes are indicated by letters (a, b, c, . . .) and appear as footnotes. If the original publication included footnotes or endnotes, they are signified by numerals (1, 2, 3, . . .) and, if footnotes, have been changed to endnotes. In other words, whereas Hostetler's original citations appear in this part as enumerated endnotes, all editorial comments in this part appear as lettered footnotes.

5

LETTER TO AMISH BISHOPS CONCERNING SHUNNING (1944)

In the following letter, addressed and mailed to Old Order Amish bishops in Iowa, Pennsylvania, Indiana, and Ohio, twenty-five-year-old John A. Hostetler condemns shunning as it is practiced in many North American Amish communities. According to Hostetler, the problem was not shunning per se, which he believed was justifiable in the case of wayward, God-defying Amish persons. The problem, wrote Hostetler, was strict shunning — that is, the extension of shunning to ex-Amish church members who left the Amish church but pursued devout Christian lives within other Christian communities.

Hostetler's complaint was, in part, a theological one. Like many twentieth-century Mennonites, Hostetler found the severe ecclesiocentrism of the Old Order Amish unjustified ("Christ is not divided," wrote Hostetler, echoing the Apostle Paul). But the practice of strict shunning was more than a theological problem to Hostetler. Having seen his father Joseph disciplined and shunned by his Pennsylvania Amish community, Hostetler knew firsthand the personal and social traumas associated with shunning. Although he did not write this letter on behalf of his father, he did mail an early draft to his parents, solicited their suggestions for improving it, and asked them to provide him with "the names of the people that should have it." Included in his father's handwritten list of potential recipients was John B. Renno, the Amish bishop who, in 1944, oversaw the church that had disciplined the senior Hostetler fifteen years earlier.

Editorial changes to the original letter are minimal in this reprinting. Obvious typographical errors (for example, "grom" instead of "from") have been changed, but the author's idiosyncratic misspellings (for example, "brethern" and "desciples") have not been altered. Similarly, the author's punctuation and style stand unchanged.

The letter is reprinted by permission of the Pennsylvania State University Archives.

C.P.S. Unit No. 53
Marlboro, New Jersey

Dear Brethern:

Christian Greetings: With help from God and his Spirit I shall attempt to write you these few lines which for some time have been on my mind. My purpose and aim in this letter is to call your attention to a few shady or questionable practices, which, according to my knowledge exist among your people, with the hope and prayer that it will edify believers in the Gospel of God. It is not my aim to unduly expose your faults to the many peoples of the world nor to overthrow or discourage your church organization and thereby boast of my own righteousness and good works. God forbid that I should boast except for what I am by his grace.[a] As a steward of God, I testify to the saving and keeping power of God. I am only a servant and a representative of the manifestation of the Gospel of Christ and as such I pray that God will bless you with a receptive heart and open mind to the message which is upon my heart.

We who confess the name of Christ should be grateful from the heart for God's manifestation of "The Way, the Truth and the Life" in these last times.[b] We claim to be Christians with a background of more than 1900 years and a heritage of faith from our anabaptist forefathers 400 years old. We should as groups of believers and Christians have made some progress in developing a truly grateful attitude and spirit of heart. But at times we wonder. Just where would we fit among those ten lepers that approached the master to be healed? Do we find ourselves among the nine who took their new life so much for granted that they could not spare the time to thank the Master, or are we like the one who out of that new life took time to offer praise and thanksgiving?[c] It is indeed regrettable that some churches within Christendom place emphasis on things unessential. What the world needs today is preachers and consistent lives unadulterated with man made opinions and humanistic objectives.

I would like to have your consideration on the subject of shunning or sometimes referred to as "avoidance". I object not to the right use of this practice in a body of Christian believers. I object to the wrong use. Let us for a moment examine the original intent of the teaching and observe its methods and the spirit in which this practice was first taught. The chief scripture passages on which this practice is based is found in I Cor 5:11, II Thess 3:14, and Rom 16:17.[d] "But now I have written unto you not to keep company, if any man that is called a brother be a fornicator, or covetous, or an idolater, or a railer, or a drunkard, or an extortioner, with such an one no not to eat. If any man obey not our word by this epistle, note that man, and have no company with him, that he may be ashamed. Now

---

a. Here Hostetler invokes Apostle Paul-like language to underscore his understanding of good works and their relationship to human righteousness: "God forbid that I should glory, save in the cross of our Lord Jesus Christ" (Gal. 6:14). All biblical quotations in Hostetler's letter and the accompanying editorial notes are from the King James Version.

b. John 14:6: "I am the way, the truth, and the life: no man cometh unto the Father, but by me."

c. Jesus' healing of the ten lepers can be found in Luke 17:11–19. Of the ten who were healed, only one, a Samaritan, returned to thank Jesus for his healing work.

d. The following quotation strings together these three disparate verses.

I beseech you brethern, mark them which cause divisions and offenses contrary to the doctrine which ye have learned, and avoid them."

We learn from history that early anabaptist believers were divided on the question of shunning. It was first introduced and taught by the Dutch and later taught by Menno Simons: Quoting from Menno: (Mennonite History in Europe, Horsch) "'Whether it be father or mother, sister or brother, husband or wife; son or daughter, without any respect of persons.' He held that such avoidance is to be observed 'with prayer, tears, and a compassionate spirit, out of great love,' its purpose being to bring the erring to repentance."[e]

From Martyrs Mirrow, P 43 (Van Braght, 1938), "Concerning the withdrawing from, or shunning the separated, we believe and confess, that if any one, either through his wicked life or perverted doctrine, has so far fallen that he is separated from God, and, consequently, also separated and punished by the church, the same must, according to the doctrine of Christ and his apostles, be shunned, without distinction, by all the fellow members of the church, especially those to whom it is known, in eating, drinking, and other similar intercourse, and no company be had with him; that they may not become contaminated by intercourse with him, nor made partakers of his sins; but that the sinner may be made ashamed, pricked in the heart, and convicted in his conscience, unto his reformation. Yet in shunning as well as in reproving, such moderation and Christian discretion must be used, that it may conduce, not to the destruction, but to the reformation of the sinner. For if he is needy, hungry, thirsty, naked, sick, or in any other distress, we are in duty bound, necessity requiring it, according to love and the doctrine of Christ and his apostles, to render him aid and assistance; otherwise, shunning would in this case tend more to destruction than to reformation. Therefore, we must not count them as enemies, but admonish them as brethern that thereby they may be brought to a knowledge of and to repentance and sorrow for their sins, so that they may become reconciled to God, and, consequently be received again into the church; and that love may continue with them according as is proper."[f]

From the foregoing quotations we get two distinct truths: First, before a member can be excommunicated and shunned it must be evident that he is out of fellowship with God and has shamefully transgressed, Second, that

e. John Horsch, *Mennonites in Europe* (Scottdale, Pa.: Mennonite Publishing House, 1942), 333.

f. Thieleman J. van Braght, *The Bloody Theater: or, Martyrs Mirror of the Defenseless Christians, Who Baptized Only Upon Confession of Faith, and Who Suffered and Died for the Testimony of Jesus, Their Saviour, from the Time of Christ to the Year A.D. 1660*, trans. Joseph F. Sohm (Scottdale, Pa.: Mennonite Publishing House, 1938), 43.

such an one must be shunned only with the spirit of love, compassion, prayer and deep concern in the hopes that he will repent of his sins, renew his relationship with God, and will want to re-unite his fellowship with the believers.

Is this the manner in which the practice of shunning is still practiced by your people? If so, then I commend you. I have been informed from reliable sources and my own experiences and contacts with your folks have convinced me that shunning has been converted into a weapon of force to use for holding church members. It is also being used as a weapon of prejudice against those who leave your branch of the Amish denomination and join themselves with other Christian believers. These facts are tragic and appalling. Are you aware of these outstanding strongholds of the Devil? Such attitudes are not in harmony with the spirit of its original intent and teaching. I cannot advise any denominational policies and practices but I do believe that the Scripture is very plain on this matter. It appears to me, from the teaching of the Bible, that any group of individuals who use the sacred scriptures for the defense of selfish interests (holding members by means of man-made legislation) is on questionable grounds. I am very much in doubt about the quality and genuineness of such a religion, and I urge you to reconsider your attitude in the light of the Scriptures, and not in the opinion and advice of human beings. Menno Simons' attitude regarding such an abominable practice is made clear by a specific example (Menn History in Europe, Horsch, P 333): "In the Mennonite congregation of the city of Emden a sister named Swaen Rutgers objected to avoiding her excommunicated husband. There were those who advised setting a time within which she must decide upon avoiding him, or lose her right of membership. Menno, in a letter regarding this case to the congregation at Emden, said that when he was informed of this threat, his heart was filled with grief. He warned the church at Emden of the evil reports which such a proceedure would cause concerning the church and the Word of the Lord. 'We have never dared to follow such a practice' he wrote. 'I shall never consent to such a course;' Swaen Rutgers was not excommunicated. In a letter written in 1588, Menno defended the same views."[g]

Menno shows that the threatening or force method is wrong! It is unscriptural! Always the spirit of love and concern must be used to restore such an one to the fold of Christ. The chief concern should be that the transgressor is restored to the fellowship with the Almighty. By using a force

---

g. Horsch, *Mennonites in Europe*, 333–34. Hostetler's quotation of Horsch, in this instance and the two instances that follow, is very close but not precise. Then again, Horsch's quotations of Simons, which he attributes to the 1871 edition of *The Complete Works of Menno Simons*, are not precise either.

method we are lowering ourselves to the standards of prejudice and hate used by militarists and worldly men; such a spirit is much different than God's word. Menno contends that love can be shown through the act of shunning without using threat.

Again, let us look at Menno's attitude toward excommunicated members. Ibid., 332, "My brethern, I tell the truth and lied not; such unmerciful, cruel opinion and practice (namely, to refuse needed aid to the excommunicated when they are in need) I hate with all my heart. Nor do I desire to be a brother among so unmerciful, cruel brethern if there should yet be any holding such an opinion, if they do not desist from such abomination and in all discretion follow love and mercy according to the example of God and Christ. For my heart cannot consent to such unmerciful treatment which exceeds the cruelty of the common heathen and Turks; by the grace of God I shall with the sword of the Lord fight against it unto death; for it is contrary to all teaching of the New Testament, and contrary to the spirit and nature of Christ, according to which all the Scriptures of the New Testament should be judged and understood."[h]

Ibid., 325, Bullinger wrote in 1561, "One cannot and should not use force to compel anyone to accept the faith, for faith is a free gift of God. It is wrong to compel anyone by force or coercion to embrace the faith, or to put to death any one for the sake of erring his faith.[i] The Lord has commanded simply to preach the Gospel, and not to compel any one by force to accept it. The true church of Christ has the characteristic that it suffers or endures persecution but does not inflict persecution on any one."[j]

There are many Christians and regenerated souls outside of one particular church group. While a visible church is necessary, yet God's call to repentance comes by the convicting power of the Holy Spirit—never by coercion from men. Salvation comes only from God through Christ as a free gift. What was Jesus' attitude toward other Christian believers who did not follow with his desciples? His admonition was "Forbid him not, for he that is not against us is on our part."[k] Is it not foolish to shun a member who finds Christ in another church or group of believers? Yea, it is more than folly. Christ is not

h. Ibid., 332. The parenthetical phrase in this quotation is bracketed in Horsch's text. Horsch meant the words to be taken as an explanatory note, not Simons's actual words.

i. Ibid., 325. The Horsch text reads "his erring faith," not "erring his faith."

j. Ibid., 325–26. Hostetler excerpts this Heinrich Bullinger quotation, which runs much longer in the Horsch text. Bullinger was not himself an Anabaptist, but he reported these Anabaptist views in a treatise he wrote against them.

k. This quotation is drawn from Jesus' response to his disciples' complaint that others were casting out demons in his name; see Luke 9:50.

divided.[l] The one purpose of shunning is to show love for the soul of the ex-communicated one in the hopes that he will repent. If and when the transgressor repents and gets right with God the shunning should be discontinued and God should be praised. When a soul finds Christ, heaven rejoices. The angels sing praises to God for the one who is restored to spiritual life. The sinner rejoices because his sins are forgiven and he has a new relationship with the Father. How can God's people keep from rejoicing? To continue shunning would be more than destructive. If that is "pure religion and undefiled before God" then I am mistaken in my understanding of Christianity.[m] I fear that such a religion is sour and a hot-bed of conspiracy. I perceive that those who practice such an attitude are not fully aware of the Bible teaching on this subject. I have nothing personally against any of your brethren, only I feel a sense of duty to warn all who are ignorantly or wilfully sinning. God will abundantly pardon all who sincerely repent and live the Holy life. "If my people, which are called by my name, shall humble themselves, and pray, and seek my face, and turn from their wicked ways; then will I hear from heaven, and will forgive their sin, and will heal their land." II Chron 7:14.

The Scriptures teach that we have no hope if we trust in ourselves and our good works. All our works are as filthy rags in His sight. "By the works of the law shall no flesh be justified. Not by works of righteousness which we have done, but according to his mercy he saved us, by the washing of regeneration, and renewing of the Holy Ghost; which he shed on us abundantly through Jesus Christ our Lord." Titus 3:5, 6.[n] "For by grace are ye saved through faith; and that not of yourselves; it is the gift of God; not of works, lest any man should boast." Heb 2:8, 9.[o] No one can live a good enough life, or do enough good to save himself.

I wish to stress the need for a positive approach toward the problem of excommunicated ones. How about the parable of the lost sheep, would not the good shepherd leave the ninety and nine and seek the one lost soul? In the case of the prodical son, did his father say I cannot receive you and not eat with you? Consider the attitude of Jesus with the woman at the well;

l. Paul addressed the problem of church divisions in 1 Cor. 1:13: "Is Christ divided? was Paul crucified for you? or were ye baptized in the name of Paul?"

m. James 1:27: "Pure religion and undefiled before God and the Father is this, To visit the fatherless and widows in their affliction, and to keep himself unspotted from the world."

n. The first sentence of the foregoing quotation is not from Titus, but rather from Gal. 2:16.

o. The verses quoted here are actually Eph. 2:8–9, not Heb. 2:8–9. Earlier drafts of Hostetler's letter confirm that Hostetler knew these verses were from Ephesians.

did he shun this moral and social outcast? No, he loved her, and so much so that he won a place in her heart.[p] What is the lesson we should get from these ensamples? It is love. God's love has more power than any earthly force or strength. Thanks to God that Jesus overcame death and the powers of darkness. If we would sell our farms and possessions—give all to the poor and wouldn't have love, it would profit nothing. Furthermore if we could speak in many languages and prophecy and even give our body to be burned, it would profit nothing without love. I Cor 13.[q] All the sweetness and roots of brotherly love come from the giver of a perfect love toward sinful men. "By this shall all men know that ye are my desciples, if ye have love one to another."[r]

In closing, I want to again emphasize that I have written out of a spirit of love and good will, without throwing disrespect on anyone. My prayer is that you will consider these problems in the light of the Holy Word and that mutually we might be strengthened in the Faith of the Lord Jesus.

An unworthy servant,

John A. Hostetler

---

p. Jesus' parables of the lost sheep and the prodigal son can be found in Luke 15. The story of Jesus' encounter with a Samaritan woman at Jacob's Well is recorded in John 4.

q. The two sentences preceding Hostetler's citation of 1 Cor. 13 constitute his paraphrased summary of 1 Cor. 13:1–3.

r. Jesus spoke these words shortly after he washed his disciples' feet and identified Judas Iscariot as his betrayer (John 13:35).

6

TOWARD A NEW INTERPRETATION
OF SECTARIAN LIFE IN AMERICA (1951)

First presented at the 1951 Pennsylvania Folk Culture Seminar, and published at the outset of Hostetler's career as a sociologist (he received his master's degree the same year this piece was published), "Toward a New Interpretation of Sectarian Life" reflects Hostetler's keen interest in revitalizing American rural life. Toward that end, Hostetler identifies certain aspects of Anabaptist "sectarian life" that, in his estimation, contribute to the sustenance of stable, healthy rural communities. Invoking redemptive language that would flavor his writing about Amish life for years to come, Hostetler claims in this article that "the survivors of the sixteenth-century Anabaptists are today maintaining communities of prophetic significance" that other Americans ignore at their peril.

Hostetler's embrace of Ernst Troeltsch's definition of sects—religious groups striving for the achievement of the New Testament ethic—creates an interesting dynamic in this piece, for it allows Hostetler to employ both the Old Order Amish and progressive Mennonites to prove his points. Clearly, however, the Amish prove more useful to him in terms of illustrating stable community life. In fact, Hostetler and other Mennonite Community Lifers were, at this very time, losing the battle to sustain among progressive Mennonites the kind of communities the Amish so poignantly exemplified. In that sense, a Troeltschian typology that lumped all Anabaptists together as sectarians obscured more than it illumined, and Hostetler would soon embrace other sociological and anthropological models.

This article first appeared in the Pennsylvania Dutchman *3, no. 4 (1951): 1–2, 7. It is reprinted by permission of Ursinus College.*

The sociological usage of the word "sect" is every bit as confusing as the psychologist's definition of "sex." In our treatment of the traditional sects in contemporary American communities, we can accept Troeltsch's criteria, those minority groups striving for personal achievement of the New Testament ethic.[a] These prophetic religionists stand in contrast to the swarm of "mushroom" cults arising from class inequalities of industrial America. Who are the sixteenth-century European sects that have survived? They are the Swiss and South German immi-

---

a. Social analyses of religion advanced by German theologian Ernst Troeltsch (1865–1923) were extremely influential in the mid-twentieth century. See especially *The Social Teachings of the Christian Churches* (New York: Macmillan, 1931).

grants, the Mennonites and Amish, and other satellites of their background and tradition.

We are witnessing today a cultural sideshow in American life to be found nowhere else in the world. Here in southeastern Pennsylvania we find a congregation of sects retaining a cultural heritage unmatched by any other ethnic extraction in North America. Here we discover a contemporary, relatively cohesive, functioning social and cultural group accommodating and at the same time conflicting with the larger society. Up to this point in history they have largely been regarded as weeds in the story of America's church expansion and development, or in the words of H. S. Bender as "exotic specimens in the zoo of the sects."[b] But we must remember that up to this point "they have often seemed to be a people without a country, wanderers on the face of the earth, having no abiding city, seeking a City whose builder and maker is God."[c] Never have they been privileged to develop their culture to its fullest bloom as we witness it today.

LANCASTER, A SECTARIAN COUNTY

What have we in Lancaster County for instance, where the sectarian culture is at its zenith? From the standpoint of sheer numbers the area contains more sects and sub-sects living side by side than any other county of its character anywhere. A diversity of social forces is creating internal rupture as well as threats of disintegration from urbanizing contacts. On the one hand there is the traditional authoritarian discipline buttressed by religious legalism with authority vested in the aged, and on the other there is unrest among the youth, a quest for religious sensation, a swing to a type of frontier revivalism, with some active Mennonite interest in the "Youth for Christ" movement and prophecy gatherings.[d] Between the two polar types there are a multiplicity of interests and sociological forces at work. A small nucleus of scholars and ministers are attempting to recapture the essence of original Anabaptism and apply it to modern times. Many, particularly Mennonites, are finding the road to wealth. Modern technology has

b. Hostetler studied under Harold S. Bender at Goshen College and worked as his research assistant on the *Mennonite Encyclopedia*. Hostetler may have picked up this "zoo" comment during his Goshen years.

c. Harold S. Bender, "In Search of a City," in John C. Wenger, *The Mennonite Church in America* (Scottdale, Pa.: Herald Press, 1966), 19. Bender was assigned to write this volume in the 1940s, but never completed it. It was completed by Wenger, who included Bender's previously written essay.

d. Founded in 1944, Youth for Christ is an evangelical parachurch ministry that focuses on youth evangelism. In the 1940s and 1950s, its signature activity was the Saturday night youth rally held in large public venues. Billy Graham was the first full-time Youth for Christ staff member.

overtaken almost every nook and corner of their lives so that it is possible for one to see a Lancaster sectarian drive a Cadillac, Packard, or Buick and at the same time cling to the beard and plain coat as a symbol of the righteous life. There exists a tremendous potential of young people.

These people possess one of the richest art and craft cultures in the New World, and it exists not in the museum but in the community and in their social life. This is Lancaster County—a sectarian society existing side by side with an industrial population, where every conceivable social process and conflict of culture continues.

One of the most appalling and pathetic facts we must face today is that no scholar, either within or without the sect, voices the direction of this culture. Like other "Dutchmen" the sectarian who has taken the trouble to get an education has not returned to the community to serve his people. We have yet a very naive understanding of the role of the sect in the American culture. Social scientists have not grasped the situation undoubtedly because they lacked insight or were themselves only superficially interested in the subject. This limited understanding of the contemporary sectarian culture may be attributed to two factors. In the first place many writers up to this point have been satisfied with only a partial view of the culture—the part they are looking for, namely sensationalism and what to them seems the most "odd." These treatments range all the way from the obscene pamphlets on newsstands to the voluminous quantity of sympathetic but often distorted articles appearing in newspapers and magazines.[e] A second factor responsible for our present limited understanding of the problem must be attributed to the bias of the sectarian himself. Take, for instance, the educated sectarian, or the individual who left the sect and is only remotely attached to his kin and community. In his declining years he romanticizes bygone days, and consequently idolizes his religious and ancestral background with a sort of "divine" halo. In this day of scientific achievement and inquiry there must be a new approach to the study of the sectarian society combining the features of unbiased and intellectual honesty in comprehending the entire culture.

THE MISSION OF THE SECTS TODAY

What is the unique mission of the sects to the American and world society? One approach to this problem would be to catalogue all the virtues of the sects,

e. The phrase "obscene pamphlets on newsstands" refers to the Pennsylvania Dutch-themed publications of Harrisburg publisher A. Monroe Aurand Jr., whose publications frequently discussed the courtship ritual known as bundling.

as well as their vices. But this we know all too well already. Besides, this has been one of the most serious pitfalls of many ethnic cultural and historical societies past, for it inevitably leads to further ethnocentrism and intellectual sterility. We have too long listened to the idolizing voices on the one hand and brash ones on the other. Let us rather penetrate beneath the surface and take cognizance of the sociological principles characteristic of this religio-centric culture. We can advance in our understanding of society only as we study it comparatively in a larger framework of scientific investigation.

The underlying hypothesis of this paper is that the survivors of the sixteenth-century Anabaptists are today maintaining communities of prophetic significance. When we appreciate that the origin of the movement was a conceptualization of voluntary association inspired by the forces of biblical ideas, we can understand their long record of faithfulness to their ideals, particularly their resistance to change. They deserve the same recognition as the standard Protestant churches with four hundred years of history. Their program was simply New Testament Christianity, the same as that professed by all Protestant churches, only they insisted that the Bible be taken more seriously than did other reformation groups. Their chief contribution to present-day American culture lies in three areas: (1) the simplicity of their theology and practicality of religion in every aspect of life; (2) the stability of community, kin, and family life combined with a sound economic program; (3) a ministry of worldwide conciliation.

I

First, note the distinguishing features of the religion. Without it the sectarian cannot eat, sleep, work, or even exist. It is not a separate compartment of life, but it is valid for all phases of life at all times. This religion has survived the fire of all sorts of criticism and persecution. The conventional accusation against Christianity—that religion is out of touch with practical life and that the churches are losing ground—is a censure that does not apply to the Amish. Their religion is about as practical as one can make it. Perhaps one reason their religion serves them so well is that they have confined it to themselves, and unlike organized Christianity at large, they are not boastingly attempting to convert the whole world. Their aims are simple and clear. In the way of ritual there is a very minimum, and nothing that cannot be easily grasped by anyone. There is no formal creed, no metaphysical formula, no elaborate theology. Religion is directed toward making the Amishman an upright man, a first-rate farmer, and a good provider for the family. It demands nothing more. Anyone can understand what an upright man and a first-rate farmer is, and there can positively be no speculation about its meaning. Given the force of religious sanction and custom, this formula, when put into effect in a society where there is a minimum of secondary group contacts, produces a life of simplicity relatively free from speculation. The Amishman lives his religion and enjoys every bit of it; at least it is a workable one to live by. It does not leave him with disillusionment, fear, and frustration, but on the contrary his devotion and the working out of it in life gives him a sense of deep satisfaction and rightness with the universe.

No Costly Trappings

The Amishman sees no need for constructing a separate and costly edifice for worship and administration of religion. As ministerial leaders are chosen by lot for life, there is no place for preliminary specialized training. Consequently, ministers receive no salary. There is not the slightest chance for a special priestly class. The economic arrangements for the maintenance of religious functions are stripped to a bare minimum. There is no expense for advertising, canvassing new members, paying the preacher's expenses, or fundraising campaigns which characteristically preoccupy other Christian churches. The organizational machinery necessary for carrying on the church is likewise a simple arrangement. There are no committees or auxiliary organizations which distract from the meetings of worship. Neither are there evening meetings during the week, which inevitably tend to divert time from farm work and separate children from parents during evening hours. The larger Protestant denominations with their changing and speculative systems of theology and creedal affirmations stand in contrast to the sect with its sharp definition of who is and who is not in the kingdom. When one joins a sect he must transform his whole life; there is no question about his conversion experience. Unlike that of joining a club or civic society, one who joins a sect must produce unconditional evidence of the intentions.

The larger denominations fulfill a mission to be sure, but they can never perform the service which the sect can render. The denomination in our world of specialization cannot be a true brotherhood in the root meaning of the term. The churches have inherited precious ethical convictions which are highly regarded, theoretically, but in actual life they are unimportant.[f] It becomes necessary for the denomination to "interpret" its creeds and traditions. It is in-

---

f. The original reads: ". . . but in actual life they are important." Given the context of the paragraph, it is likely that Hostetler meant "unimportant."

terested in preserving these noble convictions together with its theology as one would preserve tradition in books, thus passing them on in petrified form to succeeding generations. Not so with the sectarian! He has not time to write books either about himself or his history, let alone his theology. For him, the greatest achievement lies in personally fulfilling the requirements of the Christian life, being careful not to compromise with the world.

II

The quality of community maintained by the sectarian society is a second and significant contribution to the American culture. The late O. E. Baker put this concept in his own words: "Mennonite people have seemed to me to esteem and practice two great virtues—(1) integrity of the family as an institution for the reproduction of the race and transmission of Christian culture from generation to generation; and (2) ownership of the land, which is so essential to the preservation of intellectual and religious freedom."[g] To this one might add a third item, namely conscience, whose sensitivity frequently has troubled even the average citizen in contact with them. Yet, Bertrand Russell has said: "Respect for conscience, both one's own and that of others, is of boundless importance to a community, and whoever diminishes it is inflicting dreadful damage."[h] The disintegration of rural domestic life set in about 1880 and has continued with increasing rapidity up to the present day. This movement has produced, near large metropolitan centers, farming areas which have become centers of wealth and mass production manned by the hands of the relatively few. Large-scale operators have taken over the family farmer's land. The advance of technology, the decline of farm population growth, the loss of family solidarity, the threat of unemployment, and the growing interdependence of the American people are radically affecting the basic character of national life. Folk depletion is partially responsible for the momentous changes taking place in the American rural community. Despite governmental efforts in research and experimentation to conserve rural values, there has been found no successful formula to nourish the genuine values of rural life. Our industrial civilization knows only how to reintegrate individuals into mobs and masses.

g. Oliver E. Baker was a prominent student and advocate of American rural life. See *Agriculture in Modern Life* (New York: Harper and Brothers, 1939), which Baker coauthored with homesteading advocate Ralph Borsodi and M. L. Wilson.

h. Bertrand Russell (1872–1970) was a British philosopher and social critic. A religious agnostic and antiwar activist who lost his teaching post when he opposed England's participation in World War I, Russell articulated views on freedom of conscience to a wide readership.

The instability of the modern family is revealed by the frequency of divorce, separation, and desertion, not to mention other domestic disunities which come to the attention of the law courts. Urbanization and the services of specialization have reduced to a minimum the activities of common participation among family members. There are today countless social activities which divert every age group of both sexes.

The Amish System

Compare this to the Amish system! Protection from the difficulties encountered by the family is provided, not by outside services, but by the family itself. Adjustments of the marriage partners to one another through tensions and crises are imposed by economic necessity and by social pressure. Voluntary dissolution of the individual family is unthinkable. Courtship compares favorably to the patriarchal system. Marriage is viewed as a normal function of every individual, and is perhaps a matter of course. The absence of preoccupation with the conventional romantic lovemaking episode so characteristic of American youth enables the prospective mates to deal with actual life experiences. This is real preparation for marriage, as character traits are not concealed in a cloak of "romanticism" during the courtship period.

The colleges in America have directly and indirectly influenced the disintegration of the small communities. The rural youth of the country who go to college eventually drift into urban centers where their early family life and culture soon become extinct. In catering after the university, the small colleges have completely ignored the local community and its source of significant value. The philosophy of our colleges has become wedded to the "success striving" ideology so rampant in America today, and we are now reaping the fruit of it. Baker Brownell says: "The modern college has become a mechanism, along with many others, for abstracting life from its community contexts. In so doing it vitiates its own human value and helps to destroy the communal base of all significant culture. . . . Men and women, students and instructors (become) functional fragments, pieces of people in special interest groups. The college loses moral and spiritual integrity. It becomes a society of detached individuals, as Saint Paul would term them, lost souls straining for the fictions of significant life."[i]

Viewed in this perspective we see that Amish distaste for higher education makes some sense.

---

i. Northwestern University philosopher Baker Brownell advocated the importance of the "small community" and the preservation of a grassroots America. Hostetler quotes here from Brownell's "Three Corrupting Principles of College Life," *Mountain Life and Work* 22, no. 4 (1946): 8.

Neither church theology nor scientific research have devised an adequate program for community redemption. In this connection we are astounded again by the Amish economic system. Their formula for gaining wealth is the application of hard labor and modest capital to the land. This, they feel, is God's fundamental arrangement for the welfare of man, and anyone who takes a shortcut is doomed for defeat, that is, the eternal values of life are lost. Thus the most direct mode of production, the simplest, becomes the most honorable. The accumulation of wealth, such as investment in too many farms, in stocks and bonds and in speculation of various sorts, is sinful.

Some Amish Attitudes
The Amish farmer is not a manufacturer. He is neither a large-scale producer, nor a single-crop moneymaker. His first ambition is to feed, clothe, and home his family well, then he may market what is left over. The Amishman wants no more land than he and his family can properly farm. He does not believe in large-scale landholding as investment over and above his family farm. A popular notion exists than an Amishman has plenty of available cash, and that it can be dug up on demand out of his pants pocket. It is very doubtful that the Amish possess more wealth than the non-Amish, but his practice of paying bills in currency has given that impression. But more significant than this is his attitude toward wealth—its sanctioned use and how to limit its use.

This practical form of agrarian economy is sound to the core and, although lacking in modern theory, it conforms to the basic principles of a sound economic system. Whatever we may think of the theological justification for agrarianism, this policy has been with them for centuries. It is the fabric which has given them economic security through periods of prosperity and depression. Furthermore, the end product of this simple formula has made them a socially stable and financially self-respecting people.

Here, then, we have in the sectarian society hundreds of small communities scattered throughout America, and they are among the most stable of any in existence. We can come to understand the disintegration of the rural countryside as we study scientifically the culture of the sect community. While it may seem to the casual observer that Amish communities live largely to themselves, this is far from the truth. The most effective contribution which the brotherhood type of sect can make is that of building primary group relationships, and what the theologian believes is kin to early Christian communities. Americans may in the future look to the descendants of the Anabaptists for a picture of what a great community might be like. These underlying and unnoticed qualities are most urgent and important for the preservation of the larger society. Land is the foundation of the family, and until farm folks of America think more seriously about fundamental values, until they discover the qualities of the home community instead of the distant city and encourage their children to love the farm and its people, they will continue to lose their land and freedom, and with it goes their social heritage.

III

A third phase of the sectarian mission to the world is the curative work of conciliation and alleviation of human suffering. This sense of call springs more from a Christian attitude of conscience than from a reasoned set of ethical premises. Associated with the Mennonite refusal to serve in wars there has been an awareness of human pity and divine compassion. There is the compassion to help with material goods, and with it spirit and persons who will through God's blessing somehow reveal the love of Christ and lead men into His Kingdom.

Such a ministry of relief and goodwill was a major activity of America's Mennonites from 1939 up to the present. Through the facilities of the Mennonite Central Committee (established in 1920) there have been a series of responses to immediate and long-range needs extended to many nationalities and peoples around the globe.[j] From 1939 to 1949, 596 relief workers served in 20 foreign countries. Shipments of goods were personally distributed in liberal quantities on the European continent: to England, France, Holland, Belgium, Germany, Austria, Italy, Hungary, Denmark; to Egypt, Ethiopia, and Palestine; to India, China, the Philippines, Indonesia, and Japan; and finally to Paraguay, Brazil, and Puerto Rico. Cash expenditures from 1944 to 1949 were nearly three million dollars, and material-in-kind dispensed was valued at seven and one-half million, or a total of over ten million dollars for the six-year period. The Mennonites, who represent about one-tenth of one percent of America sent about fifty percent of the relief goods of private agencies to Germany during the apex of suffering. This activity demonstrated that mutual aid in the small community can be extended to the larger community, to people not intimately known.

"In 1945 the North American Mennonite churches faced the task of helping (European) Mennonite refugees to migrate and find new homes. Five years later it was a matter of record that 10,000 had been moved to Paraguay, Uruguay, Canada, and the United States. But the program continues to assist a re-

---

j. Mennonite Central Committee (MCC) is a relief and service agency of North American Mennonite and Brethren in Christ churches. Founded in 1920 in response to hunger crises in Russia, MCC seeks to bring different Anabaptist churches together for the purpose of relief and service work.

maining 2,000 . . . yet in Europe. Also about 8,000 . . . from the Danzig-East Prussia area are still dislocated in Germany. It is certain, too, that the Mennonite brotherhood has not forgotten about the thousands of brethren and sisters who remain in Russia and Siberia." (Irvin B. Horst, *A Ministry of Goodwill*, page 99.)[k]

In the version of one young scholar, the Mennonites have no better expression for what is wrong with the world than sin, and no more effective remedy than the love of God in Christ. How have Mennonites held to such a conservative doctrinal position without descending to ranting fundamentalism, and conversely, to minister to the world's physical needs without evaporating into the social sweetness and light of liberalism? It is probably due to their religious-ethical conviction that is theirs through the providence of inheritance.

No Earthshaking Accomplishments

And what do the Mennonites expect to accomplish in this program? Nothing earthshaking; perhaps nothing even noticeable in history. They entertain no hope that their few millions of dollars will banish hunger from Europe. They did not undertake the work in anticipation of stopping war. They preach in the face of the indications of history and psychology that mankind shall never get much closer to having everyone converted. And so they must feed the hungry regardless of any expectation that all will be filled.

Mennonites are theists with no apology, and they find nothing obsolescent about building their ethics upon the revealed will of God. Whether they ascertain His will aright, they are ever ready to discuss; but once having decided that the New Testament teaches peace, relief, and preaching, they no longer consider themselves at liberty to debate whether to obey simply because the commanded action appears unlikely to achieve its apparent end. For getting the hungry fed, perhaps, is not all that God desires. Perhaps the act itself of feeding, or praying, or loving, is just as important as is the full stomach, or the smooth-running society.

In summary, it is often those "remnants" who have held to religious ideals, those primary groups who have perpetuated community solidarity, that societies have looked to in reconstructing their civilization. Our problem is to obtain an objective understanding of those "remnants" in our own society. This

k. Irvin B. Horst, *A Ministry of Goodwill: A Short Account of Mennonite Relief, 1939–1949* (Akron, Pa.: Mennonite Central Committee, 1950), 99.

can be accomplished only within an adequate context in that branch of knowledge which studies social phenomenon scientifically. Although this discussion has focused on the Mennonites and Amish because of my personal acquaintance and study in this field, yet there are doubtless other minority cultures making a unique contribution to the larger society if we can acquire the techniques of discovering those values.

7

EXCERPT FROM *AMISH LIFE* (1952)

Originally published as a thirty-two-page illustrated booklet, Amish Life *epitomized John Hostetler's desire to mediate his message about Amish culture to the masses. Incensed by the bundling-heavy, Pennsylvania German-themed pamphlets of Harrisburg, Pennsylvania, publisher A. Monroe Aurand Jr., and encouraged by colleagues such as Alfred L. Shoemaker, the director of Lancaster's Pennsylvania Dutch Folklore Center, Hostetler produced* Amish Life *in cooperation with the Mennonite Publishing House, where he later accepted an editorial position. The booklet was designed by Beulah Stauffer, whom Hostetler would later marry.*

From a commercial standpoint, Amish Life *proved highly successful, eventually selling nearly one million copies. Writing in a simple, straightforward style, Hostetler addressed the questions and observations so frequently voiced by tourists, students, and others whose imaginations had been captivated by the Old Order Amish. This excerpt reiterates some of those tourist's comments; other sections, not included here, featured headings such as "Are They Flush with Money?" "Such Strange Music!" and "Courting and So Forth." In the end,* Amish Life *provided Hostetler with an avenue not only to correct misconceptions about Amish culture, but also to make his case about the significance of "small communities" for the maintenance of American civilization. Many readers were impressed by the clarity and sensitivity of Hostetler's presentation, including his graduate advisor, William G. Mather, whose introduction declared, "in this booklet the reader will receive for the first time at a popular price the true story of this much-misunderstood people."*

This excerpt, including illustrations and captions, is from the first edition of Amish Life *(Scottdale, Pa.: Herald Press, 1952). Text and illustrations are reprinted by permission of Herald Press.*

WHO ARE THEY?

You are one of the hundreds who ask this question. The answer is not so simple as one might think. The Amish people in America are not a new religious sect, but a very old one. They were a tiny offshoot of another sect, the Mennonites, who arose directly out of the Reformation struggles of the sixteenth century in Switzerland and Holland.

Mennonites (or "peaceful" Anabaptists) read the Bible seriously, but more than that they took it seriously. They said a man does not become a Christian by being baptized, or even by joining a church, but by having an inner regeneration of soul proved by outward behavior. They agreed with Luther that every man has the right to pray and have faith in God, whenever and however he wants, without the mediation of a preacher or priest. They objected to compulsion, that one must belong to this or that church depending on the particular territory in which he happens to live.

The Mennonite idea spread rapidly but everywhere met terrific opposition. Hundreds and thousands were burned at the stake. Many were placed into sacks and thrown into the river. Many were tortured in other cruel ways. The movement finally dwindled in enthusiasm as many gave up the idea of evangelism and preaching and became the quiet farmers of the hills and valleys of Switzerland and the Palatinate.

The Amish group, scholars say, developed out of the Mennonites from 1693 to 1697. Jacob Amman, a Mennonite bishop of Switzerland, emphasized the need for more serious observance of what he called "the old ground and foundation." He succeeded in gaining a considerable following, who came to be known as the Amish. He was not a reformer, but a proponent of a stricter way of life than was often practiced among the Mennonites earlier. He bequeathed to his followers a radically conservative point of view. To this day the Amish have retained his spirit as well as certain externals of a former way of life. They have clung to the forms of worship, styles of dress, and customs of centuries past.

We see, then, that both Amish and Mennonites were branches of the same tree, but today they differ in many ways. Mennonites worship in meetinghouses, maintain colleges, are greatly concerned about extending the Christian gospel through home and foreign missions, they publish books and devotional literature, and administer worldwide relief in wartime, while the Old Order Amish generally do none of these things. Some Mennonites dress "plain," but many do not. Amish adult men wear beards, use horses for farming and for "buggy" transportation; they have neither electricity nor telephones in their homes.[a]

The Amish make no attempt to "convert" the whole world, but it must be said that their aims are simple and clear. They support no "revivals," missionary activity, or organized evangelistic services of their own, and seek no proselytes. Their religion is directed toward making the Amishman an "upright man" (an honest, God-fearing, and obedient Christian) and a first-rate

---

a. In a section of *Amish Life* not reprinted here, Hostetler made finer distinctions between the various Amish and Mennonite groups, thereby complicating the simplistic Mennonite-Amish dualism that often existed in popular discourse.

FIG. 7.1 An Amish boy gets his tray filled at the serving counter in his school. His haircut and cloth suspenders are regular Amish style. Photograph by the U.S. Department of Agriculture.

farmer, and that is all. Any Amishman knows what that means. The aims of religion are clear, thus ruling out the need for a detailed creed or an elaborate theology.

The Amish are a farming and peace-minded folk. With Mennonites and other Swiss, Dutch, and German immigrants, several hundred came to Pennsylvania after 1730. Family names prominent in the early settlements were Yoder, Zook, Lapp, Hostetler, Beiler, King, and others. Joseph Schantz (Johns) in 1800 founded a colony near the present city of Johnstown, Pennsylvania, which was named in his honor. After the Napoleonic Wars ended (1815) a larger number of Amish came from Alsace and South Germany to settle chiefly in Ohio and Illinois.

WHERE DO THEY LIVE?

Today the only Amish people in the world are those in the United States and Canada, but there are no reliable figures on the total Amish population. The church membership of the Old Order Amish is given as 15,880 in the *Mennonite Yearbook* (1952).[b] A conservative estimate of the Amish population including children would seem to be about 35,000. Sociologists have found that Amish families are larger than the average American farm family. Since Amish youth do not join church until they reach the age of sixteen or more, a large proportion of their number are non-church members. Because of their large families they are one of the fastest growing denominations in America today.

Each local Amish community is divided into *Kaahre* (church districts), each containing about 15 to 30 families, or on the average about 75 members. The size of the districts is limited because of horse and buggy transportation; and because worship is held in homes, only a limited number of people can be accommodated. There is generally one bishop for each of the districts, with two to four assisting preachers and a deacon. The total number of church districts in North America is about 200 (1951). There are settlements in eighteen states and one Canadian province.

. . .

---

b. Ellrose D. Zook, ed., *Mennonite Yearbook and Directory 1952* (Scottdale, Pa.: Mennonite Publishing House, 1952), 83.

FIG. 7.2 Horses are still the principal source of power in many communities. Drawing by Ann Killins, reprinted by permission of Herald Press.

IS THEIR RELIGION REALLY DIFFERENT?

Religion is the axis around which the Amishman's world revolves. The old traditions are regarded as sacred and any new ideas in religious matters are looked upon with suspicion. Whole households come to "preaching" held every other Sunday. Men, women, and children gather in the home of a member for worship. This is made possible often by the removable partitions and doors between the large rooms on the first floor of the house. Everybody shakes hands on Sunday morning, and preachers greet each other with the holy kiss as commanded in the Bible. I Thess. 5:26. Worship begins about 9:00 or earlier and ends about noon, or sometimes later. The service consists of numerous sermons by two ministers, sometimes silent and also oral prayers which are read, testimonies (*Zeugniss*) from all ministers present, and singing.

Children learn early to sit attentively, although their preoccupation with handkerchiefs (making objects such as "mice") compensates for this. "Halfmoon pies" (in Pennsylvania) or crackers served to toddlers during mid-service also help to minimize their restlessness. The social hour and lunch (coffee, bread, butter, jams, pickles, red beets, and pie) following the service is a valuable part of the meeting. The after-church menu is standard and so established by custom. Everyone enjoys the period of visiting and good fellowship

FIG. 7.3 [Uncaptioned.] Photograph by Rusinow, Bureau of Agricultural Economics.

which follows. Not only do men discuss religious subjects, but also the happenings of the day, crops and farming, world events, and personal and community problems. Women do likewise. Young men spend their time leisurely gathering about the barn or around the buggies. Jokes, good-natured teasing, and subjects related to courtship are often topics of their conversation.

The Sunday meeting is but an outward or observable manifestation of an Amishman's religion. How religion controls his thinking, with what purpose he lives, and why he acts as he does is far more significant. Without religion the Amishman could not be Amish; he cannot separate his belief from eating, sleeping, and working. He simply could not exist without it, for the best Amishman finds it impossible to divide sacred from secular. His Christianity has survived the fire of all sorts of criticism and persecution. It is practical and "down-to-earth."

Furthermore, the staunch Amishman enjoys his religion. Far from being frustrated, his religion gives him a sense of deep satisfaction and rightness with the universe. Given the force of custom, his faith produces a wholesome simplicity of life relatively free from snobbishness and the worldliness he abhors. A few of the young people, however, rebel against the extreme formalism and find it impossible to adjust.

Amish ministers are chosen from their own congregations by "lot" for life, and there is no place for specialized training. They receive no salary. There is no need for constructing a costly church building for worship when services can be held in the homes. There is no expense for advertising, canvassing new members, or other expenses as in the larger American denominations. Not even a written record of the membership list is kept. Why should they bother with one, when everyone knows everyone else?

. . .

WHAT KEEPS THEM "SEPARATE"?

Scholars have said that the Amish culture is maintained by certain techniques of isolation, such as the use of dialect, a peculiar form of dress, and by living in semi-isolated areas. Maybe this is true, maybe not. But we must look beneath the surface to discover what those principles are that make for stability and contentment among the Amish.

The Amish family is a closely knit unit living on the farm. There is no need for the son or daughter to go to town for a job. The boy gets instruction in farm management in the barnyard and around the dinner table. The girl is taught the techniques of sewing, cooking, homemaking, and working alongside her mother and sisters. The meaning of cooperation and work is learned early in life. The many inventions which ordinarily take over the functions of the home have not affected the Amish family to any great degree. For example, they make many of their own clothes, they bake pies and bread in the old-fashioned bake oven, and they produce and preserve much of their own food. In many places modern conveniences are being accepted.

The Amish system provides "social security" for its members from the womb to the tomb, and a certain guarantee of security even beyond the tomb!

Grandfather has no need for old-age pension or commercial forms of insurance for security, for in his judgment he already has the best kind of insurance. There are no premiums to pay and his policy never lapses. To retire, he simply moves into the *grossdawdy* (grandfather) house, and the young generation takes over. If his barn burns down, his neighbors help him build a new one. If he be-

FIG. 7.4 The outside bake oven is still used for baking large amounts of bread and pies, also for drying apple "schnitz" and corn. Drawing by Ann Killins, reprinted by permission of Herald Press.

comes ill, they do his work. Should he die very suddenly, they make arrangements to have the farm operations continue.

The ordinary protection of the individual members is given by father and mother, brother and sister, uncle and aunt, and church members, not by money investments, state security, the township trustee, or by welfare agencies. Divorce, desertion, and separation do not have a chance among the Amish people. The adjustment of newly married people is of necessity made right in the home community. In fact, there is limited contact with persons outside one's acquaintances.

One reason why the Amish home is not broken is that its members spend more time in "living" and less time in leisure than is the case in the average American home. The tasks of homemaking have not been lightened by electrical appliances and similar modern inventions. The Amish mother would be horrified by the thought of working outside the home and at the same time trying to raise a family. There is plenty of time to bear children, and to "bring them up in the nurture and admonition of the Lord."[c] In a recent report of one Amish community in Pennsylvania (Mifflin County) it was found that the average completed Amish family had between seven and eight children.[d]

The Amishman enjoys a wholesome family life. However stiff others may think his religion and culture, it is a mistake to assume that he is a slave to an unhappy fate. Children born into his home will always eat well, and will be clothed and housed well. So long as he remains on the farm he will not be troubled by fear of losing his job. Nor will he wonder where the bread will come from for his wife and children.

. . .

WHAT GOOD ARE THEY?

The Amishman's attachment to the soil is about as strong as his devotion to the Bible. Obviously the two go together, and his faith and nonconformed way of life can best be expressed in a rural environment. There exists in Amish communities a generous warmth of brotherhood, mutual respect, and trust. But what more are they than hardworking, prosperous, and religious people?

Their religion forbids participation in warfare. They literally believe: "Thou shalt not kill"; "Blessed are the peacemakers"; "If thine enemy hunger, feed him"; "Overcome evil with good"; "Christ also suffered for us, leaving us an example, that ye should follow his steps"; and other Bible passages.[e] Nevertheless, they are sensitive to the sufferings of other people and they are generous contributors to foreign relief and rehabilitation, a fact not too well known. During and since World War II they contributed cash in the amount of $25,000 annually to war sufferers' relief, through the Mennonite Central Committee which coordinates the relief activities of the several branches of Mennonites. During 1948 and 1949 they gave over fifty-two thousand dollars for refugee rehabilitation. In addition, many have combined their efforts in canning meat and fruits for foreign shipment. They donated food, soap, shoes, and clothing in quantities.

Their mission to America as apostles of peace is to bring healing to a human society and to witness to a higher way of life. They do not entertain any

c. Eph. 6:4 (KJV).

d. Hostetler is probably referring to his 1951 Pennsylvania State College master's thesis, "The Amish Family in Mifflin County, Pennsylvania," 15–21.

e. Biblical quotations are from Ex. 20:13; Matt. 5:9; Rom. 12:20; Rom. 12:21; and 1 Peter 2:21 (all KJV).

utopian ideas about possessing the whole world, nor converting it. They attest that there will always be enough people to perform the task of the magistracy, the police, and the military. But they believe that candidates for the Biblical way of life, which nonresistant and obedient Christians alone can fulfill, are altogether too few.

The fifty settlements of Amish people in North America are small brotherhoods of a kind necessary to national life and well-being. The foundations of any civilization depend on the moral quality of the people living in it. Where better can such virtues as neighborliness, self-control, good will, and cooperation be found than in small communities? A civilization will thrive wherever these qualities are found, and it will break down wherever they cease to exist. Perhaps the modern hurried, worried, and fearful world could learn something from the Amish.

8

GOD VISITS THE AMISH (1954)

In this short piece, published in a family-oriented Mennonite Church periodical, Hostetler reports on a surprising — and controversial — evangelical awakening among Midwestern Amish communities. In addition to noting the factors fueling the revival, Hostetler offers a positive theological assessment that begins with the article's title and concludes with a glowing review of progressive movements in Mennonite history. According to Hostetler (although usually expressed through his informants), the revival was bringing spiritual renewal to Amish communities that, for various reasons, had grown spiritually desolate. Delineated in the article are the standard critiques of Old Order religious life long advanced by evangelically oriented Mennonites — namely, the Amish are bound to tradition, ignorant of the Bible, resistant to conversion, unwilling to claim assurance of salvation, reluctant to share their faith with others, and morally lax with their youth. That Hostetler expresses them so vividly in this article says something of his theological proclivities as a relatively young man. Soon, however, his sociological training and experience would lead him to think differently about the traditional religious sensibilities of the Old Order Amish and the efforts of those who would seek to subvert those sensibilities in God's name.

This article first appeared in Christian Living, *March 1954, 6–7, 40. It is reprinted by permission of the Mennonite Publishing House.*

"God is moving among us in these last days. One of our ministers has crucified the self more than the rest of us. He is used of God in waking us up, even the old people."

The Old Order Amish preacher who spoke these words was referring to preacher David Miller, an Amishman of Oklahoma, who preaches evangelistic messages to his own people in several states. His earnest preaching, pleading, and praying have won the respect of hundreds and thousands of Amish people.

Traditionally the Old Order Amish have not had revival meetings. The present spiritual awakening found in well over half of the fifty settlements in the United States, however, shows that there is exceptional hunger for new religious life.[a] In Ohio last year, for example, Miller was booked up for thirteen

---

a. For a historical analysis of this revival, see Steve Nolt, "The Amish 'Mission Movement' and the Reformulation of Amish Identity in the Twentieth Century," *Mennonite Quarterly Review* 75 (2001): 7–36.

days straight. He preached Sunday and weekdays, in the morning, sometimes afternoon, and occasionally after an evening hymn sing—in brooder houses,[b] in barns, and on lawns.

There are dozens of other Amish preachers like Miller who are getting "new light." They preach "biblical" messages stripped of the usual Amish singsong delivery and the old terminology.[c] While this newer preaching has brought deep satisfaction to many who have been praying for release from the power of sin and overbearing traditions, it has also brought stress and worry to those leaders who hail it as *eppes neues* (something new).

The new awakening has its roots in several forces: prayer meetings and discussions on the part of young people; the broadening experience received by a few CPS men;[d] messages sent to Amish leaders by a converted Catholic called Maniaci; the influence of revival campaigns by Mennonites; the presence of degenerate spiritual life in Amish communities; and interest in missionary work.[e] We shall discuss each briefly.

A few "concerned" Amish young people, some of whom are married, have been meeting in secret for prayer and Bible study. A few of the men who were drafted into camps during the last war found enrichment of soul through exercising personal devotional life. Some of them read the Bible extensively in English for the first time. They shared in the Sunday school, worship, and prayer meetings. Those who stuck by the Amish Church and returned to their communities have not forgotten the more valuable things they learned.[f]

Most unusual was the conversion of Russell Maniaci who is now arousing the missionary conscience of the Amish. Maniaci was a Catholic, a workingman, the head of a family in Detroit. While in a state of confusion about the adequacy of his own religion, one morning he read a newspaper account of the

---

b. Brooder houses are buildings in which young fowl are raised.

c. Hostetler's use of quotation marks around the word "biblical" indicates that he himself is not ready to brand traditional Amish sermons "unbiblical." Clearly, however, the new light camp believed that traditional Amish preaching did not invoke the scriptures directly enough.

d. "CPS men" refers to those Amish men who, during World War II, gained conscientious objector status and participated in the Civilian Public Service (CPS) instead of the military. These men typically moved far from their home communities and lived in camps numerically dominated by Mennonites. For tensions that emerged, see Albert N. Kiem, "Military Service and Conscription," in *The Amish and the State,* rev. ed., ed. Donald B. Kraybill (Baltimore: Johns Hopkins University Press, 2003), 49–56.

e. Hostetler does not address the issue of Mennonite revival campaigns in this article, though like Russell Maniaci's work, Mennonite tent revivalism elicited mixed reactions from Amish persons. For Amish reactions, see Nolt, "The Amish 'Mission Movement,'" 20.

f. For the activist effect of Mennonite-administered CPS camps on Amish participants, see David Wagler and Roman Raber, *The Story of the Amish in Civilian Public Service, with Directory* (Millersburg, Ohio: John D. Hershberger, 1986), 65–67.

Amish in Kansas who sold their farms and moved away because oil was discovered on them. They did not wish to subject themselves to the temptation to become wealthy.[g] This event so astounded Maniaci that he wrote to one of the Amish farmers concerning his religion. He was advised to contact Amish persons in his own state of Michigan. He expressed a desire to join. The Michigan Amish, not being accustomed to receive outsiders into their fellowship, advised that he contact the Mennonite mission in Detroit. Maniaci, his wife, and his family of children experienced salvation and were baptized into the Mennonite Church.[h]

Realizing that the Amish people were the ones who attracted him to Christ and to a practical Christianity, Maniaci set himself to work to arouse the Amish to do missionary work. The Amish Christian way of life, he felt with deepest sincerity, should be proclaimed wide and far. He began to produce a mimeographed paper called "Amish Mission Endeavor" in December, 1951, and sent specially prepared letters to all Amish ordained preachers explaining his conversion and the necessity of doing missionary work.[i]

He said: "My only interest is to see the Amish Church on fire for the Gospel. What about the debt that you as a leader owe to the unsaved? There are many young people in your church who are willing to launch out for the Master. They are waiting for you as a leader to lead them to a fuller spiritual service for their Master. Will you lead them or will you cause them to join other churches?"

Of his first visit to an Amish home, the home of M. E. Bontrager of Centerville, Michigan, Maniaci said: "We were treated like millionaires, and the welcome was not like that in the big city—but was real and genuine."

Many Amish have a secret conviction and interest in promoting missionary work. The first Amish Missions Conference was called by Maniaci at Kalona, Iowa, in the fall of 1950. Over 150 persons were present from several states. Annual missions meetings have been held since, but such conferences are now sponsored by Amish persons themselves. Although some preachers were se-

g. According to Nolt, the Associated Press wire service story was wrong: the Amish left Yoder, Kansas, for Fairbanks, Iowa, for different reasons. A short version of the news story can be found under the headline, "Shun Oil-Well Riches: Amish Farmers Move from Area Where New Pool is Found," *New York Times*, 7 March 1936, sec. 5.

h. For more on Maniaci, whose actual first name was Rosario, see Nolt, "The Amish 'Mission Movement,'" 14–16. Hostetler spelled Maniaci's nickname "Russel," but it was "Russell."

i. Maniaci sent his mimeographed *Amish Mission Endeavor Bulletin* to hundreds of Amish ministers, raising the ire of many, particularly with its harsh criticism of Amish traditionalism. He eventually added the words "Please Do Not Tear This Until You Have Read It" above the publication's address line. Nolt, "The Amish 'Mission Movement,'" 16.

cretly enthusiastic about the upshot of interest in missions, it sprang largely from the laity.[j]

The fourth Amish Missions Conference was held near Hutchinson, Kansas, in August last year at the home of David Miller. The theme of the three-day conference was "Witnessing—in Word, in Deed, in Truth, in Power." Twenty-five persons, all of them Amish, were assigned topics for discussion. Names appearing on the program were Graber, Beachy, Miller, Hochstetler, Stoltzfus, Yoder, Gingerich, Bontrager, Wagler, Schlabach, Nisley, Troyer, Lapp, and Weirich. States represented were: Ohio, Pennsylvania, Iowa, Indiana, Arkansas, Oklahoma, and others. The program called for periods of devotion, testimonies, and song service. There was a financial report and recommendations made by committee members.

A "Mission Interests Committee" of this interested group issues a bimonthly release entitled *Witnessing* which is edited by Harvey Graber and W. W. Wagler, and mimeographed by Andrew A. Miller of Holmesville, Ohio. Its purpose is "making known the Gospel of Jesus Christ to all mankind, with special emphasis on personal work. Distribution of the paper is free as the Lord provides."[k]

In the first issue of *Witnessing* (April, 1953) R. L. Schlabach wrote: "God, we believe, could convert men without us, but it is not His order to do so. We wonder if any man on the face of the earth has ever been converted without God using some co-worker in some way or other. At the raising of Lazarus the disciples were to take away the stone, loose the grave clothes, and let him go. From Noah to our day, God has used some human instrument as His co-worker to accomplish His work."

There is another powerful motive responsible for the Amishman's interest in spiritual revival. It is the breakdown of their older culture evidenced by drinking parties, carousals, and sex violations. Complaints from Amish parents and from others against drinking have been voiced at various times. One Amish minister said he prefers to have his children join the Mennonites rather than be exposed to the evil environment in his particular locality. A daily paper recently reported the arrest of six Amish youths at a Sunday night "singing" for selling liquor unlicensed. The officers who made the raid said there were 200 persons at the singing and that 10–13 cases of empty beer bottles were

j. An eight-member planning committee elected in 1951 was composed entirely of Amish laymen. Nolt, "The Amish 'Mission Movement,'" 18.

k. *Witnessing* actually emerged as an alternative to Maniaci's *Amish Mission Endeavor Bulletin*. Given Maniaci's strident tone, Amish leaders of the movement distanced themselves from Maniaci and started a paper they believed would be more effective in catalyzing change. See Nolt, "The Amish 'Mission Movement,'" 23.

found on the premises. This is not a true picture for all Amish, but such conditions wherever they exist provide good incentive for spiritual preaching and work among their own people.[1]

One informant told me: "The conduct among the Old Order Amish young people was far from what I thought it should be—smoking, drinking, smutty stories, lack of opportunity for service, and no Bible teaching. The young people are ignorant of the teachings of the Bible." Conditions such as these explain in part the present desire for spiritual awakening among the Amish.

Moral and spiritual decay is often associated with the loss of the traditional language. This has been true of the American Indians and other groups of people. It is true among the Amish. The Amish youngsters attend public schools and learn English well. Most of their parents no longer take the pains to teach their children to read the old High German. In fact, they never learn to write their everyday spoken language.

A former Amish mother said, "The German preaching was hard for our youngsters to understand. This caused the boys and girls to be too little concerned about their convictions at a tender age." Others who leave their church say the Amish Church gets confused in the plain teaching of salvation; "they teach the doctrine of not knowing whether one can be saved or not."[m]

More and more English words are being used by the Amish preachers. This is necessary if meanings are to be made clear. Sermons still have traces of High German, but they have been greatly "Englishized." Examples are: *Ich bin impressed* (I am impressed); *Mir hen resisting forces in uns* (There are resisting forces within us); *Der bruder hot ein calling* (The brother has a calling); *Mir dependa uff Gottes Wort* (We depend on God's Word); *Peter warr convert nei bis der core* (Peter was converted to the core); *Mir hen oft 'es lezt concept vom Wort Gottes* (We often have the wrong concept of the Word of God).

The German language is a good expressive language. But the Bible does not require the Christian to keep a specific language. There is not a single language which is more divine than any other. Therefore, it is quite likely that the Amish who speak English to their neighbors and "Dutch" among themselves will in

1. Partying continues to be an element of Amish teen life, though only for some (particularly in larger settlements). Donald B. Kraybill explains teenage Amish rowdiness as a form of "social immunization" that allows Amish teenagers to dabble in worldliness but also become resistant to it for the long haul. See Kraybill, *The Riddle of Amish Culture*, rev. ed. (Baltimore: Johns Hopkins University Press, 2001), 184–87. Outsiders, most notably Mennonites and evangelical Christians, have long been critical of Amish leaders who turn a blind eye to this sort of behavior.

m. Hostetler addresses the Old Order Amish disinclination to claim salvation in his first edition of *Amish Society* (Baltimore: Johns Hopkins University Press, 1963), noting that such assertions are viewed by the Amish as prideful (50).

the long run not be able to retain a third and separate Sunday language, the High German.

What is the meaning of the present awakening among the Amish? First of all, it is an awakening coming out of deep conflict and struggle. There are opposers to the missionary-minded Amish people. They are the sincere Old Order Amish who believe it is best not to change the old ways. The ban has been placed on some families and individuals. Stress, conflict, confusion, and misunderstandings have resulted between family members, between church districts, and between sincere Amish Christians. One Amish person said Christ's words are literally being fulfilled: "I came not to bring peace but a sword."

It is well to remember that the present spiritual awakening is not something entirely new. Again and again such manifestations have occurred in Amish-Mennonite history. One hundred years ago the Mennonite Church was faced with exactly the same problems and predicaments the Amish face today.

What were those problems? A century ago there was no general church conference, no Sunday schools where the Bible is freely discussed, no missionary activity, no wholesome young people's meetings. Almost nothing was being published. The church was using German by and large, and preaching was held every two weeks. The sad part is that young people and whole families were leaving the church by the scores and hundreds for lack of spiritual exercise. Whole churches died out, at least 20 in Ohio alone. If the Mennonites of Pennsylvania had retained their children in the church, their number today would not be 28,000 but probably well over 280,000.

The language problem among Mennonites caused widespread discussion and several divisions. The Sunday school was vigorously opposed by the more conservative-minded. It was "considered needless to the development of the Christian life." It was regarded as "the open door to lead children and young people into worldliness, vanity, and pride." But the opposition was not well grounded. According to a special study by Harold Bender, those churches which refused the Sunday school lost their young people and failed to survive. "From East to West and North to South there are literally dozens of communities where once were flourishing Mennonite congregations, where church houses were built, where cemeteries were laid out, and where the faith of the church was planted, but where now nothing remains but the cemetery or possibly the empty meetinghouse."[n] But there were men of vision and of courage such as John F. Funk and J. S. Coffman, who were kind, graceful, prayerful, and moved by the

n. Harold S. Bender, *Mennonite Sunday School Centennial, 1840–1940: An Appreciation of Our Sunday Schools* (Scottdale, Pa.: Herald Press, 1940), 32. The foregoing quotations summarizing the arguments against Sunday school can be found on page 30 of the same work.

Spirit of God. These men helped to bring the Mennonite Church through difficult times.°

Coffman was so mighty in the pulpit that some Mennonite ministers feared to invite him to their churches. They feared he would so impress the people that they would be unwilling to listen to their own ministers after he left the community. A similar fear is seizing some of the Amish communities today. Presently many sincere Amish ministers and family heads are torn between two opinions: (1) the desires for spiritual awakening including the support of the mission movement; and (2) the fear of the consequences and of losing *das alt Gebrauch* (old traditions). They ask, What will this lead to?ᴾ

Concerning missions, the mind of the Mennonite Church was divided for at least 40 years. The opposition was strong and vigorous. But today the opposition has vanished, not because of organizations and conferences but because of the prayers and honest efforts of sincere Christian workers. In the early part of the present century there was division between the Conservative Amish and the Old Order Amish. There have been progressive and Old Order tendencies which have openly split Amish communities for well over 70 years.

Traditions can be a fine thing. They help people to maintain a common community and a common mind. Every movement which is not deeply grounded in tradition is in danger of shallow doctrine and of suicide. But when a tradition blocks the direct teaching of Christ and the Spirit of God, that tradition needs to be broken.

In the years gone by it was very hard to break those traditions. It is hard today. But let us pray that God will again raise up mighty men to meet the occasion, men of vision, of spiritual earnestness, of moral conviction, and men who will obey God. God is visiting the Amish brethren.

o. For the importance of John S. Coffman as a revivalist and John F. Funk as an organizational innovator, see James C. Juhnke, *Vision, Doctrine, War: Mennonite Identity and Organization in America, 1890–1930* (Scottdale, Pa.: Herald Press, 1989). Funk appears in Bender's *Mennonite Sunday School Centennial* in a section entitled "Men of Vision and of Courage" (33).

p. Nolt's vantage point allows him to see the consequences in a way that Hostetler and the actual actors could not. By the late 1950s, the Amish persons most captivated by the revival had left the Old Order church, moving into more evangelical Anabaptist churches, Beachy Amish churches in particular. At the same time, the Old Order Amish, heretofore often called "Old Order Amish Mennonites," became "more *sectarian* than they were before that time." Nolt, "The Amish 'Mission Movement,'" 34. Emphasis in original.

9

WHY IS EVERYBODY INTERESTED
IN THE PENNSYLVANIA DUTCH? (1955)

Published just months after the stage debut of Plain and Fancy, *"Why Is Everybody Interested in the Pennsylvania Dutch?" seeks to explain the fast-expanding Amish culture market to a Mennonite readership. As the title indicates, Hostetler's field of vision extends beyond the Amish to interest in Pennsylvania Dutch culture broadly conceived, most notably the Pennsylvania Dutch Folk Festival in Kutztown, Pennsylvania. Even so, Hostetler knew by this time that the Amish were Pennsylvania Dutchland's main attraction, and he correspondingly devotes most of his article to delineating the ways in which the Old Order Amish were being commodified by their English neighbors.*

While the article is largely descriptive, Hostetler turns interpreter in its last section, venturing two reasons for this profound cultural curiosity. With respect to popular interest in the broader Pennsylvania Dutch culture, Hostetler notes that outsiders often grow fascinated with a culture when they see it disintegrating before their eyes. But in addition to offering this cultural declension hypothesis, Hostetler suggests that many twentieth-century Americans were descending upon the Pennsylvania Dutch because they were looking for spiritual sustenance, for "the eternal treasures of heaven." Interestingly, Hostetler's last paragraph begins with an inclusive phrase ("We as Pennsylvania Dutch groups"), a rhetorical ploy that allows his Mennonite readers to imagine that they have the answers people are seeking. Nonetheless, the same paragraph acknowledges that it is the decidedly plain Pennsylvania Dutch groups—those with bonnets and beards— that are most alluring to outsiders. The result is a fascinating ambiguity that may reflect Hostetler's own uncertainty in 1955: were his fellow Mennonites akin to the spiritually secure Amish, or were they merely another Pennsylvania Dutch group in cultural decline?

This article first appeared in Christian Living, *August 1955, 6–9, 38. It is reprinted by permission of the Mennonite Publishing House.*

Never in the history of this country has there been such a genuine public curiosity about the Pennsylvania Dutch. Minority groups such as the Amish and the Mennonites who three or four centuries ago were condemned as heretics, apostates, blasphemers, and stubborn nonconformists, are now looked upon as carriers of a culture worthy of admiration. This widespread interest is evident not only in decorative art and in literature, but also in everyday affairs, in food, festivals, travel, gift shops, national advertising, and drama. Why this surge of public interest? Why are the Amish who want no publicity at all—not even favorable comment—foremost in publicity among all the Pennsylvania Dutch groups?

I

For the past several years the Pennsylvania Dutch Folk Festival held at Kutz-town, Pennsylvania, has attracted forty to sixty thousand people.[a] The annual four-day celebrations attempt to show how the Dutch lived in pioneer days and how well they have kept alive their culture. The background, scope, and contribution of the Pennsylvania Dutch to America are discussed by various specialists. There are demonstrations of powwowing, folk singing, dialect speech-making, moving day, folk games, storytelling, apple butter cooking, *schnitzing*, traditions, and superstitions. There are interesting demonstrations of crafts—pottery making, wheel making, and basket making. The costumes of the "Plain People" are put on display, carefully explained and demonstrated by sympathetic outsiders. The average jaywalker attending the festival can, if he wants, learn the distinction between Amish and "Black Bumper" bonnets; he can learn to distinguish an Amish bishop's hat from other styles of Amish hats. He can go as deep as he wants into "spook" stories and legends and into the finest detail of culture complexity.

Another Pennsylvania Dutch attraction, held annually for the seventh time this year, is the Hershey, Pennsylvania, festival. Last year Hershey attracted an estimated 135,000 people. The three days of festivity offered a blend of Penn-sylvania Dutch agriculture, crafts, funmaking, storytelling, and featured the appointment of a state *Lotwaerrick* (apple butter) queen, a Dutch *Fendue* (auc-tion), worship services in the dialect, square dancing, Dutch skits, musical en-tertainment, cigar making, glass blowing, candle dipping, weaving, and fa-vorite Dutch dishes. Seven and one-half tons of chicken, three-quarter ton of cabbage, three-quarter ton of beans, five hundred pounds of butter, and ninety gallons of vinegar were consumed by this crowd. A mile of paper tablecloth was used to cover the tables, where twelve lines, each capable of serving 100 persons every 15 minutes, served the interested multitude.

The Ohio Swiss Cheese Festival at Sugarcreek, Ohio, right in the heart of the largest Amish settlement in the nation, seems to have exceeded even the Hershey crowd last year. From every corner of the state and from many other states, people poured into Sugarcreek until the town was packed. An estimated 200,000 persons were present to listen to Polka Harmoniers, Pop Farver's or-chestra, to witness alpenhorn blowing, Swiss flag throwing, and the yodeling

---

a. Sponsored by the Pennsylvania Dutch Folklore Center, the Kutztown festival was inaugurated in 1950. See Don Yoder, "25 Years of the Folk Festival," *Pennsylvania Folklife* 23 (Folk Festival Supplement, 1974): 2–7.

Swiss cheese makers. Photographers swarmed everywhere recording the colorful ceremonies. Radio, television, and reporters were present to secure adequate coverage. The crowd consumed about a ton of hamburger, huge quantities of pies, cakes, soft drinks, and milk products. The Swiss cheese makers sold 13,400 pounds of cheese and a ton of Trail Bologna.

Pennsylvania's people are more tradition conscious, certainly more "Dutch" conscious, than those of other states. Lancaster County is the center for most of the Dutch fanfare. There are a number of commercial agencies and some professional societies who promote the Dutch trade. Hotel Brunswick serves Dutch dishes and has arranged regular weekend Lancaster County tours for the thousands of tourists who want to see the Dutch country. Alfred Shoemaker of the Pennsylvania Dutch Folklore Center, Franklin and Marshall College, has spearheaded publications, folk festivals, tours, dialect broadcasting, and the systematic collection of folk tales.[b] The American Society of Travel Agents met in Lancaster for their annual meeting and were told how Lancaster could become the tourist mecca of the nation. Representatives of the Swedish-American Steamship Lines recently visited Lancaster to pick up a few tips on Dutch food, especially shoofly pie.

. . .

II

The stage too has shared in the Pennsylvania Dutch "revival." "Out of This Wilderness" was an outdoor drama of the Pennsylvania Dutch played last year at Selinsgrove. In it the life story of the German people who fled from religious and political oppression is presented with mingled emotions. Portrayed are Conrad Weiser, Chief Shikellamy, Count Zinzendorf, Chief Seneca George, George Gabriel, and other Pennsylvania heroes.

"Papa Is All," a stage performance of an eccentric domineering father of a (Reformed) Mennonite setting, is still appearing at open-country summer theatricals.[c] "By Hex" was staged in Lancaster County last summer. Among other scenes it has in it the role of an Amish bishop who leads his group in the

---

b. For more on Shoemaker, see Chapter 3.

c. Patterson Greene, *Papa Is All* (New York: Samuel French, 1942). Reformed Mennonites, also known as Herrites (after founder John Herr), believed that early nineteenth-century Lancaster County Mennonites had departed from the strict practices of Menno Simons and, like the Amish a century earlier, called for stricter disciplinary practices. In the early twentieth century, they captured the attention of novelist Helen Reimensnyder Martin, who used them to poke fun at Pennsylvania Dutch people and practices.

way he feels is right.[d] To get the feel of being Amish two of the members of the cast dressed in Amish garb, false beard, and straw hat and visited Lancaster and nearby villages. In meeting Amish people on the street nods were exchanged, but this was about as close as the imitators could get.

The most sensational of all the plays on the Pennsylvania Dutch is "Plain and Fancy." It has been playing on Broadway since February and seems to have promise of popularity for a long time to come.[e] This musical has been publicized widely through newspapers, television, and radio, and reviews of it have appeared in leading magazines. The play is based upon Lancaster County Amish. Broadway's formula is not necessarily to present people as they are, but its interest seems to deal with showmanship and lust without giving too much offense. Photographs show that the costuming is not at all genuinely Amish, and the music is jarring, brassy, and worldly for the most part. But the play does leave the impression that the Amish are admirable people, if one can overlook the hexing, shunning, and drunkenness which is what Broadway wants from the Amish. The most admirable part is a song "Plain We Live" sung by a chorus of farmers as a declaration of Amish principles. It is the best statement of Amish credo coming from a secular source.[f]

Brooks Atkinson, the seasoned *New York Times* critic, gives an admirable word for the Amish, but as regards the play he states that "the subject of the Amish is one that Broadway has not really mastered in Plain and Fancy."[g]

The Amish theme as a result of the play has invaded the fashion world. A fashion editor recently advised that any girl who wants to be different should try an Amish hairdo, or that the girl whose permanent is wearing out might be "very fashionable indeed" with an Amish hair style.

III

Another aspect of the public interest in the Pennsylvania Dutch is the trinket and gift shop trade, the commercialization of especially the Amish. There are

d. John Rengier, Howard Blankman, and Richard Gehman, *By Hex* (New York: Dramatist Play Service, 1956). *By Hex* appeared on the New York stage in 1956, one year after *Plain and Fancy*'s debut. Like *Plain and Fancy*, the plot revolved around the shunning of the Amish protagonist.

e. Written by Joseph Stein and Will Glickman, *Plain and Fancy* opened at the Mark Hellinger Theatre on 27 January 1955.

f. The text of "Plain We Live" was printed in a sidebar in the original publication of this article. Sung by Amish farmers, it contrasted mainstream American life (book learning, anxiousness, and war making) to Amish life (hard work, commitment to tradition, and peaceable living).

g. Atkinson's review was published as "Amish Musical Arrives," *New York Times*, 28 January 1955, 14.

not only a range of pamphlets on the Dutch from bundling to hex signs, but a whole configuration of crafts, handwork, ironwork, etc., in roadside Dutch gift shops.

What can one find by visiting several shops in and around Lancaster? First of all there are those traits of culture which belong to the "good old days" and they are not peculiar only to the Amish. Here are some of them: wheelbarrow, potbellied stove, frying pan, hand iron, trivets, coal bucket, rocking chair, footstool, corner cupboard, grandfather clock, well house and hoist with draw bucket, pitcher, horseshoe ash tray, chest, coffee pot, coffee grinder, wall telephone, wooden sink, and others. Anything which becomes out of date, or is taken out of usage in our society, becomes valuable as a trinket.

Also in those shops are traits of culture which are contemporary Amish: cast-iron Amish boys sitting on a bench, Amish dolls, Amish subjects on a swing, standing, sitting, carrying a pig, carrying a goose, carrying a bag, in a buggy, on a seesaw, milking a cow, smoking, and Amish figures used as cup and saucer, as designs on other dishes, flower holders, and in numerous other ways. Tulips, birds, hex signs, and other Dutch themes repeat themselves in various ways on many of these trinkets.

On many of these gadgets are choice phrases from Pennsylvania Dutch colloquialisms: "Ach Vell, chust help yourself"; "Look the window out and see who's comin' the gate in"; "Your secret is shut up in me like it was dead once"; "When you come up, come over"; "Ach don't be so dumb like"; "Save the desk once" (on an ashtray); "Life chust makes so fast"; "To school we must go yet."

For $3.95 one can purchase a forged horseshoe coat and hat rack "made exclusively for our customers by a local blacksmith from two pony shoes and one horseshoe such as the Amish use." An Amish 3–D jigsaw puzzle is made by a local craftsman and sells for $1.25. An Amish doll family with Papa and Mamma and Amos and Katie costs about $8.00. There are a host of other things advertised as "Amish Stuff"—Dutch talk tea towel, wall plaques, aprons, shoofly pie baked and shipped anywhere in the world, Amish candy, etc., etc.[h] What are people interested in? Some are interested in differences, in oddities, freaks, relics, ruins, and residuals, while others are interested in wonder phenomena, magic and mysterious acts. Some are honestly inquisitive, and those weary of life seek diversion in mass gatherings where their troubles disappear for a time.

Most people who think they are interested in the Pennsylvania Dutch are

h. One of the first Lancaster County tourist enterprises, Dutch Haven, sported large signs on its building advertising "Amish Stuff."

not interested in the Pennsylvania Dutch at all, but in a small segment of the Dutch. Technically speaking there are no Pennsylvania Dutch people, for they may or may not belong to Pennsylvania and they are not Dutch at all. The Pennsylvania Dutch, as they are popularly known, are a group of people (of Swiss, Alsatian, and Palatine origin) who earlier shared (and still share to a certain extent) a common variant of a High-German Rhinelander dialect, who settled in Pennsylvania in the eighteenth century and later.[i]

The Pennsylvania Dutch are in reality a very heterogeneous group of people. Some of them have almost nothing in common except that they live in the state of Pennsylvania. Religiously there are three general types of Pennsylvania Dutch: Church People, so called because the adherents belonged to established state churches (Lutheran and Reformed) when they immigrated; the Moravians; and the Plain People (also called sects). Each has formed a cultural pattern of its own and differs radically from the others.

Among the Plain People (so called for their plainness in dress) are the Mennonites, Amish, Dunkards (or Brethren), and the River Brethren. The Mennonites and the Brethren have lost most of their plain dress. Probably because of their persistency in keeping older dress and unworldly ways the Amish have gotten more attention than any of the Pennsylvania Dutch or Plain People's groups. They are currently photographed and popularized so much that most people think all Pennsylvania Dutchmen are plain. Naturally the public is more intrigued by beards, barndoor britches, and half-moon pies than by an obsolete Pennsylvania Dutch culture which is submerged in the broader American society. That explains why the Amish have gotten the most publicity.

IV

What is the effect of the public interest on the Plain People themselves? The public is demanding information and asking more questions than ever before, but most of the Plain groups have ignored such inquiries or passed them off lightly. The plainer the group, the more apathetic it is to any demands from the public. The Amish publish nothing about themselves for the outsider, in

i. Hostetler was correct that the Pennsylvania Dutch were "not Dutch at all" in the common sense of being from Holland. However, the term "Dutch" had been used since the eighteenth century to denote immigrants from the Rhine Valley, and in that respect the Pennsylvania Dutch were indeed "Dutch." See Don Yoder, "Pennsylvania Germans," in *Harvard Encyclopedia of American Ethnic Groups*, ed. Stephan Thernstrom (Cambridge: Harvard University Press, 1980), 770.

fact regard such activity as nonessential, and it is therefore left to the discretion of others.

Some complimentary things have been said about the Plain People. Here are just a few statements taken from feature articles: "Sturdy, apple-cheeked, severely dressed in black." They "did not know that their laborious conservation of barnyard manure and their century-old method of rotating crops was scientific until the schools of agriculture and the Farm Bureau came to tell them so." There is "admiration for their perseverance and hard work, [they] never speak about their religion, never moralize to others about theirs, and are very good helpers and neighbors." "The black-frocked, peace-loving people . . . are as picturesque as any in America." "There are no finer farmers in all the world than the Amish." "Behind their severity there is a solid culture that produces happiness as well as abundance." "Their religion keeps most of them firm in habits that anyone can regard with sincere respect."

Values such as these account for serious but detached interest in the Dutch. These qualities are what most people want, and many therefore respect the Plain groups for their disciplined values. These statements in turn make the Plain groups conscious of their mission in the world. It gives them a sense of importance and distinction and helps to thoroughly convince them that they must maintain their plain and separate culture. On the other hand, favorable statements from outsiders occasionally make some sectarian members proud and self-righteous about their way of life, and they thus contribute to the spiritual decline of their own group.

Some sociologists think that whenever the traits of a small group culture come to have a curiosity value within the larger society, it is an indication that the small group culture is disintegrating. A careful comparison of "Dutch" traits in gift shops and those in the "Dutch" society would probably show which of the culture traits are on the way out.ʲ

There are numerous illustrations from other cultural groups than can be given as examples. Cases in point are the Western Cowboy and the American Indian vestigials dramatized and reappearing in juvenile and leisure activity. Another example is rural life as a whole in this country. Rural traits of culture common fifty or a hundred years ago today have a curiosity value. The horse, the domesticated ox, open well, waterwheel, wagons, sleighs, kerosene lantern, sod or log houses, scythe, blacksmithing, rural costume, the country school, the country swimming hole, the old country store, and earlier farm implements—all reap-

j. The association of "curiosity value" with cultural disintegration was particularly prominent among those who studied Native American cultures. See, for instance, James Slotkin, *The Menomini Powwow: A Study in Cultural Decay* (Milwaukee, Wis.: Milwaukee Public Museum, 1957).

pear in modern themes in commercial gift shops, and in hundreds of other ways as reminiscent of bygone days. Though these traits have not completely disappeared, they are sufficiently scarce to become valuable as interesting curiosities by the larger society.

We conclude from this that the public's interest in the Pennsylvania Dutch is partly accounted for by the sociological disintegration of the Dutch groups. While disintegration may not be a direct cause of the public interest, there does seem to be an association between the two.

Twentieth-century man is culturally insecure and spiritually confused. Frustrated and basically rootless he retreats into the primitive and seeks new idols to take the place of the ones that seem to have failed him. He is in search of something he cannot seem to find. Modern man may be retreating from moral responsibility in the struggle for freedom from enslavement to himself. The American countryside, once a community of neighbors and friends who shared common social and survival problems, has now been translated into an individualistic and urban-like existence. Modern man has no roots in a community, and as David Riesman has pointed out, he lives with a crowd but is more lonely and more insecure than ever before.[k]

We as Pennsylvania Dutch groups are probably more inclined to overlook the basic and most important need of people who inquire of us. We are in great danger of smiling wryly at people's curiosity about our bonnets, beards, and cultural trappings, forgetting that their underlying need and frequently their desire is for knowledge of a spiritual life that leads to the eternal treasures of heaven.

---

k. Hostetler refers here to Riesman's book, *The Lonely Crowd: A Study of the Changing American Character* (New Haven: Yale University Press, 1950).

10

THE AMISH USE OF SYMBOLS AND THEIR
FUNCTION IN BOUNDING THE COMMUNITY (1964)

Published shortly after Amish Society, *"The Amish Use of Symbols" illustrates Hostetler's growing attraction to anthropology as he underscores both the roots and the functions of dress and grooming practices in Amish communities. In contrast to other interpreters, Hostetler refuses to attribute Amish dress and grooming patterns to biblical mandates, but rather locates these patterns in history. In some cases, he writes, the Amish embraced and then assiduously conserved European practices that their neighbors abandoned. In other cases, the Amish chose a visible path of resistance from the start, refusing to adopt European dress and grooming practices that were otherwise widely embraced.*

Whatever their underlying causes, these distinctive practices should not be regarded as trivial, Hostetler contends, for they serve as effective (albeit nonverbal) "means of communication" both to English outsiders and to Amish insiders. With respect to outsiders, Amish dress and grooming serve as buffers, communicating the practitioners' separation from worldly trends and fashions. With respect to insiders, dress and grooming patterns communicate differences between various Amish groups as well as an individual's degree of conformity to a given group. Hostetler admits that some Amish persons find this conformity stifling, a situation that compels some to transfer their loyalty to a different set of symbols. At the same time, the symbolic world of Amish society provides many Amish people with psychological and social support—a sharp contrast to modern industrial society, where symbols associated with dress often divide people from one another, foment competition between them, and contribute to status anxiety.

This article first appeared in the Journal of the Royal Anthropological Institute 94, no. 1 (1964): *11–22. All of the drawings accompanying the text are by Beulah Stauffer Hostetler; they appeared in the original, as did the captions. The article is reprinted by permission of the Royal Anthropological Institute and Blackwell Publishing.*

The Old Order Amish people in the United States and Canada have become increasingly known for their distinctive stable communities and their ability to resist the general cultural influences of the American society (Hostetler 1951). Amish farms have remained unmechanized and relatively self-sufficient while the typical American farm has become highly mechanized and dependent on outside sources for consumer products. Yet the Amish are efficient. The Amish community has remained a religiously oriented community, close to the soil, conscious of weather and nature, while in rural America there has been a tendency to accept secular orientations of the meaning of life and of overcoming the forces of nature with technology. While the modern scientific world is determined to use technical change and invention to make the world a better place to live, the Amish have turned from such goals to seek refuge in traditional and otherworldly sources.

In North America the Amish number about 20,000 baptized members of about 43,000 persons with their children. They have become extinct in Europe. They live in twenty states in the United States and in the province of Ontario in Canada, though eighty per cent of all Amish live in three states: Pennsylvania, Ohio, and Indiana. The Amish are descendants of Jacob Ammann, a Mennonite leader in Switzerland who led a successful division from the Mennonite group in 1693 to 1697, on issues that involved a more orthodox way of life, including the practice of shunning excommunicated members, of footwashing, and the wearing of distinctive traditional styles of clothing. The Amish like the Mennonites migrated to Pennsylvania (Smith 1929) from Switzerland and the Palatinate between 1727 and 1756, and from the Waldeck and Hesse-Cassel region in Germany between 1830 and 1850. From 1820 to 1860 many Amish from Alsace, Bavaria, and Montbeliard came directly to Ontario and to Illinois, Ohio, and Iowa. In all there are about fifty geographic settlements of Amish in America. Each settlement is composed of 'church districts', or congregational units of about ninety members, who meet for worship in their dwellings every two weeks. They drive horses instead of automobiles for transportation and maintain semi-closed communities through a spoken dialect known as 'Pennsylvania Dutch' which resembles a language used earlier in the Palatinate. Their population growth is increasing steadily even though many of their young people leave the Amish way of life. This comes about through large families and not by gaining any converts from their neighbours as the Amish do not proselyte or engage in missionary work.

The ability of the Amish to withstand the pressures of the American scene, urbanism, and technology, suggests that they use effective ways for maintaining group consciousness. The Amish are a multi-bonded group, sharing not only one but many ties in common. Some of these mechanisms of isolation have been reported by social scientists in the past (Kollmorgen 1942), but there has been little conceptualization of maintenance mechanisms. The Amish hold a number of shared mechanisms in common which tend to form a consistency of culture so as to provide for the elementary needs of the individual from the cradle to the grave. Some of these mechanisms are the following. The dialect used by the Amish provides a guide to a social reality that is different. All new members are their own offspring and they are assimilated gradually by a majority of the older members. Physical property, including farms which were the abode of the forefathers, and preference for certain soils and topography come to have sentimental attachments. Common traditions and ideals which have been revered by the whole community from generation to generation embody the expectations of all. There are formal church rules which guide the members in their conduct with each other and with outsiders. The specialists, the lifetime ordained persons, carry on the functions of the church and enable it to act as a unit in maintaining separation from the world. The size of each Amish church district is kept to a minimum which enables the group to function as a small, informal, and informally controlled church, whereas largeness would make consensus more difficult. There are special means to resist shock such as mutual aid activities in times of fire, death, and sickness. The Amish baby grows up strongly attached to those of its kind and remains indifferent to contacts outside its culture. These maintenance mechanisms, when integrated, are effective in maintaining continuity.

There is another means whereby separatism is maintained which has been largely overlooked by students of Amish life. I refer to the use of visual symbolism in maintaining psychological boundaries. Symbolism provides a basis for action in meeting the future, it assures both group unity and longevity (Langer 1948). The Amish person is born into an environment which gives him symbolic and spiritual support. A symbol is a visible object that represents an idea or a quality. Symbols are intensely operative in both religious and secular social movements. Christianity, for example, in its earlier stages utilized effectively the representations of the fish, the dove, the lamb, and many other symbols.

The Amish cannot adopt the symbols of world civilization because they are not in sympathy with the 'world'. Symbols in world society, such as cathedrals, skyscrapers, automobile styling, or even ensigns displayed on the coat, they would not adopt as their own. How do folk societies, or a simple religious society such as the Amish, work out their symbolism if they cannot take their cues from the industrialized world?

The writer of this article was raised in an Amish family, but left the Amish culture at the age of seventeen to acquire an education. Following his doctoral programme he devoted some time to the observation of Amish life from the vantage point of a scientist. By bringing both personal experience and scientific method to bear on the whole question of personality and culture, and of marginality, considerably more insight can be brought about than by use of only personal experience or scientific method alone. In this article the writer wishes to advance the hypothesis that visual symbols, especially those associated with dress, serve the group with effective mechanisms for maintaining group consciousness and for integrating the charter values of the sectarian society.

Symbolism performs the function of language. Where life is governed by signs and symbols fewer words are needed for adequate communication. No two languages are sufficiently similar so as to represent the same social reality.[1] Symbolism along with language is the channel by which beliefs and attitudes are communicated to the growing child, clarifying the place one is to take in adult life and in the community. Symbolism is an effective means of communication to the outsider, but even more effective to the insider. The symbols distinguish the conformist from the nonconformist. Associated with these symbols are some linguistic, ritualistic, and small group principles that powerfully condition Amish life.

In Amish life, dress becomes highly symbolic of one's attachment to the group, and of one's place within the society.[2] There is not just one culture trait, as black broad-brimmed hats for men, or black shawls for women, which become important but the whole style and complex of dressing is symbolic to all members. Styles of dress were not enacted and formally agreed upon when the Amish originated, but they are the product of convention and institutionalized behaviour patterns resulting from long periods of association. Consensus on the symbols is achieved by intimate informal small group associations over long periods of time. Material differences become symbolic in that those who conform are ranked highest by members of the community. Dress becomes identified and integrated with a total way of life.

In this paper we shall discuss the symbols of Amish life as manifest in dress. There are many other in-group symbols to be sure, but the manner of dressing becomes one of the most important entities of group consciousness and awareness. Here we shall examine Amish grooming and dressing in some detail, noting especially its symbolic and sociological function in bounding the community. The treatment will also throw some light on the origin[3] of Amish styles of dress as diffusion phenomena of past cultures.

THE BODY

The Amish do not disfigure the body. Tattooing is not allowed, nor the ornamentation of the body with cosmetics, bracelets, and jewelry. The only exception is that people may wear rings as a treatment for rheumatism, but this is

FIG. 10.1 Contemporary Amish hair style.

functional and not ornamental. The hair of the women must be long and un-cut, parted in the middle only, and combed down the sides. Girls' hair from infancy is braided and with adolescence is put up in the back. The beard must begin to appear at baptism for Amish men though the young men during the courtship period manage to keep it very short. At marriage they dare no longer to trim it.

In 1525 when the Anabaptist brotherhood originated, and for several decades thereafter, the beard was commonly worn by men of all classes except the Catholic priests. As early as 1568 the Anabaptists passed a resolution forbid-ding the trimming of the beard and hair 'according to worldly fashions'. After the French Revolution, Napoleon's soldiers began wearing moustaches with-out beards in order to look more fierce. At about the same time, and probably in reaction to this practice, both the Mennonites and Amish began shaving their upper lips. Both groups wanted nothing to do with the military. Both groups have consistently opposed the moustache down to the present time. On the other hand, many men during the last century with no Amish affiliation wore beards and shaved their upper lips, as photographs in museums will show. But the Amish so consistently and uniformly followed this practice that this type of beard became known colloquially as the *Täuferbart* or Anabaptist beard (Umble 1955–9).

The Amish men today wear their hair bobbed (Fig. 10.1). It is cut below the ear or slightly above the ear lobes, depending on locality, and never shin-gled. The hair length is an index to the conservatism of the group. This hair

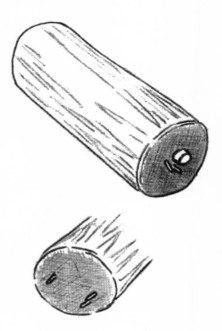

FIG. 10.2 Instrument used in Europe (nineteenth century) for making hooks-and-eyes.

style was common in the eighteenth century and the Amish have retained it. An Amish member makes himself subject to the sanctions of the church by wearing his hair too short.

HOOKS-AND-EYES

Buttons appeared as ornaments in the thirteenth century and the ruling classes began to use them functionally to fasten their garments a century later. Hooks-and-eyes preceded buttons, which were for some time regarded as ostentatious by non-cosmopolitan people. The Amish, supporting this view, rejected them. Like all people of earlier times, the Amish spun their own cloth and made their own clothes and fasteners. A few Amish grandfathers in America still pass the time by making hooks-and-eyes (Fig. 10.2) but most of the Amish buy their supply at the store. Buttons have made inroads into Amish dress as they are worn today on trousers, shirts, sweaters, and, in some regions, on overcoats. Some groups permit buttons on work jackets but in all Amish groups the coat and vest on the Sunday dress must have hooks-and-eyes. In fact, all Amish today wear buttons, but tradition has prescribed where and when.

FIG. 10.3 Amish broadfall trousers.

TROUSERS

The homemade trousers of the Amish men are sometimes called broadfall trousers. They also are an adaption of Old World styles. Amish trousers do not have a fly-closing, but a latch which buttons at the sides and along the front waist, something like sailors' pants (Fig. 10.3). Unbuttoned, the latch hangs down, which probably explains why the trousers were nicknamed 'barn-door pants'. The trousers are held around the waist by a three-inch band that buttons in front. In the Palatine this style of trouser was common. The latch was called *Latz*, *Faltäre*, or *Klappture*. The latch of the Palatine style was narrower than that of the Amish today. Broadfall trousers were still worn in the Palatinate about sixty years ago. The *Lederhosen* in Germany still have the *Latz* (Fig. 10.4).

The common practice of wearing knee-length breeches during the eighteenth century was drastically changed by the French Revolution. The breeches were rejected along with the aristocracy by the revolutionary soldiers who wore long trousers. The Amish eventually adopted the long trouser, although breeches are known to have been worn by the Amish in Europe and by some of them when they came to America.

Regionalism among the Amish is expressed in the way a man's trousers are held up. The number of suspenders, how they are made, and the way in which they are worn become symbolic of belonging to this or that Amish group. Such differences also serve to distinguish one kind of Amish from another in the same locality as in Mifflin County, Pennsylvania, for example, where there are nine different groups of Amish and Mennonites. Here the most traditional of all Amish groups, the Old School (nicknamed Nebraska Amish), forbid

FIG. 10.4 Modern *Lederhosen* of Germany.

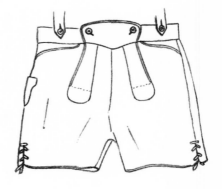

the use of all suspenders. Trousers are held up by means of a laced-up crotch at the rear of the broadfall trousers. The Old or Byler group (nicknamed Bean-soup Church) shared this ban on suspenders until recent years when it permitted the same practice as the Renno group, one homemade black elastic suspender fastened by a single button at each end. The Speicher group permits the use of two plain suspenders, including the privilege of store-bought suspenders, crossed at the back. Preschool boys of the 'one suspender group' may wear their single suspender with a large slit through the middle to allow the head to come through which keeps the suspender in place. The Swartzen-druber Amish, the most formalistic group in Ohio, wear two suspenders but instead of crossing them they must form a 'Y' at the rear. These forms have given rise to nicknames among the Amish: 'One Suspender Amish' or among the Amish *Schwentzli*, meaning 'tail', and 'Two Suspender Amish'. They are highly symbolic of group identity and illustrate the slowness and unequal way in which culture changes.

Palatine trousers were worn without suspenders in the sixteenth century. Suspenders were worn by commoners in the seventeenth century, both the single and double style. In the Rhineland suspenders were often made and decorated by the girls who gave them to their boyfriends as betrothal gifts.

THE HAT

Hats, like the length of the hair, distinguish the Amish man from the outsider. They also symbolize status within the group. When a boy at the age of two leaves behind a dress to wear trousers for the first time, he must also have a stiff jet-black hat with three or more inches of brim. One firm manufactures twenty-eight different sizes and nearly as many styles of Amish hats. The bridegroom in Pennsylvania gets a 'telescopic' hat which is worn during the early married years. Grandfather's hat has a four-inch crown and a four-inch brim. The bishop's hat has a 4½–inch crown, slightly rounded, and a wide seam around the brim. The 'stovepipe' hat with a slightly different shaped crown is worn by the rank and file of Amish fathers. While the outsider may regard these differences as trivial, this is not so to the insider. These are symbols which communicate whether people are fulfilling the expectations of the society. A boy who wears a hat with too short a brim is liable for sanction. The Old Order Amish are in the same way distinguished from more progressive groups by the width of the brim and the band around the crown. Thus when my father's family moved from Pennsylvania to Iowa, one of the first adaptations made was to cut off some of the brim. This made us acceptable to the new community but at the same time typified other changes that were in the making.

A black hat with a low crown and wide brim was worn by the peasants of the Rhineland and also by the waggoners, or teamsters, from Lorraine. The brim was flappy and was sometimes worn folded under in one or more ways. When folded up on three sides it was given the name *Nebelspalter*.[4] It also became the soldiers' hat and later, strangely enough, the hat of the Amish.

THE COAT

An Amish man has three types of coats, a jacket or vest which is worn under the Sunday dress coat, a *Wamus* or ordinary coat for work or dress, and a *Mutze* which is worn to church after baptism. Again, all of these have special significance in that there is a proper time and place to wear these garments. All have hooks-and-eyes with the exception of some who permit buttons on work coats, which appears to be the first step of departure from the old order.

All of these garments were common in Europe (Becker 1952, p. 82) and they have been retained with modifications. A short jacket had been worn for centuries. The *Wams* (or *Wamus*, in Pennsylvania Dutch) was a popular coat for young and old made of dark blue cloth and worn over the vest. The collar became wide and sometimes stood up, then it was called *Kummetkragen*, or horse collar. The nineteenth-century immigrant Amish men wore modest collars on their coats.

The *Mutze* is the distinguishing apparel of the baptized Amish male. He may appear in full dress with a *Wamus* when he goes to town, when he visits his relatives, but for preaching he wears the *Mutze*. This garment is longer than the ordinary coat and has a split tail in the back. It signifies full obedience to the church, and of course to the baptismal vow. Why this particular style rather than any other became a distinctive church garment, can scarcely be explained. Here is a custom which also had its origin in the ordinary dress of the Rhineland. The *Mutzen* or *Swilchmutzen* (long *Mutzen*) as it was called was made of bleached linen or hemp and was worn at home and at work. In the northern part of Alsace, especially when lined in red, it was almost like an elegant garment.

In full dress, the shirt of an Amish person is only slightly visible. The old line Amish use homemade patterns that call for no collar and the buttons appear only halfway down the front. The shirt is put on by slipping it over the head. In Europe the shirts were made of linen, therefore white in appearance. There is still a group of 'Old School' Amish who ban all other colour but white for shirts, even for work. Most Amish wear white shirts on Sunday but blue also is common.

WHITE CAPS

A most distinguishing feature of the Amish woman's costume is the white cap or *Kapp* worn on her head. Girls from the age of about twelve to marriage wear a black instead of a white cap for Sunday dress, and a white one at home. The cap is worn at all times, except for sleeping, and in some homes there are even special sleeping caps.

Amish caps are very similar to those worn by Palatine women during the nineteenth and as early as the fifteenth century (Becker 1952, pp. 44, 84, 90, 108). (Compare Figs. 10.5 and 10.6.) In Europe this headpiece was called *Häubchen*, but there were other local and regional names within the Palatinate such as *Kappe*, *Ziehaube*, and *Nebelkapp*; dialect names given it were *Betz* and *Saumagen*. The caps in the western part of the Palatinate were always white. The *Ziehhaben* (draw-bonnets) were the counterpart of the Amish bonnet today as they were drawn over the cap[5] (Becker 1952, p. 118).

In the Palatinate only married women wore the *Häubchen*. Girls sometimes carried wreaths or flowers on their heads on very special occasions, but not until marriage (unless they reached the age of about forty without marrying) were they permitted to wear caps. The expression *unter die Haube kommen* (to come under the cap) meant that a girl was to be married. Though the Amish headpiece of today has undergone some changes in detail, the pattern is essentially the same as that worn by the Palatine women of earlier centuries.

FIG. 10.5 Amish *Kapp*, *Halsduch* and *Läpple*.

Regional variations in style, colour, and design of the caps in Germany were so distinct that one scholar mapped the Palatinate by the kind of caps worn by the women. Today the Amish caps in Pennsylvania are different from those in Ohio and elsewhere. While the cap is essentially the same in all Amish communities, these slight variations are important ways in which one community or one kind of Amish is distinguished from others (Hostetler 1963, p. 137).

Among the American Mennonites of Swiss origin the cap has become a 'prayer cap', or 'prayer veiling', as it is often called. When the Mennonite women began to adopt the prevailing styles of headdress in America in the nineteenth century, the Mennonite leaders began to point out the significance of women having their heads covered. Wearing this cap is given religious sanction with Paul's teaching to the church at Corinth: 'But every woman that prayeth or prophesieth with her head uncovered dishonoureth her head.'[a] With some Mennonite women the cap is still a part of the ordinary household dress but with most it is worn only at times of public worship. With the Amish it is a matter

a. 1 Cor. 11:5 (KJV).

FIG. 10.6 *Kapp* worn by Palatine women about 1800. (Adapted from Becker, p. 88.)

of custom to wear the cap. However, when Amish life begins to change generally, then there is a tendency to justify the cap for religious reasons as do the Mennonites. As an effort to develop a conscience against bundling and immoral courtship, one Amish writer stated that when the head covering is removed the power which a woman ought to have is also gone.

THE CAPE

Women's dress is generally a bit more colourful than that of the men, as there is more variation in solid colours. One-piece dresses are made from traditional patterns, and over the bodice an Amish woman wears what she calls a *Halsduch,* which plain Mennonite groups call 'a cape'. In the Palatinate this was called *Brusttuch* or breastpiece (Becker 1952, pp. 90, 132). (See Fig. 10.7.)

The *Halsduch* is a triangular cloth about thirty inches long. The apex is fastened at the back and the two long ends go over the shoulder and after embracing the front, are pinned around the waist. These garments also distinguish married women from the unmarried and the old from the young. Girls wear white capes and white aprons for Sunday which are fastened to their dresses with numerous straight pins. Married women wear capes and aprons which match their dresses.

FIG. 10.7 *Halsduch* of Palatine women of about 1850. (Adapted from Becker, p. 4.)

THE *LÄPPLE*

The *Läpple*, or bustle, is the Amish counterpart of *Lappen* or small flap (Fig. 10.5). Amish women in Pennsylvania and other parts of eastern United States wear this mysterious small flap at the rear of the waist. Not even the Amish women can tell why they wear it except as a fulfilment of tradition. It has no apparent function other than ornamental, but it does have a striking symbolic value.

The bustle is clearly a carryover from a European usage. The *Lappen* in Europe was an extension of the bodice or jacket (Fig. 10.8) and extended down over the waist from four to six inches (Becker 1952, p. 129). The apron strings were sometimes tied over it. In the Rhineland and in Alsace this overlap extended all round the back if not the whole of the waist.

The Pennsylvania Amish have retained a small *Läpple* only at the back. It is no longer an extension of the bodice, but a rounded piece of cloth fastened to the skirt instead. The more progressive Amish have abandoned it altogether. There are regional variations in the width of the *Läpple*. An almost infallible rule is that the width of the bustle varies in direct proportion to the conservatism of the Amish group. A woman wearing a wide *Läpple* is supposed to be more *demutig* (lower or conservative) than one wearing a very small and

FIG. 10.8 Palatine counterpart (about 1810) of the
Amish *Läpple*. (Adapted from Becker, p. 89.)

abbreviated one. When the *Läpple* is explained to the midwestern Amish, they
are surprised to learn of this custom and usually reply, 'it is nonsense'.[6]

THE SCOOP STRAW HAT

One of the oldest survivals of European dress is the 'scoop hat' worn by the
'Old Schoolers' of Mifflin County, Pennsylvania (Fig. 10.9). This group has also
retained other older traits of dress and still do not allow the white cap nor the
bonnet. Instead, these women wear a black kerchief on the head which was a
Palatine custom (Becker 1952, p. 123). In Ontario the Amish wear a black
kerchief over the white cap.

   This homemade straw hat, having a crown of about one inch, and a wide
floppy brim, is bent down at the sides and tied with ribbons under the chin.
Upside down, this hat resembles a hand scoop for shoveling grain, hence 'scoop
hat'. It is still worn in the field for making hay just as it was in the Palatinate
in the sixteenth century (Becker 1952, p. 126). These hats were also used widely
in Alsace and Switzerland. The girls at Weissenburg wore them on top of their
small white cap. It was common earlier to wear a felt hat of similar design in
winter.

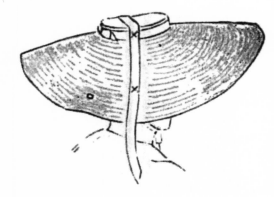

FIG. 10.9 The eighteenth-century 'scoop' hat still worn by some Amish.

The flat hat was widely used in the United States among the Amish as far west as Iowa but also in Ontario.[7] In the twentieth century other headgear, mainly bonnets, took its place.

SYMBOLIC CHANGES AND STRESS

We have shown how in the Amish society the symbolic channels of communication function in maintaining separatism and continuity. These symbolic representations are today fixed upon the people and their dress as distinct from the rest of the world. The language of dress forms a common understanding and mutual appreciation among those who share the same heritage. To the outsider, however, and to people of diverse heritages the symbols are difficult to understand and thus communicate very little. The Amishman in turn has difficulty accepting the symbols of the outside world. They are a constant reminder of danger to him.

But the same symbols which give momentum to Amish life become divisive factors with the appearance of subgroupings within an Amish community. For example, of five Amish groups in one area with slightly differing dress, each 'looks at the church above with suspicion, and the church below with compassion'. When a different set of symbols capture the loyalty of a group of Amish, let us say young people, then there are grounds for misunderstanding. Physical isolation and homogeneity of culture go together and a close correlation exists between them so as to make them one. If we take isolation and homogeneity of a folk culture as the independent variable, we may expect to find with the loosening of isolation such dependent variables as disorganization, individualization, and secularization of culture. The signs and symbols of Amishness, in other words, function at their best in a physically isolated as well as psychologically isolated community.

Disorganization comes about with the lessening of physical isolation as the outside world encroaches upon the small isolated community. As a result there is contact and linkage between the Amish and the surrounding world. In this way the traditional symbols come to have diverse meanings to the folk of the community. When Amish culture changes it does so unevenly. Machines, for example, are accepted more readily among the Amish than are those social practices which usually go along with the machine civilization. This unequal change in numerous and very obvious illustrations shows cultural lag. In some Amish communities we find an extreme phase of lag which we call formalism. The removal of traction wheels from a new tractor which is used only for belt power is one example. Evidence of unusual lag in the many folkways and mores that still persist long after the Amish people have ceased to have faith in their value. When conservatism and traditionalism are excessive as is the case in some Amish communities, intellectual stagnation for the rising generation is usually the result. Conflict between the members of one phase of Amish culture and the supporters of another then become inevitable. The laggards and the reactionaries then oppose the progressives, and this furnishes the climate for a breakdown in culture and a regrouping of the folk society.

SUMMARY OBSERVATIONS

The development of symbols in this small religious sect group is associated with intimate associations over long periods of time, probably under conditions where physical isolation and little mobility is possible. It was in the New World that the Amish for the first time became conscious of a distinctive, uniform dress, different from that of their Scotch, Irish, Huguenot, Quaker, and other neighbours. As protection against change and absorption in the 'melting pot', they 'froze' the costume which they brought with them to the shores of America. The practice served well to perpetuate their closely-knit communities in America.

The world in which the Amish live is different from the non-Amish or 'English' world, as the Amish call it, and is so represented by the symbols. It is not merely the same world with different labels attached. The Amish maintain a symbolism which embodies a social reality, a way of life that teaches how people should live and what they should believe. Group symbols strengthen a culture, but when language changes the symbols also change. When the Amish person loses his Pennsylvania Dutch dialect and takes on the English language he loses the symbols and the social reality which they represent. Not only the Amish but many linguistic groups know how difficult it is to change their language without losing their way of life or their religion.

This limited study suggests that there exists an essential difference between symbolism in a civilization and symbolism in a folk culture (Ortega y Gasset 1957, Chapter 11). In a simple society symbolism has its origin in informal associations rather than in formal processes. The symbolism of the Amish is achieved neither by parliamentary processes nor by voting. Custom and conformity to traditional ways of doing things determines the symbol. The symbols of our progressive civilization are derived from speculation, from formal and rational procedures, from scientific pursuits, from economic competition, and from the signs of material achievement. Slogans, trade marks, flags, and laws arc enacted deliberately and rationally. In Amish society the symbols are the products of intimate human association, of consciousness of kind (Cooley 1915, p. 23) and not the result of rational processes. This is well illustrated in the style of dress of the Amish in that a whole complex of dressing becomes formalistic and symbolic of a total way of life.

A final observation is that in Amish society the symbolism centres not upon human achievements, whether economic or material, but upon the people themselves and upon their dress. It is indeed interesting that a society which places emphasis on personal trustworthiness and religious devoutness should inadvertently centre its symbols in styles of clothing.

REFERENCES

Becker, Karl August. 1952. *Die Volkstrachten der Pfalz*. Kaiserslautern.

Cooley, Charles H. 1915. *Social Organization*. New York.

Hostetler, John A. 1951. *Annotated Bibliography on the Amish*. Scottdale, Pa.

Hostetler, John A. 1959. *Amish Life*. Scottdale, Pa.

Hostetler, John A. 1963. *Amish Society*. Baltimore, Md.

Kollmorgen, Walter. 1942. *Culture of a Contemporary Rural Community: The Old Order Amish of Lancaster County, Pennsylvania*. U.S. Dept. of Agriculture. Washington, D.C.

Langer, Susanne K. 1948. *Philosophy in a New Key: A Study in the Symbolism of Reason, Rite, and Art*. New York.

Ortega y Gasset, José. 1957. *Man and People*. New York.

Smith, C. Henry 1929. *The Mennonite Immigration to Pennsylvania in the Eighteenth Century*. Norristown, Pa.

Umble, John S. 1955–9. Art. 'Beard', in *The Mennonite Encyclopedia*. Scottdale, Pa.

NOTES

1. Edward Sapir makes this point in *Selected Writings of Edward Sapir* (University of California Press, 1949), p. 162. Folk or primitive mentality relates action not only to a direct end as we perceive it, but also to rite, taboos, and decorative art of a religious and symbolic nature, as reported by Franz Boas, *The Mind of Primitive Man* (1911), pp. 198–99. A deviation from customary meanings and from the performance of customary acts creates strong sentiments of abhorrence. Sigmund Freud (*Totem and Taboo*, 1918) recognized the psychological character of ritual and taboo not as purposeful in themselves but as motivating a feeling of compulsion. Acts are performed from a sheer inward need. Highly spontaneous acts that represent taboo and conformity are normal in a folk society.

2. The scholarly work of Don Yoder, 'Plain Dutch and Gay Dutch: Two Worlds in the Dutch Country', *The Pennsylvania Dutchman* (Summer 1956), recognizes the function of dress among the 'Plain People'. Although climatic conditions are underlying factors in the amount of clothing required by most human societies, it becomes one of secondary importance among the Amish. See James B. Kelly, 'Heat, Cold and Clothing', in *Scientific American* (February 1956). John C. Wenger, 'Dress', in *The Mennonite Encyclopedia,* provides additional sources.

3. Fortunately the history of Palatine costume is well documented. Karl August Becker (1952) represents not only the work of his own lifetime, who was aged eighty-five when the author met him in 1954, but also his own father who made costume his special interest. On seeing photographs of contemporary American Amish styles Becker excitedly noted likenesses and elaborated on the evolution of Palatine styles. Palatine dress differed according to region and social class so that one cannot say that the Amish styles are typical of the whole range of Palatine ways of dressing. Like other facets of social change, borrowing in this instance is selective. Traces of Alsatian and Swiss usages may also be found among the Amish.

4. The word *Nebelspalter*, literally meaning 'to cut the fog', is an interesting description for a hat. With brim folded under on the sides its appearance was high and sharp and looked distinctive. The women later used the name *Nebelkappen* for a distinctive cap.

5. Doubt has been suggested by some scholars as to whether the Amish brought the bonnet to America. The work of Becker leaves no doubt that the bonnet, or at least its forerunner, was common among the Palatines. Other treatments of bonnet history are: Mary Jane Hershey, 'A Study of the Dress of the (Old) Mennonites of the Franconia Conference 1700–1953', *Pennsylvania Folklife* (Summer 1958); Priscilla Delp and John A. Hostetler, 'History Makes Bonnets', *Christian Living* (December 1955); and H. S. Bender, 'Bonnets', in *The Mennonite Encyclopedia.*

6. The irrationality of custom becomes apparent in this instance as has been observed by sociologists in other societies, particularly by Emile Durkheim.

7. The 'flat hat' has been called various names: 'scoop hat', 'skimming-dish hat', 'beaver hat', 'shaker hat', and various nicknames.

11

PERSISTENCE AND CHANGE
PATTERNS IN AMISH SOCIETY (1964)

This essay, which recapitulates important analytical elements of Amish Society, *was reprinted in a variety of venues. The basis of its popularity is clear. In addition to being readable, it summarizes Hostetler's foundational argument about the Amish "charter" before proceeding to a lively discussion of factors that challenge conformity to the charter. Filled with well-chosen illustrations narrated in Amish voice, the essay provides readers with an intimate but discreet view of the tensions that stress Amish society.*

Although the essay was reprinted as late as 1990, some of its claims would become dated during Hostetler's career, most notably his assertion that nonfarming occupations are "marginal" to Amish society. Moreover, Hostetler's contention that the Amish "are less and less able to satisfy the psychological and social needs of their individual members" appears to have overstated the actual trajectory of Amish life, which remained remarkably stable over the course of his career. It is conceivable that Hostetler's boyhood experience contributed to his grim assessment, particularly in light of the fact that this statement appears in the essay's section on "the forbidden fruit" of higher education. Of course, even Hostetler admits (early in the essay) that his analysis of Amish life is drawn in part from his own experience "as a participating member of the culture." Later in the essay, he underscores his personal experience again, though this time as a scholar of Amish life. In a section on Amish singings, Hostetler notes that Amish boys are often suspicious of English boys who crash their parties, adding with a wink that these young boys are not unlike their elders who "are wary of the outsider who wants to write a book about them."

This article first appeared in Ethnology 3 (1964): 185–98. *It is reprinted by permission of the Department of Anthropology at the University of Pittsburgh.*

The student of human society finds explicitly developed moral postulates in human institutions which Malinowski (1944:52) calls the "charter." The charter is "the system of values for the pursuit of which human beings organize." It is "an organized system of purposeful activities." In Amish society behavior is oriented to absolute values, involving a conscious belief in religious and ethical ends entirely for their own sake and independent of any external rewards. This orientation to *Wert-rational*, or absolute values, as Max Weber (1947:305–306) states it, requires of the individual unconditional demands. Regardless of personal considerations the members are required to put into practice what is required by duty, honor, personal loyalty, and sacrifice. Behavior is tradition-directed by unwritten norms. In Amish society there is an almost automatic reaction to habitual stimuli which guides behavior in a course which has been hallowed by the habit of long experience.

The consistency of "charter" in Amish society has been noted by a number of social scientists. Gillin (1948:209–220), for example, has termed the Amish culture "remarkably compatible with the various components of its situation." Kollmorgen (1942:105) observed that the integrative aspects of the culture "must have qualities that make for survival." Huntington (1956:introduction) states that in Amish society "Each community is integrated, but not self contained." Freed (1957:55) has noted the absence of class differences in Amish society as a factor in the acceleration of change.

The generalization that the Amish are a stable people, consistent in their moral values, has led to several misconceptions and overstatements about Amish social organization. One recent source (Schreiber 1962:58), for example, states that "juvenile delinquency is unknown among the Amish." Consistency of major points in the charter does not mean that Amish life is relatively free from stress, sustained personal conflicts, or rebellious behavior.

It will be the purpose of this paper to develop five elements in the Amish charter which demonstrate a high degree of consistency. They are formulated from careful observation in a number of contemporary communities, from the original documents (Gascho 1937), and from personal experience as a participating member of the culture. Second, evidence for sustained personal conflicts in this seemingly "remarkably compatible" culture will be presented. The evidence is based upon depth interviews with Amish and former Amish persons and reveals stress patterns of the following character: thwarted motivations for higher education, the practice of marginal occupations, the presence of suicidal behavior, and rowdyism. Third, it will be shown how persons with unresolved personal conflicts make meaningful contacts with out-groups by means of acculturation agents.

THE CHARTER

Separation from the World. The doctrine of separation is an expression of the Amish view of reality, which is one of "nonconformity to the world." The conception of reality is conditioned by a dualistic view of human nature. Although the natural, "created" world is amoral, the world of man is categorically divided into the pure and impure, light and darkness, and the powers of good and of evil. Separation from the world is based upon this dualistic conception of reality, and it is expressed in life situations, in ecology, and social organization. Separation is furthermore based upon explicit scriptural passages which validate the practice: "Be not conformed to this world . . ." and "Be ye not unequally yoked together with unbelievers."[a] The ark of safety for the member is within the community, and not outside of its beliefs and customs. This doctrine forbids marriage with outsiders, it prohibits members from establishing business partnerships or sustained associations with outsiders, and it keeps intimate human associations within the ceremonial community.

Biblical Tradition. The whole of the Old and New Testaments, in the German language, and to some extent the Apocrypha as well, constitute the sacred writings for the Amish. The codifications and moral principles have their basis in the teachings of Christ and his proclamation of a kingdom. The Amish have perpetuated the teachings of the sixteenth-century Anabaptists from whom they are direct descendants, having been an offshoot of the Swiss Brethren in the late eighteenth century.[b] Some of their teachings and practices are taken literally from scriptural texts, e.g., the refusal to retaliate or bear arms, to swear oaths, or to hold public office, the observance of adult baptism, the footwashing ceremony, and mutual concern for the aged and poor. They refuse to accept or to pay social security on the grounds that it is insurance; they pay taxes without qualms of conscience, but compulsory insurance is another matter. The vow of baptism involves not only confession of faith in the Trinity but the promise to remain in the narrow path of "obedience" to the rules of the believing community.

The Ordnung *or Rules of Order.* The rules of order of the church are clearly understood by all baptized members, and the individual is committed not only to obedience but to active maintenance of the rules. Marriage, always occurring after baptism and not before, admits the individual to even greater responsibility for promoting and "building the church." The body of rules and traditions which govern behavior are rarely specified in writing; they are essentially a body of sentiments and taboos intimately shared among the members. The rules are taken for granted, and it is usually only the questionable or borderline issues which are specified in the "examination" service preceding the semiannual communion service. A change in the rules, either toward relaxation or formalization, requires a members' meeting where each person is asked to give assent to the unanimous recommendations of the ordained functionaries. The bishop is, of course, the spokesman. The rules are not strictly the same in all communities. Those which are most nearly universal in the

a. Rom. 12:2 and 2 Cor. 6:14 (KJV).
b. The Amish emerged in the late seventeenth century, not the late eighteenth century.

twenty states where the Old Order Amish live are the following: no electricity, telephones, automobiles, central heating systems, or tractors with pneumatic tires; beards but no moustaches for all married men; long hair (which must be parted in the center if parted at all); hooks-and-eyes on dress coats; and the use of horses for farming and for travel within the community. No formal education beyond grade eight is also a rule of life.

Meidung *or Shunning.* Shunning is a technique of keeping the fellowship "clean" or purged from habitual transgressors. Although a means to an end, it is so important in the total life of the society that it becomes prominent in the charter. Shunning is applied after the offender has been formally excommunicated from the fellowship by vote of the assembly. In such a state the transgressor cannot enjoy normal relations with other members of the church. He may not eat at the same table in the home. Married couples may not sleep in the same bed, and church members may not receive gifts or favors from one who is under "the ban." The offender can be restored if he so desires after a period of shunning by confessing violation of the taboos and by expressing repentance. A member can be excommunicated not only for lying or for adultery but also for buying an automobile, for possessing a driver's license, or for cutting the hair too short. Persons who voluntarily leave the church to join more relaxed groups, such as factions who drive automobiles or Mennonite groups, are excommunicated and shunned for life. They are regarded as "vowbreakers" and apostates. Members are in duty bound to regard them in this way, and any member who sides with the offender is also excommunicated. Shunning is regarded by the "strict" Amish as absolutely essential as a disciplinary measure. That it should continue to be rigidly practiced was one of the main issues on which the Amish separated from the Swiss Brethren.

Agrarianism. The Amish worldview is conditioned by firsthand experience with nature. The ordered seasons, celestial objects such as the moon and stars, and the world of growing plants and animals provide the Amish with a sense of order and destiny. Hard work with the soil, where muscles and limbs ache from daily toil, provides human satisfaction. All family heads are required to limit their occupation to farming or to closely related activities such as operating a sawmill, carpentering, or masonry. Hard work, thrift, and social concern for the believing community find sanction in the Bible. The city by contrast is held to be the center of worldly progress, of laziness, of nonproductive spending, and often of wickedness. Man occupies his right place in the universe when he is caring for the things in "the garden," that is, the plants and animals created by God. The Amish agrarian experience for several centuries has been conducive to isolation characteristic of the ideal-typical folk society

(Redfield 1947:293–308), which greatly strengthens their religious outlook on life.

The above five elements of the Amish charter demonstrate a high degree of consistency and integration. Contradictions of belief appear to be at a minimum. Agrarianism, for example, is compatible with the doctrine of separation from the world. Conformity to absolute values is expressed by adherence to the biblical formulations as interpreted by the functionaries. Powerful social controls are exercised through institutionalized rules (*Ordnung*) and shunning (*Meidung*) of offenders.

HIGHER EDUCATION: THE FORBIDDEN FRUIT

Despite the internal consistency of the charter, an increasing number of Amish persons find meaningful and satisfying experiences outside of the Amish society. As the American rural community becomes more urban the Amish, with their small familistic type of society, are less and less able to satisfy the psychological and social needs of their individual members. When individuals find personal fulfillment outside of the Amish community the relationship to the traditional community is altered. As marginal persons they frequently experience great personal stress; the individual is no longer sure of himself or of the values which he has traditionally held. Problem areas then arise within the society which threaten elements within the charter. Families who live on the fringe of the larger settlements of Amish appear to be exposed to greater stress than those living in "solid" communities.

One of the areas of internal conflict is the desire of young people to obtain education beyond the elementary grades. Attendance at high school is prohibited by the Old Order Amish, and such ambitions are blocked. The increased emphasis on education in American society as a prerequisite for adult living makes learning very attractive to the Amish boy or girl. The following life-history documents reflect the rewarding experiences of outside learning and show how such satisfying behaviors are legitimized to other members of the Amish society.

Our first case is that of an ex-Amish person whom we shall call Sam. Sam recalls his early interest in schooling, leading to his decision to enter college:

> I always loved school from the day I started. My parents didn't start me until I was seven so I wouldn't have to go to high school. They thought I couldn't learn very well, and I wanted to show them I could.

When my mother was young she taught school. She wanted to go on to school but never had a chance. I sort of caught this desire from my mother. It made me mad when my father kept me home for a day's work. Sometimes, when I was to stay at home, I would switch into my school clothes at the last minute and get on the bus.

Sam was adept in making friends at school and during his last grades in school, he said, "I hated that I came from such a backward family." His animosity over his backwardness grew as he learned to know his classmates and especially a certain non-Amish girl.

We were always the top two in the class. I could beat her in arithmetic, but she always beat me in reading. It was always tit for tat between us. We were always together in those early years. I always hated that I was an Amishman. My older brother was a "good boy" and listened to daddy but was always getting into trouble. Sunday after Sunday I would go to church, and all we would do after church was sit out in the buggies and tell filthy stories. I was the cockiest guy, I guess, as I was more or less the leader of our group of boys. My, how I used to get whippings from my father. I hear other people brag how they thank the Lord for their whippings, but mine just did not make sense.

With the completion of grade school Sam wanted to go to high school but could not. "I felt there was nothing to do but stay home and work for Dad till I was twenty-one. My life was terribly lean during those years." Sam was baptized in the Amish church. After he reached legal age he was exposed to a wider association of friends, most of them Mennonites. Following his release from service he entered a Mennonite college. Although for some years he attempted to retain his Amish affiliation, eventually he became a member of the Mennonite Church.

Another case is that of Rebecca, who turned from her Amish background at the age of eighteen without having been baptized.

I read a great many books and anything I could get my hands on. I tried to persuade my father to let me go to high school. But he would not. After grade school I was Amish for another six years, and this was a very difficult time in my life. My dissatisfaction began to show in physical ways. I had no energy. I was anaemic. Nothing interested me. I didn't fit in with the Amish young people, and I sort of despised them for their lack of learning. I made attempts to be popular among the Amish and dated a few times, but I didn't like it very much. I was pretty lonely, and it was a very miserable time for me. I was the oldest of eight, and mother kept on having children. This tied me down, and I was constantly resenting this. I was always running away to read, and I hid books. When mother was not watching I would read everything I could.

When I was eighteen, I thought mother had reached the age when she could have no more children. Finally, I thought I could begin to see daylight, have a little more time to myself, and keep the house neat without working so hard. Then I learned that mother was pregnant again, and this was the last straw. I simply could not face this. I went to the basement and just cried. I told father that I had had enough, I was leaving. While I was packing my suitcase, mother became upset. Father knew that mother needed my help. So we worked out a compromise. Father said if I would stay until the baby was born, the next year I could go to Bible school. This was enough for me; then I could get away and go where there was a library and read.

A third case is that of a lad whom I shall designate as Chris.

I wanted to go to high school so badly that I remember crying about it, trying to persuade my parents. They gave us county-wide achievement tests after grade eight, and I found out I was the highest in the county. I competed from grade one through grade eight very closely with a girl who went on and became valedictorian. In the accumulative tests which included all eight grades I had all A-plusses except two. My principal talked to my father several times and told him I had possibilities. I was only fourteen, so my father made me repeat the eighth grade the next year. After getting all A-plusses in grade eight I barely got As the second time. I was very athletic, though, and even though I was not going on to high school the principal let me go all out for athletics. All the time the kids and neighbors (non-Amish) wanted me to go on to high school. In my second year in the eighth grade I quit when April came because it was time to start plowing. I went home, and I remember how terrible I felt.

With all his chums now in high school, the lad returned to the principal and explained his painful experience. The principal gave him ninth grade books, and Chris promised that he would study them and appear for the semester tests.

I hardly touched the books, but I took the first semester test and got all As and Bs. But I finally gave up and returned the books. But I knew I would never stay Amish because the principal convinced me the Amish should not keep their children home from school. He told me I had brains. He told me I could be more than a farmer.

Such experiences frequently result in a reconsideration of the basic provision of the Amish charter which unilaterally forbids any formal training beyond the elementary grades. The Amish leaders know that they must consider the problem of finding teachers for their own private schools in areas where school consolidation has been put into effect. So long as the one-room public school served the Amish, they did not need to face the problem of securing teachers. Presently there are about 150 privately operated schools whose teachers are Amish, most of them offering no more than an elementary education. The realization that education is needed to prepare teachers for their own schools has helped to legitimize the teacher role. A few members have entered college for preparation without bringing upon themselves the sanctions of *Meidung*. The role of these persons as agents of change within the Amish society may have the effect of modifying the charter in the future.

MARGINAL OCCUPATIONS

The Amish charter requires that persons aspire to be laborers on farms and eventually farm owners. Investigation of current occupations reveals exceptions to this rule. Old Order Amish girls who have taken training as nurses have not remained Amish. There are no Amish physicians, and this role appears not to be a likely one. One unusual occupation is that of an Amish girl who is employed as a registered technician. She completed high school by correspondence, and by borrowing books from a local high school she qualified for a high school certificate. She had always anticipated the vocation of nursing. Upon counseling with a Director of Nursing, she learned that a professional uniform would be required for a trained nurse and that no exception could be made. She knew that she could not remain loyal to the Amish church if she followed this vocation, so she began training for work as a technician. She commuted to a college and completed the required courses. As a registered technician she is not required to wear white shoes or white stockings, and she may wear a white coat over her Amish uniform while on duty. The hospital officials have been very cooperative in helping the girl find security in her new vocation. Safeguards were taken not to give publicity which would jeopardize her relationship to the Amish church. When photographs of her graduating class appeared in the papers, for example, hers was omitted. Her Amish friends believe that, if she keeps the *Ordnung* otherwise, she may be able to continue her profession.

Sickness, incapacity, or chronic illness of a family head may lead to marginal occupations of a nontraditional type. Daniel, a man in his fifties, always loved farming. According to a neighbor, "He has been in many things." As a result of an accident in his youth, "he had surgery done on his head and has suffered many headaches since. He has taken many pills from different doctors, which now affects his heart." Besides being a sales agent for seeds, which allows him to travel in many Amish settlements, he also has been engaged in dynamite blasting as custom work. In this business he served as a supplier of dynamite for hardware stores in his region of the state. He ordered the dynamite by carload lots and stored it in a stone quarry on his farm. This occupation was perhaps more compatible with farming than many.

The question may be raised why Amish persons who are really marginal remain within the Amish community. One young Amishman, after many years of trying to remain loyal to the Amish faith, gave up, saying, "I would rather be a conservative Mennonite than a liberal Amishman." But many who are allowed to exercise a small degree of marginality prefer to remain with their kin and community. A marginal occupation may be tolerated by the community so long as it does not constitute a direct threat. However, when a person takes his marginal occupation seriously and wishes to excel, as in nursing, teaching, or business, the stresses created tend to exceed the limits of toleration.

Marginal persons who persist in their deviation, as in the cases above, frequently become effective agents of change. They create favorable attitudes toward behaviors usually forbidden. An Amish father who invokes no sanction against his son for buying an automobile becomes an innovator. Family heads who merely refrain from taking negative sanctions against violators are in a favorable position for introducing change, especially if they are from families of high status. Agents of change may accept the goals of their society but use other than institutional means for achieving the goals.

SUICIDE

The frequency of suicides, even in the face of strong biblical injunctions against taking life, suggests the presence of unresolved personal conflicts. While most common among single unmarried Amish males, suicide also occurs among adults who occupy key positions (Hostetler 1963:283). Two well-informed persons in one community could recall fifteen suicides, fourteen of whom were males and most of them under the age of 22. This period in life appears to be the most crucial for acceptance or rejection of the basic values of the culture. Persons "without values" (Durkheim 1951) to direct a course of action revert to apathy and despair. Anomic suicides reflect one aspect of personal disorganization. Religious functionaries who are charged with maintaining the *Ordnung* are subjected to extraordinary role stress. The threat of strong negative sanctions for suggesting alternative courses of action contributes to anxiety and conflict in persons charged with maintaining the norms.

One of the most dramatic instances of suicide was that of a very prominent leader who hanged himself to the surprise of the entire Amish community. The reason for his sudden "disgraceful act" remained a mystery to his kin and his close friends. Upon close examination of the case it is clear that the ordained man was caught between contradictory expectations.

The rate of suicide among the Amish may be higher than that of the rural United States population in general—possibly even as high as that for rural Michigan (Schroeder and Beegle 1953), which exceeds that of the urban population. This impression derives from a survey based on the memory of informants in one large community, but we shall not know conclusively until a complete investigation has been made. The Amish would need to have but four suicides per year to approximate the rate for the United States at large (10.3 per 100,000).[c]

ROWDYISM

"Running wild" is tolerated in the normal life of the young unmarried adult male. The number of young persons who defect permanently varies considerably with each community. After marriage the individual generally conforms to the rules of the community and accepts seriously the norms of its culture. Before marriage, however, there is a great deal of rowdyism and other forms of antisocial behavior in reaction against the traditional norms. This has become

c. In 1986, Hostetler coauthored an article with Donald B. Kraybill and David G. Shaw that concluded that the Amish suicide rate in Lancaster County was higher than the Lancaster County rural average for the forty-year period from 1944 to 1983. However, the same study indicated that the Amish suicide rate had dropped dramatically over this period, and for the last decade (1974–1983) was significantly lower than average. See "Suicide Patterns in a Religious Subculture: The Old Order Amish," *International Journal of Moral and Social Studies* 1 (1986): 249–63.

especially manifest in the largest Amish settlements, where it is associated with the relaxation of traditional controls.

The geographic boundaries of the community have expanded beyond the limits encompassed by a horse and buggy. This poses no problem for the adult ceremonial community, which has explicit recognized boundaries. But for the young people of courting age there are no geographic boundaries. One result has been the development and differentiation of informal special-interest groups, especially in connection with the institution of Sunday evening "singings." Sharp differentiations are expressed in the names and modal behavior of the various "singings." According to one young man:

> The Groffies are the most liberal, then the Ammies, and then the Trailers. Each has a number of subgroupings and interests, and under the Groffies, for instance, there are the Hillbillies, Jamborees, and Goodie-goodies. The Hillbillies occupy the hill country, the Jamborees are the most unruly, and the Goodie-goodies are so called because they are the Christians.

These groups maintain social distance and display various forms of antagonism. "There are times when one gang has cut the harness of another to pieces, or they have unhooked the horses of the others and let them run off." Differentiation is also expressed in patterns of smoking, entertainment, dating, and the use of automobiles.

Indulgence in antisocial acts, within the religious community as well as outside of it, occurs with greater frequency as individuals experience problems of stress. Stealing chickens or grain and selling these products, or trading them for a dance floor for a night, is not unknown. One juvenile said: "We used to see who could do the best job of swearing and being the biggest blow gut. If there was anything daring to be done, I had to show the boys I had the nerve to do it." Problems associated with drinking alcoholic beverages have come to the attention of the wider community. There have been a number of arrests of Amish for violation of the liquor laws. After complaints from neighbors, the police conducted several raids on Sunday night singings. On one occasion, officers reported more than a dozen cases of empty beer bottles, and several youths were arrested for drunkenness. Although parents are concerned about the mischief of the boys, they appear helpless. After one arrest at a singing, an Amish father said: "What can I do? I know it's wrong for minors to drink beer, but the boys would get down on me if I didn't allow it."

Outsiders are not welcome at Amish singings and are chased off the grounds if not invited. One outsider, who was a farmhand but had worked for an Amish family, decided to attend a nearby singing. He was surrounded by a score or more of Amish boys and was accused of wanting their women and of spying. He did not escape without a beating. Just as the staunch Amish are wary of the outsider who wants to write a book about them, so the young too are suspicious of the stranger as a possible intruder.

ACCULTURATION AGENTS

After a period of permissive "wildness" the typical Amish young man returns to a state of conformity, for baptism and marriage, and to serious observance of the moral postulates of the society. Those who cannot or will not be induced to accept the basic elements in the charter usually make successful linkages with outsiders who bridge the gap between the Amish and the surrounding alien culture.

Acculturation agents are those non-Amish persons outside the Amish society but adjacent to it who are in unique positions to assist the marginal Amish person, e.g., members of nearby churches, physicians, businessmen, officers of the law, and neighboring farmers. They are the middlemen who mediate between the small and the great society.

To obtain a valid driver's license (forbidden by the *Ordnung*) an Amish youth must have some kind of assistance before he applies for a permit at the police headquarters. Usually he will have learned how to drive an automobile from a friend or relative in the Amish Mennonite religious group, or in some cases from an employer if, for instance, he has been employed by a non-Amish construction firm. Amish youth who wish to qualify for college entrance frequently fulfill their high school requirements by taking special examinations administered by the state. Assistance in applying for the proper forms and in acquiring the knowledge and tutorial instruction necessary to pass the examinations is often obtained from a school principal or a non-Amish friend.

Owing to their ignorance of the ways of the outside world, the Amish are sometimes exploited by outsiders, e.g., by charging an exorbitant price for an automobile. Automobile salesmen, salesmen of musical instruments, insurance salesmen, and issuers of driver's licenses do business secretly with young Amish people so that their parents and the public do not discover such activities and the special procedures involved. When Amish youth are arrested or convicted, their names are often withheld from the newspapers if they request it. Frequently a postman or mail carrier will hold certain mail until he sees the recipient personally, so that parents will not be aware that a family member has received a forbidden item such as an insurance policy or a driver's license.

Young Amish men who have been stopped for speeding, or for legal charges having to do with the condition of an automobile, e.g., a faulty muffler, are known to have been released because a police officer "favored" or was in sympathy with them. Many have passed driver's examinations with a little bribery. Some examining officers have the reputation among Amish youth for passing them easily on driver examinations. Even persons under the legal age have been issued licenses, as well as trustworthy youths who have not had adequate driver training. In return for pies, rolls of bologna, and home-cured hams these "agents" provide licenses under conditions which Amish youth can meet.

There are gasoline service stations which permit Amish boys to park their automobiles with them. One used car salesman allows boys to keep their autos on his lot when they are not driving them on the understanding that they will buy the automobiles from and service them with his firm. A number of service stations receive much Amish patronage on weekends.

Increasing numbers of Amish youth, minors included, patronize bars and liquor stores because they are trusted and favored by many outsiders and rarely cause trouble. In general, the Amish young people enjoy an excellent reputation among outsiders because they are usually honest and industrious. There appear, however, to be a few outsiders who cooperate with the elders and parents to keep the young people "in line."

For those who leave the group, making the initial break with the culture takes place in a number of ways and is usually an adjustment to stress. Some run away from home without making a successful contact with outside reference groups. A boy aged sixteen suddenly disappeared one Saturday afternoon. The first sign of his leaving was the discovery of his Amish hat a mile away from home. The father was alarmed but could do nothing but wait hopefully. The next day a neighbor received a phone call from a large city stating the exact place where the runaway boy could be picked up. The boy had discarded his Amish clothing, had his hair cut in a barber shop, and traveled to the city, then became despondent and gave up. Unknown to any of the family members the boy had entertained the notion of running away for many months as a result of an unhappy encounter with his father.

Four Pennsylvania boys, two of whom were members, made their departure after midnight by walking and thumbing their way to Ohio. The first sign of their leaving was the discovery of their long shorn hair in an upstairs bedroom. Within two weeks all were back in their native community, though not all returned to their homes. Two of them joined the army, and the other two soon

married girls outside the Amish faith. A former Amish father, when asked
why boys sometimes run away, said:

> Who wouldn't? All the teaching they get is *Attnung* [*Ordnung*] and
> the command from their parents "*Du bliebst Deitsch*" ["You must stay
> Dutch"]. Parents are too rigid in their demands and punishment. My
> brother ran away from home last year, and I can tell you why. Dad was
> awful rough with him. He gave us boys one licking after another. Even
> when I was eighteen he tried to lick me, but that's when I said, "It's
> enough." I didn't let him.

Slipping outside the Amish community with intent to return appears to be
more common now than in former years. As outside pressures exert themselves
on small neighborhoods, and as young members have more and more knowledge about outside affairs, "having a fling" with the world and returning has
become institutionalized. Thirty or forty years ago it was not uncommon for
two or more Amish persons to go west and work their way with the harvest
from Texas to North Dakota. They usually returned and after marriage settled
down as members in the Amish community.

Two brothers purchased an automobile "to see the world." One of them said:

> We traveled all over the United States and visited practically all the
> states. We just cut a huge figure eight all over the United States. We
> were interested in traveling, and we told our parents, and then bought
> a car. We each had a half share and after returning I sold my share.

The boys left in the spring and returned in the fall.

Another type of exodus is typified by a boy who left as usual on Monday
morning for work on a nearby non-Amish farm.

> I did not want to leave this way, but I decided I would write my par-
> ents a letter after I was away so they wouldn't need to worry about
> me. I stayed away several weeks. Then, because I was not of legal age,
> I got a warning from the courthouse. I told my boss I did not think
> the warning meant anything because I was sure my father would not
> go to law. Then in a few days I got a phone call from my dad, and he
> asked if I am coming home. I told him I would come home to visit
> but I didn't feel too welcome. I said I could not stay home. So he said
> he would have to go to the courthouse. Then I knew he was not kid-

ding. My boss went to the courthouse to find out what would happen. He found out they could only take me home, but they could make it bad for him as my employer. So I left his place and on the advice of a friend went to Florida. While down there I also got a warning from the courthouse, so I went to see them about it. They said Florida authorities could do nothing, but the Pennsylvania authorities could come and get me, but it would cost them a lot of money and they probably would not. After they heard my story, they told me not to worry.

Another young man gave the following account:

I did not run away at night. After my father accused me of something I had not done, I just put on my old straw hat and walked down the road. I wanted to join the army but was too young. I worked for an English farmer not far away who hated the Amish. My father saw me in town one day and asked me why I don't come home. I said, "I'm not coming home now nor will I ever come home."

The young man then joined a traveling medicine show which visited his home town.

They needed a boy to help. Of course I was interested. I had read a lot about circuses, so I joined the show. We traveled all over the state. I ran the popcorn machine, took the tent down, and cleaned up the papers and mess afterwards. The show did not get into any of the Amish communities. I would sell tickets at the door, and if the ropes needed tightening I did that. On my birthday the recruiting officer got in touch with me. I left and joined the service.

CONCLUSION

The Amish charter embodies elements which tend to be consistent with each other. But consistency does not assure conformity. Amish life is not free from personal stress and sustained conflict. The experiences related in the above case materials reveal problems of thwarted motivation and problems of socialization common to marginal persons. The role of "agents of change" within Amish society and of "acculturation agents" outside the society gives rise in multiple ways to meaningful personal contacts in the larger American society. Alterations of behavior patterns occur, forcing a reevaluation of the charter. Unless the charter is reinterpreted, inconsistencies develop between doctrine and practice, and these may lead to anomie, fragmentation, and demoralization. The central doctrines remain essentially the same, but the applications change. Separation from the world, for example, remains a central doctrine, but slight modifications in dress, in mechanization, and in other living habits occur in the process of solving the existential problem and of coping successfully with the environment.

The Amish response to change, especially when it threatens the charter, characteristically takes the form of fragmentation and division over what appear to the outsider as hairsplitting issues. Divisions are rarely peaceful or the result of deliberations. Instead, the relations between different ceremonial groups are commonly characterized by *Meidung* and animosity. Some settlements have as many as five different kinds of Amish, with different symbolic behavior systems, who practice ritual avoidance in relation to all others. These subsystems function so as to prevent further change. Each group expels its marginal persons and controls marriage and intergroup associations. The large number of small and extinct communities of Amish is evidence of such fragmentation (Mook 1955; Umble 1933).

But extinct settlements do not mean failure of the community—only failure of its spatial dimension. The Amish take their social institutions with them to other areas where group fulfillment can be successfully resolved. Complete disintegration is rare, for staunch families generally migrate if they dislike their community or the conditions in it. Migration is frequently the only alternative for those Amish who wish to shun all progress. Amish who cannot put up with change frequently sell their farms and move to other settlements, often across state lines. Those who moved from Pennsylvania to Ontario in recent years said: "We want to go back fifty years; things are going too fast there." Thus a father faced with the possible threat of the automobile or the tractor may write to an uncle or a distant relative in another state and ask, "How are things there?" In prospecting for a new location, the strictness of *Ordnung* there is as important to him as the price of land.

Migration, for the Amish, is one of the most important factors in resisting acculturation. Freed (1957:55) has observed that specialists and class differences are essential to the maintenance of the Jewish *shtetl* of Eastern Europe. By contrast, the Old Order Amish, who have no occupational class differences and no specialists, are able to survive by migration. Had they not migrated from Europe to America they would have become extinct long ago. Indeed, those who remained in Europe have coalesced with other Protestant sects or with Catholics (Hostetler 1955). Migrations are normally directed to new localities rather than old ones, but there is also constant family mobility between communities.

All cultures exert pressures on the individual, and in Amish culture, as in that of French Canada (Hughes 1943:216), such pressures generate feelings of resentment. Like the French Canadians, the Amish have not had to absorb their own "misfit people," their own "toxic by-products." Their misfits and marginal persons, following their excommunication by the Amish, are absorbed by neighbors of other religions. Discontent finds expression in a variety of complaints, and rowdyism has exceeded institutionalized boundaries and become a serious problem. Marginal personalities have emerged among individuals who have identified themselves with the dominant out-group but have encountered relatively "impermeable barriers" (Kerckhoff and McCormick 1955:54).

Amish communities, like other separatist communities, find themselves in a problematic situation. Amish society is faced with the problem of community self-realization and personal fulfillment for each new generation of members born into it. The problem must be solved within the range of its limited potentialities and by means of its available natural and human resources and its own unique local heritage. The constant striving to achieve the goals of the charter has given rise to distinctive patterns of deviancy and stress.

BIBLIOGRAPHY

Durkheim, E. 1951. *Suicide*. Chicago. (Original edition, 1897).

Freed, S. A. 1957. "Suggested Type Societies in Acculturation Studies." *American Anthropologist* 59:55–68.

Gascho, M. 1937. "The Amish Division of 1693–1697 in Switzerland and Alsace." *Mennonite Quarterly Review* 11:235–266.

Gillin, J. P. 1948. *The Ways of Men*. New York.

Hostetler, J. A. 1955. "Old World Extinction and New World Survival of the Amish: A Study of Group Maintenance and Dissolution." *Rural Sociology* 20:212–219.

———. 1963. *Amish Society*. Baltimore.

Hughes, E. C. 1943. *French Canada in Transition*. Chicago.

Huntington, G. E. 1956. "Dove at the Window: A Study of an Old Order Amish Community in Ohio." Unpublished Ph.D. dissertation, Yale University.

Kerchoff, A. C. and T. C. McCormick. 1955. "Marginal Status and Marginal Personality." *Social Forces* 34:48–55.

Kollmorgen, W. M. 1942. "The Old Order Amish of Lancaster County, Pennsylvania." United States Department of Agriculture, Rural Life Studies 4:1–105.

Malinowski, B. 1944. *A Scientific Theory of Culture, and Other Essays*. Chapel Hill.

Mook, M. A. 1955. "A Brief History of Former, Now Extinct, Amish Communities in Pennsylvania." *Western Pennsylvania Historical Magazine* 38:33–46.

Redfield, R. 1947. "The Folk Society." *American Journal of Sociology* 52:292–308.

Schreiber, W. I. 1962. *Our Amish Neighbors*. Chicago.

Schroeder, W. W., and J. A. Beegle. 1953. "Suicide: An Instance of High Rural Rates." *Rural Sociology* 18:45–56.

Umble, J. S. 1933. "The Amish Mennonites of Union County, Pennsylvania." *Mennonite Quarterly Review* 7:71–96, 162–190.

Weber, M. 1947. *The Theory of Social and Economic Organization*. Glencoe.

12

THE AMISH WAY
OF LIFE IS AT STAKE (1966)

Published one year before the founding of the National Committee for Amish Religious Freedom, "The Amish Way of Life is at Stake" demonstrates Hostetler's willingness to advocate for Amish causes and his ability to reach popular audiences. In this particular instance, the cause was Amish educational practices that violated Iowa state regulations. More specifically, the Amish of Buchanan County, Iowa, unable to secure certified teachers for their private schools, nonetheless refused to send their children to the consolidated town school. Local officials sought to compel compliance, first by fining Amish parents, then by forcing Amish children onto a bus bound for the consolidated school. The latter incident received wide publicity and led to intervention by Iowa governor Harold E. Hughes, who mandated a cooling-off period. In 1967, the Iowa legislature amended its school code, allowing religious groups to apply for exemptions from certain educational standards.

Hostetler's advocacy work would increase in the years ahead. In addition to helping found the National Committee for Amish Religious Freedom, Hostetler served as the committee's expert witness in a variety of legal proceedings. Most significant in this regard was Hostetler's testimony in Wisconsin v. Yoder, *a compulsory school attendance case that wound its way to the U.S. Supreme Court, which ruled on behalf of the Amish defendants. Hostetler's anthropologically informed testimony was crucial in these cases, for he effectively underscored the integrity of Amish opposition to certain government mandates. As he notes in the article below, Amish resistance to these regulations should not be construed as stubbornness or selfishness, but rather as rational, religiously informed opposition "based on integrated principles and on a background of almost two centuries of sociological experience."*

This article first appeared in Liberty, *May–June 1966, 12–13. Copyright © 1966 John A. Hostetler. Reprinted by permission.*

The conflict over the Amish school issue fills me with mixed emotions.

I can sympathize with the educational spokesmen, for I am an educator.

I can also sympathize with the Amish, for as an Amish boy, religion was important to me.

I can sympathize with the local persons who are inclined to think that stubbornness rather than religion is the real issue.

Perhaps most of us can appreciate the problem faced by Governor Hughes, who must manage the peacekeeping function between people who feel so strongly in opposite directions.[a]

By birth I was Amish and for twelve years I tilled Iowa soil. Against the mandates of Amish culture I attained an education and have taught in several universities. I have conducted research among minority groups in the United States and Canada.[b]

The Amish opposition to education, however stubborn and economic it may appear to those who are not Amish, is based on integrated principles and on a background of almost two centuries of sociological experience.

A whole way of life for them is involved if education goes beyond the limits of conscience and if education is taken over by a secular system. Studies conducted in underdeveloped countries, and American communities, reveal that the high school is indeed the most effective leveler of human beings. The transition from a rural to an urban society is made complete with the consolidation of schools. The Amish know intuitively what scientists know empirically, that their way of life is at stake.

Faith, farm, and family are the three postulates in the Amish charter. Farming in a simple and modest way is a focal point in their religion. The Amish religion demands the loss of land, goods, or self, for conscience sake if required, without retaliation through legal means or by force. If the Amish man must lose his Iowa land, his faith requires that he accept the consequences as the judgment of God upon him for the price of faithfulness.

The issue is not a question of law, but of the interpretation of the law. A law requiring certification of teachers is based on the assumption that the proper amount and kind of courses will serve the public good. Those requirements represent the collective judgment and ignorance of educators and lawmakers. What group of experts is sufficiently learned to know when a teacher should be certified to teach and what courses are the best ones in teacher preparation?

But the law requiring minimum standards for teachers is, nevertheless, essential with its limitations. It has a purpose and an intent, for it provides a guide or baseline for the common good. But the law must be interpreted with a knowledge and understanding of cultures if it is to maintain its function.

Some laws, like stopping at a red light, must be widely understood and made

---

a. The reference here is to Iowa governor Harold E. Hughes. For a detailed consideration of the Iowa conflict, see Donald A. Erickson, "Showdown at an Amish Schoolhouse," in *Public Controls for Nonpublic Schools*, ed. Donald A. Erickson (Chicago: University of Chicago Press, 1969), 15–59.

b. Hostetler's advocacy on behalf of religious minorities included the Canadian Hutterites as well. See "Hutterite Separatism and Public Tolerance," *Canadian Forum* 41 (1961): 11–13.

absolute if they are to achieve their intended good. In the area of values, religion, and education, laws (if made) require interpretation and a latitude of understanding if their intent is to achieve the public good.

A sufficiently broad understanding of the certification law would take into account the following knowledge as applied to the Amish culture:

1. The Amish are a culture group whose religion pervades all aspects of their life.
2. The Amish are changing their culture pattern at a slow but voluntary rate. This voluntary rate of change is retarded by enforcement of laws affecting religion and values. Amish youth who are highly motivated will break with their culture and continue their goal of higher education. Community studies show that as high as one-third of the offspring do not join the church of their parents.
3. The Amish educational ideals are not in conflict with those of the larger society.
4. The public good is served if the illiterate and the disadvantaged are brought to enlightenment and self-help through state laws. The public good is not served if the same law forces people to violate their religion, their morality and their nativistic and economically self-sufficient institutions.

The fear of some that if the Amish do not come up to minimum standards, then the door will be open to all kinds of cults and disorderly groups who want to evade education, has little ground. Pennsylvania has no certification requirements for teachers in private schools, but asks only that instruction be in the English language and in subjects approved by the state.

Although we have our share of lawless people, they are not the Amish, who have maintained freedom of religion, as well as the assets of a nativistic culture, which is no small contribution to our American life.

13

OLD ORDER AMISH CHILD REARING
AND SCHOOLING PRACTICES: A SUMMARY REPORT (1970)

From 1966 to 1969, John A. Hostetler and Gertrude Enders Huntington received funding from the U.S. Office of Education to explore Amish socialization practices (Huntington did most of the fieldwork, frequently living with Amish families and schoolteachers). Their study had a very specific goal: to provide a scientifically grounded rationale for exempting the Amish from certain state educational mandates that, in their view, threatened the future of Amish society. "It is astonishing," Hostetler wrote in 1968, that so little research had been done on this problem. More specifically, little effort had been made "to look at the problem from the level of culture and personality," and "to find out if there is a 'way of life'" that justifies Amish resistance to broad societal mandates regarding education ("The Amish Socialization Study: A Research Project," Mennonite Quarterly Review 42 {1968}: 69). *Hostetler and Huntington's research sought to correct that deficiency.*

The following article summarizes the results of their research (for a more detailed account, see their book Children in Amish Society: Socialization and Community Education, *published in 1971). In it, Hostetler outlines the cultural assumptions that informed Amish educational goals, delineates six life cycle stages in which Amish socialization occurred, and reports findings from various personality and educational skills tests. In the end Hostetler deems false the assumption that schoolchildren educated in public schools are higher achievers than privately educated Amish children. Moreover, while admitting that Amish schools do not enable their students to pursue certain vocational paths, Hostetler argues that Amish children "are not deprived of meaningful aspiration and participation in the goals of {Amish} culture." All told, Hostetler and Huntington built a convincing case for Amish exceptionalism, a case that was affirmed in 1972 by the Supreme Court's* Wisconsin v. Yoder *ruling.*

This article first appeared in Mennonite Quarterly Review 44 (1970): 181–91. *It is reprinted by permission of the* Mennonite Quarterly Review.

The problem of schooling in Amish society is particularly instructive to those who are concerned with education in culturally different communities as distinguished from culturally "deprived" communities. Several previous studies have advocated special programs for the Amish pupils or have advocated forced assimilation. The purpose of the present study was not to resolve the policy conflict of the Amish school versus the public school, but rather to understand the life participation level of Amish schooling in the context of their own culture by examining such questions as: How do Amish children perform in the light of their own cultural goals and values? In what ways do they differ from other children in their capabilities and learning patterns? These and related questions were explored in a research project covering a span of thirty-eight months ending August 31, 1969. (The project has been explained in the [*Mennonite Quarterly*] *Review* of January 1968, pp. 68–73.) The purpose of this report is to present a brief summary of the major findings. Greater detail is available in the final report.[1]

GOALS AND METHODS

The investigation had four specific objectives: (1) the formulation of their basic beliefs with respect to their view of child nature and the education of children; (2) the construction of the age categories as defined by the culture with a description of the socialization practices; (3) the discovery of the achievement levels of schoolchildren on standardized tests; and (4) the development of generalizations with respect to changes in the social patterns affecting the education of children in "traditional" and "emergent" lifestyles. The methods very briefly were as follows:

To construct the basic beliefs (charter) with respect to the view of child nature, historical (from the sixteenth century) and contemporary source documents were examined for the range of Amish conceptions of human nature and child nature. The underlying assumption is that every culture provides guidelines for child rearing and that these guidelines can be constructed, whether the society be literate or nonliterate. A bibliography of source materials ranging from the sixteenth century to the present time was carefully examined, and conclusions are presented in the form of postulates with respect to the Amish view of child nature.

Observation and description of socialization practices required participant-observation in Amish communities. As a resident in the community the anthropologist member of the research team occupied a farmhouse, identified with a specific family, its network of kinship and visiting patterns, ceremonial activity, and the daily routine of farm and community activities.[2]

A sufficient number of schools and communities cooperated to facilitate the study of the performance of pupils on carefully chosen standardized school tests. A basic criterion for the selection of the tests was that they be "proven" and suitable for normal and "healthy" children rather than those which measure deviant or abnormal traits of personality. Random sampling of all Amish pupils was obviously impossible, but every effort was made to acquire representative groups of schoolchildren in the various grades and desired categories. Representativeness was recognizable on the basis of affiliations within communities, size of school, and experience of the teachers, and agricultural or nonagricultural features of the community. The fourteen Amish schools tested were located in Ohio, Indiana, Michigan, Iowa, and Ontario. The control group consisted of pupils in modern rural public schools, selected for their social and economic similarity to the Amish schools.

In addition to a control group of non-Amish children, sample populations were tested in four additional social contexts: (1) Amish in all-Amish public schools; (2) Amish in private (parochial) schools; (3) Amish in public schools with non-Amish; and (4) non-Amish in public schools with Amish.

The pupil sample sizes varied with the type of test and are given in the discussion.

FINDINGS: THE VIEW OF CHILD NATURE

An extensive examination of the sources was made for both the European period (from about 1525 to 1780) and for the American period (1780 to the present). Postulates[3] derived from the European sources indicate a view of child nature as follows:

1. All human nature is believed to be inherently carnal (evil), but children are believed to be in a state of innocence, having potentialities for good.

2. Parents are responsible for training their children and are morally accountable to God for teaching them right from wrong and for transmitting to them a knowledge of salvation.

3. Children are urged not to be idle but to learn to read and write so that they may acquire a knowledge of the Scriptures. Learning manual skills that are useful for making a living is encouraged along with literacy.

4. Children during their age of innocence are regarded as pure and not in need of ceremonial baptism. Should they die in their innocence, original sin[a] is not imputed to them on account of the

---

a. Here Hostetler is contrasting the Amish to other Christians who believe(d) that unbaptized children, because of the stain of "original sin," were subject to God's judgment upon death.

death of Christ. Their entrance into adulthood and into the church-community is through a knowledge of the Scriptures, followed by faith, and finally by baptism after attaining adulthood.

5. Obedience to parents and ultimately to God is a cardinal virtue. Children are not to be self-willed, but well-mannered, quiet, and humble in the presence of others.

6. Acceptance of mature social responsibility is through total commitment to a believing church-community, materially and spiritually separated from worldly standards, including association and marriage with other members of the believing community, and a personal willingness to suffer persecution or death in order to maintain the faith.

An analysis of the sources from 1780 to the present resulted in the formulation of these additional postulates:

7. Although children are believed to have an inherited sinful nature through no fault of their own, they are loving and teachable, and with the proper environment are capable of assuming responsibility to God and man for their actions by the time they become adults.

8. As a learner, the child is viewed as a passive receptor of correct attitudes and facts. Independent thinking and inquiry are encouraged so long as such thinking does not challenge the basic religious values of the culture. How children learn is of less direct interest than what is learned.

9. The family and—to a lesser extent—the school are believed to have the primary responsibility for training the child for life. Limited individualism is encouraged within the concept of faithful adult behavior as the model for the child. It is believed that the child must have an explicit relationship to his parents, siblings, church, community, and school to achieve adequate training for adult life.

10. The school is viewed as an instrument for teaching the children the needed literacy and skills to live as productive adults in an environment where values taught in the home are continuous and function throughout life. The home and the church rather than the school are responsible for the religious training of the young.

FINDINGS: AGE-GRADING AND SOCIALIZATION

During his development the Amishman passes through a series of six more or less well-defined age stages, each with its own expectations for achievement and behavior. Socialization does not stop with arrival at adulthood but continues throughout life. The age stages are as follows:

1. *Infants: Birth to Walking.* In infancy children are generally referred to as "babies."
2. *Preschool Children: Walking Until School Age (At Six or Seven Years).* In this second stage children are referred to as "little children." Sometimes they are spoken of as "children at home," although that phrase more often refers to all children who are unmarried and still eat and sleep under the parental roof.
3. *Schoolchildren: Six or Seven to Ages Fourteen to Sixteen.* Children attending school are referred to as "scholars" by the Amish. These children are fulfilling the eight years of elementary schooling required by the state in either public schools or Amish schools.
4. *Young People: Fourteen or Sixteen Until Marriage.* These young people have completed eight years of schooling and therefore can do a full day's work. Those who finish before the age of sixteen must, in some counties, attend an Amish vocational school.[b] But even though day school is finished by fourteen, most young people are not full participants in this age stage until they are sixteen. After baptism there is a modification of behavior, and the baptized member is no longer a full participant. The draft, which removes Amish young men from the community for two years of alternative service, has not become integrated into the age patterning of the culture.[c] It can affect either young people or adults.
5. *Adults: Marriage Until Retirement.* Baptism signifies religious adulthood, but marriage and the birth of the first child brings social adulthood. Generally the time interval between baptism and mar-

b. These schools, which typically demand a half-day per week of classroom vocational training and four-and-a-half days per week of experiential, out-of-classroom learning, are described in John A. Hostetler and Gertrude Enders Huntington, *Children in Amish Society: Socialization and Community Education* (New York: Holt, Rinehart and Winston, 1971), 71–79.

c. This article, published in 1970, was written during the Vietnam War and the corresponding U.S. military draft. The draft ended in 1973, which has made this particular issue (the place of alternative service in the Amish life cycle) moot, at least for the present.

riage is relatively short. The major activity during adulthood is child rearing.

6. *The Aged: Retirement Until Death.* Adults generally retire sometime after their youngest child has married and started to raise a family. They move from the big house into the grandfather house, or to the edge of the village. They are cared for by their children and exert a conservative influence as they fulfill their accepted role of admonishing their children.

THE GOALS OF AMISH SCHOOLING

The goals of Amish schools are consistent with Amish culture and generally parallel with American educational goals. Just as the goal of public schools is to produce individuals with "the best chance of understanding and contributing to the great events of his time," so the goal of Amish schools is to produce Amish Christians able to understand and contribute to the small events that will help perpetuate their community here and in eternity. Amish school standards are designed to establish the foundations of a society of "useful, God-fearing, and law-abiding citizens." Although the Amish goals are not identical with those of the larger society, they are not antithetical, for both systems strive to produce useful, law-abiding citizens. The Amish will not tolerate the removal of their children to a distance from their homes, or placing them into large groups with narrow age limits, or teaching skills useless to their way of life, or exposing them to values and attitudes antithetical to their own. These conditions develop when schools become large and bureaucratic. Then the Amish establish their own schools, and when this is not possible they migrate to other states or counties where they can raise their children to thrive on co-operation and humility rather than competition and pride of achievement.[d] The Amish stress humility, the elimination of self-pride, mutual encouragement, persistence, the willingness to attempt a difficult task, and love for one another. For the Amish, education is primarily social rather than individual. Its goal is not "the freedom which exalts the individual" but social cohesion and social responsibility. Teaching the children to get along together in work and play is as important as teaching the academic subjects, and both are essential to the Amish community.

d. In the thirty-plus years since this article was written, the Amish have continued to construct and operate their own schools so that private schooling is now the dominant educational paradigm in Amish communities.

Amish teachers are as much concerned with the development of Christian character as with the teaching of facts. There is more concern with giving the pupils "correct knowledge" than teaching them "critical thinking." Only within the framework of the material presented are the children taught to think for themselves. In a secular school, with a scientific orientation, children's rational powers are trained to enable them to attempt to solve the "riddles of life, space and time." In the Amish school these are not believed to be riddles that need to be solved by man; truth does not have to be sought, for it has already been revealed (in the Bible) and is there for those willing to believe. Because the Amish and the public school have two such different concepts of what truth is and how it is to be obtained, their teaching methods are different: the Amish stress "believing," memorization and drill, while the public schools stress "questioning." Most Amish want their children to study history and geography; however, in schools where history is taught, facts are learned and interrelationships are not stressed. Secular man searches for pattern and meaning in history, and for reasons and explanations of distant events. Religious man (the Amish) does not need to; he knows the world is orderly and is so ordered by God.

FINDINGS: SCHOOL TESTS AND DRAWING EXERCISES

The Amish pupils tested within the normal IQ range. The Amish schools generally out-performed pupils in the public schools in achievement tests,[4] scoring below the non-Amish in language tests but well above the public school pupils in the quantitative phases of testing. In reading comprehension, knowledge and use of reference material they did as well as non-Amish; and in spelling, word usage, and arithmetic problem solving they did much better than the non-Amish. Amish pupils learn to do well in those subjects that are considered basic to education: reading, writing, and arithmetic. A summary for each of the tests follows:

SRA Intelligence Test.[e] This test was given to 115 Amish and a control group of 61 non-Amish. The overall or composite score differences between the Amish and non-Amish were not statistically significant, whether the Amish were in public schools or in Amish schools, or in a public school where some or all the pupils were Amish. Amish pupils who were in public schools with about equal Amish and non-Amish enrollment scored higher than their non-Amish class-

---

e. Designed by Louis Leon Thurstone (1887–1955) and Thelma Gwinn Thurstone (1897–1993) and published by Science Research Associates (SRA) in the 1950s and 1960s, the SRA Tests of Educational Ability provided general measures of language, reasoning, and quantitative abilities for grades 4–12.

mates. The IQ scores of the Amish pupils in Amish schools varied little from grades five to eight.

When scores were compared on the basis of subject (language, reasoning, and quantitative) the Amish scored lower than the non-Amish in the language aspect of the test. The differences were statistically significant.

Iowa Tests of Basic Skills (Achievement Tests).[f] Here the Amish scored higher than the non-Amish pupils in spelling, word usage, and in arithmetic, but were surpassed by the non-Amish in vocabulary. All these differences were statistically significant. In vocabulary all groups tested scored below the national norm, and all of the Amish categories scored lower than the non-Amish. The highest scores among the Amish were made by the pupils in private schools rather than those in public schools.

In reading comprehension all groups tested were lower than the national norm; the differences between the Amish and non-Amish were not statistically significant.

In spelling the Amish in three different social contexts scored higher than the non-Amish. Only the Amish scored above the national norm. The best showing among the Amish was in the Amish school rather than the public school.

In word usage the Amish scores exceeded the non-Amish, and the difference was statistically significant. Amish pupils in private schools had higher scores than Amish pupils in public schools. Those Amish enrolled in public schools with about an equal number of non-Amish pupils made the same scores as those in public schools with a totally Amish enrollment.

In the knowledge and use of reference material all groups tested were from five to nine months below the national norm. The variance between the groups was not statistically significant. The best showing was made by the Amish who were in public schools where the total enrollment was composed of Amish children.

In arithmetic problem solving the Amish private school population had scores higher than the national norm and higher than the non-Amish school population. The difference was statistically significant. Pupils in Amish schools had higher scores than Amish pupils in public schools regardless of whether they were segregated or mixed with non-Amish pupils in the public schools.

In the Iowa Test scores for Amish private schools for grades five through

---

f. The Iowa Test of Basic Skills (ITBS) is a battery of tests designed and overseen by the College of Education at the University of Iowa. The ITBS's areas of testing in the 1960s included vocabulary, reading comprehension, spelling, word usage, and arithmetic problem solving.

eight, the scores tend to improve with each grade in those subjects in which the Amish do well: spelling, word usage, and arithmetic.

Stanford Achievement Test.[g] In this test the scores of 468 Amish pupils in public schools from grades one through six were compared with the scores of 1290 non-Amish pupils' scores from the same schools. The Amish performed equally well with the non-Amish on language and vocabulary and tended to be better achievers in arithmetic than the non-Amish by the time they reached grades five and six.

Goodenough-Harris Drawing Test, IQ.[5] This nonverbal test of intelligence was given to 389 Amish and 78 non-Amish pupils. The pupil was asked to draw a man, a woman, and himself. The total point scores for the man-drawing were used as a measure of intelligence using 100 as a mean standard IQ score.

The Amish scored slightly above the national norm, having a score of 101.6. Boys scored slightly higher than girls. Pupils in private Amish schools made higher scores than Amish pupils in public schools, even when the pupils in the public schools were all of the Amish faith.

A comparison of the Goodenough-Harris scores and the SRA IQ test scores from the same schools shows that the former tend to be higher than the latter.

In a school where there were about equal numbers of rural white, black, and Amish children, the Amish scored slightly lower than the rural whites and higher than the blacks.

Cultural differences were reflected in the Amish children's drawings between those who were in Amish schools and those in public schools. The drawings by the Amish pupils in the most traditional schools clearly reflected their traditional culture. Amish children in public schools who drew themselves tended to identify more with "English" or alien symbols than did the children in private schools.

Myers-Briggs Type Indicator.[6] The test contains indices for determining each of four basic preferences that presumably structure the individual's personality. It is designed to discover the cognitive aspects of how people perceive and form conclusions. It is not an ability test. These four indices are central to the test: Extroversion or Introversion, Sensing or Intuition, Thinking or Feeling, and Judgment or Perception, indicated respectively as EI, SN, TF, and JP.

The test was given to 251 Amish and 78 non-Amish pupils. The Amish pupils clearly fell into the ISFJ personality pattern, which according to the test manual is described as:

g. Designed in 1923 by Stanford University psychologist Lewis Madison Terman (1877–1956), the Stanford Achievement Test (SAT) continues to be used as an assessment tool for schoolchildren in the areas of language, vocabulary, and mathematics.

Quiet, friendly, responsible and conscientious. Works devotedly to meet his obligations and serve his friends and school. Thorough and painstaking, accurate with figures, but needs time to master technical subjects, as reasoning is not his strong point. Patient with details and routine. Loyal, considerate, concerned with how other people feel even when they are in the wrong.

The control group (non-Amish in an agricultural setting) were ESFP in their personality pattern, and this type is described by the test manual as:

Outgoing, easy-going, uncritical, friendly, very fond of a good time. Enjoys sports and making things, restless if he has to sit still. Knows what's happening and joins in helpfully. Literal-minded, tries to remember rather than to reason, is easily confused by theory. Has good common sense and practical ability, but is not at all interested in study for its own sake.

Introversion rather than extroversion was most frequent among the Amish pupils in private schools. The control group was decidedly extroverted. Amish in public schools tended to be less introverted and were more similar to the non-Amish pupils who attended the same schools.

Sensing rather than Intuition was preferred in all the groups tested, but the group having the highest proportion of Sensing were the pupils in Amish private schools. The SF types are pronounced among the Amish, even when compared to norms for rural high school pupils. When compared to various occupational groups the Amish have a Sensing-Feeling score approximating that of sales and customer relations employees, and least like research scientists or science students.

Feeling rather than Thinking was preferred in all of the groups tested, but the Amish had the highest percentage of this type. Amish in public schools tended to have fewer Feeling and more Thinking types.

Judgment rather than Perception was highest among the pupils in Amish private schools and decreased among the pupils in all-Amish public schools. Only in the public school where they were mixed with the non-Amish did the Amish have a greater percentage of Perception than Judgment types.

Occupational Aspirations.[7] Children's essays on "What kind of work I want to do when I grow up, and why," were grouped into traditional and nontraditional categories. The majority of the children in the survey illustrate successful Amish socialization. They are confident of what they will be doing as adults and know they are receiving the technical and psychological training needed for adult life. Most of the children chose occupations of the traditional type— farm or farm-related. The proportions of traditional occupational choices ranged widely among the nine schools, apparently reflecting some heterogeneity of occupational patterns in various communities. The proportion of nontraditional choices by the children was greater than the proportion of actual nontraditional occupations of the household heads.

Responses from a multicultural school, consisting of Amish, blacks, and rural whites, showed that the Amish pupils still preferred the traditional occupations of their culture. Amish girls showed a marked interest in professional occupations such as teaching and nursing, but many were interested in housekeeping, cleaning, cooking, or helping others in the family. The choices of blacks and rural white pupils were more heterogeneous than the Amish and touched on a great variety of interests.

Freehand Drawings. Amish drawings are clearly distinguishable from the drawings of suburban schoolchildren when asked to draw "my home" and "my happy time." Amish children included more cooperative group activity in their drawings, more work-related activities, and more outdoor activity. There is a demonstrable association between the content of the house drawing and intimate knowledge of Amish culture and spatial details of the environment. Use of color in quantity and variety differed from one school to another.

Amish children represent their external environment unusually early in the developmental sequences. This is manifest by the early consistent use of the baseline and the sky, down to the horizon, both of which indicate representation of spatial relationships. There is early use of detail in many of the drawings. These features are important criteria of social growth. The de-emphasis on the self and the importance of the family and the community in Amish society make the child aware, at a very young age, of the external environment. These children depict the external environment (other people and objects) as being important rather than subjective or individual feelings.

CHANGE: TRADITIONAL AND ELEMENTARY LIFESTYLES

Generalizations with respect to the impact of social change are presented in a dichotomy of "traditional" and "emergent" lifestyles. "Traditional" lifestyles are characterized by preference for the tried as opposed to changing methods of child rearing and by communal consensus in contrast to individualistic decision making. "Emergent" lifestyles are characterized by differentiation of social patterns, receptivity to new methods of child training, and developed interest in rational efficiency and verbalization of belief as opposed to nonverbal symbols of sharing. Although the emergent type follows the modernizing or transitional groups of Amish, its manifestation does not strictly follow church affiliations.

The traditional Amish believe that babies are incapable of sin: young children can be disobedient but not sinful. They see the child as having potentialities for both good and evil, and it is the parents' responsibility to create an environment that encourages Christian qualities and discourages the non-Christian qualities. The traditional Amish are confident of their babies, their preschool children, and even their school-age children as long as they can protect them within the family and community and shelter them from "the world."

The emergent Amish tend to verbalize the sinfulness of the child. More emphasis is placed on physical punishment and the cleansing effect of pain than is the case with the Amish traditional pattern. The traditional Amish do not stress feelings of guilt, for wrongdoing can be completely forgiven when acknowledged humbly and replaced by proper behavior. The emergent Amish emphasize guilt as a necessary Christian emotion. The emergent Amish reflect greater contact with fundamentalist emphases that were common in the United States during the mid-nineteenth century.[h]

The traditional Amish community is more supportive of its members, while the emergent community is more judgmental. The traditional Amish religion is practical and ritualistic, and the emergent lifestyle is by contrast more theological and mystical. The traditional form is characterized by a high degree of shared experience rather than by rational theological understanding.

The emergent Amish are more dependent upon the larger society outside their immediate community than are the traditional Amish. In the latter, the need for human support and interaction are met within the community. The traditional Amish structure age categories and rituals more consistently with supportive customs than do the transitional Amish groups. The emergent Amish support missionaries who leave the community to work in the world. Their religious style is more individualistic, as is evidenced by an emphasis on personal emotional crisis of rebirth. Typically the traditional Amish person can grow steadily towards adulthood in a supportive community, while the emer-

---

h. Hostetler's use of the word "fundamentalist" with respect to mid-nineteenth-century American Protestantism is anachronistic, since the rise of Protestant fundamentalism is usually tied to the late nineteenth and early twentieth centuries. He is likely referring to theological emphases that have been common in American evangelicalism for at least two centuries, and remain prominent today.

gent Amish person needs a personal integrative experience to overcome the discontinuity he experiences as a member of a transitional culture.

GENERAL OBSERVATIONS

The assumption that children in public schools are better achievers on standardized tests than Amish children in private schools is not supported by the data. Furthermore, the tests were familiar to many pupils in the public schools and were probably "biased" in the direction of the non-Amish populations.[i] By contrast, the Amish were not accustomed to taking standardized tests, and their teachers in most cases were uncertified by state standards and had no more than an eighth-grade formal education. Variation was observed among Amish schools, however, and no conclusions can be made about schools not included in our sample.

The Amish children are not deprived of meaningful aspiration and participation in the goals of the culture. Although there are individuals who, when they leave the traditional culture, appear to have personal problems of stress and adaptation to the larger culture, they do not become liabilities to the larger society. They are generally motivated individuals in terms of occupational adjustment and goals.

The Amish have demonstrated that local control by a culturally divergent group can work even when judged by American public school standards of achievement. Our investigation shows that local control (with no funding from the government) can work well even though the parents have a limited educational background (eight years at the most), speak English as a second language, and are culturally different from the prevailing American culture. Amish parents are generally satisfied with the schools, the children who graduate from them are well prepared for adult life, and even as judged by public school standards (on standardized tests) the children are adequately taught. All of this has quietly been achieved in a day when there is a great deal of discussion in the urban and state school system about the validity of local control in the public schools.

The Amish have devised a vocational training program that teaches not only technical skill but also the associated "worker's etiquette." The vocational role

---

i. In *Children in Amish Society*, Hostetler and Huntington note that the standardized educational tests they administered were designed by persons with a "very different philosophy of education" from the Amish philosophy of education (89). Moreover, they write, Amish children sometimes encountered test items that assumed cultural knowledge that their communities would have deemed inappropriate for them to learn.

is taught as well as the job skill. Adolescents learn much faster by actual participation than by talking about participation. Working at real jobs outside the school walls helps the young to envision their adult roles and their place in the society. The Amish, like their Anabaptist forebears, stress training for life participation (here and for eternity) and warn of the dangers of "pagan" philosophy and the intellectual enterprises of "fallen man." They are not opposed to education but to having their children trained in a way of life that emphasizes analytical science and technical competence to the exclusion of folk wisdom.

The Amish have rejected certified teachers in favor of qualified teachers. The Amish teacher must transmit the Amish culture to the children as well as teach them basic educational skills. Certified non-Amish teachers are incapable of teaching Amish children "by the example of their lives." Perhaps the concept of "qualified teacher" in addition to "certified teacher" should be considered for schools serving specific cultural groups. Teacher certification as generally practiced is too narrow, for it excludes persons who may be best qualified to teach children of culturally divergent groups.

The Amish have been able to stop, at least temporarily, the onslaught of *Techne*.[j] They have scant legal protection and little guarantee other than public sentiment for the maintenance of their schools in which their children are learning the skills and attitudes required of their culture. Were it not for the Amish appeal to religious freedom, their communities would long since have been forced out of their pastoral "poverty" into the economic mainstream where they would either have contributed more to the gross national product or would have added to the welfare rolls already swelled with unhappy individuals drifting between the culture they no longer have and the middle-class American culture they do not fully embrace.

NOTES

1. The report is entitled *Educational Achievement and Life Styles in a Traditional Society, the Old Order Amish.* U.S. Department of Health, Education, and Welfare: Office of Education, 1969. 523 pp. A limited number of copies are available from the author, Professor of Sociology and Anthropology, Temple University, Philadelphia, Pa.

2. Gertrude Enders Huntington's contribution to the fieldwork and to the analysis is gratefully acknowledged.

---

j. Why Hostetler uses the Greek word *techne*, rather than the English term *technology*, is not entirely clear. It is likely, however, that he wanted his readers to perceive technology as a cultural system that affects lives, relationships, and conceptions of meaning, rather than as mere items of hardware that make tasks easier.

3. The method for construction of postulates is discussed by Francis L. K. Hsu, *The Study of Literate Civilization* (New York, 1969), chapter viii.

4. The project director is indebted to Wayne E. Miller for assistance in the testing phase of the research, which also formed the basis of his Ph.D. dissertation, "A Study of Amish Academic Achievement" (Faculty of Educational Administration, University of Michigan, 1969).

5. Dale B. Harris, *Children's Drawings as Measures of Intellectual Maturity* (New York, 1963).

6. Isabel Briggs Myers, *Manual: The Myers-Briggs Type Indicator* (Princeton, N.J., 1962).

7. A method of investigation employed by Mary E. Goodman, "Values, Attitudes, and Social Concepts of Japanese and American Children," *American Anthropologist*, LIX, 979–99.

14

FOLK MEDICINE AND SYMPATHY
HEALING AMONG THE AMISH (1976)

John A. Hostetler's concern about the health and vitality of Amish culture extended to the physical and psychological health of its individual members. For instance, in the 1960s he and his wife Beulah Stauffer Hostetler worked closely with Victor A. McKusick and other Johns Hopkins University medical researchers to track, diagnose, and prevent genetic maladies in Amish populations. "Folk Medicine and Sympathy Healing among the Amish," written about a decade later, focuses more generally on Amish approaches to medical health that, according to Hostetler, demonstrate a pragmatic amalgamation of folk and scientific medical practices. On the one hand, Hostetler observes, the Amish have embraced scientific medicine more readily than most other aspects of "worldly" culture, particularly in response to critical, incapacitating illnesses. On the other hand, in cases of chronic illnesses, the Amish continue to rely on a vast storehouse of traditional medical practices, ranging from herbal remedies to reflexology to Braucherei ("sympathy healing").

Hostetler's concern with physical health in the Amish community had an existential grounding: as an Amish teenager he had suffered from stomach ailments that made it difficult for him to do the work expected of Amish farmers. Later in life, he sought to influence situations in which his Amish friends and subjects were jeopardizing their health through ignorance or, in some cases, by principle. In one instance he wrote an editor at an Amish-run publishing concern, encouraging him to publish an article on tooth and gum care (John A. Hostetler {JAH} to David Luthy, 10 February 1975, Hostetler Papers, Box AL04.02). A few years later Hostetler wrote his nephew and his nephew's wife, encouraging them to counter ideas circulating in Pennsylvania's Big Valley that Amish bishops opposed polio vaccines (JAH to Jesse and Fannie Detweiler, 11 May 1979, Hostetler Papers, Box AL05.07). In these cases and others, Hostetler did more than report about Amish life. He sought to shape Amish society in ways that, from his perspective, would enhance its existence..

This article was first published in Wayland D. Hand, ed., American Folk Medicine: A Symposium *(Berkeley and Los Angeles: University of California Press, 1976), 249–58. It is reprinted by permission of the University of California Press.*

Every known society has developed methods for coping with threats to health and well-being. Each has created a body of therapeutic knowledge in keeping with its ongoing culture. As a member of a folk society,[1] the sick individual will act according to the norms and assumptions held by his society. Decisions about treatment and who should provide the treatment depend upon the knowledge made available to the individual from his culture. The healing arts of the folk society are frequently regarded by literate people as a queer collection of errors and superstitions. The tendency of modern medical institutions and their personnel to scorn folk concepts of illness and treatment has delayed unnecessarily long the much needed perspective of the holistic therapeutic processes. This conference is a concrete step, a historic venture, in exploring knowledge derived from two of man's greatest sources of knowledge, the oral tradition and science. It is to be hoped that we will learn more about the integration of these methods of healing.

"Folk medicine," as Don Yoder has so effectively pointed out, "has many *gesunkenes Kulturgut*[a] items in its repertory."[2] Modern healing practices deriving from folk medical knowledge are today in all probability very limited; and when a breakthrough is made, it is "accidental." There are practitioners, grandmothers, and sages in mass culture who as individuals perpetuate a knowledge of folk beliefs and curing. This is idiosyncratic behavior rather than a cultural phenomenon. When we come to the Old Order Amish, however, we are dealing with an enclave of humanity, a segment of interrelated people who have retained a style of living that is credible in its "strain toward consistency."[3] The function and place of folk medicine in the process of consistency remains yet to be thoroughly investigated. Though the Amish are not in every respect an ideal-typical folk society,[4] they have retained many of its basic characteristics—distinctiveness, smallness, homogeneity, and self-sufficiency. The Amish derive from the sixteenth-century Anabaptist tradition and along with other Germanic-speaking peoples migrated from Switzerland and Germany to the United States in the eighteenth century. They have grown in population, almost wholly from natural increase, from about eight thousand in 1905 to approximately seventy thousand in 1970. Eighty percent of their population is located in the three states of Pennsylvania, Ohio, and Indiana.

Aside from my personal knowledge of folk medical practices as a product of growing up in an Old Order Amish home, I have collected data on this subject in connection with my fieldwork over the past twenty years. The sources for this paper are personal interviews with Amish informants and with physicians who serve the Amish people and a content analysis of the Amish newspaper, *The Budget*. The Amish rules of discipline prevent members from securing higher education; thus they have no physicians among their members. In

---

a. This German phrase means "diminished cultural goods" or "diminished cultural value"; in other words, folk medicine retains certain ideas that are no longer esteemed by elite, academic medical professionals.

order to understand folk medicine in Amish society, I maintain, we must observe the totality of Amish medical practices and observe how both folk and scientific knowledge function in a cultural system.

ATTITUDES TOWARD SICKNESS

Concern for the sick constitutes a subject of major interest in every Amish community. *The Budget* (a weekly) reflects the attitudes, happenings, and interests of the Amish people from scores of communities in the United States and Canada and covers illness, diagnosis, and treatment. An analysis of the content indicates that the Amish are extremely health conscious.[5] Scribes who report illnesses frequently give lengthy and detailed reports of not only the ailment, but also the method of treatment and the progress of the patient. Scribes invite readers to send letters to the sick person. It becomes the duty of members to visit, especially the chronically ill and the aged relatives.

Modern medical terminology forms a substantial part of the Amish medical vocabulary. The range of complaints and diseases varies widely in Amish writings. Treatment for an ailment is generally that prescribed by the modern medical profession, although there are also terms used that designate home remedies, patent medicines, and traditional forms of treatment.

Modern science has penetrated the Amish culture to a far greater extent than have other aspects of "worldly" culture, such as new forms of recreation and leisure. The services of clinics, hospitals, and physicians constitute linkages with outside social systems. While the Amish have maintained boundaries against some dominant values of American culture—the automobile, radio, television, and even technological improvements—they have erected no boundaries against hospital and medical care. There is no need to resist health improvement, since such values are not in conflict with the values of their religion. Medical science constitutes no direct threat to the breakdown of the community. The Amish, as a culture group, find nothing in the Bible which prevents them from using hospitals, dentists, fluoridation, surgeons, or anesthetists. Yet folk beliefs and cures are still practiced for some types of illnesses.

The penetration of medical science into Amish life, the acceptance of scientific explanations of disease and treatment, suggests that medical knowledge may be one of the points most vulnerable to the inroads of change in a folk culture. Children at early ages are exposed to outside health and hygiene practices in the public school. Where health and life are at stake, new concepts of disease and treatment are not labeled "too worldly." There is, however, a selective principle which determines the method of treatment. For critical, incapacitating illnesses such as appendicitis, infections, and broken bones, scientific modes of healing are accepted. For chronic, nonincapacitating malfunctions or for treatments not responding to scientific modes of healing, folk treatments tend to play an important role.

Illnesses which are not understood or do not respond to treatment bring both scientific and folk sources of knowledge into the experience of the sick person. Much of the medical knowledge does not get into the columns of the Amish newspaper. The space devoted to health advertisements in *The Budget* is consistent through the years from 1890 to the present. This is a source of folk knowledge for the chronically ill reader, but it is also a form of borrowing. The advertisements are from non-Amish sources. The patent names for these remedies have varied greatly over the years, but the ailments they would cure remain about the same. Remedies for rheumatism and arthritis are most numerous, but there are also tonics, vitamins, and bitters to cure constipation and to relieve itch and other ailments. Tranquilizers and sedatives are also advertised.

Many Amish have told me, "Too many pills and strong medicine is not good for a person." For persons who believe in bone therapy and have a fear of "strong medicine," advertisements have considerable appeal. Teas and homemade formulas constitute another source of Amish medical treatment. "They use all kinds of teas for all kinds of ills and I don't interfere with it unless I know it to be detrimental," said one physician.

FOLK TREATMENTS

Amish folk medicine is composed of the two recognized branches of folk medicine: (1) natural folk medicine (use of natural phenomena, herbs, plants, minerals, and animal substances for curing), and (2) occult folk medicine (the use of charms and supernatural forms of support).[6] Both are maintained by a strong oral tradition through which, for example, knowledge of plant lore as well as charms are transmitted from generation to generation. In recent years the traditional Amish use of herbs and plants has been reinforced by the health movements in the larger American culture. I shall mention two specific linkages. One is William McGrath,[b] a convert to the Anabaptist faith (though he did

---

b. The original, which reads "though he did join the Old Order Amish," was probably intended to say "did not." William McGrath was a convert to the Amish faith, but he joined the more progressive Beachy Amish, not the Old Order Amish.

not join the Old Order Amish), who has privately published a book entitled *God-Given Herbs for the Healing of Mankind* (1970), now widely circulating among the Amish people.[7] The book combines "What the Bible Says About Sickness and Health" (chapter 1) with healing methods, natural healing, herbs, and testimonials. The second illustration is the rather widespread acceptance by the Amish of the method of "reflexology," or zone therapy, attributed to Eunice D. Ingham.[8] This treatment proposes that the proper massaging of the nerves in the toes has beneficial effects on the head, neck, spine, stomach, digestive system, and other parts of the body. The Amish not only patronize non-Amish foot masseurs, but some have taken the required course to become certified as foot massage specialists.

Occult practices in various forms, including sorcery, have been observed by those who have done fieldwork in Amish communities. The five widespread theories of disease and treatment based on magical causation as reported by Clements[9] have been observed in the Amish by Janice A. Egeland.[10] They are: (1) imitative and contagious magic; (2) intrusion of a disease-causing object; (3) soul loss, in which the victim's soul is thought to have been stolen and he is left to fall ill and die; (4) spirit intrusion, in which a person is believed to be possessed by a spirit; and (5) breach of taboo.

A common form of healing among the Amish is *Brauche* or *Braucherei*, which may be translated as "sympathy healing," or "secrets of sympathy."[11] The English equivalent is usually rendered as *powwowing*, though the cultural and psychological context is very different from that of the Indian medicine man. The traditional Amish have retained this source of knowledge from the ancient past. Though it is a source of mysterious power based on the use of incantations, it is not witchcraft, as the more progressive and evangelistic affiliations of the Amish would have it.[c] The old charms used in this connection were in the German language. Many of the charms and recipes I have found in family Bibles are in the English language.

Brauche is usually performed by one of the older Amish members in the community. Practitioners receive no remuneration for their services. The patient does not always need to be present when the actual incantations are performed, but the patient must believe in the practice to experience healing. One who desires to acquire the skill can obtain it only from an older person of the opposite sex after promising that the formula will be kept secret. The chief fea-

---

c. Hostetler is referring here to groups like the Beachy Amish, who maintained the Amish name even as they adopted more modern technologies (for example, car ownership and electricity) and embraced more evangelical assumptions about the Christian faith.

tures of *Brauche* are the silent repeating of certain verses or charms at appropriate times. It is performed for hemorrhaging, toothache, burns or scalds, the common cold, bed-wetting,[d] wild fire, mortification, sores in the mouth, and warts.

There are several Amish folk practitioners of varied reputation. One regularly visits Amish communities in several states in the interest of "curing." He claims to posses a special gift of healing. He asserts that his practice is neither *Brauche* nor powwowing but says he can tell what is wrong with a person by simply laying his hands on that person.

Amish persons who turn from scientific personnel to folk practitioners show little preference for Amish over non-Amish practitioners. One state inspector who investigates "quack healers" states that invariably he finds Amish patients at the offices of these healers, sometimes far from an Amish settlement.

The general tendency to rely on oral tradition and testimony, so characteristic of the whole Amish culture, is specifically manifest in the areas of the healing arts.

A mysterious ailment called "livergrown" (*a-gewachse*—literally meaning "hidebound" or "grown together") is common among Amish infants. Livergrown is thought to be caused by too sudden exposure to the outside atmosphere or by being shaken up by a buggy ride. The symptoms are similar to colic in babies. A sure diagnosis of the ailment is made by placing the child on his abdomen on a table, then bringing together, if possible, the left arm and the right foot (or vice versa) of the child. If the two do not come together with ease, the child has livergrown. The only cure for this illness is *Brauche*. This ailment and its cure is cited by Brendle and Unger in their extensive collection of folk medicine among the Pennsylvania Germans.[12] Livergrown seems to have no equivalent in modern medical terminology.

The biblical practice of anointing with oil has never found widespread acceptance among the Amish, as it has in some of the Mennonite groups, although there are instances when it is observed.[e] No record of the practice of anointing exists among the Amish or Mennonite groups in Europe.

Certain types of illnesses are taken to the physician and other types to the folk practitioner. Critical, incapacitating malfunctions are taken to the scientifically trained practitioner, while the chronic, nonincapacitating ailments are treated by the folk practitioner and by traditional means. For a sudden illness, broken bones, wounds, or pregnancy, the physician is consulted first. For

d. "Wild fire" is the colloquial term for erysipelas, a bacterial skin infection.
e. For the biblical injunction supporting this practice, see James 5:14.

nameless pains and long-standing disorders or for ailments which do not respond to the physician's treatment, *Brauche*, folk diagnosis, and folk treatment are prescribed. Chiropractors and naturopaths are believed to treat the "causes" of illnesses, while medical doctors tend to be regarded as specialists in treating the "effects." The former is believed to work with the slow but fundamental forces of nature; the latter gives immediate but short-range treatment by an injection of "strong" chemicals. The latter is considered necessary in emergency cases but is regarded as inferior to the slow working "natural" causes.

The Amish have a standard practice known as "changing doctors." This is upsetting to the medical practitioner, but to the Amish it is a means of achieving social integration by acquiring all available means of healing.

PHYSICIANS AND THE AMISH

Many physicians who serve the Amish express the opinion that there is a difference in symptomatology between Amish and non-Amish patients. In an effort to discover whether the Amish have complaints and symptoms that are different from non-Amish, I conducted a survey among physicians in four states.[13] Forty-six physicians cooperated in the survey, which was conducted by the interview and direct mail method. Eighty percent of these physicians had been in professional contact with the Amish for more than ten years, and over half estimated that they had been consulted by over one hundred Amish persons during the preceding year. On a checklist of symptoms, there was a high degree of consensus on some of the items.[14] Consensus does not prove that the physicians are right. There is, however, a somewhat greater than random chance that they might be, as indicated by applying tests of significance to the data.

The Amish are believed to have more of the following symptoms than non-Amish patients (significant at the 0.01 percent level of confidence): obesity, fats in the diet, salt in the diet, and capacity to endure pain. They are believed to have more chronic bed-wetting after the age of six and more chronic digestive disturbances but are believed to show more dependability in personal relationships than non-Amish clients. The physicians were of the opinion that there is a difference in physical and mental health between Amish and non-Amish patients (though not significant at the 0.05 level of confidence). Amish patients were judged to have less fainting, nervous tics, hysterical seizures, stuttering, chronic headaches, eczema, spastic colitis, arterial hypertension under the age of forty, coronary heart disease, complaints of menstrual disorders, aggressiveness in personal relationships; nevertheless, they were considered to have less general good mental health.

Amish patients are believed to have fewer of the following symptoms than non-Amish patients, as indicated by clinical judgments of the physicians (significant at the 0.01 percent level of confidence): chronic insomnia, chronic use of sleeping pills, drug addiction, extreme alcoholism, chronic nightmares, food allergies, and syphilis. Amish patients were also believed to have fewer of the following additional symptoms than non-Amish (significant at the 0.05 percent level of confidence): amnesia, suicide, peptic ulcers, complaints of poor appetite, coronary heart disease, malingering,[f] fear of death, parental concern over enuresis, parental emphasis on early toilet training. They also showed less interest in birth control information.

Little or no difference between Amish and non-Amish patients is thought to exist in the frequency of the following symptoms: hypochondriacal complaints, asthma, hay fever, sleepwalking, cancer, chronic constipation, kidney malfunctions, urinary tract infections, arterial hypertension over age forty, arteriosclerosis, hypertensive complications in pregnancy, worry about illness, feeling of personal inadequacy, average life expectancy, and general good physical health.

Many of these professional clinical judgments substantiate what we would expect. As a rural people, the Amish work hard and have no difficulty sleeping at night; therefore they need no sleeping pills. Their traditional teachings have generally prevented them from alcoholic excesses. They want large families, since children are not an economic liability but rather an asset to the farm. They do not lack good appetites and apparently have less heart failure than people who work in offices and in nonfarm occupations. Once on the way to recovery, getting over an illness is not difficult, and they show little anxiety over the fear of death. The Amish infant is generally not forced into early toilet training.

Some Amish symptoms are probably associated with conditions of stress and culture change. Amish persons are believed to lack aggressiveness in personal relationships and manifest less general good mental health according to the physicians. Chronic bed-wetting after the age of six and more digestive disturbances suggest the presence of social and cultural problems. The Amish apparently complain about illness as much as other people.

Most of the physicians cooperating in the study offered comments about

---

f. In medical terminology, malingering is the feigning or exaggerating of physical or psychological symptoms for some tangible gain.

their Amish clients, their social relations, and their health conditions. Their observations may be summarized as follows:[15]

1. The Amish are generally regarded as being desirable patients by physicians.
2. The Amish, in the view of medical doctors, pay less attention to preventative medicine; physicians attribute this to a lack of formal education.
3. The Amish are more inclined than other patients toward using home remedies and patronizing unscientific practitioners.
4. The Amish have special health problems that are associated with social and cultural changes.

Thirty-one of the forty-six physicians believed that the incidence of possible hereditary pathologies was greater among the Amish than among non-Amish patients. Since 1965 the Amish have made a significant contribution to medical genetics by permitting medical scientists to study their hereditary problems.[16] Several recessive genetic disorders have been found to have a relatively high occurrence: a rare type of anemia, phenylketonuria, hemophilia, six-fingered dwarfism, and a new form of dwarfism affecting the growth of cartilage and hair. Because the Amish are a well-defined population and have good family records, it is possible to trace many of the cases to a common ancestor. The Amish prohibit first-cousin marriages, but even though they appear not to marry close, there has been much intermarriage for generations in confined communities.

SUMMARY AND CONCLUSIONS

The relationship between medicine and social change is still a field which deserves much investigation. Medicine in any society, in a broad sense, is understood as we understand its relation to integration and the culture. In a changing world, medicine, as well as other social institutions, is influenced by the forces that are changing the general social order.

In Amish society changes occur selectively, by the processes of reinterpretation and syncretism. In Amish tradition there are no manifest beliefs that militate against the use of hospital or surgical methods. Nevertheless, it would appear in the case of the Amish that the practice of folk medicine persists in a culture that places a premium on isolation. Major innovations flow outward from cities to country. The sixty or more Amish settlements in the United States are agrarian communities with a preference for isolation from the general society. The Amish have preserved what the society around them has discarded long ago. In pioneer times the Amish and many rural people lived far from a physician. In case of sudden illness they were forced to use those cures at hand or to search the memory for those treatments used by their forefathers. Amish culture is slow-moving and, by tradition, slow to accept new ideas. The old ways are not only familiar ways but preferred ways in a society that ranks "practical" above "theoretical" knowledge. "Folkways" are ranked high in the scheme of things, while "new ways" are ranked lower. In a society that places a high value on face-to-face associations, the advice of a friend (especially an old person) concerning medical treatment carries more weight than the advice of a scientifically trained man. This is especially true in a society that is suspicious of higher learning in general.

Finally, the folk concepts of disease, diagnosis, and treatment are culturally consistent with the whole of Amish culture. In a mentality of slowness, of suspicion against newness, of uncertainty in general about the outside world, the old conservative ways are preferred. Another reason for the persistence of folk medicine is that the Amish are probably experiencing psychotherapeutic results which they do not find in the highly rational non-Amish world. That effective results are obtained from any number of folk treatments contributes to the persistence of folk medicine. This is a phenomenon which anthropologists and the medical sciences have yet to probe further.

NOTES

1. "Folk society" in this discussion connotes the model developed by Robert Redfield: a small, isolated, traditional, simple, homogeneous society where oral communication and conventionalized ways are important in integrating the whole of life. See "The Folk Society," *American Journal of Sociology*, 52 (January, 1947), 292–308.

2. Don Yoder, "Folk Medicine," in *Folklore and Folklife: An Introduction*, ed. Richard M. Dorson (Chicago: University of Chicago Press, 1972), p. 191.

3. The phrase is from W. G. Sumner, *Folkways* (Boston: Ginn and Co., 1906).

4. For a discussion of the Amish as a folk society see J. A. Hostetler, *Amish Society* (Baltimore: Johns Hopkins University Press, 1968), pp. 3–22; and for a thorough anthropological study see G. E. Huntington, "Dove at the Window: A Study of an Old Order Amish Community in Ohio" (Ph.D. diss., Yale University, 1956).

5. For a detailed discussion of the analysis of *The Budget* on matters of health vocabulary, see table I in J. A. Hostetler, "Folk and Scientific Medicine in Amish Society," *Human Organization*, 22 (Winter 1963–1964), p. 271.

6. Yoder, *op. cit.*, p. 192.

7. William R. McGrath, *God-Given Herbs for the Healing of Mankind*, 3d ed. (n.p., 1970). 87 pp. Distributor: Dan J. B. Byler, Route 2, Seymour, Missouri.

8. Eunice D. Ingham, *Stories the Feet Can Tell* (n.p., n.d.). 109 pp. plus "Reflexology Chart." Distributor: Post Office Box 948, Rochester, N.Y.

9. Forrest E. Clements, "Primitive Concepts of Disease," *University of California Publications in American Archaeology and Ethnology*, 32 (1932), 185–252.

10. From an address at Johns Hopkins University School of Medicine, June 1, 1965. Also Janice Egeland, "Beliefs and Behavior as Related to Illness: A Community Case Study of the Old Order Amish," 2 vols. (Ph.D. diss., Department of Sociology, Yale University, 1967). For a limited study of the Iowa Amish medical practices, see Thomas McCorkle and J. von Herringen, "Culture and Medical Behavior of the Old Order Amish of Johnson County, Iowa," mimeographed, State University of Iowa, Institute of Agricultural Medicine Bulletin no. 2 (Iowa City, Iowa, 1958).

11. *Brauchen (Brauche, Braucherei)* was commonly practiced in Europe. See Fritz Heeger, *Pfälzer Volksheilkunde: Ein Beitrag zur Volkskunde der Westmark* (Neustadt/Weinstrasse: Verlag Daniel Meininger, 1936), pp. 19–31. Sympathy healing connotes a high degree of empathy and forms of community involvement. See also G. F. Helfenstein, . . . *Hausschatz der Sympathie* (1839). *Powwow* (meaning "to counsel" or "confer") as applied to faith healing may be "a fundamental misapplication of meaning," says John Joseph Stoudt, in *Sunbonnets and Shoofly Pies* (New York: A. S. Barnes Co., 1973), p. 174.

12. T. R. Brendle and C. W. Unger, *Folk Medicine of the Pennsylvania Germans* (Norristown, Pa.: Pennsylvania German Society, 1935), pp. 192–195.

13. The survey was conducted in 1961 and involved Pennsylvania, Ohio, Indiana, Iowa, and Ontario. The results were published in Hostetler, *Human Organization*.

14. The checklist was used with the permission of J. W. Eaton and R. J. Weil and appears in their book *Culture and Mental Disorders* (Glencoe, Ill.: The Free Press, 1955), pp. 233–237.

15. For quotations supporting these generalizations, refer to Hostetler, *Human Organization*.

16. Hereditary diseases have been studied by Victor A. McKusick at Johns Hopkins University School of Medicine, by his students and associates and by other medical scientists. See especially V. A. McKusick, et al., "The Distribution of Certain Genes in the Old Order Amish," *Cold Spring Harbor Symposia on Quantitative Biology* 29 (1964), 99–114; and Harold E. Cross, *Genetic Studies in an Amish Isolate* (Ph.D. diss., School of Medicine, Johns Hopkins University).

15

THE AMISH AND THE LAW: A RELIGIOUS
MINORITY AND ITS LEGAL ENCOUNTERS (1984)

In "The Amish and the Law," John A. Hostetler explores the relationship of the Old Order Amish to the American legal system from two distinct perspectives. The first half of the article explores interpersonal conflict among the Amish, using case studies to illustrate both the roots and the (non)resolutions of these conflicts. The second half of the article moves beyond internal Amish disputes to highlight situations in which Amish people and communities, for reasons of conscience, found themselves in conflict with the state. In both cases, Hostetler underscores the reticence of Amish people to resort to "worldly" means in the face of conflict; that is, he highlights the disinclination of Ordnung-abiding Amish persons to defend themselves and their property in courts of law. This disinclination is not an absolute refusal — Hostetler notes various examples of Amish uses of the law. Still, he demonstrates how long-standing Amish theological commitments embedded in their charter (for example, separation from the world and nonresistance) combine to make them distinctly nonlitigious relative to the larger society.

For Hostetler these issues were of more than academic concern. In the article's first half he tells the story of his father's difficulties with the Peachey Amish church, capably suggesting that, in many cases, the roots of Amish conflict run through many layers of soil and are thus quite difficult to unearth. With respect to Amish conflict with the state, Hostetler's account draws from his personal experience as a legal advocate for the Amish. Given their countercultural perspectives, Hostetler writes, the Amish often find themselves in precarious legal situations, a precariousness that is further exacerbated by the historically rooted Amish belief that suffering and redemption go hand in hand. For his part, Hostetler was unwilling to see Amish persons suffer unnecessarily at the hands of worldly people and institutions, and his advocacy sought to create space for them on America's pluralistic landscape.

This article first appeared in the Washington and Lee Law Review *41 (1984): 33–47. It is reprinted by permission of the* Washington and Lee Law Review.

I. INTRODUCTION

The Old Order Amish, who arrived on American shores in colonial times from about 1727, have survived in the modern world in distinctive and viable small communities. They are the most traditional of several branches of Mennonites originating from the Swiss Anabaptist movement of 1525,[1] having resisted modernization more successfully than most. In planting and harvesttime one can see their bearded men working the fields with horses and their women hanging out the laundry in neat rows to dry. Many American people have seen Amish families, with the men wearing broad-brimmed black hats and the women in bonnets and long dresses, in railway depots or bus terminals. Although the Amish have lived on the fringes of industrialized America for over two and a half centuries, they have moderated its influence on their personal lives, their families, communities, and values.

Thirty years ago, social scientists predicted that the Amish would be absorbed into the larger society in a few decades. It was reasoned that once the vitality of European customs was exhausted, like a run-down clock, the Amish would be assimilated into the dominant society.[a] The predictions were wrong. Moreover, the Amish population has more than doubled in thirty years. In 1950, there were an estimated 33,000 Amish persons in the United States. Today, the Amish population stands at approximately 90,000. Amish communities are in twenty states and in one province (Ontario) of Canada. None remain in Europe.

Compulsory school attendance laws were problematic to the Amish people for decades. The Amish felt that attendance at secondary schools, private or public, was contrary to their religious faith. Sending their children to high school, they asserted, would endanger their own faith community by preparing their children for a way of life outside the redemptive community. In *Wisconsin v. Yoder*,[2] the United States Supreme Court agreed. The Court ruled that compulsory schooling as applied to those Amish children who have completed the elementary grades, but are not yet sixteen years of age, unjustifiably interfered with the free exercise of the Amish religion in violation of the First and Fourteenth Amendments. The Court recognized that states have the responsibility of improving the education of their citizens, but measured this interest against the legitimate claims of the free exercise of religion. A recognized authority on church and state, Leo Pfeffer, called *Wisconsin v. Yoder* "a landmark case in American constitutional history."[3] The ruling confirmed the right of the Plain People to be let alone, a right which Mr. Justice Brandeis called, "the most comprehensive of rights and the right most valued by civilized men."[4]

My purpose here is not to comment on the legal consequences of the Court's ruling, for commentaries in professional journals are abundant. Rather, I shall describe the religious and cultural context of disputes within the Amish com-

a. Hostetler frequently makes this reference in his writings, though he never cites the social scientists who made that prediction. In any case, it was quite common for early- and mid-twentieth-century observers to predict the demise of the Amish. See, for example, Cornelius Weygandt, *A Passing America: Considerations of Things of Yesterday Fast Fading from Our World* (New York: Holt and Co., 1932), 168.

munity as distinguished from conflict with state governments or with outsiders. Further, I shall discuss some of the problems of a minority group that is prevented by its own ideology from using the courts as a means of dispute settlement, how Amish disputes enter the courts, the problems encountered by the legal profession in representing the Amish, and the ultimate resolution of such disputes. These issues come into sharp focus if we understand the religious and philosophic basis of the Amish faith community.

II. THE CHARTER OF THE AMISH COMMUNITY

A. A Redemptive Community

The Amish people are engaged in a social discourse with reality that requires them to build and maintain a redemptive community.[5] They view themselves as a Christian body suspended in a tension field between obedience to an all-knowing Creator on one hand and the forces of disobedience on the other. Central to their worldview is the story of creation in the Genesis account, the Garden of Eden, with its many plants, animals, birds, and fishes. Because of the "fall", human beings became heir to a disobedient or carnal nature which is under the curse of death. Redemption from death and restoration to eternal life is believed to be possible. Of his own free will the individual must acknowledge his natural sinful status, accept the love-gift of God (the substitutionary suffering and death of the Son of God), and live obediently in a disciplined community of believers.

The articulation and maintenance of a brotherly community is a love-response to God and distinguishes Anabaptist groups from most Protestants. The model for this community (the teaching and examples of Christ, especially in *Matthew* 5, 6, and 7) are the attributes of submission, humility, forgiveness, brotherly love, and nonresistance. The community is made up of "surrendered" members with Christ-like incarnated spiritual qualities. As a corporate offering to God, the brotherly community must exist "without spot or blemish" (*Ephesians* 5:27; 1 *Peter* 1:19; 2 *Peter* 3:14) and must be "a light to the world" (*Matthew* 5:14). By living in a state of harmony and constant struggle to be worthy "as a bride for the groom" (*Revelation* 21:2), the community must be vigilant, living on the edge of readiness. Within the community the gift of God is shared and reciprocated among the members, for since God loves all, "we ought also to love each other" (1 *John* 3:23).

Separation must be maintained between those who are obedient to God and those who are proud and disobedient. The community must be "nonconformed to the world" (*Romans* 12:2). The Amish are mandated to live separate from the "blind, perverted world" (*Philippians* 2:15) and to have no fellowship with "the unfruitful works of darkness." The Amish try to be "in the world but not of it" and hence claim the status of "strangers and pilgrims" (1 *Peter* 2:11). As a believing community, the Amish strive to be a "chosen generation" (1 *Peter* 2:9), "a congregation of the righteous," and a "peculiar people" (*Titus* 2:14) prepared to suffer humiliation or persecution.

B. *Ordnung*

Amish mythology and religious ideals are binding on individual members. Loyalty to God is judged by obedience and conformity to the community's rules of discipline. These rules, called *Ordnung*, enacted by each congregation, stipulate the ways in which members may interact with outsiders. Members may not be "unequally yoked with unbelievers" (2 *Corinthians* 6:14). On such grounds business partnerships or conjugal bonds with outsiders are forbidden. Strife and violence have no place in the community or in the life of members. Members may not function as officers or caretakers of the political or worldly society. The community rules clarify what is considered worldly and sinful, for to be worldly is to be alienated from God. Some of the rules have contextual support from biblical passages; others do not. Regulations that cannot be directly supported by biblical references are justified by arguing that to do otherwise would be worldly. The old way, *das alt Gebrauch*, is the better way.

Separation from the world means that one must be different from the world. Being different is more important, within limits, than specific ways of being different. The Amish feel some affinity to other Anabaptist "plain" groups, for example, Hutterite and Old Order Mennonite, who differ from them in specific ways such as dress and grooming, but who teach and maintain separation from the world. An overriding commitment to the practice of separation from the world also helps to explain why the Amish are not disturbed by slightly different rules in other Amish communities.

The rules of the Amish church-community cover a wide range of human behavior. Although there are slight variations among Amish communities, the most universal norms include the following: no high-line electricity, no telephone in the home, no central heating system, no automobiles, no tractors with pneumatic tires, and horse-drawn machinery must be used for farming. Married men must wear beards but moustaches are not allowed. Members must dress in plain and traditional styles of clothing. No formal education beyond the elementary grades is a rule of life. No meetinghouses are allowed, because members gather in farm homes for worship services. Adults only may become members of the *Gemeinde*, or congregation, by voluntary choice by taking the vow of water baptism. The baptismal vow includes the promise to abide by the *Ordnung* of the church. Some of the Amish rules, those recorded at special ministers' conferences, have been published, but the functioning *Ordnung* of each local group remains unwritten. These rules represent the deliberations of the ordained leaders with the endorsement of the members at a special "preparatory" service held semiannually before the communion service. Twice each calendar year, the members must affirm the rules and express their unity with all other members before taking communion. Unless there is unanimous expression of "peace with God" and unity with all believers, there can be no communion service. Offenses must be confessed and wrongs made right.

Interpreting the essence of Christianity as a love-community, a voluntary *Gemeinde* of the believing, is central to Anabaptist teaching. It cost the Amish and their ancestors, the Swiss Anabaptists of the sixteenth century, great sacrifice of blood and much harassment to establish this concept of the church-community. It meant severing their relationships with the state-church reformers, specifically the Reformed Church of Zwingli, and deportation and disfranchisement of themselves as citizens. Although highly valued as skillful farmers in Germanic countries, the Amish were denied the rights of ownership. They were totally dependent on the goodwill of lesser rulers for a peaceful existence. Only after coming to America did the Amish have the opportunities to buy land and to organize unique communities never realized in the Old World.

III. DISPUTE SETTLEMENT WITHIN THE COMMUNITY

A. Excommunication and Shunning

Much of the Amish ritual consists of maintaining the high standards of purity and the unity of the community. The disobedient and those who cause disunity must be excluded, for a blemish cannot be tolerated in the "bride" offered to God. The "old leaven", disorderly and carnally minded members, must be purged from the group. Most offenses in the community are violations of the rules, or actions by persons who, frequently without their knowledge, become the focus of disunity. Economic disputes occur infrequently. The offender in an Amish community must be dealt with in the manner stated in *Matthew* 18:15–17:

If your brother sins against you, go and show him his fault, just between the two of you. If he listens to you, you have won your brother
over. But if he will not listen, take one or two others along so that
every matter may be established by the testimony of two or three witnesses. If he refuses to listen to them, tell it to the church; and if he
refuses to listen even to the church, treat him as you would a pagan.[b]

Excommunication from membership is exercised after the offender has been
properly warned and remains unwilling to acknowledge his transgression. The
ordained leaders attempt to be loyal to every instruction of the Word, to avoid
offending the weak believers, and to cause the sinner to examine himself and
repent. Until they are restored to full membership, excommunicated persons
must be shunned. Social avoidance, *Meidung*, or shunning is the practice of re-
stricting member associations with persons who have been excommunicated.
Members must neither "eat with" nor "keep company" with such a person (1
Corinthians 5:11). The doctrine of avoidance is taken from *Romans* 16:17, where
the apostle instructs the believer to "avoid" those who work against the unity
of the church. In the sixteenth century, social avoidance was exercised by the
Anabaptists against "fanatical" persons including the Munsterites, Baden-
burgers, and the Davidians.[c] A century and a half later, Jacob Ammann, founder
of the Amish group, reintroduced the practice among the Swiss Mennonites
in 1693–1697 which resulted in a church division. The Amish today practice
shunning as taught by Ammann. While the Mennonites do not practice shunning at the domestic table, they do exclude offenders from participation in the
communion or ceremonial "table".

The following instances of disputes within the community are not necessarily representative, but they are illustrative. Disagreements within the community are typically settled between the parties, and the offenses are forgiven and
forgotten, but frequently not without economic loss and personal humiliation.

B. Examples

Case No. 1. A newly married couple, Susie and Sam Yoder,[6] settled on a farm
beside the bride's parents, Lydia and Eli Miller. Because the Yoders' acreage

---

b. New International Version.

c. These three apocalyptically oriented groups (the Davidians, followers of David Joris, are often called
Jorists) had various connections with sixteenth-century Anabaptists, and are often considered Anabaptists
themselves. See George Hunston Williams, *The Radical Reformation* (Philadelpia: Westminster Press, 1962),
362–86.

was small, the Millers donated and later deeded forty acres of their farm to the young couple. For ten years, all was neighborly and pleasant. Then Sam's father, who was known to be economically well off and adept in matters of finance, persuaded his son to sell his farm, including the lands donated to him by his wife's parents, Lydia and Eli Miller. Sam was to relocate in a more prosperous region closer to his own father. When the young couple announced their decision, the Miller family was dismayed. The two families stopped talking. After examining the records in the courthouse, Miller discovered that he had unknowingly signed over his lands to his son-in-law's father who was listed as having power of attorney for the young couple. Since Miller was a minister of the church, ostensibly an example of Christian character in the brotherhood, he had double reason for not contesting the transaction or seeking legal recourse. The estimated value of the "lost" acreage was 100,000 dollars. The transaction passed without contest and without publicity.

Case No. 2. Two large chicken houses on the farm of Joe Lapp burned to the ground. The losses were estimated at 170,000 dollars. Fire marshals who investigated the cause of the fire brought charges against Lapp for intentionally spreading liquid fuel on his premises for the purpose of collecting insurance. Lapp was brought to trial and a jury found him not guilty. The dispute and trial received full coverage in the local press. Lapp was excommunicated for hiring a lawyer to defend himself in court.

During the course of the trial, additional facts and accusations were reported. According to an Amish spokesman, Lapp was also excommunicated from the Amish church for operating a truck, a direct violation of Amish *Ordnung*. He denied owning a truck, but witnesses said they saw him driving the vehicle.

At the time of the fire, Lapp had insurance coverage of 245,000 dollars. He had increased his coverage with the Amish Aid Plan one month prior to the time of the fire, and three months earlier he had taken 82,000 dollars additional coverage from a non-Amish insurance agency. For several months Lapp tried, unsuccessfully, to sell his farm and egg business. At the time of the fire he had already bought a farm for 300,000 dollars in an adjoining county with the intention of moving.

Lapp rejected the sanctions of the Amish church, and said he would seek another religious affiliation that was more friendly. The Lapp family had previously had two fires on their property, and in one had lost a young son. The Amish Aid Committee deliberated whether they should pay a claim by a person who had been excommunicated. After consultation with the Amish bishops, the claim was paid in full. Lapp did not seek reinstatement with the Amish church.

The record suggests that Joe Lapp was hard-pressed financially. Whether or not he burned his own chicken houses, he may have overstepped the Amish rules. Although he claimed that he did not drive a farm truck nor personally own one, he had purchased a truck in the name of his business firm and paid nonmembers for operating the vehicle. In doing this, he acted like a few Amish engaged in small businesses such as painting, plumbing, and the building trades.

Case No. 3. In a highly publicized case, Andrew Yoder, an excommunicated Amish member of Wayne County, Ohio, in 1947 retaliated by suing each of four Amish ordained officials for 10,000 dollars each.[7] Yoder had been excommunicated and shunned after he joined an Amish group that permitted the use of automobiles. Claiming that he needed an automobile to transport his daughter to the doctor for frequent medical attention, Yoder began to attend a meetinghouse Amish church that allowed automobiles. Yoder claimed economic hardships as a consequence of the shunning. In a trial by jury, Yoder was awarded 5,000 dollars in damages. When the defendants made no attempts to pay, the farm of Bishop John Helmuth was put up for sheriff's sale. Such lawsuits are rare, but several have occurred. In some cases there appears to have been envy between individuals or families, in which in journalistic parlance, spite turned into 'mite', a derogatory rendering of *meide* or *meidung*, meaning to shun. In long-standing shunning cases, the divisive consequences on individuals and family members are far-reaching.

Case No. 4.[d] Henry Zook was an enterprising farmer, involved in construction, saw-milling, cattle raising, maintaining a dairy herd, and horsetrading. At the age of forty-seven, he became the focus of criticism, possibly also of envy among other Amish members. Regarding dress and grooming, he and his family more than conformed to Amish rules. Nevertheless, after a sequence of accusations, each followed by visits from the ordained officials, he had been excommunicated for reasons he could not accept. His wife requested that she be excommunicated with him. At the outset the accusations appeared to be petty and insignificant, but they became more serious. Pride was manifested in his various farm enterprises. Eventually he was accused of embezzling the estate of which he was the executor.

After a lapse of three years, reconciliation seemed remote. The couple had no inclination to liberalize by joining another Amish affiliation. When it became apparent that no reconciliation was possible, the family sold their Pennsylvania farm and moved to Iowa "to get away from church trouble." On their

---

d. This case recounts the experience of Hostetler's father, Joseph, who was excommunicated from his Amish church in 1929. For further details, see Chapter 4.

arrival in Iowa the couple applied for membership in the Amish church. They were received as members on confession of their faith. When the Pennsylvania bishop learned that the couple had been granted membership, he wrote the Iowa bishop explaining that if he did not promptly exclude the couple and honor the Pennsylvania shunning policy, the whole Iowa Church would be excluded from fellowship. Not prepared for a confrontation, the Iowa bishop promptly complied with the Pennsylvania ultimatum, excluded the couple, and advised them to return to Pennsylvania to make the necessary reconciliation. After four separate journeys to Pennsylvania to "make peace", no satisfactory reconciliation was achieved. After seven years of living without membership in any church, the couple joined a Mennonite congregation only after their grown children had done so and at the urging of the Mennonite bishop. Relatives and friends who remained faithful to the Amish church were obliged to shun the couple as long as they lived, a span of over forty years.

What had Henry Zook done to merit exclusion? No single offense was singled out. One obtrusive fact remains: he "talked back" to his accusers and to the ordained Amish officials, something that no excommunicated person must ever do if he wishes to be reinstated. As indicated, no amount of argument, justification, or logic will aid in reconciliation. A submissive attitude is absolutely necessary.

Backstage there were informal contributory factors that help to explain the accusations against Henry Zook, many of which were in the nature of harassment. Zook, it was learned in later life, had insisted that one Amish family, the Hertzlers, should not be invited to the wedding of his oldest daughter. All other families in the church were invited, but the Hertzlers were singled out as "not-invited". It was Hertzler, an older uncle of the bishop, who had initiated a series of accusations against Henry Zook. The young bishop felt morally compelled to pursue the allegations of his uncle. Why did Henry Zook insist that Hertzler be excluded from the wedding? Because Hertzler in the previous year excluded Henry from the wedding of his own daughter.[e]

C. The Pressure to Conform

Social ills associated with jealousies between neighbors or family lines frequently lie in the background of Amish disputes. When transgressions are

---

e. The person with whom Joseph Hostetler was in conflict was Ezra Renno. See Chapter 1.

clearly in evidence as in the case of moral lapses, and when the offender accepts the accusation, the threat of exclusion is a powerful technique for assuring conformity. In rare cases, excommunication can turn "sour".

This may occur when the accused person feels he is a victim of spite, unjust accusation, and is dealt with in an arbitrary manner. A person in such circumstances has no recourse, no court of appeal, and no alternative, for only the church has the power "to bind or to loose" (*Matthew* 16:19). An excommunicated person must, in keeping with Amish practice, show submission even if he considers himself innocent. Should such a person seek justice for himself or engage in arguments, he will certainly bring shunning on himself. The reason for this extreme action is that the church-community as the "bride of Christ" cannot tolerate arrogance or disunity.

The Amish, who work so hard to maintain unity and uniformity, nevertheless suffer the consequences of individual deviation or of persons who cannot achieve the high ideals. They fear the prospect of a fragmented social order. The symbols over which they may polarize into divisions are diverse. In the past, divisions have focused on the shape or color of a garment, the style of a house, carriage, harness; or the use of labor-saving machines. Members typically tend to suppress their feelings since no one wishes to become the object of publicity or of fostering disunity. Instead of disputing, those members who may be dissatisfied with the prevailing *Ordnung* may move to a more compatible Old Order community or start a new settlement.

IV. FIRST AMENDMENT ISSUES

A. Education

Wisconsin v. Yoder was preceded by several decades of uncertainty and a history of legal confrontations unfavorable to the Amish.[8] The Amish opposition was remarkably uniform in the various states, but the legal attempts to enforce attendance took various forms. A Kansas court found "[t]he question of how long a child should attend school is not a religious issue."[9] Most court decisions acknowledged that the Amish have sincere beliefs, but failed to see how Amish worship was violated. The notion of confining religious practices by defining religion was a serious challenge.

In Lancaster County, Pennsylvania, a large consolidated school supported by federal funds was planned for East Lampeter Township in 1937. The Amish leaders were concerned about its meaning and initially were divided as to the action to be taken. One element wanted to withdraw its children from the public schools. Others feared disobeying the law. An Old Order Amish School Committee of sixteen members was formed, to which representatives of the Old Order Mennonites were also invited. An attorney advised the Amish to use the legal process to stop construction of the school. A petition signed by 3,000 persons was sent to state officials. It asked for eight months of schooling per year, exemption from schooling after completion of the elementary grades, and the privilege of attending one-room schools. The petition was of no avail and the new consolidated school was soon built.

Children in Pennsylvania were required to attend school until their seventeenth birthday, but those engaged in farmwork were permitted to apply for a farm permit at the age of fifteen. Many, however, had repeated the eighth grade in order to stay out of high school and were still not old enough to apply for a farm permit. The conflict erupted when schools were no longer willing to tolerate the practice of allowing the Amish children to repeat grade eight. School officials tried withholding the farm permits. The state threatened to withhold funds from districts that did not comply with the law. When the parents did not send their children to the consolidated high school, they were summoned to court and fined. They refused to pay the fines on grounds that this would admit guilt. The parents were then sent to the county jail. Anonymous friends and businessmen frequently paid the fines to release the parents from prison. Some were arrested as many as ten times.[f]

Attorneys and friends of the Amish who took the case to the courts found no legal solution. After many confrontations, Governor George Leader in 1955 arranged a reinterpretation of the school code and introduced a compromise plan, the Amish vocational school. Under this plan, the pupils performed farm and household duties under parental guidance, kept a daily journal of their activities, and met in classes three hours per week. The schools were required to teach certain subjects, and to file attendance reports, but teachers were not required to be state certified.

Other states began to follow the Pennsylvania plan. In Ohio, there were many legal attempts to force the Amish to attend the public school. In Indiana, the State Superintendent of Schools encouraged the Amish to organize their own schools and develop standards in keeping with their prerogative as a religious body. In all of these states, the Amish began to form their own country schools, hiring experienced teachers who had retired from the public school system.

f. See Thomas J. Meyers, "Education and Scholing," in *The Amish and the State*, rev. ed., ed. Donald B. Kraybill (Baltimore: Johns Hopkins University Press, 2003), 88–92.

When this was no longer possible, they staffed the schools with their own Amish teachers.[g]

The Amish in Hardin County, Ohio, had established a private school in 1954. The teacher had had no college training, and apparently no experience as a teacher. John P. Hershberger was tried and found guilty of failing to cause his children to attend school as required by the compulsory education laws of Ohio. The court found no question of religious freedom in the case. The issue was whether the instruction provided in the private school was equivalent to the instruction given in the public schools. The court said it was not. Hershberger was fined and ordered to comply with Ohio law.

Hershberger then moved to Wayne County, Ohio, where he and other Amish parents were charged with child neglect for failing to send their children to school. Following numerous court delays, the children were found to be neglected and the parents were ordered to surrender their children to the custody of the Child Welfare Board. On the appointed day, the parents appeared without the children. The parents claimed they could not find the children and the judge sentenced them to jail for contempt of court. The truant officer was sent to the Hershberger farm where he found some twenty children all dressed alike. When "he asked for Andy Hershberger, he received twenty answers, all in Pennsylvania Dutch."[10] There was public sympathy for the jailed parents. The judge ordered the parents released on condition that they return with the children on Friday. The parents appeared on Friday, but without the children. The bishop agreed to have the children appear in school on Monday. On Monday they did not appear. When it became apparent that the Amish were going to appeal the contempt order, the Wayne County Board of Education dropped the charges against the Amish.[11]

The controversy in Iowa during the mid-1960s illustrates the complex differences between local, county, and state authorities and the Amish.[12] In the Amish settlement in Buchanan County, Iowa, school authorities forced their way into an Amish private school in order to compel the children to board a bus to take them to the consolidated town school. The press got wind of impending events and recorded the scene as frightened youngsters ran for cover in nearby cornfields and sobbing mothers and fathers were arrested for non-compliance with an Iowa school law. The Iowa incident became the subject of worldwide publicity. School officials were deluged with adverse reactions from people who sympathized with the Amish.

The emergence of a number of educational and legal problems in operating

g. Ibid., 93–95.

nonpublic schools prompted Donald A. Erickson, of the University of Chicago, in 1967 to plan a two-day National Invitational Conference on State Regulation of Nonpublic Schools on "Freedom and Control in Education." Attending were members of state departments of education, members of the legal profession, representatives of religious denominations operating private schools, and a few university professors. In another expression of concern, a group of citizens in 1967 organized the National Committee for Amish Religious Freedom with a Lutheran pastor, Rev. William C. Lindholm, as chairman. The immediate task was to appeal to the United States Supreme Court a Kansas Supreme Court decision against Amishman Leroy Garber.[13] A number of religious leaders, politicians, and educators wrote articles in national magazines advising conciliation. Governor Hughes[h] of Iowa said, "I am more willing to bend laws and logic than human beings. I will always believe that Iowa and America are big enough in space and spirit to provide a kindly place for all good people, regardless of race, or creed."[14]

It was against this background that the United States Supreme Court settled the long-standing controversy on May 15, 1972. Since the Amish would not initiate legal action, one of their members asked the National Committee for Amish Religious Freedom for assistance. The committee hired attorney William B. Ball, an expert in constitutional law and religion, and raised the needed funds. In laying the groundwork for a First Amendment religious issue, Mr. Ball attempted to show that a true religious liberty claim was involved, that the state was interfering with the Amish religion, and that despite the state's interests in compelling children to attend school, the Amish position did not present any significant threat to society.[15] As in previous court cases, the county court and the circuit court ruled that even though the Amish were sincere, the compelling interest of the state was greater. When the case reached the Wisconsin Supreme Court, it ruled that the state had failed to prove its case. The Department of Education in Wisconsin was not satisfied to let the matter rest. It appealed to the United States Supreme Court, which granted a review of the case. Wisconsin argued that compulsory education is necessary to maintain the political system, that the state has a right to free the children from ignorance, and that only legislatures can determine educational policy. The Supreme Court held to the contrary, at least with respect to the Amish.

Why did this far-reaching case emerge in a remote Amish community in Wisconsin and not in Lancaster County, Pennsylvania, or Holmes County, Ohio, where there are large concentrations of Amish? How was the Amish disdain

h. This refers to Harold E. Hughes, who served as Iowa's governor from 1963 to 1969.

for legal suits overcome? The geographic and cultural context of the case was significant. The cheese-making Swiss Americans of Green County, Wisconsin (New Glarus) were indifferent to the Amish in their midst. The local school officials were ambitious in promoting education and the educational standards of the state. The Amish settlement was new and small. There were twenty-four Amish families living in the community. There was no residing bishop, and the bishop overseeing the ceremonial functions of the New Glarus group did not prevent the defendants from seeking legal advice from the National Committee for Amish Religious Freedom. An Amish bishop in Iowa, however, expressed fear of taking the issue to court.[i] The Amish are extremely careful and usually reluctant to permit others to litigate in their behalf.

The legal counsel for the Amish avoided the pitfall experienced by attorney Shepard Cole who represented the Amish in their case against the Social Security Administration in 1961. After Cole had completed all the necessary legal work, the Amish bishops changed their minds as they ascended the steps of the Federal District Court in Pittsburgh and asked that the case be dropped. In *Wisconsin v. Yoder*, this circumstance was avoided.

The National Committee for Amish Religious Freedom placed the problem of Amish education on a broader base than was possible for the local Amish community or the Mennonite denomination, thus giving it national perspective. Public opinion had become favorable to the Amish as a result of previously publicized incidents. The Amish defendants were not disciplined by their church for allowing the National Committee for Amish Religious Freedom to litigate in their behalf. In the Amish view, the Wisconsin Department of Education was the aggressor. The Department was the party that appealed the case to the United States Supreme Court. That was important to the Amish participants.

The threat of the large school and its associated values has been stopped, at least temporarily for the Amish. It is clear that the Amish will not tolerate the removal of their children from their homes to distant schools where they are placed in large groups with narrow age limits, taught skills useless to their way of life, and exposed to values contradictory to their culture.[16] Although they have won the legal protection in some respects, they have little guarantee other than public sentiment for the maintenance of their schools. The certification of teachers remains a problem in a few states. For example, a newly formed Amish community in Nebraska in 1978 was forced to leave that state

i. Dan M. Bontrager wrote to the National Committee for Amish Religious Freedom on 19 May 1969: "There are other old order Amish settlements in Wisconsin and they seem to get along. And remember if you loose [sic] things will be worse." Copy of Bontrager letter in Hostetler Papers, Box AL06.22.

in 1982 following unsuccessful attempts to operate their own schools. This can happen even though the Amish willingly comply with state requirements of attendance, length of the school year, length of the school day, health and safety standards, and the teaching of basic skills.

B. Compulsory Insurance

The Amish opposition to compulsory insurance was widely publicized when Social Security benefits were extended through Public Law 761, January 1, 1955, to cover self-employed persons, including farmers. A delegation of bishops made numerous trips to Washington seeking exemption from the tax and its benefits. Before congressional committees, they contended that "Old Age Survivors Insurance is abridging and infringing to [sic] our religious freedom."[17] In support of their stand, they said the Bible teaches "if any provide not . . . for those of his own house, he hath denied the faith, and is worse than an infidel." (1 Timothy 5:8). To pay social security tax, the Amish say, is to admit that the government has a responsibility for aged Amish members, and to admit this is to deny the faith. They foresaw that this alliance with government would make future generations dependent on the government. Federal means of providing for these needs were viewed as purely secular if not sinful.

Some Amish paid the self-employment tax and others maintained bank accounts against which levies could be made. The Internal Revenue agent met with the Amish to persuade them to comply with the law. When this failed the Internal Revenue Service took legal action to seize horses from as many as thirty delinquent Amish farmers. Valentine Byler of New Wilmington, Pennsylvania, for example, was approached on May 1, 1961, by law enforcement officers on his farm. Three horses were unhitched, taken to market and sold. His tax and the expenses of transporting and feeding the horses were deducted from the proceeds, and the balance was returned to him. The incident received such widespread publicity that the Internal Revenue Service placed a moratorium on further enforced collections, pending a test of constitutionality. Finally, on July 30, 1965, President Lyndon Johnson signed Public Law 89–97 to provide medical care for the aged under the Medicare section of the Social Security Act. Section 319 of the bill contained a subsection permitting an individual to apply for exemption from the self-employment tax.[18] The applicant must be a member of a religious body, conscientiously opposed to social security benefits, that makes reasonable provision for its own dependent members. The waiver applies only to self-employed persons and not to individuals who are employees and work for wages. The Supreme Court has ruled that Old

Order Amish employers must withhold wages from employees who are Amish, even though such employees refuse old age pensions.[19] Those Amish who engage in business or manufacture are faced with still other compulsory entanglements such as unemployment insurance, accident compensation, and workers' compensation taxes.

When the Occupational Safety and Health Administration of the United States Department of Labor ruled that employees in construction and carpentry work must wear hard hats, the Amish refused to give up their traditional broad-brimmed felt hats. Hard hats would in effect obliterate their identity as Amish persons. They had no dispute with the safety standards, but since the regulation affected their own safety, and not the safety of others, they considered the requirement a violation of their religion. After four hundred Amish were furloughed from their construction jobs in Allen and DeKalb counties in Indiana, they sought and won an exemption from the regulation. They did not file suit. Rather, they asked for an exemption, which was granted in June 1972. When the safety of others is directly involved, as in the laws requiring lights on horse-drawn vehicles and SMV (slow-moving vehicle) emblems on the rear of such vehicles, the Amish generally comply. Only in a few regions have the Amish objected to SMV emblems on grounds that they are too ostentatious for their way of life.[j]

V. AMISH USES OF THE LAW

Like their Anabaptist founders, the Amish acknowledge the necessity of government and its prerogative to rule over its citizens. Rebellion against the government would be considered un-Christian and unthinkable. The function of the state is to maintain order in the natural or carnal world. The Amish do not run for public office and they avoid any kind of political activity that would require the use of force, for this would violate the higher law of Christian love as they understand it. They are admonished to suffer injustices rather than instigate lawsuits or defend themselves in the courts. They are forbidden to take oaths, serve on juries, or collect debts by using the courts. The Amish have an outstanding reputation as law-abiding citizens. However, in matters that violate their conscience and religion, they resolutely stand their

---

j. For a thorough consideration, see Lee J. Zook, "Slow-moving Vehicles," in Kraybill, ed., *The Amish and the State*, 145–60.

ground, and as a consequence they have advanced the cause of religious liberty for all Americans.

In practice, some Amish have made use of the law in the past, depending on the circumstances and their conscience. Some family heads are more inclined to use the law than others. When fined for refusing to send their children to high school, Amish parents have refused to pay. In some cases, attorneys have represented them in courts. Their ambivalence about going to court was expressed by an Amishman who remarked, "The trouble with a lawsuit is that if you lose you lose, and if you win, you lose too (in good will)." Some Amish have a superstitious fright of going to court, fearing that if the powers of evil are coerced, greater evil and catastrophe will result. Although holding public office is forbidden, voting in local or national elections is not. Voter turnout is heaviest in local township elections.

Controversies that have drawn the Amish into community conflict with the non-Amish have generally centered on cultural values or beliefs rather than on economics or power. The Amish pay federal, state, and local taxes, as well as property taxes. A few Amish have been jailed for contempt for failing to secure building permits, in violation of municipal zoning ordinances. In one community, zoning would require installing septic tanks on their farms, using certified plumbers, and the elimination of outdoor toilets. Some Amish communities are not prepared to make the change.

There have been no studies of acts of violence against the Amish. Amish are frequently helpless, as pacifists, to defend themselves or their property. Members typically do not report acts of violence or destruction of private property to law enforcement officials. Rancorous behavior, threats, deliberate destruction, vandalism, and arson are known to occur and are most likely underreported. In the community of Berne, Indiana, an Amish infant was killed by a rock thrown into an Amish buggy at night by four juveniles from the local village.[20] For several weeks, juveniles routinely were spending their evenings throwing rocks at Amish buggies. A woman in Ohio was shot in the face. Firecrackers are frequently thrown at Amish horses. The Amish are easy targets, since most know that they will not prosecute.

The Amish are well aware that they cannot halt modernization nor throw industrialization off their backs. The most they can hope for is tolerance for their religious communities, existing as pockets in rural America. They have no interest in allying themselves with an agrarian movement or a political party. Their community life is precarious in a world enamored with the illusion of having power over nature. As they view the general decay of sensibilities in the outside world, they maintain a willingness to suffer as may be necessary for their redemption.

NOTES

1. For standard descriptions of Amish culture see generally J. A. Hostetler, Amish Society (1980); William I. Schreiber, Our Amish Neighbors (1962); Calvin G. Bachman, The Old Order Amish of Lancaster County, Pennsylvania (1942, 1961).

2. Wisconsin v. Yoder, 406 U.S. 205 (1972).

3. Leo Pfeffer, Compulsory Education and the Amish 136 (A. N. Keim ed. 1975).

4. Olmstead v. United States, 277 U.S. 438, 478 (1928).

5. J. A. Hostetler, Amish Society 75–92 (1980) (more extensive treatment of "The Amish Charter").

6. All names appearing in the disputes described here are fictitious except concerning the Andrew Yoder case. See infra note 7.

7. John H. Yoder, Caesar and the Meidung, Mennonite Q. Rev. 23, 76–98 (April 1949).

8. See A. Keim, From Erlanbach to New Glarus, reprinted in Compulsory Education and the Amish 1–15 (A. N. Keim ed. 1975); see also Paul Ruxin, The Right not to be Modern Men: The Amish and Compulsory Education, 53 Va., L. Rev. 925–52 (1967).

9. Ruxin, supra note 8, at 945.

10. Id. at 943.

11. Ohio has not modified any of its laws to meet Amish objections. The state issued a report entitled Amish Sectarian Education, Research Report No. 44, Ohio Legislative Service Commission (1960). See also F. S. Buchanan, The Old Paths: A Study of the Amish Response to Public Schooling in Ohio, Ph.D. dissertation, Ohio State University (1967).

12. Donald A. Erickson, Showdown at an Amish Schoolhouse: A Description and Analysis of the Iowa Controversy, reprinted in Public Controls for Nonpublic Schools 9–60 (Donald A. Erickson ed. 1969) (full description). See also Harrell Rodgers, Jr., Community Conflict, Public Opinion and the Law: The Amish Dispute in Iowa (1969).

13. In a 4–3 decision, the Kansas Supreme Court declined to hear the case. See Donald A. Erickson, The Persecution of Leroy Garber, reprinted in Compulsory Education and the Amish (A. N. Keim ed. 1975).

14. William Lindholm, Do We Believe in Religious Liberty—for the Amish? (1967).

15. See William B. Ball, Building a Landmark Case: Wisconsin v. Yoder, reprinted in Compulsory Education and the Amish 114–23 (A. N. Keim ed. 1975).

16. J. A. Hostetler & G. E. Huntington, Children in Amish Society (1971) (description of Amish educational philosophy and schooling).

17. Our Religious Convictions against Social Security (April 1960).

18. I.R.C. § 1402(g) (1982) (exemption for members of specified religious faiths); see I.R.C. § 1402(h) (1982) (definition of self-employed).

19. United States v. Lee, 455 U.S. 252, 256–61 (1982).

20. Barry Siegel, A Quiet Killing in Adams County, Rolling Stone (Feb. 19, 1981) (full report of incident).

16

MARKETING THE AMISH SOUL (1984)

In March 1984, John A. Hostetler was asked by the Pennsylvania Bureau of Motion Picture and Television Development to advise Paramount Pictures in the production of Witness, *an action-romance featuring Amish themes and characters. Hostetler refused the bureau's request, though not without offering his advice: tell Paramount Pictures to leave the Amish alone. In the following months, Hostetler would mount a campaign to exert pressure on Pennsylvania state officials to pull the plug on the film and others like it in the future. The campaign failed, but Hostetler and his allies (including some Old Order Amish leaders) did gain a few moderate concessions from the bureau, which promised not to promote the Pennsylvania Amish as subjects for future films.*

"Marketing the Amish Soul" outlines Hostetler's concerns, which revolved around three foci. First, the film violated Amish sensibilities against having their images and sacred symbols portrayed in a Hollywood film, something Hostetler called a "symbolic intrusion" into their lives. Second, the moviemaking process and the publicity generated by the film boded ill for real-life Amish people, particularly those in Lancaster County. Third, Hollywood's portrayal of the Amish was bound to be inauthentic, thus planting false impressions in the minds of moviegoers. Critics charged Hostetler with overstating his case against the film (would Witness *really "signal a milestone in the erosion of the social fabric of the Amish community"?) and, in other instances, challenged his assumption that religious groups should be granted control over the way they are portrayed. Still, Hostetler's views gained broad circulation and widespread approbation, particularly among Mennonites and Lancaster County residents already troubled by the commercial spectacle of Amish-themed tourism.*

This article was published in Gospel Herald, 26 June 1984, 452–53. Copyright © 1984 John A. Hostetler. Reprinted by permission.

Paramount Pictures, a Hollywood firm, is making a major commercial movie in the heart of the Amish community in Lancaster County. The plot, we are informed, concerns a murder in Philadelphia and an affair between a police detective and an Amish widow. The filming is to be completed by late June.

This event marks a major symbolic intrusion into the Amish community. It is well known that the plain people dislike having their pictures taken, basing their objections on the "graven image" (Deut. 5:8).[a] Why, then, has the movie industry entered this community?

---

a. Deut. 5:8 (KJV) reads: "Thou shalt not make thee any graven image, or any likeness of any thing that is in heaven above, or that is in the earth beneath, or that is in the waters beneath the earth."

In their search for the exotic, the entertainment world is looking for new turf. But the real reason is that the Commonwealth of Pennsylvania solicited Hollywood to come into the area on grounds of attracting more money into the state. James Pickard, Secretary of Commerce, says his newly created Bureau of Motion Picture and Television Development is run by two energetic persons, Michelle Casale and R. S. Staab. We have been informed that since the creation of the Bureau in 1977, 27 moviemakers have chosen Pennsylvania as the site of their filming, and all fifty states are now competing for Hollywood business.

When Mr. Staab asked me to serve as a consultant for the authenticity of the production earlier this year, I declined, saying I thought the project was inappropriate. I stated my objections in a letter and strongly suggested that the project be dropped. The National Committee for Amish Religion, via its counsel William B. Ball, asked Governor Thornburgh to abandon the movie. There has been no response from the governor or state agencies.[b]

Meanwhile state and Paramount representatives sought a suitable Amish farm, and assurance that up to fifty Amish buggies and sufficient Amish hats and clothing could be secured to make the movie. Offers were made to Amish people for their help. The Amish bishops warned their members not to take part.

One Amish farmer was offered $200,000 in cash for the exclusive use of his farm.[c] The family would have had to move, but the crops and livestock would be taken care of, and in six weeks the family could have moved back again. The Amish farmer declined. Another was offered full payment for the restoration of his barn which a short time earlier had burned to the ground if he would permit the barn raising to be filmed for the movie. He declined the offer. Paramount then found a Mennonite farm couple who allowed the use of their farm to make the movie. Offering exorbitant money, which the Amish understood as bribes, undoubtedly tempted some but only strengthened the resolve of others.

One Amish woman turned from a carriage to a photographer who had just snapped her picture; she said, "You are stealing from us, you are taking our soul."

b. Hostetler turned down Staab's request in a letter dated 13 March 1984. William Ball, writing on behalf of the National Committee for Amish Religious Freedom, sent his letter to Governor Richard Thornburgh on 30 April 1984. On 26 June 1984, Hostetler wrote his own letter to Thornburgh, asking the governor to stop Hollywood firms from doing in the future "what Paramount Pictures has done this summer." James Pickard, Pennsylvania's Secretary of Commerce, responded to Hostetler on Thornburgh's behalf on 19 July 1984, defending filmmakers' right "to exercise their craft based on the same principles of personal freedom that allow the Amish to practice their culture." All letters in Hostetler Papers, Box AL06.16.

c. Director Peter Weir denied this in Jon Ferguson, "Angry Weir Defends Film Against 'Lies,'" *Lancaster Intelligencer Journal*, 29 June 1984, 1–2.

By posing as a stranger interested in Amish ways, the actress who was to play the part of an Amish woman, was received into an Amish home for several days. When her real identity was discovered the family asked her not to return. Asked about the incident, the film director replied, "There have been worse deceptions."[d]

What are the religious issues and social consequences of featuring violence and transgression of fundamental mores in an Amish context? How strong is the Amish objection to the "graven image" in view of the tourist traffic for many years in Lancaster County?

The objection to photographing remains firm. Although tourists have snapped many pictures of Amish people and local persons have made documentary films for historic and instructional purposes, a Hollywood film is something else.

Hollywood is in the entertainment business. They want access; they want the freedom to fictionalize and to alter reality in any way that will entertain with maximum profit. Their productions generally flow liberally with violence and violation of standards of morality.

The Amish people have retained a pattern of living that is open and friendly with visitors on a face-to-face basis. Their faith forbids them to use coercion. They are vulnerable and easily exploited. They are harmless and pacifists, and in the historic sense "defenseless Christians." Moviemakers know that they will not retaliate.

Through the years the Amish people have earned the respect of the public. Local merchants and industries have exercised restraint rather than blatant exploitation. It is ironic that the state of Pennsylvania, the "Quaker state," is itself instrumental in the exploitation of long-standing religious communities, and against their consent. It appears that neither the state nor the Pennsylvania Dutch Tourist Bureau or the county commissioners have exercised sufficient sensitivity.

The movie will signal a milestone in the erosion of the social fabric of the Amish community. Divorce, violence, and taking human life will be made thinkable and more commonplace in a community relatively free from these ills. The deterioration of trusting relationships, the acceleration of human blight,

---

d. The statement "There have been worse deceptions" was not made by director Peter Weir, but rather by producer Edward Feldman (see Chris Conway, "But the Amish are Displeased by the 'Intrusion,'" *Philadelphia Inquirer*, 11 May 1984, D-8). In a subsequent interview with the *New York Times*, Kelly McGillis denied that she had failed to identify herself as an actor (see Constance S. Rosenblum, "A Young Actress Adopts Old Ways," *New York Times*, 3 February 1985, 17). Director Weir also denied that McGillis had been deceptive in gaining access to an Amish home (see Ferguson, "Angry Weir Defends Film," 1–2).

and the presence of leisure seekers overrunning the Amish landscape and entering one-room schools will become more common. By gaining surreptitious entrance into Amish homes, schools, and gatherings, intruders with cameras will destroy much of the friendly disposition the Amish have for visitors.[e]

Are these erosions worth $3,000,000 which the commonwealth says will be gained in revenue? What can be done? Social and moral outrage is about the only alternative. The production of a Hollywood film here is sure to set a precedent for more to follow, unless action is taken to prevent it. Mennonites and other churches can sensitize their members to the issues. Letters to the editor of any Pennsylvania newspaper will help. Phone Governor Dick Thornburgh at his toll-free office number: 1–800–932–0784. Hundreds of calls will help.

At issue is a principle that goes far beyond an Amish inconvenience. If the state government follows a policy of stimulating the economy without regard for the religious life of its citizens and the welfare of its communities, then all religious groups may suffer the loss of liberty in one way or another.

For years the American Indians were pictured by moviemakers as bloodthirsty savages. They suffered harm from these widely disseminated images which planted erroneous impressions in millions of people. The Indians finally grew tired of having their symbols sold for entertainment and laughter. They now have their own police force, and the states in which they live require a license before moviemakers may enter.

The right to be "left alone" is a right which Supreme Court Justice Louis Brandeis called "the most comprehensive of rights and the right most valued by civilized men."[f] We believe the Amish people have earned the right to be left alone from those who would market their sacred symbols for shallow entertainment and pecuniary gain.

e. The final sentence of this paragraph refers not to the moviemakers (who did not film Amish people, let alone do it surreptitiously), but rather to tourists and photographers who, in Hostetler's estimation, would be emboldened by the movie's existence.

f. Hostetler's quotation draws from Brandeis's dissenting opinion in *Olmstead v. United States*, 277 U.S. 438 (1928), a case concerning the government's use of evidence obtained by wiretapping: "They [the makers of the Constitution] conferred, as against the government, the right to be let alone—the most comprehensive of rights and the right most valued by civilized men."

17

A NEW LOOK AT THE OLD ORDER (1987)

In 1987, Penn State University's Department of Agricultural Economics and Rural Sociology invited alumnus John A. Hostetler, then sixty-eight years old, to deliver its sixth annual M. E. John Memorial Lecture. Hostetler's presentation, entitled "A New Look at the Old Order," assembled an array of conceptual issues that Hostetler wove around the theme of Amish survival. The survival of the North American Amish had long been one of Hostetler's chief concerns, and he frequently challenged forces that, from his perspective, threatened Amish vitality. Now that he neared retirement, however, he was just as interested in making sense of their survival, for despite contrary predictions, the Amish had survived in twentieth-century America — not only survived, but also thrived. The Amish have "no tricks" in this regard, wrote Hostetler, but they do have unique and, in the case of silence, subtle cultural practices that have served them well. In sum, "the cultural energy of the Amish remains vigorous."

As much as Hostetler's "New Look" pertained to the Amish and their unique cultural resources, the lecture was, in a certain sense, also about him. In it he notes his career-long disciplinary migration toward anthropology, and he criticizes the tendency of scholars (a tendency sometimes evident in his earlier work) to explain cultures by invoking broad, theoretical models. These models can be useful, Hostetler concedes, but scholarship with an "anthropological touch" is often more revealing. Hostetler uses that touch in this piece, which he concludes with a familiar refrain: the Amish are an important national resource, one which their American neighbors would sacrifice at their own peril. Of course, the difference between proclaiming that message in 1987 and proclaiming it in 1950 was vast, for in 1987 Hostetler could point to a host of other pundits who were saying the same thing. Hostetler's concern for Amish survival remained, but it was now coupled with the recognition that his high view of Amish life had been vindicated in the court of public opinion.

This piece was first published in the Rural Sociologist *7 (1987): 278–92. Copyright © 1987 John A. Hostetler. Reprinted by permission.*

Gene Logsdon is a small farmer, author, and columnist. He lives in Ohio. As a neighbor of the Amish people he has won their friendship and has monitored their farm management practices. Recently (Logsdon 1987:74) he wrote:

> The Amish have become a great embarrassment to American agriculture. Many "English" farmers, as the Amish call the rest of us, are in desperate financial straits these days and relatively few are making money. As a result it is fashionable among writers, the clergy, politi-

cians, farm machinery dealers, and troubled farm banks to depict the family farmer as a dying breed and to weep great globs of crocodile tears over the coming funeral. All of them seem to forget these small, conservatively-financed family farms that are doing quite well, thank you, of which the premier example is the Amish.

Amish farmers, as Logsdon points out, are still surviving in the present crunch despite (or because of) their supposedly old-fashioned ways of farming. When an Amish farmer occasionally does get into difficulty, it is because he has listened to the promises of modern agribusiness instead of heeding traditional wisdom. Even when this happens, his brethren in the community will generally come to the aid. Moreover, the Amish continue to prosper without government subsidies and to disregard a "get big or get out" philosophy. Logsdon observes, interestingly, that the Amish do not work as hard physically as he and his father did when they were milking 100 cows with all the modern conveniences.

Mechanized farmers have downgraded the Amish for their "hair-splitting ways" with technology, such as using tractors for stationary power but not for field work. The Amish contend that this keeps their community intact while yet being efficacious for farming. A motor-powered baler, corn harvester, or hay crimper pulled by horses appears ridiculous to a modern agribusinessman. But such innovation saves many thousands of dollars over buying more mechanized equipment for the same work. The Amish reason that tractors would tempt their members to expand acreages and accumulate large debts while driving other Amish off the land. Following such temptations, Logsden contends, is why American agriculture today finds itself in such deep trouble.

Amish church rules, which restrict members from using the most modern technology, have given rise to ingenious ways of economizing. Woodworking enterprises and shops are operated with diesel-powered hydraulic or air pumps instead of an electric motor for each tool. The small repair shops, furniture shops, printing plants, and many other enterprises make a small profit where non-Amish operations fail. The Amish landscape is active and alive in most cases with bustling shops and small businesses. Homes are inhabited by young couples with children and grandparents are not banished. Schools, churches, roadside stands, and often cheese factories dot the countryside. Logsdon asks us to compare the Amish areas of the nation with the decaying towns and empty farmsteads of land dominated by large-scale agribusiness. The local economy of the Amish feeds into the regional economy of which it is a part.

According to Wendell Berry, a Kentucky small farmer, poet, and critic, the differences between Amish occupied farmlands (in the states of Iowa, Illinois, and Indiana) and Midwestern farming country are as great as that between a desert and an oasis. He writes (Berry 1981:249):

> In typical Midwestern farming country the distances between in-habited houses are stretching out as bigger farmers buy out their smaller neighbors in order to "stay in." The signs of the "movement" and its consequent specialization are everywhere: good houses stand-ing empty, going to ruin; good stock barns going to ruin; pasture fences fallen down or gone; machines too large for available doorways left in the weather; windbreaks and woodlots gone down before the bulldozers; small schoolhouses and churches deserted or filled with grain.

There is more life in the Amish country—more natural life, more animal life, more human life. Because the Amish farms are smaller, many of them a hun-dred acres or less, Amish neighborhoods are more densely populated than most rural areas.

Amish farming has a complicated structure. It is at once biological and cul-tural, rather than industrial or economic, and defies standard bookkeeping. There are unaccountable values, expenses, and benefits. Not only is the accoun-tant confronted with biological forces and processes, but also with spiritual and community values that cannot be quantified. Because of such mysteries, Amish farming practices have been ignored, says Berry. By contrast, conven-tional agriculture or "agribusiness" is simple arithmetic.

A half-century ago, the Amish were viewed by many as an obdurate sect living by oppressive customs, exploiting the labor of their children. Thirty years ago Amish parents were sent to jail for not allowing their children to go to school beyond grade eight. They were seen as a group who renounced both modern conveniences and the American dream of progress. Today, the Amish are esteemed as meticulous farmers, practicing the virtues of thrift and hard work, and as islands of sanity in a culture obsessed with economic indicators and technology run rampant.

Thirty-five years ago sociologists predicted that the Amish would be ab-sorbed into the larger society in a few decades. The predictions were wrong. The Amish population has tripled in the last 35 years, standing today at ap-proximately 100,000.

The tendency to reexamine the Amish stance is not confined to agricultural professionals. My files are bulging with letters from people, including children and old folk who ask me how to become Amish. A man from California writes:

> I am interested in joining the Amish. Just how does one do that? I am 53 years old and my wife is 47. Do you have the address of the Amish? They don't have any Amish here in California, do they? Please send me their newspaper and bill me. I shall pay you later. They have the real true religion for sure. Our society is sick—[with] greed for money and real estate. I was raised a Roman Catholic. They went down the tubes with Vatican II.

A ten-year-old girl named Jessie has written:

> When I grow up I want to live like the Amish, with no electricity or cars. I really would believe their way and live it. I live in a rural part of New York state, in a small house with ten acres and a brook. I love nature and to live simply. My great grand mom was a Mennonite. Would you know the address of an Amish boy or girl?

Cindy Jensen, a mother in Wisconsin, wrote:

> I understand that the Amish communities are located in Wisconsin. Could you pinpoint the townships for me? As part of the education of my children, I would like to expose them to the lifestyles of others. I am intrigued by the Amish, and their flourishing nature. Their survival in this crazy world is astonishing.

Thirty years ago our national magazines described the Amish as a "dying breed." It was reasoned that once the vitality of the European customs (like dress and language) were exhausted, like a run-down clock, the Amish would be assimilated into the dominant society. Today they are featured in national magazines as hearty Americans. Earlier, the state of Michigan prosecuted the Amish for maintaining uncertified schools. But in 1976 *Michigan Farmer* chose the Amish for their bicentennial feature. In the premier issues of *Country*, a "new type of magazine for those who live in or long for the country," the reader is introduced to a major feature in color (Miller 1987:62–64) entitled, "We Love Being Amish."

AMISH SURVIVAL PATTERNS

The Amish have no tricks or mechanisms which other groups such as the Essenes, Orthodox Jews, or monastic orders have not utilized for maintaining their identity.[a] Sociologists today could offer the Amish no improvement by way of techniques for the transmission of their values. They are their own practicing sociologists. The Amish embrace a social charter that requires a way of thinking distinguished from worldly thinking. They practice limited geographic isolation by living in rural areas. Social isolation is maintained by codes allowing only limited participation in wider human affairs. Consumptive aspirations are guarded by meaningful rules against luxuries. A symbol system delineates the "redemptive community" from worldly civilization. A separate language, dress, and grooming practices specify the cultural boundaries. In addition to such obvious explanations, a hidden dimension must be mentioned: the Amish past is alive in their present. Their singing of the martyr hymns while the world around is tuned to rock and roll illustrates this dimension.

University professors have taught their students to think of the Amish as a cultural island, or as a traditional cultural system left over in the modern world, a type labeled as sect, folk, or *Gemeinschaft* society.[b] The Amish may be viewed from any one of these theoretical perspectives, but such models leave out much that is relevant for understanding the inner dynamics.

Edward Hall (1976:10) states that man is a model-making organism par excellence. Models serve a useful function. They enable the participant in a culture to cope with enormous complexities. But models are incomplete and arbitrarily exclude things. What they exclude may be more important than what they include. They provide us with fragmented glimpses of the whole. The models with which graduate students learn to picture the Amish must be abandoned for a more comprehensive view.

Some models are more fashionable than others. When I was a graduate student, acquiring a high degree of Parsonian "social systems" terminology was "in."[c] Currently, sociologists are engulfed in mathematical models trying to express certain qualities, quantities, and relationships. Many studies of Amish culture

a. The Essenes were a disciplined, semi-ascetic Jewish sect that arose in Palestine around 150 B.C.E. and survived until the end of the first century C.E.

b. For Hostetler's own use of these theoretical perspectives, see *Amish Society* (Baltimore: Johns Hopkins University Press, 1963), 3–9; and "The Amish: A Cultural Island," in *Readings in Sociology*, 3d ed., ed. Edgar A. Schuler (New York: Thomas Y. Crowell, 1967), 89–105.

c. Hostetler is referring to the theoretical work of Talcott Parsons, for example *The Social System* (Glencoe, Ill.: Free Press, 1951).

have utilized sociological models. They answered the questions which were hypothesized but they yielded fragmented knowledge. As stated earlier, models leave out much that is important. This is particularly the case in approaching the study of community and ethnic or religious subcultures.

Anthropologists have done a better job, focusing predominantly on the more incomprehensible, the nonverbal, and the holistic aspects of social and cultural behavior, or that which is unmeasurable or ambiguous. In the rest of my talk I shall attempt to deal with the question of Amish survival patterns, using an anthropological touch in looking at what theoretical models have "left out" and then I will return to the contemporary widespread perceptions of Amish culture.

Four factors are important in explaining Amish survival. They are: (1) the maintenance of an explicit redemptive community; (2) restraint in the uses of technology; (3) a strong familial bond associated with manual labor and training in the practical arts; and (4) the effective uses of silence.

THE MAINTENANCE OF A "REDEMPTIVE" COMMUNITY

Without taking into account how the Amish view themselves, all else in their culture is virtually incomprehensible. Like people everywhere, the Amish are engaged in a social discourse with reality. They ask themselves, "What is the meaning of life and of existence?" They view themselves as a Christian body suspended in a tension field between obedience and disobedience to an all-powerful Creator.

Central to Amish belief is the biblical story of Creation in the Genesis account—the Garden of Eden, with its many plants, animals, birds, and fishes. This mythological setting is umbilically related to their hoped-for rural environment. The Amish perceive themselves as the recipients of an undeserved gift from God. Thus, they live in a moral predicament; they must prove themselves worthy, faithful, grateful, and humble. God's offer of redemption obligates the Amish to reciprocate, by offering in return a corporate community incarnated with the attributes of the deity. Righteousness, sacrificial suffering, obedience, submission, humility, and turning the other cheek is Godlike. As a corporate offering, this community must be "without spot or blemish" (Eph. 5:27), existing in a state of brotherly love and union, in a state of readiness, and in constant struggle to be worthy (Rev. 21:2). Two of the more important paradigms which guide the individuals in making choices are *humility vs. pride*, and *submission vs. alienation*.

Pride leads to knowledge which is counterproductive to the knowledge of God. Disobedience yields knowledge that comes from "the evil one" and will lead to the broad path of destruction. The knowledge of God, in contrast, comes from obedience to God and leads to the narrow path of redemption. Amish education goals for their children and their antipathy toward humanistic worldly knowledge are grounded in this understanding.

Separation must be maintained between those who are obedient and those who are rebellious against God. There is, therefore, a continuous tension between the two spheres. The Amish believe that as individuals and as a community they must live separate from the "blind, perverted world" (Phil. 2:15) and have no relationship with the "unfruitful works of darkness" (Eph. 5:11). They know they are "in the world but not of it" (I Pet. 2:11). The symbols of the redemptive community are explicit and even a young child can distinguish the appropriate community symbols from the worldly ones.

Living in a redemptive community, separated from the world, is essential to salvation. Amish sermons are replete with passages emphasizing separation. I John 2:15–17 (Jordan tr.)[d] reads:

> Do not love the world system, or the things that keep it going. If anyone loves the world order it is not the Father's love that is in him. For everything that's in the world system—the hankering for physical comforts, the hankering for material things, the emphasis on status— is not from the Father but from the carnal world order. The world system with its hankerings is collapsing, but he who lives by the will of God moves into a new age.
>
> So don't be surprised, brothers, if the world system hates you. We ourselves are convinced that we have switched from death to life because we love the brethren.

Much of Amish ritual consists in maintaining the purity and unity of the community. The disobedient or those who cause disunity must be expelled, for a blemish cannot be tolerated in that which is offered to God. Disorderly members must be purged from the group (I Cor. 5:7). Twice each year the church-community enacts the necessary ritual to cleanse and purify the corporate body through self-examination and purging. Strife, war, and violence have no place

---

d. "Jordan tr." refers to a paraphrase of the New Testament text by twentieth-century activist Clarence Jordan, founder of Koinonia Farm near Americus, Georgia.

in the community nor in the life of the believer. To hold public office or function as a politician in the unbelieving world would be unthinkable.

Interpreting the essence of Christianity as community, a voluntary communion of believers, is central to Anabaptism. It cost the Amish and their ancestors, the Swiss and Dutch Mennonites of the sixteenth century, great sacrifices of blood and torment to establish this concept of church-community. Their protests are based on the story of their martyrs, whom the world hated. It meant severing their relationships with the state church reformers, specifically the Reformed Church of Zwingli, and suffering deportation and disenfranchisement of themselves as citizens. Although highly valued as skillful farmers in many countries, the Amish were denied the rights of ownership. They were totally dependent on the goodwill of lesser rulers for their existence. Only after coming to America, from 1727–1770, did the Amish have the opportunity to buy land and organize what are today unique church-communities never realized in Europe.

MODERATION IN THE USE OF TECHNOLOGY

Soil has for the Amish a spiritual significance because it was created by God in the Garden. Man's first duty is to dress the garden, to till it, and manage it as a good steward. Secondly, man is to keep the garden, that is, to protect it from exploitation. Stewardship is continuous, and will terminate in a day of reckoning. This view of land implies not only sustenance for life, but also a place that is attractive and orderly. If treated violently or exploited selfishly, the land will yield poorly, leaving mankind in poverty. This view of land contrasts sharply with a so-called "modern" view, which sees man's role as that of an exploiter of nature. To damage the earth means, for the Amish, to destroy one's own offspring.

The charter of Amish society requires that members make their living from farming; if not from farming, then from occupations of a rural or semi-rural character. The Amishman does not farm for monetary rewards. On the contrary, he works and saves so that he can buy a farm to support himself and his family, in order to enjoy work even at the cost of some inconvenience. The joys of living together are not traded off for progress. The Amish will accept some progress, but they will not let it destroy their community life. Moderation is an important principle in Amish survival.

The Amish are selective in choosing the inventions and machines that will influence their lives. They see nothing inconsistent in using magic markers and driving a horse and carriage. Pocket calculators or battery-operated razors do not threaten family solidarity. They see no contradiction in forbidding a telephone in the home but permitting its use from a pay station. The telephone is an umbilical cord tied to a dangerous worldly influence. You will not talk so long or so often at a pay booth down the road. Electricity from the public utilities (high line) is another matter. The Amish know that once they plug into an electric socket, they will have changed their whole way of thinking, their relationship to the Garden of Eden, and to the world. With it will come all the conveniences that would wipe out simplicity, humility, and dependence upon each other.

The worldly metaphor, which stresses bigger and more efficient machines, stands in sharp contrast to Amish thinking about the use of tools. The logic of bigger technology points toward infinite industrial growth and infinite energy consumption. The energy crisis for the Amish is not one of supply or of technology, but a question of morality. In respect to energy, and the balancing of human life with machines, the Amish have mastered for themselves one of the contradictions so puzzling to modern society. By holding big technology at a distance they have maintained the integrity of their family and community life. They have escaped many of the poisonous side effects of ambitious technology—haste, aimlessness, destruction, violence, waste, and disintegration. Through the centuries, the Amish have developed an intuitive awareness of the dangers of large-scale enterprises, not only in applied economics and technology, but in the management of human relationships including schools.

FAMILIAL BONDS, MANUAL LABOR, AND PRACTICAL TRAINING

Social roles are clearly defined in the Amish family unit. The farm is the Amish man's kingdom. He is in charge of the barn, the animals, the sowing and harvesting. His wife is the general manager of household affairs; her domain is the house, garden, and general appearance of the lawn. She is in charge of cooking, gardening, preserving food, cleaning, and caring for the children. Her participation and formal vote is important in major decisions.

Personal relationships are typically quiet and responsive. Respect is the norm of behavior. Home and family are effective socializing and training agencies. Within the family, children are reared in a secure, predictable, and stable environment. Here children are taught to work, accept responsibility, and to participate in meaningful roles. Home is a place of security, a center for life, and a place of belonging for all family members. Grandparents are typically living nearby. They have their own living quarters, means of travel, and the two families learn to assist each other without intruding.

The goals of Amish education are three—to acquire humility, simple living, and respect for the Creator. When the controversy over whether Amish children must attend public high schools reached the U.S. Supreme Court in 1972, the state of Wisconsin argued that the Amish were free to worship as they please; how, therefore, could anyone say their religious liberty was being violated? The notion of confining religion by defining it thus was a serious challenge—a line of reasoning that would have seriously threatened the Amish communities. By appealing to the First and Fourteenth Amendments, the Amish were able to demonstrate to the courts that their religion was not simply a matter of worship, but a way of life expressed in community.

Amish child rearing emphasizes cooperation, responsibility, humility, and skills which are learned thoroughly. The schools are located in the Amish farm environment, taught by Amish persons, and conducted in an atmosphere of trust. Many of the Amish schools use discarded books from the public systems. The old books are preferred because they have less science, less reference to television, and less discussion of ego-centered activities. Books supporting conspicuous consumption, militaristic superiority, and sex education are avoided. The older books, such as *McGuffey Readers*, stressing pride in the beauty of the nation rather than technological "progress," coincide with Amish values.[e] Books that stress the virtues of honesty, thrift, and purity without a heavy religious vocabulary are sought. Schools fit the child to become a part of the community. The dignity of tradition rather than change is emphasized. Amish schools function to prepare the young to live simply, with minimum reliance on middle-class values and on the mass communication systems of modern society.

THE MULTIPLE USES OF SILENCE

Anabaptist communities with minority status have invariably found the outside world to be hostile. They have learned that the powers of evil may be re-

e. *McGuffey Readers*, named for their initial compiler William Holmes McGuffey (1800–1873), are a series of reading textbooks for schoolchildren. First published in 1836, *McGuffey Readers* underscored virtues like cleanliness, industriousness, honesty, and courage, and they were used widely in nineteenth-century America. They continue to be used today, particularly by home schooling parents. More than 120 million copies are in print.

leased without warning. One elder who entertained outsiders on his farm said to me: "You can't plant sense in worldly men's minds, but we are quiet and sometimes it works." In their confrontation with the hostile world, the Amish have encountered many uncertain and unpredictable situations. Like the Apache Indians (Basso 1972), Amish will often "give up on words." Silence, moderation, ineptitude, or resignation is frequently the Amish pattern of response.

Silence has many functions in the Amish community. Amish conversions (rebirth experiences) tend to be silent rather than assertive. The Amish assembly for worship begins with silence. Between hymns there are long periods of silence. The entire assembly kneels for silent prayer; the praying ends with a scuffling, or a clearing of the throat by the minister. Prayers before and after meals are periods of uninterrupted silence. Sundays at home are spent in relative silence—hammering, building, and secular workday sounds are prohibited. Relaxed conversation, resting, and walking are silences that blend with the sacred.

Silence is a defense against sudden change, an appropriate response to fright or supernatural intervention. Silence is appropriate during severe thunderstorms or in moments of disaster, accident or death. In early morning or late at night around the farm, in spring or in winter, in sunshine, rain, or snow, when animals and hay are under cover of roof, the environment accommodates many shades of silence.

Silence is a way of living and forgiving, a way of embracing the community with charity and the transgressor with affection. The member who confesses all before the church is forgiven, and the sin is never spoken of again. The reinstatement of an excommunicated member requires submission and humility. "Talking back" would be unthinkable. Silence can aid in the restoration of good human relationships. By remaining silent when others would ask questions, one avoids the ugly subjects that would introduce disharmony. Silence in the face of hooligan behavior by the young allows adults to absorb the faults of the immature. When cheated in a shady financial deal, an Amish farmer may prefer to remain silent for fear of creating a scene.

In Amish life, silence is a resource, not a sign of introspection. Silence is a partnership with others, supporting the individual at work, at worship, and in facing the objective world. The person cultivating silence (as distinguished from solitude) lives above verbal contradictions. The Amish are spared many of the arguments about words of Scripture or theology over which others will haggle. For them, absolutes do not exist in words, whether in creeds or in position papers, for all such arguments are silenced by the character and example of Christ himself.

The individual who is given to silence does not consciously need to order everything. Much is ordered covertly, and in silence there is room to work out contradictions. Silence is a resource that is always at one's disposal. Many noises, including "needless words," are a displeasure to God, for once they are spoken, words can never be taken back and never stricken from the record. They will surface again on the day of judgment. Oaths are unneeded; a simple "yes" or "no" is sufficient, and "anything beyond this comes from the evil one" (Matt. 5:36, 37). There is the silence of pacifism, of turning the other cheek—which reaches back to the martyrs and to Christ himself, who refused to answer the question of Pilate and who suffered silently on the cross. When confused by a bureaucrat, outwitted by a regulation, or cursed by a worldly man, the Amish response is often silence. Silence becomes a difficult argument to refute.

Preoccupation with words, whether spoken or written, prevails in the outer world among those who emphasize literacy, rationality, and individuality. Study, reasoning, exegesis, and record keeping lead to a way of thinking that is primarily linear in emphasis. Instead of collective unity there is a multiplicity of thought, which leads to individual revelations and individualistic knowledge.

The practice of moderation in speech is, for the Amish, supported by their charter, that is, by the biblical teachings in respect to the use of speech. Sermons routinely stress passages related to speech behavior, especially from the Book of James: "you must be slow to speak" (1:19, New English Bible) and "quietly accept the message planted in your hearts" (1:21); the tongue "represents . . . the world with all its wickedness" (3:6); "it pollutes our whole being; it keeps the wheel of our existence red-hot, and its flames are fed by hell" (3:6); "No man can subdue the tongue. It is an intractable evil, charged with deadly venom" (3:8).

Wise sayings in Amish culture stress the virtue of silence. A motto hung on the wall of a workplace reads: "It is better to keep silent, even at the risk of being taken for a jackass, than to open your mouth and remove all doubt." A motto in an Amish school reads: "You can always tell a wise man by the smart things he does not say." Any tendency toward cleverness, pride, and showmanship in memorizing Scripture is discouraged.

In a recent Amish periodical, a father discussed some of the dangers of swimming in the farm pond and how to avoid them. While under the water he advised keeping the mouth shut, but admonished the reader that when not under water it is also a good general practice.

Studies of Amish personality type (Hostetler and Huntington 1971) support these observations on the modest use of speech. On the Myers-Briggs Type

Indicator (Hostetler and Huntington 1971:80), the Amish scored predominantly as ISFJ (Introverted-Sensing-Feeling-Judgmental) rather than ENTP
(Extroverted-Intuitive-Thinking-Perceptive); the former type is "quiet, friendly,
responsible and conscientious; thorough, painstaking, accurate; loyal, considerate, concerned with how other people feel."

SOME IMPLICATIONS

The cultural energy of the Amish remains vigorous. Thy have not yet been
swept aside by the proverbial broom of civilization.

In the late twentieth century, not being "swept out" by modernity is a momentous achievement. In his assessment of modernity Peter Berger (1977:61)
states that:

> The forces of modernization have descended like a gigantic steel ham-
> mer upon all the old communal institutions—clan, village, tribe,
> region—distorting or greatly weakening them, if not destroying
> them altogether. The capitalist market economy, the centralized bu-
> reaucratic state, the new technology let loose by industrialization, the
> consequent rapid population growth and urbanization, and finally the
> mass media of communication—these modernizing forces have caused
> havoc to all the social and cultural formations in which human beings
> used to be at home, creating radically a new context for human life.

Modernity, says Berger, is marked by "homelessness." There are severe discontents arising from modernizing processes, and there is a widespread long-
ing for the restoration of community, and for "redemption" from the alienating power of modernity. Prophets and psychologists have been telling us
for decades that the pace of modern life is detrimental to physical and emotional well-being. However, perpetual striving for convenience, property, protection, and status is perceived as dehumanizing in some cultures. For the
Amish, modernity contradicts the teachings of Jesus.

Through the decades, the Amish have had to negotiate with modernity. They
regarded it not as a miracle or some kind of magic, but as a sort of disease, an
abnormal and deeply destructive deviation from the way mankind was intended
to live. But the Amish know that modernity is not simply a matter of either/or;
it is a proposition to be negotiated. There is, as has been noted (Berger 1977),

no totally modernized society. Some societies are still, however, more whole than are others.

Throughout their history the Amish have frequently moved to new areas of settlement rather than make accommodations to modernization. But with the shrinking availability of land they have begun to make certain concessions to modern economic practices. A recent study (Kraybill 1987) suggests that the Amish have survived not merely by erecting barriers to isolate themselves, but have interacted with the surrounding society in ingenious ways.

They have negotiated with modernity on some things but not with others. They have not traded off their language, their community life, the training of their children, their distinctive dress, nor their way of farming with horses. They have made no concessions with birth control, divorce, or conscientious objection to war. These are nonnegotiable aspects of their culture.

In other ways, they have accepted changes; for example, they do so by freely riding in automobiles while yet refusing to drive or own them. These smaller concessions baffle the modern mind. Kraybill (1987:1–4) has suggested that some of these accommodations can be expressed in the form of riddles:

> *The tractor riddle*: Why do Amish farmers use modern tractors around the barn and silo but refuse to use them in the fields?
> *The household riddle:* Why are modern bathrooms and kitchens acceptable in homes but electrical appliances are not?
> *The telephone riddle*: Why are telephones taboo in Amish homes but permitted at the end of the farm lane and in shops?
> *The power riddle*: Why do Amish shops and manufacturing concerns readily use technology powered by air and hydraulics but refuse to use electricity from the public utilities?
> *The equipment riddle*: How is it that certain types of modern farm machinery—horse-drawn haybalers, for example, are widely used but forage harvesters and self-propelled combines are forbidden in the field?

To the outsider such concessions may appear to be contradictory. To the participant in Amish life they are natural and necessary. They hold in restraint the adverse influences of modernization on their personal lives, their families, and communities.

Faced with the perpetual "progress" of modernization, the Amish are dubious of its future promises. They ask themselves: Why do modern societies build nuclear weapons that can harm the earth if not destroy it altogether? Why do highly educated people deposit their aging parents in institutions isolated from family, friends, and grandchildren? Why do well-paid individuals leave their church, family, community, and neighbors in pursuit of even higher paying jobs and live at great distances from their homes?

What has the dominant society gained from the Amish? What is the worth to the nation of—in Kephart's (1976) term—this "extraordinary group"? The answer defies simple accounting.

The Amish have been productive farmers through most of their history in North America. They have functioned as mediating structures (Berger and Neuhaus 1977) through the centuries, paying their taxes without grudging, but they have consistently refused military service, public office, and affluent lifestyles. They lament the loss of community and the trusting relationships nurtured in family neighborhoods, church, voluntary associations and the growth of alienating bureaucracies of public life. They have enjoyed, for the most part, the fundamental right to be left alone.

The Amish have also become a national resource for genetic studies and for a variety of academic inquiries yielding doctoral dissertations in demography, psychology, sociology, history, education, language, religion, literature, and musicology, They have become the object of prizewinning news reporters, photographers, filmmakers, and publishers of cookbooks and tourist literature. Amish areas have become a mecca for tourists; their communities are the national center for quilt production.

All cultures have backstages—ills, incongruities, and tragedies—concealed from public view. The Amish also have their tragedies, but that is the subject for another discourse. The Amish are well aware that they cannot halt industrialization nor throw it off their backs. The most they can hope for is tolerance for their religious communities, existing as pockets in rural America. As they view the general decay of sensibilities in the world of disobedience, they maintain a willingness to suffer as may be necessary for their redemption.

REFERENCES

Basso, Keith. 1972. "To give up on words: silence in Western Apache culture." Pp. 67–86 in Pier Giglioli (ed.), *Language and Social Context: Selected Readings*. New York: Penguin Books.

Berger, Peter L. 1977. *Facing Up to Modernity: Excursions in Society, Politics, and Religion*. New York: Basic Books.

Berger, Peter L., and Richard John Neuhaus. 1977. *To Empower People: The Role of Mediating Structures in Public Policy*. Mercer (PA): American Enterprise Publishers.

Berry, Wendell. 1981. *The Gift of Good Land*. San Francisco: North Point Press.

Hall, E. T. 1976. *Beyond Culture*. New York: Doubleday.

Hostetler, John A., and Gertrude E. Huntington. 1971. *Children in Amish Society*. New York: Holt, Rinehart and Winston.

Kephart, William M. 1976. *Extraordinary Groups: The Sociology of Unconventional Life-Styles*. New York: St. Martin's Press.

Kraybill, Donald B. 1987. Negotiating with Modernity: The Riddle of Amish Culture. Unpublished manuscript.

Logsdon, Gene. 1987. "The Amish—a great embarrassment to American agriculture." *Whole Earth Review* (Spring): 74–76.

Miller, Edna. 1987. "We love being Amish." *Country* 1 (premier issue): 62–64.

18

TOWARD RESPONSIBLE GROWTH AND STEWARDSHIP OF LANCASTER COUNTY'S LANDSCAPE (1989)

First presented as a lecture to the Lancaster Mennonite Historical Society, the following article demonstrates John A. Hostetler's willingness to reflect theologically on social issues and problems. In this case the problem was the development of Lancaster County farmland, an endeavor that, according to Hostetler, was destroying one of the nation's greatest natural resources. Hostetler's assessment ranges widely, noting in turn the productivity (and renown) of Lancaster County's farmland, the history of Anabaptist agricultural endeavors, and the ecological and cultural crises that were poisoning the environment and disrupting rural communities. But the core of Hostetler's argument is theological: God's gift of good land demands careful stewardship, and Lancaster Countians were failing in that regard, forsaking God's blessings for leisurely living and material consumption. Hostetler concludes his analysis on an apocalyptic note. "No law of the universe decrees that humanity must transform the earth into a hell," he writes, but "we now face the danger of exploiting ourselves out of existence."

Hostetler's late-career focus on farmland preservation (in 1988 he convened a conference on "Land, Ethics, and Community Values") was the extension of a related concern that spanned his career: the health and vitality of Anabaptist communities, particularly Old Order communities. Victims of soaring land prices and declining land availability, numerous Old Order families had migrated from Lancaster County in the 1970s and 1980s. As Hostetler notes, such migrations were nothing new in Anabaptist history; nonetheless, it was painful for him to watch the transformation of the landscape that, for over two centuries, had served Anabaptist farmers well. Even more painful to him was the recognition that progressive Lancaster County Mennonites, some of whom were selling their farms to developers or developing farmland themselves, were exacerbating the problem more than they were solving it. Assuming the role of prophet-in-residence, Hostetler offered this jeremiad in hopes of rekindling Mennonite embers of faithfulness.

This article was first published in Pennsylvania Mennonite Heritage *12, no. 3 (1989): 2–10. Copyright © 1989 John A. Hostetler. Reprinted by permission.*

How can the people of God be stewards of the land and, at the same time, sojourners? Such an apparent contradiction is expressed by Yahweh in the Old Testament: "The land shall not be sold forever. For the land is mine; for ye are strangers and sojourners with me."[1] This essay flows from exploring the hidden meaning of the fruitful paradox between caretaking and sojourning.

CULTURAL LANDSCAPE

For more than two centuries Lancaster County, Pennsylvania, has been a unique place because of its cultural and religious inheritance. This includes an interdependence between merchants and farmers, and between diverse religious groups who respected each other's boundaries and peculiarities. In North America religious freedom was first practiced in William Penn's Pennsylvania, not in New England where trials were held for suspected witches; Friends (Quakers) suffered harassment and death.

Penn's colony, including Lancaster County, was unique because most of its inhabitants exercised restraint, moderation, and a sense of care about each other. Several of its long-established industries have made very important contributions by their informed and sensitive economic policies. Even today the county has many distinctive, attractive traits, notably the beauty of the landscape and the way it is nurtured.

The United States has been enormously favored with farmland. Only about 11 percent of the earth's surface is high quality farmland, and at least one-eighth of this land exists within U.S. borders.[2] The greatest concentration of fertile soil in the U.S.—perhaps in the world—exists in the Midwest, particularly Iowa; the next greatest concentration is found in Lancaster County.

Lancaster County is the nation's highest producer of agricultural products on unirrigated land. Most of the five thousand farms are family-owned and family-operated. About 20 percent or one thousand of these farms are occupied by the horse-farming population of Old Order Amish and Old Order Mennonites. In the United States only 1.5 percent of the population is engaged in farming in the nation, but in 1975 less than 10.9 percent of the total Mennonite population were farmers.[3]

One of the wealthiest men in the world wrote this letter:

> I have visited Lancaster County for almost fifty years. It is my idea of paradise. Lancaster County is a unique national treasure. "Growth" is bound to destroy it. I wonder if the State of Pennsylvania could be persuaded to set aside Lancaster County or a part of it as a permanent oasis, protected from every kind of exploitation. A sort of national park. I would be happy to help pay for it.[4]

Robert Rodale of Rodale Farms, Emmaus, Pennsylvania, proposed the idea of creating some kind of national farmland area so that people can enjoy the sheer beauty and uniqueness of the landscape. He pleaded, "Save these deep and fertile fields. Preserve at least this one place where we can see how a true and natural life can be lived."[5]

Unfortunately, since about the late 1970s Lancaster County has been afflicted with a cancerous disease known as "overgrowth"—unmanaged and out of control. Two recent publications have explicitly documented the growth patterns in Lancaster County and the major changes resulting from them.[6] Lancaster County has the highest rate of population growth for the thirteen municipal units in the state. About five thousand people are added to the county's population every year. Fifteen thousand acres were earmarked for development in 1987 and 1988. Since 1978 income from farming has declined while income from business, industry, and tourism has soared.[7]

Lancaster County is losing farmland today at a greater rate than Bucks County, Pennsylvania, which is no longer a land of cows and corn but a landscape of commerce, congestion, and corporate headquarters. Once a farming paradise, Lancaster County now suffers from traffic congestion, large areas designated for shopping centers, deterioration of water quality, the "need" for government services, suburban growth, overburdened school systems, water and sewage problems, noise, air pollution, trailer parks, "strip" development, and crime. The number of shopping "outlets" has grown from seventeen to one hundred and seventy-five in six years. Utility companies with a surplus of energy are promoting it vigorously in the heart of the Amish country. Lancaster County alone produces twenty-five acres of garbage twenty-five feet deep per year.[8]

TESTIMONY OF HISTORY

What have we learned from historical experience that will help us in the present predicament? Amish and Mennonites are the spiritual descendants of a sixteenth-century movement known as the Radical Reformation. By "radical" we mean returning to the original or the essence. Modern scholarship is still interpreting the meaning of this awakening, also called Anabaptism.[9]

The Anabaptist vision has been regarded as a spontaneous outbreak of a spiritual rather than a social reformation, though the social consequences were enormous. The Anabaptist founders did not formulate what we today would call a comprehensive worldview. No systematic theology was necessary to comprehend that "the earth is the Lord's and we are his people." Instead, they focused on the burning issues of their time. They redefined the meaning of being Christian, insisted on separation of church and world, and sought to live as a disciplined community, maintaining a loving brotherhood as the way in which the kingdom of God was to be realized.

Although the founders insisted that the community of believers must live in harmony and achieve a redemptive relationship in God's created world, they did not theologize about the use of land. Present-day Mennonite theology and land ethics need serious reexamination, although one could argue that not more theology is needed but more determination to practice what we implicitly know from our heritage.

The Mennonites and Amish in Switzerland and the Palatinate developed strong rural communities after a period of persecution. By nurturing the sub-marginal soils in places where they were banished, they gained a reputation for management skills which set a trend for generations.[10] Their enterprising farms distinguished them from the native populations and served them well in achieving cultural and religious isolation.

Land ownership was almost impossible because large farms were seldom available. In some cases restrictive laws prevented Mennonites from owning land. Among South German Mennonites a tradition developed that Mennonites ought not own land, but as "strangers and pilgrims" they should remain renters.

A general reputation for honesty and hard work permitted Mennonites to obtain long leases on some of the best farms owned by the nobility. In fact, the nobility sought them out. The order and beauty of the Mennonite and Amish farms in France led to a popular belief among their neighbors that they possessed some kind of divine favor others did not have.

Except for the first decades of sixteenth-century urban origins, the Mennonites in Switzerland have been farmers, engaged in cheese making, cattle raising, and weaving. When these Swiss Brethren went to Germany, France, and Pennsylvania, they brought with them innovative methods of farming such as the use of animal manure, crop rotation, and methods of conservation.[11]

Mennonites in the Netherlands, Belgium, and northwest Germany were not farmers during their sixteenth-century origins, though some Frisian Mennonites did farm later in that century. Some migrated to Prussia where they practiced agriculture for four centuries. Their chief contribution was land drainage. They made arable the lands lying below sea level, and for these capabilities they were invited to settle in the Vistula River delta. The huge drainage project, which took several generations to complete, spanned a frontage of forty miles and only could be accomplished by people who had a strong sense of communal continuity. The Prussian Mennonites also excelled in dairy farming, cheese making, orchard keeping and gardening.[12]

In Russia the Mennonites developed a distinctive settlement pattern and a viable agricultural economy. They located their colonies on large tracts of land which were divided further into "daughter" colonies. The government required this village type of settlement. Mennonite villages became ethnic and cultural islands in the Ukraine. Here they developed large-scale manufacturing of farm equipment, which they sold far beyond their own communities.[13]

Cultural historians have long claimed Amish and Mennonite farmers and colonizers as examples of stable but highly productive communities. They learned these skills not from books, but from necessity in their struggle to survive. Other circumstances furthered their success—faith in the Christian virtue of hard work, the practice of frugality and simplicity, large and well-ordered families, freedom from the arbitrary traditions of the state churches, and the practice of moderation.

What we have learned from more than four centuries of Amish and Mennonite land use is instructive, supportive, and complimentary. We were often a people without a country, wanderers on the face of the earth. Our God does not reside in one location, either in Jerusalem, the Netherlands, Zurich, Molotschna, or New Holland.[a] Soil wherever and whatever—black loam or hard clay—was used for building communities. These communities were not commodities, but were essential to worship and redemption. When the world would not tolerate us any longer, we moved on as sojourners to rebuild in a frontier situation.

The presence of a thriving Mennonite community in the Paraguayan Chaco today is a prime example. Here is a land of poor, sandy soil, far from a river, with little rainfall, hot winds, bad water quality, and far from markets. On entering Paraguay as refugees in the 1920s and 1930s they knew nothing about the natural resources of the region, but they drew upon spiritual and communal resources to adapt.[14] This story repeats itself again and again. Today Mennonite communities are scattered over the globe in over forty countries.

---

a. These latter four locations are cited because of their signficance in Anabaptist-Mennonite history. Zurich is typically considered the birthplace of the Anabaptist movement. The movement soon spread to the Netherlands, where it was embraced by future leader Menno Simons, from whom the term *Mennonite* derives. In the early eighteenth century, Prussian Mennonites migrated to the Ukraine, where they founded the thriving Molotschna colonies. Mennonites and Amish immigrants to North America settled in Lancaster County, where some of their descendants continue to farm land near the town of New Holland.

PRESENT ECOLOGICAL CRISIS

Is this historical experience a match for the complexities we now face in the modern world? Human technology has chalked up a string of unparalleled accomplishments. We have probed the surface of other planets, plumbed the subatomic microsystems, and opened up anthropomorphic and genetic libraries to general reading. But even as we marvel at our own brilliance, we are poisoning water and soil with chemical and radioactive waste, raking away topsoil and changing rain into acid. We casually turn up the atmospheric thermostat while our minds are wandering elsewhere. We have destroyed many species of plants and animals whose value will never be known. Unfortunately, all of these trends are accelerating, not abating.

What has gone wrong with our ability to keep the garden? Our current predicament is real: an imperiled ecology, world hunger and starvation, depletion of resources, environmentally-caused diseases, vanishing wilderness, uncontrolled technologies and economies, and endangered species on land and in water. Our nation produces 275 million tons of toxic wastes a year. Six major Atlantic Ocean fisheries and five along the Pacific have been closed. A large hole in the Antarctic ozone layer has been discovered with the aid of orbiting satellites.

Two events since World War II have overshadowed all of these calamities— splitting the atom and the artificial transplanting of the gene. Humanity has invaded the natural world as never before. By accident or in anger, humankind can extinguish its own existence and even can collapse the systems that support life on earth.

Enormous forces in our society are crying for economic growth. All political candidates, national or local, yield the same rhetoric. Growth is hailed as the answer to all the problems. Nobody has suggested that we have enough to meet our material needs. People naturally tend to want more and to be impatient with less. Consequently, both human nature and economic policies of expansion are most often opposed to enlightened restraint.

Our sensate culture makes it difficult to maintain the elusive middle way between poverty and luxury. Among the cultural groups practicing consumptive austerity, few are more effective than the Old Order communities and the Hutterites who live corporately. The promotion of such enlightened consumptive austerity is generally ignored by the mass media.

For many years North American society primarily lauded work and achievement. Now many people concentrate on fun, display, pleasure, leisure, and drama.[15] Scholars and the scientists are cataloging the sins and conceits of our culture.[16] They name traits such as excessive egoism, smothering bureaucracy, dehumanizing technology, pervasive envy, greed, self-display, and obesity. Advertising upholds consumer spending as the answer to human problems of discontent, loneliness, sickness, weariness, and a long list of wants. The most pervasive sickness in North America, according to Mother Teresa, is loneliness.

When stability appears in our economy and community life, the media calls it "stagnation." When the industrialized nations have sufficient oil the media calls it "a glut." Current misguided economic thinking would have us perpetually restless and discontented.

For most of five thousand years of recorded history, humankind has lived in a relatively symbiotic relationship with nature by acknowledging that human life depends on living in a proper relationship with the environment. The taming of wild animals and plants was one of the most significant events in the history of humankind.

Only yesterday, as it were, did we begin to add chemicals to the soil and alter the growth pattern of cells in animals and humans. We have eaten freely of the tree of knowledge of good and evil. We are no longer informed by sensitive feedback from nature because we have poisoned the soil, water, and the atmosphere. Fascination with technology has further alienated humanity from the spiritual dimensions of existence.

This alienation appears in factory farms where millions of farm animals are forced to live in cages or crates barely larger than their own bodies. Because factory farms deprive their animals of exercise, fresh air, and wholesome food, they are a breeding ground for disease. Veal calves are not fed mother's milk, but an antibiotic formula that often causes severe diarrhea.[17] One-third of the chickens that reach the market today are contaminated with antibiotics. These drugged products contain strains of bacteria that play havoc with human health. Salmonella poisoning in humans is reaching epidemic proportions, yet the U.S. Department of Agriculture does not prevent tainted meat from being sold.

What can we learn from ancient cultures with respect to agricultural wisdom—people who have farmed not for four centuries but forty centuries?[18] Anthropology is the study of human beings—their subsistence, culture, language, communities, and values. My colleagues in anthropology study Samoans, Eskimos, Gypsies, and other remote people in the world. My career has led me to study North American rural communities. The requirements for all forms of life may be summed up in five elements: soil, water, air, sunlight, and community.

Community is an essential requirement for every one of us. Without it we would not grow up to be human. Community is an extension of the love of parents. Infants will die without it. Yet in the modern world little recognition is given to the maintenance of community. There is no way to do one-minute parenting. There is no way to pay attention in a hurry. Nurturing friendships and family relationships takes time. Arriving at a sense of wholeness and well-being also takes time.

Two of the most vital concerns of primitive peoples, anthropologists inform us, are propagation and nutrition. Universally people have a reverent attitude toward fertility and food, the primary link between the tribe and divine providence.[19]

This relationship between the supernatural and the tribe is expressed in what anthropologists call totemism—in essence, a covenant relationship. Each tribe selects its totem or symbol from the available animal or plant species which is important to its well-being and subsistence. The group maintains attitudes of gratitude and high respect for the spiritual forces represented by the totem. Although each tribe has a different species totem, they have in common a system of magical cooperation with one common purpose, the abundance of food. Ritual acts support the beliefs of primitive societies and provide strength and endurance in the pursuit of the dangerous, the useful, or the edible. Abundance without gratitude and dependence on the mysterious invite catastrophes. Such catastrophes have their counterparts in biblical accounts concerning the fall and the flood.

BIBLICAL ECOLOGY

If we turn to the biblical account of the creation we find a kind of survival manual for living rightly on this planet. This account has informed our conscience and has influenced our sojourn. These teachings include three principles.[20]

First, the Creator is the owner of the earth and of all its creatures, including humankind. "The Lord God planted a garden eastward in Eden"[21] and he "took the man, and put him into the Garden of Eden to till it and to care for it."[22] We can deduce that the garden had a natural setting, required protection and care, and produced food for the good of humanity. Yet a condition was attached: "Of the tree of knowledge of good and evil, thou shalt not eat of it; for in the day that thou eatest thereof thou shalt surely die."[23] At the heart of our problem today is the question of who owns the land? Humankind is prone to claim ownership to the detriment of God's creation.

Second, the Creator gave humankind responsibility for earthkeeping and stewardship. The word "dominion"[24] describes this responsibility; it is no license for arrogance or ownership. Since God gave Adam and Eve this dominion before the fall, a sinless dominion is required. An old Jewish teaching states that if people use their dominion to destroy the very thing over which they have dominion, they make fools of themselves because they no longer have dominion over anything.[25]

Third, humanity must give the earth its rest or Sabbath. "There shall be a Sabbath of solemn rest for the land."[26] If the commandments are obeyed, the people will dwell securely in the land. The land will yield its fruit, people will eat their fill, and the loss of one year's production will be more than recovered in the other six years. If these commandments are not obeyed, then the land will be devastated. We must refuse to allow the enemy from within or without to divert the charge given to us by God at the creation of the world.

Mennonite farmers in some communities have practiced soil regeneration principles, not as a ritual event on the calendar but in keeping with the principle of wholeness. The land is given a year's rest, cultivated but not seeded, in places such as Montana, Alberta, and Saskatachewan.[27]

After the first six busy days of creation, God rested and enjoyed the fruits of his work. Similarly, the land must be given its time for regeneration, recuperation, and putting things back together again.

Jesus Christ's teaching in content and form, using examples of nature such as birds and flowers, are fundamentally ecological. Dominion must be exercised as service. Jesus came not to be served but to serve. "Do nothing from selfishness and conceit" writes Paul.[28] The human race is described in the Scriptures as needing redemption from bondage, greed, selfishness, and various forms of idolatry. The apostle Paul offers a vision of restoration: "Creation itself will be set free from its bondage to decay and obtain the glorious liberty of the children of God."[29] This is accomplished in the redemptive work of Jesus Christ's death and resurrection. "All things" are reconciled with God through Christ.[30]

Christian theology asks the believer to give "thanks unto the Father, which hath made us meet to be partakers of the inheritance of the saints in light," and who has "delivered us from the power of darkness."[31] If this statement appears naive to us, perhaps the scientific, evolutionary worldview rules over us— a view which in all probability is "metaphysically blind, cosmologically deaf, and spiritually dumb."[32]

Having eaten of the tree of knowledge, humanity must now live with the prospect of extinction. In accepting a purely egocentric outlook humankind has undertaken to rearrange both the human and nonhuman worlds so that human life will prosper on its own terms rather than God's terms. The problematic assumptions of our contemporary world are that humanity has the capacity to enjoy life by solving all problems through science, technology, politics, and economics.[33]

In the book of Genesis the fall of humanity led to this climax. "The Lord . . . was sorry that he had made man on earth, and he was grieved at heart. He said, 'This race of men who I have created, I will wipe them off the face of earth— man and beast, reptiles and birds. I am sorry that I ever made them.'"[34] Then follows the account of the flood and of Noah, who was called "a blameless man of his time."

OPTIONS

Today we are confronted with limited options. Our choice depends on who we are, how we perceive ourselves in relation to nature and creation, and from whom are we taking orders. Jesus Christ asked his followers to do three things: "Follow me," "Take up your cross daily," and "Forsake all." Whoever will not forsake all, cannot be His disciple. He also reminded all persons that they "cannot serve God and mammon."[35]

1. Become a prophet. In the same manner that the Hebrew prophets spoke against unfaithful rulers, so the prophets of our day must warn against arrogance, greed and excessive love of money. Mennonites and Amish have shied away from prophecy, often taking refuge under the canopy of silence. With respect to agricultural life and soil stewardship they have had few prophets. Two are the late Orie O. Miller and Howard Raid.[b] When asked to name the greatest threat to the Mennonite Church today, Miller replied, "Affluence."[36] Howard Raid of Bluffton, Ohio, wrote: "We should seek to build community and not personal empires."[37]

2. Emigrate. We can follow the example of Isaac when the Philistines stopped up his wells and there was no water for his cattle.[c] When others harass you, clog your roads, or arrest you, move to new lands. The pattern has been repeated again and again in our history. Let the pleasure seeking world have Lancaster County.

There is something to be said for sojourning. Jesus said: "And everyone that hath forsaken houses . . . or lands for my name's sake, shall receive an hundredfold, and shall inherit everlasting life."[38]

b. Orie O. Miller (1892–1977) was a Mennonite businessman who served as executive secretary of both Mennonite Central Committee and the Eastern Mennonite Board of Missions and Charities; Howard Raid (1912–2004) was a longtime professor of economics and business at the Mennonite-affiliated Bluffton College.

c. Isaac's conflict with the Philistines is recorded in Gen. 26.

3. *Cooperate.* We urgently need new social models of community organization and planning inspired by faith and love to offset dangerously homogenized thinking. Our most useful weapon is our spiritual heritage and resources. The imagination of a small group of persons or one person is potentially a thousand times more creative than all the factories that devise program and products.

We must ask some hard questions. Is Lancaster County ecologically and environmentally unique? Does trading the most fertile soil in the world for shopping malls add to our country's ecological credibility? If we trade ecological resources for "increased shopping pleasure,"[39] what have we gained?

The challenge is to work together. Here in this county we have sixty separate municipalities working individually. Each has its own ordinances and policies. In the German Palatinate, where most Pennsylvania Amish and Mennonites originated, there were forty-four different sovereign mini-states, each with its own language, laws, monetary system, religion, and units of weights and measures. This gave rise to continuous quarrels and feuding. We still have some problems cooperating with a comprehensive or larger governing unit.

4. *Choose austerity and simplicity, not affluence.* One predicament is that stewardship, good management, and austerity results in the accumulation of capital. Success drives us up the evolutionary ladder of affluence, of "bettering" ourselves with a high standard of living. The Old Order groups in our midst have prevented this by keeping the size of their economic productivity within scale and by using technologies that do not overstep the boundaries of reverence. Capital remains in the community to support newly married couples and to finance new settlements.

The response of Mennonites to economic success is more varied, for most "feel caught between the traditions of the past and the escalating demands of the present."[40] Some Mennonites who formerly kneeled in prayer, washed each other's feet during worship services, and affirmed each other with a handshake and the biblical kiss of peace, now observe rituals associated with sports and pecuniary events. Many have become wealthy and some extremely wealthy.

Sharing and giving to the needy people of the world is appropriately emphasized through such organizations as Mennonite Central Committee. Contributions are channeled to education, relief, and volunteer services. Gifts in kind, clothing, food, and housing are provided after fire, tornado, or other disasters. Sharing the material goods which emerge out of affluence is honorable but does not eliminate the task of stewardship.

Many people are searching for a means to escape from the excesses of consumerism and affluence. They seek a caring community not based on the market economy where nurture, stability, and self-reliance are possible. Mennonites can help these seekers. We should not impose austere poverty on those who would not have it, but on the other hand, we should not force increased luxury on those who do not want it. The strain of living simply will not move the millions, but it still nourishes those with sensitive imaginations and those who try to follow the simple teachings of Jesus with regard to repentance and sharing.

The enormous materialistic endeavor of our society in some sense has provoked the desire for simpler living. Only those who have too much can aspire to live on less. Only those surrounded by bigness can decide that smaller is more beautiful. If our society has made widespread abundance possible, it has also made it difficult to sustain a simpler way of life in the midst of prosperity.

Affluence does not distinguish between what is wise and useful and what is merely possible. Affluence demands impossible endless growth, whereas austerity can help us enhance the joy of sharing, friendships, and close relationships. An excess of material possessions can damage or destroy the good community relationships that we desire.[41]

5. *Choose betterment, not biggerment.* What can be measured by pecuniary standards is no substitute for quality. We are wise when we determine what is enough rather than how much is possible. The fewer our wants, the greater our freedom from having to serve them.

Not all growth is good. Shortsighted growth would have us measure the worth of life in financial terms. For example, to achieve full employment we need more people who are lacking something, who are disabled or deficient. To serve the growth economy we need more people with crooked teeth, more family disarray, more failing automobiles, more psychic malaise, more educational failures, more people in need of legal services and more people who are underdeveloped in some way. Growth in the economy entails our capacity to identify more and more deficiencies. Such shortcomings, it is reasoned, are good for the economy.

6. *Choose stewardship.* Stewardship requires us to care and to nurture what we have. Progress tells us to throw away what we have and to get something else. Shortsighted economic growth no longer brings us a sense of well-being. Psychological economy, or the richness of one's human relationships and the enjoyment of them, matters more than one's material possessions. If you are a landowner in Lancaster County, don't treat your acreage solely as a commodity. This is a landscape belonging to us all. People before you respected the land, cultivated the well-being of their community, and practiced stewardship. Follow their example.

Even when growth is ecologically possible, ethical factors often should limit its desirability. The basic needs of the future must take precedence over the luxuries of the present. The corrosive attitudes that foster affluence include greed, acquisitiveness, glorification of self-interest, technological pride, and gradualism. Gradualism is the disease of accepting convenience without thought, deferring to the power of wealth, striving for high status, and, for religious believers, mistaking these for the blessing of God. Our secular environment has enthroned efficiency and convenience so that almost nothing is generally true and almost nothing is generally false. One is free, given the premises of gradualism, to do as one pleases.

7. *Draw the line.* Gideon Hershberger, an Amishman, sat in a Minnesota jail in 1988 because his conscience would not allow him to abide by a state law mandating a red triangle on the rear of his buggy. Instead, he used plain reflective tape. To some this is quibbling over insignificant details, but Hershberger did draw the line between the modern ways of the world and his loyalty to God.[d] In Lancaster County a line between worldly success and the redemptive community is still drawn by the horse-farming people of the Old Order groups. Their technologies do not overstep the boundaries of reverence. Mennonite and Amish history and heritage have taught its adherents to be moderate in the uses of prosperity, power, pride, and pleasure. It is not prosperity and material growth that have made Lancaster the garden spot of the world.[e] For about three centuries the Mennonites and the Amish people in this county have been afraid of prosperity. They were afraid of pride, manipulative power, the use of force, and they were afraid of pleasure. Is it any wonder that this rare lifestyle has become the focus of enchantment?

8. *Practice redemptive hospitality.* People from all over the world come to Lancaster County because it reminds them of their earlier home environment. People who have witnessed the destruction of natural resources are becoming aware that Lancaster County is a national treasure and they grieve for the destruction of its beauty. We have the equivalent of the Grand Canyon or the California redwoods.[42] Agriculture is the historic foundation for this remarkable story.

Many visitors to the area are not prepared for what they see. Lord Snowden was shocked by what seemed to him a gross invasion of privacy. He writes: "Nothing had prepared me for the exploitation I would find of these peaceful, enormously hardworking people. I never imagined I would come away so deeply moved and affected by their way of life."[43] Other visitors have asked for in-

---

d. For details of the Hershberger case, see Lee J. Zook, "Slow-moving Vehicles," in *The Amish and the State*, rev. ed., ed. Donald B. Kraybill (Baltimore: Johns Hopkins University Press, 2003), 154–60.

e. This phrase, "the garden spot of the world," refers to Lancaster County's reputation as "the Garden Spot of America," a reputation that was established by 1800. See David Walbert, *Garden Spot: Lancaster County, the Old Order Amish, and the Selling of Rural America* (New York: Oxford University Press, 2002), 19–20.

structions for visiting the area have returned with similar reactions: "I will never go there again. I felt that I was intruding on their private life."

The unplanned growth of tourist attractions is a gross violation of the otherwise orderly character of the landscape. The high profile of advertising and merchandising which pervades not only gift and book shops, but also tourist "information centers," convey an air of commercialism that is an affront to more sensitive persons.

People who come here to speak with the Plain People, who expect to drive through their villages, or who want to "touch the hem of their garment" are often totally dismayed.[f] Everything is so commercial," they say. Is the genuine image of Mennonites and Amish buried in the clutter of mammon—tourist brochures, postcards, slides, and cash registers? Although we try to be unpretentious, we have much to achieve in developing a visceral, emotive, and quiet exchange with visitors.

Places where visitors can meet with natives without intimidation are virtually nonexistent. Buying, selling, asking for directions, or traffic accidents are the major contexts for social interaction. Places that were formerly village stores for supplies and useful to the Old Orders have been taken over by merchants who expect to sell their products to tourists. Here the Plain People, known by tradition as person-to-person people who are caring, sharing, and hospitable, have an opportunity. Visitors who stay with host families overnight probably experience the greatest rewards.

CONCLUSION

Gregory D. Cusak of the Iowa Department of Agriculture and Land Stewardship cautions us:

> Farming is the only 'industry' essential for our continued existence: our very lives depend upon the nutritional value, purity, availability, and cost of the food produced by America's family farmers. Their welfare, therefore, is of the greatest importance to us all. . . .
>
> Agriculture intimately involves us directly with the soil, water, and other living creatures of God's Creation. Working with the rhythms of the good earth, farmers are co-creators with God of the fruits of the

---

f. The reference here is to Luke 8:43–48, which recounts the story of a hemorrhaging woman whose bleeding stops when she touches the hem of Jesus' robe.

earth upon which all of us depend. The nature of that relationship—whether it is in harmony with the Creator's plan or in opposition to it—determines whether we are either responsible stewards of God's bountiful gifts, or irresponsible destroyers of both our heritage and of our children's future.[44]

What does an Amish and Mennonite understanding of Christian faith mean with respect to stewardship and earthkeeping in the world today? Too often otherworldly piety has caused indifference to earthkeeping. Yet the history of many Amish and Mennonite communities provides us with examples of people who have lived for godliness and contentment within their environmental limits. The Bible, the plow, and community are the most distinctive totems in Amish and Mennonite agricultural history. Although not acclaimed as successful by worldly standards, they knew when enough was really enough. They read the gospel and infused it into their farms, their work, their self-sacrifice, and their reverence for God.

Long ago Joshua confronted God's people with a choice: "Choose this day whom you will serve, whether the gods your fathers served . . . or the gods of the Amorites, in whose land you dwell."[45] Who are the gods of the Amorites today? They are the short-term gratifications that subvert our spiritual sensitivities. We serve other gods when we exceed the boundaries, when we seek success rather than faithfulness, practice convenience rather than commitment, follow efficiency instead of contentment, and seek pleasure in riches instead of pleasure in doing the will of the Creator. As an Amishman once observed, persecution has never been fatal to Christianity but prosperity has often smothered true faith.[46]

To be a just steward is our calling and our finest achievement. However, we now face the danger of exploiting ourselves out of existence, although no law of the universe decrees that humanity must transform the earth into a hell. God wills that we forsake these other gods and tend the garden as both caretakers and sojourners.

NOTES

1. Lev. 25:23 (KJV).

2. Joe Paddock, Nancy Paddock, and Carol Bly, *Soil and Survival* (San Francisco: Sierra Club Books, 1988), p. 4.

3. J. Howard Kauffman and Leland Harder, *Anabaptists Four Centuries Later* (Scottdale, Pa.: Herald Press, 1975), p. 60.

4. Letter to Richard Armstrong, March 1988.

5. Robert Rodale, "Protecting the Amish Lands," *Organic Gardening* (Dec. 1988): 21.

6. Robert J. Armbruster, *Lancaster: The (Bitter)Sweet Smell of Success* (Lancaster, Pa.: Lancaster Chamber of Commerce and Industry, 1988); Ed Klimuska, *Lancaster County: The (Ex?) Garden Spot of America* (Lancaster, Pa.: Lancaster Newspapers, 1988).

7. Klimuska, *Lancaster County: The (Ex?) Garden Spot of America*, p. 1.

8. Armbruster, *Lancaster: The (Bitter)Sweet Smell of Success*, p. 25.

9. J. Denny Weaver, *Becoming Anabaptist: The Origin and Significance of Sixteenth-Century Anabaptism* (Scottdale, Pa.: Herald Press, 1987).

10. Jean Séguy, "Religion and Agricultural Success," trans. Michael Shank, *Mennonite Quarterly Review* 47 (July 1973): 179–224.

11. Ernst H. Correll, *Das Schweizerische Täufermennonitentum: ein soziologischer Bericht* (Tübingen: J. C. B. Mohr, 1925), p. 24.

12. Johann Driedger, "Farming among the Mennonites in West and East Prussia," *Mennonite Quarterly Review* 31 (Jan. 1957): 16–21.

13. David G. Rempel, "The Mennonite Commonwealth in Russia: A Sketch of Its Founding and Endurance," *Mennonite Quarterly Review* 47 (Oct. 1973): 259–308 and 48 (Jan. 1974): 5–54.

14. J. W. Warkentin, "Carving a Home out of the Primeval Forest," *Mennonite Quarterly Review* 24 (Apr. 1950): 142–148.

15. Daniel Bell, *The Cultural Contradictions of Capitalism* (New York: Basic Books, 1976).

16. Christopher Lasch, *The Culture of Narcissism* (New York: Norton Pub. Co., 1978), p. 31.

17. Advertisement by Humane Farming Association, *Harpers'*, February 1989, p. 71.[g]

18. F. H. King, *Farmers of Forty Centuries, or Permanent Agriculture in China, Korea, and Japan* (Mrs. F. H. King, 1911; Emmaus, Pa.: Rodale Press, 1973).

19. Bronislaw Malinowski, *Magic, Science and Religion* (New York: Anchor Books, 1954).

20. Calvin B. DeWitt, "Ecological Issues and Our Spiritual Roots," unpublished address at Conference on Land, Ethics, and Community Values, at Elizabethtown College, Elizabethtown, Pa., July 22, 1988.

21. Genesis 2:8 (KJV).

22. Genesis 2:15 (NEB).[h]

23. Genesis 2:17 (KJV).

24. Genesis 1:28 (KJV).

25. DeWitt, "Ecological Issues and Our Spiritual Roots."

26. Leviticus 25:4; see also Exodus 23:11 (RSV).[i]

27. Observations and conversations by John A. Hostetler.

28. Philippians 2:3–11 (RSV).

29. Romans 8:21 (RSV).

30. Colossians 1:20 (RSV).

31. Colossians 1:12–14 (KJV).

32. Vincent Rossi, "Christian Ecology Is Cosmic Christology," *Epiphany Journal* (Winter 1987): 52.

33. David Ehrenfeld, *The Arrogance of Humanism* (New York: Oxford University Press, 1981), p. 16.

g. This citation, now correct, was incomplete and incorrect in the original.

h. "NEB" is an abbreviation for New English Bible.

i. "RSV" is an abbreviation for Revised Standard Version.

34. Genesis 6:5–7 (NEB).

35. Luke 14:33; Luke 9:23; Matthew 6:24 (RSV).

36. Orie O. Miller, in "The Mennonite Story," film by Eastern Mennonite Board of Missions and Charities, Salunga, Pa., 1970.

37. Howard Raid, "Changing Agriculture and the Mennonite Community," unpublished address at 1986 Triennial Meeting of Mennonite Health Plan and Mennonite Aid Plan of the U.S.A. at Normal, Ill.

38. Matthew 19:29 (KJV).

39. "Outlets Make Lancaster County a Better Place to Shop," *Penn-Dutch Traveler* (Oct. 21, 1988–Nov. 4, 1988): 1.

40. Paul W. Cohen, "Can Mennonites Survive Success?" *New York Times* (Nov. 8, 1987): 119.

41. David E. Shi, *In Search of the Simple Life* (Salt Lake City: Gibbs M. Smith, Inc., 1986), p. 309.

42. Richard Armstrong, "A Place Called Lancaster," unpublished script for 1988 slide set compiled by Lancaster Alliance for New Directions (LAND).

43. Lord Snowden, "The Plight of the Amish," *McCall's* (April 1972): 88.

44. Gregory D. Cusak, "The Rural Crisis and the Theology of the Land," *Epiphany Journal* (Fall 1987): 46.

45. Joshua 24:15 (RSV).

46. Gideon L. Fisher, *Farm Life and Its Changes* (Gordonville, Pa.: Pequea Publishers, 1978), p. 372.

The Life of John A. Hostetler: A Chronology

1918 Born on 29 October, in Pennsylvania's Kishacoquillas (Big) Valley near the Mifflin County town of Belleville; the fifth of seven children of Joseph and Nancy Hostetler.

1929 Joseph Hostetler, John's father, excommunicated from the Peachey Old Order Amish church in the Big Valley.

1930 Hostetler family moves to Kalona, Iowa, where they fellowship with an Old Order Amish church.

1935–36 John declines baptismal instruction in the Amish church; begins attending East Union Mennonite Church.

1941–42 Attends Hesston Junior College and Bible School, a Mennonite institution in Hesston, Kansas.

1942–45 Enters Civilian Public Service during World War II; serves in a variety of capacities in Colorado, Maryland, New Jersey, North Carolina, and Pennsylvania.

1947–49 Attends Goshen College, a Mennonite college in Goshen, Indiana; graduates with a B.S. in sociology; assists Harold S. Bender with the four-volume *Mennonite Encyclopedia*.

1949 Marries Hazel Schrock on 4 June. Enters graduate program in rural sociology at Pennsylvania State College (later University) in State College, Pennsylvania; studies with sociologist William G. Mather and anthropologist Maurice A. Mook.

1951 Hazel Schrock Hostetler dies in childbirth on 20 Feburary; infant, Susan, dies at birth. John receives M.S. from Pennsylvania State College; thesis topic is "The Amish Family in Mifflin County, Pennsylvania." Publishes *Annotated Bibliography on the Amish*.

1952 *Annotated Bibliography on the Amish* awarded the International Folklore Association's Chicago Folklore Prize. Publishes *Amish*

Life; the popular booklet, still in print, sells nearly a million copies.

1953   Marries Beulah Stauffer on 14 February. Daughters Ann, Mary, and Laura born in 1954, 1956, and 1962. Receives Ph.D. in rural sociology from Pennsylvania State University; dissertation topic is "The Sociology of Mennonite Evangelism."

1953–54   Studies in Heidelberg, Germany, on a Fulbright Scholarship at the Alfred Weber Institute; research topic is the Amish in Europe.

1954   Publishes *Mennonite Life*. Accepts job as editor at Herald Press, the Mennonite Church's book publishing concern in Scottdale, Pennsylvania.

1958   Publishes a history of the Mennonite Publishing House, *God Uses Ink*.

1959   Accepts teaching position at the University of Alberta in Edmonton, Alberta; while in Canada, becomes acquainted with the Hutterites.

1962   Accepts teaching position at the Ogontz campus of Pennsylvania State University in Abingdon, Pennsylvania.

1963   Publishes first edition of *Amish Society*; later editions released in 1968, 1980, and 1993, with total sales reaching 100,000 copies. Begins collaboration on genetic studies of the Amish with Johns Hopkins University professor Victor A. McKusick; studies later expanded to include Hutterite subjects.

1965   Accepts teaching position at Temple University in Philadelphia, Pennsylvania; serves as associate professor from 1965 to 1967, as full professor from 1967 to 1985. Publishes *Hutterite Life*.

1967   Publishes *The Hutterites in North America*, coauthored with Gertrude Enders Huntington; second edition published in 1980, revised edition published in 1996.

1970–71   Studies Hutterite origins in Europe while on sabbatical in Vienna, Austria.

1971   Publishes *Children in Amish Society*, coauthored with Gertrude Enders Huntington; revised edition, *Amish Children*, published in 1992. Serves as expert witness in *Wisconsin v. Yoder*, which ruled in favor of an Amish defendant who challenged a Wisconsin state law requiring children to attend school beyond eighth grade (the U.S. Supreme Court decision was handed down in 1972).

1974 Publishes *Hutterite Society*. Publishes *Communitarian Societies*.

1979 Serves as distinguished visiting professor at the College of William and Mary in Williamsburg, Virginia.

1979–80 Serves as expert witness in a variety of court cases (in Ohio, Ontario, Pennsylvania, and Saskatchewan) involving persons from plain and/or communal groups.

1984 Rallies opposition to *Witness*, a Hollywood film featuring Amish characters and settings and filmed on location in Lancaster County, Pennsylvania.

1986–89 Serves as director of the Young Center for the Study of Anabaptist and Pietist Groups at Elizabethtown College in Pennsylvania.

1986–92 Lectures widely on the Amish and related topics for the Pennsylvania Humanities Council.

1989 Publishes *Amish Roots: A Treasury of History, Wisdom, and Lore*.

1993 Feted at 300th anniversary conference marking Amish beginnings; release of Festschrift, *The Amish and the State* (edited by Donald B. Kraybill), which honored Hostetler as a "champion of religious liberty."

2001 Dies 28 August, at age of 82, in Goshen, Indiana.

The Publications of John A. Hostetler: A Bibliography

The following bibliography lists the published writings of John A. Hostetler. The entries have been divided into four categories, with each category arranged chronologically from the earliest publication to the most recent. The four categories are (1) books, monographs, and booklets; (2) book chapters and encyclopedia articles; (3) journal and popular articles; and (4) book and journal reviews.

In a certain sense, Hostetler published many more items than appear in this bibliography—if by "published" we mean that he communicated formally developed ideas to an audience via the spoken or written word. This bibliography, however, operates with a stricter definition of what constitutes a "publication;" it includes only publications that were circulated via text. It does not, therefore, include his unprinted public lectures, conference presentations, or sermons, nor does it include written works that were developed for a specific audience and not made available to a general readership (for example, research reports). Put simply, this bibliography lists Hostetler's written work, published in a textual medium and made available to a wide readership.

I. BOOKS, MONOGRAPHS, AND BOOKLETS

1949   *If War Comes: A Condensation of the Book, "Must Christians Fight?"*,
by Edward Yoder. Scottdale, Pa.: Herald Press. [booklet]

1951   *Annotated Bibliography on the Amish: An Annotated Bibliography of
Source Materials Pertaining to the Old Order Amish Mennonites.* Scottdale,
Pa.: Mennonite Publishing House.

1952   *The Amish in American Culture.* Harrisburg, Pa.: Pennsylvania
Historical and Museum Commission. [pamphlet; new editions
published in 1956, 1972, and 1994]
Amish Life. Scottdale, Pa.: Herald Press. [booklet; revised editions
published in 1959 and 1981]
Participation in the Rural Church: A Summary of Research in the Field,
with William G. Mather. State College, Pa.: Pennsylvania State
College, School of Agriculture-Agricultural Experiment Station.

1954   *Mennonite Life*. Scottdale, Pa.: Herald Press. [booklet; revised editions published in 1959 and 1974]
The Sociology of Mennonite Evangelism. Scottdale, Pa.: Herald Press.

1957   *An Invitation to Faith: The Mennonite Fellowship*. Scottdale, Pa.: Herald Press. [booklet]

1958   *God Uses Ink: The Heritage and Mission of the Mennonite Publishing House After Fifty Years*. Scottdale, Pa.: Herald Press.

1963   *Amish Society*. Baltimore: Johns Hopkins University Press.

1965   *Hutterite Life*. Scottdale, Pa.: Herald Press. [booklet]
Education and Marginality in the Communal Society of the Hutterites. Washington, D.C.: U.S. Department of Health, Education, and Welfare, Cooperative Research Program of the Office of Education.

1967   *The Hutterites in North America*, with Gertrude Enders Huntington. New York: Holt, Rinehart and Winston.

1968   *Amish Society*, rev. ed. Baltimore: Johns Hopkins University Press.

1969   *Educational Achievement and Life Styles in a Traditional Society, the Old Order Amish*. Washington, D.C.: U.S. Department of Health, Education, and Welfare, Office of Education, Bureau of Research.
Conference on Child Socialization. Washington, D.C.: Department of Health, Education, and Welfare, National Institute of Mental Health.

1971   *Children in Amish Society: Socialization and Community Education*, with Gertrude Enders Huntington. New York: Holt, Rinehart and Winston.

1974   *Communitarian Societies*, with Eric Michaels and Diane Levy Miller. New York: Holt, Rinehart and Winston.
Hutterite Society. Baltimore: Johns Hopkins University Press.
Cultural Transmission and Instrumental Adaptation to Social Change: Lancaster Mennonite High School in Transition, with Gertrude Enders Huntington and Donald B. Kraybill. Washington, D.C.: Office of Education, National Center for Educational Research and Development.

1975   *Selected Hutterian Documents in Translation, 1542–1654*, with Leonard Gross and Elizabeth Bender. Philadelphia: Temple University Communal Studies Center.

1977   *Fertility Patterns in an American Isolate Subculture*, with Eugene P. Ericksen, Julia A. Ericksen, and Gertrude E. Huntington. Philadelphia: Temple University, Departments of Sociology and Anthropology.

1980   *Amish Society*, 3d ed. Baltimore: Johns Hopkins University Press.
        The Hutterites in North America, fieldwork ed., with Gertrude Enders
        Huntington. New York: Holt, Rinehart and Winston.

1982   *The Amish*. Scottdale, Pa.: Herald Press. [the "old" *Amish Life*,
        retitled]

1983   *Amish Life*. Scottdale, Pa.: Herald Press. [new edition of *Amish Life*]
        Mennonite Life. Scottdale, Pa.: Herald Press. [new edition of *Mennonite Life*]
        Hutterite Life. Scottdale, Pa.: Herald Press. [new edition of *Hutterite Life*]

1984   *A Bibliography of the Old Order Amish: Sources Available in English*,
        with Nancy L. Gaines. Philadelphia: Temple University Communal
        Studies Center.

1989   *Amish Roots: A Treasury of History, Wisdom, and Lore*. Baltimore:
        Johns Hopkins University Press.

1992   *Amish Children: Education in the Family, School, and Community*, 2d
        ed., with Gertrude Enders Huntington. Fort Worth, Tex.: Harcourt
        Brace Jovanovich College Publishers. [revision of *Children in Amish
        Society*]

1993   *Amish Society*, 4th ed. Baltimore: Johns Hopkins University Press.

1996   *The Hutterites in North America*, 3d ed., with Gertrude Enders
        Huntington. Fort Worth, Tex.: Harcourt Brace College Publishers.

2. BOOK CHAPTERS AND ENCYCLOPEDIA ARTICLES

1951   "Evidences of Cultural Change among the Amish." In *Proceedings
        of the Eighth Conference on Mennonite Educational and Cultural Problems*,
        87–96. Newton, Kans.: Council of Mennonite and Affiliated
        Colleges.

1955   "Pennsylvania's Plain Folk." In *New Aims in Rural Life: Proceedings
        of the Thirty-Fourth Conference of the American Country Life Association*,
        ed. Paul C. Johnson, 20–26. Chicago, Ill.: Prairie Farmer Publish-
        ing Co.
        "Arkansas County [Ark.] Amish Mennonites." In *Mennonite Ency-
        clopedia*, 1:158. Hillsboro, Kans.: Mennonite Brethren Publishing
        House; Newton, Kans: Mennonite Publication Office; Scottdale,
        Pa.: Mennonite Publishing House. Also, "Beiler, Hans," 1:267;
        "Belleville, Pa.," 1:272; "Butler County, Mo.," 1:486; "Calhoun

County (Mich.) Old Order Amish," 1:491; "Colfax County, N. Mex.," 1:635. [Entries from the *Mennonite Encyclopedia*, 4 vols., are listed as they appear in the encyclopedia itself; brackets indicate editorial notes by David Weaver-Zercher, whereas parentheses appear in the text of the encyclopedia entries.]

1956   "Defiance County (Ohio) Old Order Amish." In *Mennonite Encyclopedia*, 2:26. Also, "District Superintendent," 2:74; "Fayette County (Ill.) Old Order Amish," 2:318; "Fort Vermilion, Alberta," 2:356; "Funk, Joseph," 2:423; "Funk, Joseph, Press," 2:423–24; "Geauga County, Ohio, Old Order Amish," 2:441; "Gosper County (Nebraska) Old Order Amish," 2:551; "Hostetler (Hostetter, Hochstetler)," 2:818.

1957   "Ixheim," with Pierre Sommer. In *Mennonite Encyclopedia*, 3:58. Also, "Johns, Joseph," 3:116; "Juniata [County, Pa.]," 3:128; "Kaufman, Isaac," 3:158; "Kent County, Del., Old Order Amish," 3:166; "Lawrence County (Pa.) Old Order Amish," 3:300; "Lebanon County [Pa.] Amish," 3:303; "Madison and Union County (Ohio) Amish," 3:435; "Mattawana Mennonite Church," 3:538; "Menno Township, Mifflin Co., Pa.," 3:585; "Mennonite Book and Tract Society," 3:594; "Mercer County, Pa.," 3:655; "Mifflin County [Pa.]," 3:683–84; "Monroe County (Miss.) Amish," 3:741.

1959   "Old Order Amish." In *Mennonite Encyclopedia*, 4:43–47. Also, "Our Bi-Monthly Letter," 4:98; "Pennsylvania-German Culture," with Arthur D. Graeff, 4:142–44; "Princess Anne County (Va.) Amish Mennonites," 4:219; "Raber, J. A.," 4:241; "Snyder County (Pa.) Amish," 4:557; "Suspenders (Amish)," 4:664; "Verhandlungen der Diener-Versammlung," 4:813; "Zook, Shem," 4:1040.

1960   "An Amish Church Adopts the Automobile." In *Social Systems: Essays on Their Persistence and Change*, ed. Charles P. Loomis, 241–46. Princeton, N.J.: Van Nostrand.

1961   Introduction to *The Old Order Amish of Lancaster County*, by Calvin George Bachman. Lancaster, Pa.: Pennsylvania German Society.

1964   "Hutterite Separatism and Public Tolerance." In *Social Problems: A Canadian Profile*, ed. Richard Laskin, 164–72. New York: McGraw-Hill.

1967   "Persistence and Change Patterns in Amish Society." In *Beyond the Frontier: Social Process and Cultural Change*, ed. Paul Bohannan

and Fred Plog, 289–306. Garden City, N.Y.: Natural History
Press.

"The Amish: A Cultural Island." In *Readings in Sociology*, 3d ed.,
ed. Edgar A. Schuler et al., 89–105. New York: Thomas Y.
Crowell.

1969   "Persistence and Change Patterns in Amish Society." In *Perspectives
in Marriage and the Family: Texts and Readings*, ed. J. Ross Eshleman,
168–85. Boston: Allyn and Bacon.

"Amish and Hutterite Socialization: Social Structure and Contrast-
ing Modes of Adaptation to Public Schooling." In *Conference on
Child Socialization*, ed. John A. Hostetler, 283–305. Washington,
D.C.: Department of Health, Education, and Welfare, National
Institute of Mental Health.

1970   "The Hutterites: Fieldwork in a North American Communal
Society," with Gertrude Enders Huntington. In *Being an Anthropolo-
gist: Fieldwork in Eleven Cultures*, ed. George D. Spindler, 194–219.
New York: Holt, Rinehart and Winston.

1971   "The Amish: A Cultural Island." In *Readings in Sociology*, 4th
ed., ed. Edgar A. Schuler et al., 85–98. New York: Thomas Y.
Crowell.

1974   "Education in Communitarian Societies—The Old Order Amish
and the Hutterian Brethren." In *Education and Cultural Process:
Toward an Anthropology of Education*, ed. George D. Spindler,
119–38. New York: Holt, Rinehart and Winston.

"Communal Socialization Patterns in Hutterite Society," with
Gertrude Enders Huntington. In *Sociology Canada: Readings*, ed.
Christopher Beattie and Stewart Crysdale, 109–33. Toronto:
Butterworth and Co.

1975   "Aspects of Personality in a Communal Society." In *Socialization and
Communication in Primary Groups*, ed. Thomas R. Williams, 95–105.
The Hague: Mouton.

"The Cultural Context of the Wisconsin Case." In *Compulsory
Education and the Amish: The Right Not to be Modern*, ed. Albert N.
Keim, 99–113. Boston: Beacon Press.

1976   "Folk Medicine and Sympathy Healing among the Amish." In
American Folk Medicine: A Symposium, ed. Wayland D. Hand,
249–58. Berkeley and Los Angeles: University of California Press.

"The Amish Elementary School Teacher and Students," with

Gertrude Enders Huntington. In *Schooling in the Cultural Context: Anthropological Studies of Education*, ed. Joan I. Roberts and Sherrie K. Akinsanya, 194–205. New York: David McKay Co.

1978   "Aspects of Personality in a Communal Society." In *Community, Self and Identity*, ed. Bhabagrahi Misra and James Preston, 281–91. The Hague: Mouton.

1979   "Conditions of Technological Development: Amish Society." In *Technology and Change*, ed. John G. Burke and Marshall C. Eakin, 168–74. San Francisco: Boyd and Fraser.

1980   "Amish." In *Harvard Encyclopedia of American Ethnic Groups*, ed. Stephan Thernstrom, 122–25. Cambridge: Harvard University Press.

"Hutterites." In *Harvard Encyclopedia of American Ethnic Groups*, ed. Stephan Thernstrom, 471–73. Cambridge: Harvard University Press.

"The Old Order Amish on the Great Plains: A Study in Cultural Vulnerability." In *Ethnicity on the Great Plains*, ed. Frederick C. Luebke, 92–108. Lincoln: University of Nebraska Press.

1983   "Amish." In *Brethren Encyclopedia*, 1:25–26. Philadelphia: Brethren Encyclopedia, Inc.

1984   "The Plain People and the Art of Survival." In *Germans in America: Retrospect and Prospect*, ed. Randall M. Miller, 110–21. Philadelphia: German Society of Pennsylvania.

"Silence and Survival Strategies among the New and Old Order Amish." In *Internal and External Perspectives on Amish and Mennonite Life*, ed. Werner Enninger, 81–91. Essen, Ger.: Unipress.

1985   "The Plain People: Historical and Modern Perspectives." In *America and the Germans: An Assessment of a Three-Hundred-Year History*, vol. 1, ed. Frank Trommler and Joseph McVeigh, 106–17. Philadelphia: University of Pennsylvania Press.

1986   "An Amish Wedding." In *Active Writing*, ed. Timothy H. Robinson and Laurie Modrey, 149–52. New York: Macmillan.

Introduction to *Amish and Amish Mennonite Genealogies*, by Hugh F. Gingerich and Rachel W. Kreider. Gordonville, Pa.: Pequea Publishers.

"The Hutterites: Fieldwork in a North American Communal Society," with Gertrude Enders Huntington. In *Being an Anthropologist: Fieldwork in Eleven Cultures*, ed. George D. Spindler, 194–219. Prospect Heights, Ill.: Waveland Press.

1987   "Education in Communitarian Societies—The Old Order Amish
        and the Hutterian Brethren." In *Education and Cultural Process:
        Anthropological Approaches*, ed. George D. Spindler, 210–29.
        Prospect Heights, Ill.: Waveland Press.
        "The Old Order Amish and the Gentle Art of Survival." In *Quest for
        Faith, Quest for Freedom: Aspects of Pennsylvania's Religious Experience*,
        ed. Otto Reimherr, 99–107. Selinsgrove, Pa.: Susquehanna Univer-
        sity Press.

1988   Foreword to *Community for Life*, by Ulrich Eggers. Scottdale, Pa.:
        Herald Press.
        "The Case of Jane: Psychotherapy and Deliverance," with Mervin R.
        Smucker. In *Essays on Spiritual Bondage and Deliverance*, ed. Willard
        M. Swartley, 179–91. Elkhart, Ind.: Institute of Mennonite Studies.
        "Hollywood Markets the Amish," with Donald B. Kraybill. In
        *Image Ethics: The Moral Rights of Subjects in Photographs, Film, and
        Television*, ed. Larry Gross, John Stuart Katz, and Jay Ruby, 220–35.
        New York: Oxford University Press.

1990   "Mennonites." In *Dictionary of American Immigration History*, ed.
        Francesco Cordasco, 504–7. Metuchen, N.J.: Scarecrow Press.
        "Persistence and Change Patterns in Amish Society." In *American
        Culture: Essays on the Familiar and Unfamiliar*, ed. Leonard Plotnicov,
        25–40. Pittsburgh: University of Pittsburgh Press.

1992   Foreword to *After the Fire: The Destruction of the Lancaster County
        Amish*, by Randy-Michael Testa. Hanover, N.H.: University Press of
        New England.

1993   "The Plain People: An Interpretation," with Calvin Redekop. In
        New and Intense Movements, ed. Martin E. Marty, 105–16. New York:
        K. G. Saur.

1995   Foreword to *The Plough and the Pen: Paul S. Gross and the Establish-
        ment of the Spokane Hutterian Brethren*, by Vance Joseph Youmans.
        Boone, N.C.: Parkway.

1996   "The Amish as a Redemptive Community." In *The Amish: Origin
        and Characteristics, 1693–1993*, ed. Lydie Hege and Christoph
        Wiebe, 346–54. Ingersheim, Fr.: Association Française d'Historie
        Anabaptiste-Mennonite.

1998   "The Amish and Their Land," with Maurice A. Mook. In *Base-
        ball, Barns, and Bluegrass: A Geography of American Folklife*, ed.
        George O. Carney, 195–210. Lanham, Md.: Rowman and
        Littlefield.

3. JOURNAL AND POPULAR ARTICLES

1935   "Some Effects of Tobacco and Alcohol." *Words of Cheer*, 5 May, 2.

1940   "The Secret to Success." *Christian Monitor*, May, 141, 147.

1941   "The Active Christian." *Christian Monitor*, February, 43–45.

    "Impressions." *Christian Monitor*, August, 234–35.

1943   "Christian Principles of Money Management." Parts 1–5. *Youth's Christian Companion*, 14 February, 465–66; 21 February, 475, 480; 28 February, 482–83; 7 March, 493–94; 14 March, 501–2.

    "An Attempted Alliance Between Faith and False Philosophy." *Christian Doctrine: A Bimonthly Supplement to the Gospel Herald*, December, 826–28.

1944   "The Christian Attitude Toward Liberal Trends of Thought." *Gospel Herald*, 24 February, 1018–19.

    "The Sin of Vain Criticism and Empty Reasoning." *Christian Monitor*, May, 136–37.

    "Prayer Changes Things." *Gospel Herald*, 25 August, 418–19.

    "Spirit-Controlled Intellect." *Gospel Herald*, 3 November, 617–18, 631.

1945   "Christian Books in Public Libraries." *Gospel Herald*, 18 May, 124.

    "The Christian Challenge to Peace." *Gospel Herald*, 31 August, 412.

    "The Peace Challenge of Civilian Public Service." *Christian Monitor*, September, 230.

    "An Open Door." *Gospel Herald*, 14 September, 445.

    "Church Hospitals for the Mentally Ill." *Gospel Herald*, 19 October, 548–49.

1946   "Youth Leadership." *Gospel Herald*, 22 February, 897–98.

    "Mennonite Relief in China." Parts 1–6. *Christian Monitor*, July, 206–7; August, 243–44; September, 270–71, 278; October, 302–4; November, 335–37; December, 366–67.

    "Youth for the Church." *Gospel Herald*, 10 September, 516–17.

    "Destinies." *Gospel Herald*, 24 December, 830.

    "The Joy of the Lord." *Gospel Herald*, 24 December, 821–22.

1947   "Shall We Feed the Literature Hungry?" *Gospel Herald*, 28 January, 952–53.

    "Consider These Little Ones." *Youth's Christian Companion*, 30 March, 417–18, 424.

    "Little Ones in China." *Youth's Christian Companion*, 30 March, 418.

"Joseph Funk: Founder of Mennonite Publication Work, 1847."
Gospel Herald, 23 December, 817–18, 831.

1948   "Pioneering in the Land of the Midnight Sun." *Mennonite Life*,
April, 5–9.

"The Mennonite Conception of the Church and Its Implications for
a Youth Program." *Gospel Herald*, 20 April, 365–68.

"A Brief History of the Amish." Parts 1 and 2. *Mennonite Historical
Bulletin* 9, no. 2:1–3; no. 3:2–3.

"The Life and Times of Samuel Yoder (1824–1884)." *Mennonite
Quarterly Review* 22:226–41.

"Rethinking Rural Work." *Gospel Herald*, 28 December, 1225–26.

1949   "Report of Conjoint Committee Meeting." *Gospel Herald*, 19 April,
364–65.

"The Settlement in the Peace River Country." *Mennonite Community*,
May, 18–23.

"Amish Pioneer of Somerset County." *Pennsylvania Dutchman* 1, no.
14:6.

"Current Work of the Peace Problems Committee." Parts 1–2.
Gospel Herald, 28 June, 614; 12 July, 660.

"Shem Zook of Mifflin County, the Amish Publisher and Writer."
Gospel Herald, 27 September, 955.

"Amish Problems at Diener-Versammlungen." *Mennonite Life*,
October, 34–38.

"Amish Pioneer of Somerset County." *Mennonite Historical Bulletin*
10, no. 4:1, 3.

"The Amish in Gosper County, Nebraska." *Mennonite Historical
Bulletin* 10, no. 4:1–2.

Untitled article on Amish settlers in Centre County, Pennsylvania.
Budget, 27 October, 10.

"The Life of Henry A. Mumaw." *Gospel Herald*, 22 November,
1147, 1157–58.

Untitled article on Amish family histories. *Budget*, 1 December, 2.

1950   "Amish in Centre County." *Pennsylvania Dutchman* 1, no. 24:6.

Untitled article on early settlers in Centre County, Pennsylvania.
Budget, 23 February, 2.

"Why Do Rural Communities Decline?" *Mennonite Community*,
March, 24–25.

Untitled article on Mifflin County, Pennsylvania, settlers and
American Indians. *Budget*, 30 March, 2.

Untitled article on extinct Amish communities. *Budget*, 13 April, 2.

"A Brief History of the Amish." Parts 1–4. *Budget*, 18 May, 3; 25 May, 3; 1 June, 3; 22 June, 3.

"Evangelization Through Colonization." *Mennonite Community*, June, 12–13.

"Amish Family Histories: An Annotated Bibliography." *Pennsylvania Dutchman* 2, no. 8:5–6.

1951   "Caesar and the Amish Again." *Gospel Herald*, 23 January, 78–79.

"On Marriage Customs." *Gospel Herald*, 20 February, 178.

"An Amish Baptismal Service." *Gospel Herald*, 27 February, 202–3.

"The Amish in Center County, Pennsylvania." *Mennonite Historical Bulletin* 12, no. 2:2–3.

"Toward a New Interpretation of Sectarian Life in America." *Pennsylvania Dutchman* 3, no. 4:1–2, 7.

"A More Excellent Way." *Gospel Herald*, 20 November, 1123.

1952   "Dead Statistics as Index to Evangelism." *Gospel Herald*, 15 January, 53–54.

"Farmers' Organizations and the Nonresistant Conscience." *Mennonite Community*, February, 17–19, 32.

"Brotherly Love." *Gospel Herald*, 12 February, 150.

"The Amish in American Culture." *American Heritage*, Summer, 4–8.

"Research, Magic, and Prayer." *Gospel Herald*, 12 August, 785–86.

1953   "Social Suicide and Community." *Mennonite Community*, February, 16.

"Do College Trained Persons Lose Their Religion?" *Mennonite Community*, May, 16.

"The Rural Church—Is It Free of Class Distinctions?" with W. G. Mather. *Science for the Farmer* 1, no. 1:5–6.

"Can Communities Witness?" *Mennonite Community*, July, 6–8.

"Looking Ahead." *Gospel Herald*, 21 July, 683.

"Sociological Aspects of Mennonite Evangelism." *Gospel Herald*, 4 August, 729–30.

"Isms Versus Christian Community?" *Mennonite Community*, September, 16.

"The Impact of Contemporary Mennonite Evangelistic Outreach on the Larger Society." *Mennonite Quarterly Review* 27:305–30.

1954   "Faith and Works in Minnesota." *Christian Living*, January, 22–24, 43–44.

"God Visits the Amish." *Christian Living*, March, 6–7, 40–41.

"Vom Leben der Amischen in Amerika." *Pfälzische (Germany) Heimatblätter*, March, 21–22.

"The Last Amish Church in Deutschland." *Budget*, 22 July, 1, 6.

"Healing Arts and Cures." *Christian Living*, August, 7–9, 38.

"Religious Mobility in a Sect Group: The Mennonite Church." *Rural Sociology* 19:244–55.

"How to Get Your Book in Print," with Beulah Hostetler. *Christian Living*, October, 25–27.

"Folk Art and Culture." *Christian Living*, November, 4–5.

1955   "The Amish Faith." *Wooster (OH) Daily Record*, 28 February, 18.

"A Week at Woerschweilerhof," with Beulah Hostetler. *Pennsylvania Farmer*, 9 July, 5, 27, 33.

"The Hostetler Family." *Mennonite Historical Bulletin* 16, no. 3:5–6.

"Why is Everybody Interested in the Pennsylvania Dutch?" *Christian Living*, August, 6–9, 38.

"Old World Extinction and New World Survival of the Amish: A Study of Group Maintenance and Dissolution." *Rural Sociology* 20:212–19.

"What Is a Mennonite?" Parts 1–3. *Lancaster (Pa.) New Era*, 17 October, 17; 18 October, 19; 19 October, 19.

"What Is an Amishman?" Parts 1 and 2. *Lancaster (Pa.) New Era*, 20 October, 15; 21 October, 15.

"History Makes Bonnets," with Priscilla Delp. *Christian Living*, December, 14–18.

1956   "Conference Historian Called Home." *Mennonite Historical Bulletin* 17, no. 1:7. [anonymous news note]

"Why is Everybody Interested in the Pennsylvania Dutch?" Parts 1 and 2. *The Morning Call*, 7 January, 6; 14 January, 10.

"Heidelberg—Famed Old City of Beauty and Culture." *Pennsylvania Farmer*, 14 January, 82–84.

"Some Shameful and Disturbing Facts." *Gospel Herald*, 14 February, 145–46, 165.

"Revived Interest in Pennsylvania-German Culture." *Mennonite Life*, April, 65–72.

"Pennsylvania German Culture," with Arthur D. Graeff. *Mennonite Historical Bulletin* 17, no. 2:1, 4.

"District Conference Historians." *Mennonite Historical Bulletin* 17, no. 3:3. [anonymous news note]

"Westmoreland-Fayette Historical Society." *Mennonite Historical Bulletin* 17, no. 3:6. [anonymous news note]

"The Changing Pattern of Pennsylvania German Culture, 1855–1955: The Mennonites and Amish." *Pennsylvania History* 23:330–34.

"Research on Family Names in Germany." *Budget*, 5 July, 6.

"Concern, 1956." *Gospel Herald*, 10 July, 652.

"The Amish and the Public School." *Christian Living*, September, 4–6, 41–43.

"Amish Costume: Its European Origin." *American-German Review* 22, no. 6:11–14.

1957   "Joseph W. Yoder (1872–1956)." *Mennonite Historical Bulletin* 18, no. 1:1–2.

"Mennonite Reader Interests (1864–1908)." *Mennonite Historical Bulletin* 18, no. 1:4–5.

"Heimatstelle Pfalz." *Mennonite Historical Bulletin* 18, no. 1:8. [anonymous news note]

"The Mennonite Book and Tract Society, 1892–1908." *Mennonite Quarterly Review* 31:105–27.

"Our Tradition and Our Scholars." *Gospel Herald*, 8 January, 25–26, 45.

"Tradition and Your Community." *Christian Living*, March, 4–6, 28.

"Problems of the German Farmer." *Pennsylvania Farmer*, 9 March, 10, 26–27.

"New District Historians." *Mennonite Historical Bulletin* 18, no. 2:4. [anonymous news note]

"The Amish and Their Land," with Maurice A. Mook. *Landscape* 6, no. 3:21–29.

1958   "Titles Printed (Not Published) by John F. Funk and the Mennonite Publishing Company." *Mennonite Historical Bulletin* 19, no. 1:3, 5.

"After Fifty Years." *Christian Living*, March, 12–13, 36–37.

"Yoder School." *Christian Living*, September, 3–7.

"Public Schools, Amish Cooperate in Maryland Educational Effort." *Wooster (OH) Daily Record*, 17 September, 5.

"Dutch College." *Pittsburgh Press*, 21 September, 8–9.

1959   "The Amish, Citizens of Heaven and America." *Pennsylvania Folklife* 10, no. 1:32–37.

"What is a Growing Country Church?" *Christian Living*, June, 4–7, 29.

"Why Young People Don't Grow Up." *Christian Living*, August, 6–7, 37.

"Learning from the Bible." *Christian Living*, December, 20–21.

1960   "Divisive Forces in the Church Today." *Gospel Herald*, 8 March, 201–2, 221–22.

"Fanaticism Then and Now." *Christian Living*, September, 23–25.

"The Hutterites in Perspective." Parts 1–3. *Canadian Mennonite*, 25 November, 7–8; 2 December, 7; 9 December, 7–8.

1961   "Hutterite Separatism and Public Tolerance." *Canadian Forum* 41:11–13.

"The Communal Property Act of Alberta." *University of Toronto Law Journal* 14: 125–28.

"The Amish and Their Land," with Maurice A. Mook. Parts 1–4. *The Morning Call*, 8 July, 6; 15 July, 6; 22 July, 6; 29 July, 6.

"Amish Family Life: A Sociologist's Analysis." *Pennsylvania Folklife* 12, no. 3:28–39.

1962   "Hutterian Brethren: A Way of Community." *Christian Living*, January, 14–17, 34–35.

"Education and Assimilation in Three Ethnic Groups," with Calvin Redekop. *Alberta Journal of Educational Research* 8:189–203.

1963   "The Hutterite Socialization Study." *Mennonite Quarterly Review* 37:239–42.

"Folk and Scientific Medicine in Amish Society." *Human Organization* 22:269–75.

1964   "The Amish Use of Symbols and Their Function in Bounding the Community." *Journal of the Royal Anthropological Institute of Great Britain and Ireland* 94, no. 1:11–22.

"The World's War Against the Amish." *Johns Hopkins Magazine*, February, 4–11.

"Social Problems and Value Conflicts." *Ogontz Campus News*, 28 February, 3–4.

"Persistence and Change Patterns in Amish Society." *Ethnology* 3:185–98.

"Education and Boundary Maintenance in Three Ethnic Groups," with Calvin Redekop. *Review of Religious Research* 5:80–91.

"Memoirs of Shem Zook (1798–1880): A Biography." *Mennonite Quarterly Review* 38:280–99, 303.

"Genetic Studies of the Amish: Background and Potentialities," with Victor A. McKusick and Janice A. Egeland. *Bulletin of the Johns Hopkins Hospital* 115:203–22.
"The Distribution of Certain Genes in the Old Order Amish," with Victor A. McKusick, Janice A. Egeland, and Roswell Eldridge. *Cold Spring Harbor Symposia on Quantitative Biology* 29:99–114.
"Dwarfism in the Amish," with Victor A. McKusick, Roswell Eldridge, and Janice A. Egeland. *Transactions of the Association of American Physicians* 77:151–68.

1965   "The Amish: Rural Communities of Love." *Fellowship*, January, 19–21.
"Study in Heredity." *Christian Living*, February, 32, 36–37.
"Genetic Studies of the Amish: A Summary and Bibliography," with Victor A. McKusick. *Mennonite Quarterly Review* 39:223–26.
"Dwarfism in the Amish: II. Cartilage-Hair Hypoplasia," with Victor A. McKusick, Roswell Eldridge, Janice A. Egeland, and Utai Ruangwit. *Bulletin of the Johns Hopkins Hospital* 116:285–326.

1966 "   A Note on Nursing Practices in an American Isolate with a High Birth Rate," with Gertrude E. Huntington. *Population Studies* 19:321–24.
"Minority-Majority Relations and Economic Interdependence," with Calvin Redekop. *Phylon* 27:367–78.
"The Amish Way of Life is at Stake." *Liberty*, May/June, 12–13.

1968   "The Amish Socialization Study: A Research Project," *Mennonite Quarterly Review* 42:68–73.
"Communal Socialization Patterns in Hutterite Society," with Gertrude Enders Huntington. *Ethnology* 7:331–35.

1969   "Amish Genealogy: A Progress Report," with Beulah S. Hostetler. *Pennsylvania Folklife* 19, no. 1:23–27.

1970   "Socialization and Adaptations to Public Schooling: The Hutterian Brethren and the Old Order Amish." *Sociological Quarterly* 11:194–205.
"Total Socialization: Modern Hutterite Educational Practices." *Mennonite Quarterly Review* 44:72–84.
"A Bibliography of English Language Materials on the Hutterian Brethren." *Mennonite Quarterly Review* 44:106–13.
"The Hutterian Confession of Faith: A Documentary Analysis," with Laura Thompson. *Alberta Journal of Educational Research* 16:29–45.

"Old Order Amish Child Rearing and Schooling Practices: A Summary Report." *Mennonite Quarterly Review* 44:181–91.

"Mennonite Central Committee Material Aid, 1941–1969." *Mennonite Quarterly Review* 44:318–23.

1972 "Amish Schooling: A Study in Alternatives." *Council on Anthropology and Education Newsletter* 3, no. 2:1–4.

1976 "Maurice A. Mook (1904–1973): An Appreciation." *Pennsylvania Folklife* 26, no. 2:34–37.

1977 "The Plain People: An Interpretation," with Calvin Redekop. *Mennonite Quarterly Review* 51:266–77.

"Old Order Amish Survival." *Mennonite Quarterly Review* 51:352–61.

1979 "Fertility Patterns and Trends among the Old Order Amish," with Julia A. Ericksen, Eugene P. Ericksen, and Gertrude E. Huntington. *Population Studies* 33:255–76.

1980 "The Cultivation of the Soil as a Moral Directive: Population Growth, Family Ties, and the Maintenance of Community among the Old Order Amish," with Eugene P. Ericksen and Julia A. Ericksen. *Rural Sociology* 45:49–68.

1981 "Discourse and Cultural Survival: An Amish Case." *Working Papers in Culture and Communication* 3, no. 2: 23–38.

1982 "The Amish Tradition." *Liberty*, January/February, 15–19.

1984 "Marketing the Amish Soul." *Budget*, 30 May, 2.

"Marketing the Amish Soul." *Gospel Herald*, 26 June, 452–53.

"Professor Protests 'Witness' Filming," by Amy Hostetler. *Lancaster (Pa.) Intelligencer Journal*, 28 June, 1–2. [includes written statement by John A. Hostetler about *Witness*]

"The Amish and the Law: A Religious Minority and Its Legal Encounters." *Washington and Lee Law Review* 41:33–47.

1985 "'Witness' Violated Amish Integrity." *Harrisburg (Pa.) Patriot News*, 6 March, A10.

Clayton, Dawn. "John Hostetler Bears Witness to Amish Culture and Calls the Movie *Witness* 'A Mockery.'" *People*, 11 March, 63–64. [interview]

"History and Relevance of the Hutterite Population for Genetic Studies." *American Journal of Medical Genetics* 22:453–62.

1986 "The Plain People and the Art of Survival." *Pennsylvania Magazine* 5, no. 1:24–30.

"A Century of Life Together." *Christian Living*, March, 8–12.

"Suicide Patterns in a Religious Subculture: The Old Order Amish," with D. B. Kraybill and D. G. Shaw. *International Journal of Moral and Social Studies* 1:249–63.

1987   "A Visit to the Historic Immigrant Hochstetler Homestead." *Mennonite Family History* 6:67.

"A New Look at the Old Order." *Rural Sociologist* 7:278–92.

"New Zealand's 'New' Christian Community." *Christian Living*, October, 2–3, 6–9.

"Maintaining a Redemptive Community in Today's World: A Conversation with John A. Hostetler." *Sunstone*, November, 47–48. [interview]

1988   "Coping with Modernity: Introduction." *Brethren Life and Thought* 23:151–53.

1989   "Rules of Speaking and Their Mediation: The Case of the Old Order Amish," with Werner Enninger, Joachim Raith, and Karl Heinz Wandt. *Zeitschrift fur Dialektologie und Linguistik* 64:137–68.

"Toward Responsible Growth and Stewardship of Lancaster County's Landscape." *Pennsylvania Mennonite Heritage* 12, no. 3:2–10.

"Paradise Lost? Lancaster County Threatened." Parts 1–4. *Mennonite Weekly Review*, 22 June, 8; 29 June, 6; 6 July; 6; 13 July, 6.

1990   "Managing Ideologies: Harmony as Ideology in Amish and Japanese Societies," with Robert L. Kidder. *Law and Society Review* 24:895–922.

1992   "What I Learned from My Heritage." *Mennonite Family History* 11:106–10.

"An Amish Beginning." *The American Scholar* 61:552–62.

1993   "The Society of Brothers who Call Themselves Hutterites: Some Personal Concerns." *KIT Newsletter*. November, 8–9.

n.d.   "Expelled Bruderhofers Members Speak Out." Peregrine Foundation Web site, http://www.perefound.org/em-s_sp.html.

4. BOOK AND JOURNAL REVIEWS

1947   "The Mennonitisches Lexikon." Parts 1–5. *Gospel Herald*, 7 October, 580; 14 October, 612; 21 October, 628; 28 October, 660; 4 November, 676.

"The Mennonite Encyclopedia." Parts 1–6. *Gospel Herald*, 9 December, 789; 16 December, 804; 30 December, 852; 6 January, 4; 13 January, 28; 20 January, 52.

1948 "The Mennonite Quarterly Review." *Mennonite Community*, May, 29–30.

1949 Review of *Mennonite Piety Through the Centuries*, by Robert Friedmann. *Budget*, 25 August, 2.
Review of *The Pennsylvania Dutchman*. *Budget*, 1 September, 2.
Review of *Descendants of Daniel Bender*, by C. W. Bender, D. B. Swartzendruber, and Elmer G. Swartzendruber. *Budget*, 8 September, 2.
Review of *The Maryland Germans: A History*, by Dieter Cunz. *Budget*, 15 September, 2.
Review of *Mennonite Colonization: Lessons from the Past for the Future*, by J. Winfield Fretz. *Budget*, 22 September, 2.
Review of *Pennsylvania Songs and Legends*, by George G. Korson. *Budget*, 29 September, 5.
Review of *Hostetler, or, the Mennonite Boy Converted: A True Narrative*, by "A Methodist Preacher." *Budget*, 6 October, 5.
Review of *The Pennsylvania Dutch Cook Book*, by Ruth Hutchison. *Budget*, 13 Octo-ber, 9.
Review of *Alaska Today*, by Webster Denison. *Budget*, 20 October, 3.
Review of *Old Order Amish Church Districts of Indiana*, by Levi D. Christner and Eli J. Bontrager. *Budget*, 3 November, 2.
Review of *Service for Peace: A History of Mennonite Civilian Public Service*, by Melvin Gingerich. *Budget*, 10 November, 2.
Review of *The Small Sects in America*, by Elmer T. Clark. *Budget*, 17 November, 2.
Review of *Traditionally Pennsylvania Dutch*, by Edward C. Smith and Virginia Van Horn Thompson Smith. *Budget*, 24 November, 2.
Review of *Little Known Facts about the Amish and the Mennonites*, by A. Monroe Aurand Jr. *Budget*, 8 December, 2.
Review of *Geschichte der Mennoniten,* by Daniel K. Cassel. *Budget*, 15 December, 2.
Review of *Folk Art of Rural Pennsylvania*, by Frances Lichten. *Budget*, 22 December, 2.
Review of *Barbara Hochstetler-Christian Stutzman Geneology*. *Budget*, 29 December, 2.

1950 Review of *Pennsylvania Dutch American Folk Art*, by Henry J. Kauffman and C. Geoffrey Holme. *Budget*, 5 January, 2.

Review of *The Long Crooked River (the Susquehanna)*, by Richmond E. Myers. *Budget*, 12 January, 2.
Review of *Family Record of Jacob Guengerich and Barbara Miller and Their Descendants*, by David R. Bontrager. *Budget*, 19 January, 2.
Review of *Etched in Purple*, by Frank J. Irgang. *Budget*, 26 January, 2.
Review of *Youth and Christian Citizenship*, by Melvin Gingerich. *Budget*, 2 February, 2.
Review of "The Very Remarkable Amish," *Collier's*, by Richard B. Gehman. *Budget*, 9 February, 2.
Review of *Marriage and the Family*, by Meyer F. Nimkoff. *Budget*, 16 February, 2.
Review of *Descendants of Jacob Byler and Nancy Kauffman (Byler)*, by Amanda D. Mast and Barbara Swartzentruber. *Budget*, 2 March, 2.
Review of *The Doctrines of the Mennonites*, by John C. Wenger. *Budget*, 9 March, 2.
Review of *Centennial Memoir: The Life Story and Genealogy of Abraham and Mattie King Yoder*, by Isabelle King Yoder. *Budget*, 16 March, 2.
Review of *Mennonite Quarterly Review*. *Budget*, 23 March, 2.
Review of *Descendants of Christian Byler and Mary Kaufman (Byler)*, by Phoebe Byler. *Budget*, 30 March, 2.
Review of *Geneaology of the Descendants of Christopher Esh*, by Benjamin L. Blank. *Budget*, 6 April, 2.
Review of *History, Descendants of Peter Hershberger and Elizabeth Yoder, 1810–1950*, by Eli P. Hershberger, Eli D. Hershberger, and Katie Hershberger. *Budget*, 20 April, 2.
Review of *Conrad Grebel, c. 1498–1526: The Founder of the Swiss Brethren Sometimes Called Anabaptists*, by Harold S. Bender. *Budget*, 27 April, 2.
Review of *The Fulfillment of Prophecy*, by Chester K. Lehman. *Budget*, 4 May, 2.
Review of *Jack Miner and the Birds*, by Jack Miner. *Budget*, 11 May, 2.
Review of *Proceedings of the Fourth Mennonite World Conference*. *Budget*, 18 May, 2.
Review of *Kinder-Lieder zum Gebrauch für Schulen*, by Ervin N. Hershberger. *Budget*, 25 May, 2.
Review of *Rural Social Systems*, by Charles P. Loomis and J. Allan Beegle. *Budget*, 1 June, 2.
Review of *The "Deep River" Girl*, by Harry J. Albus. *Budget*, 8 June, 2.

Review of *American Wild Flowers*, by Harold N. Moldenke. *Budget*, 15 June, 5.

Review of *Law on the Farm*, by Harold W. Hannah. *Budget*, 22 June, 2.

Review of *House for You to Build, Buy, or Rent*, by Catherine Sleeper and Harold R. Sleeper. *Budget*, 6 July, 2.

Review of *Mennonite Yearbook and Directory*. *Budget*, 13 July, 2.

Review of *Mennonites in Europe*, by John Horsch. *Budget*, 20 July, 2.

Review of *Mennonite Community Cookbook: Favorite Family Recipes*, by Mary Emma Showalter. *Budget*, 27 July, 2.

Review of *Women in the Old Testament*, by Norah Lofts. *Budget*, 3 August, 2.

Review of *Gospel Herald*. *Budget*, 10 August, 2.

Review of *How To Avoid Financial Tangles*, by Kenneth C. Masteller. *Budget*, 17 August, 2.

Review of *Mennonite Community*. *Budget*, 24 August, 2.

Review of *Paraguayan Interlude: Observations and Impressions*, by Willard H. Smith and Verna Smith. *Budget*, 7 September, 5.

Review of *If War Comes: A Condensation of the Book, "Must Christians Fight?"*, by Edward Yoder, condensed by John A. Hostetler. *Budget*, 14 September, 2.

Review of *Handbuch für Prediger*, by Eli J. Bontrager and L. A. Miller. *Budget*, 21 September, 2.

Review of *The Tobias Schrock Family Record, 1823–1950*, by Martha A. Habegger Schrock. *Budget*, 5 October, 2.

Review of *Pennsylvania Agriculture and Country Life, 1640–1840*, by S. W. Fletcher. *Budget*, 5 October, 2.

Review of *Descendants of Benjamin Beachy*, by William D. Beechy. *Budget*, 12 October, 2.

Review of *Pennsylvania Game News*. *Budget*, 26 October, 4.

1951   "Recent Textual Treatments of the Amish." *Mennonite Quarterly Review* 25:133–36.

Review of *Separated unto God: A Plea for Christian Simplicity of Life and for a Scriptural Nonconformity to the World*, by John C. Wenger. *Gospel Herald*, 18 September, 918–19.

"A Book on Colonization: With Lessons for Today." *Mennonite Community*, October, 24–25.

1952   Review of *High Bright Buggy Wheels*, by Luella B. Creighton. *Pennsylvania Dutchman* 4, no. 8:6.

1953   "The Mennonite Reaction to Wartime Experience." Review of
Service for Peace: A History of Mennonite Civilian Public Service, by
Melvin Gingerich, and *The Mennonite Church in the Second World War*,
by Guy F. Hershberger. *Pennsylvania Dutchman* 4, no. 15:9–10.
Review of *Blue Hills and Shoofly Pie in Pennsylvania Dutchland*, by
Ann Hark. *Pennsylvania Magazine of History and Biography*
77:359–60.
Review of *High Bright Buggy Wheels*, by Luella B. Creighton.
Mennonite Quarterly Review 27:86.

1954   Review of *Blue Hills and Shoofly Pie in Pennsylvania Dutchland*,
by Ann Hark. *Mennonite Quarterly Review* 28:78–79.
Review of *The Quaker Approach to Contemporary Problems*, ed. John
Kavanaugh. *Christian Living*, May, 27.
Review of *The College and the Community*, by Baker Brownell.
Christian Living, June, 25.

1955   Review of *Profile of America: An Autobiography of the U.S.A.*,
ed. Emily Davie. *Christian Living*, February, 34.
Review of *Im Schweisse Deines Angesichts*, by Walter Quiring. *Christian Living*, March, 35.
Review of *Folk Art Motifs of Pennsylvania*, by Frances Lichten.
Christian Living, April, 35.
Review of *Down on the Farm: A Picture Treasury of Country Life in
America in the Good Old Days*, by Stewart H. Holbrook. *Christian Living*, April, 35.
Review of *Sing and Dance with the Pennsylvania Dutch*, by Ruth L.
Hausman. *Mennonite Quarterly Review* 29:167–68.
Review of *Bibliography of German Culture in America to 1940*, by
Henry A. Pochmann and Arthur R. Schultz. *Christian Living*,
July, 35.
Review of *American Ways of Life*, by George R. Stewart. *Christian Living*, October, 35.
Review of *Amishland*, by Kiehl Newswanger and Christian
Newswanger. *Pennsylvania Magazine of History and Biography*
79:393–94.

1956   Review of *In Search of Utopia: The Mennonites in Manitoba*, by
Emerich K. Francis. *Christian Living*, March, 35.
Review of *The Origin and Development of Early Christian Church
Architecture*, by J. G. Davies. *Christian Living*, April, 35.

Review of *The Christian View of Science and Scripture*, by Bernard L. Ramm. *Christian Living*, April, 35.

Review of *Culture and Mental Disorders: A Comparative Study of the Hutterites and Other Populations*, by Joseph W. Eaton. *Christian Living*, April, 35.

Review of *Grand Deception: The World's Most Spectacular and Successful Hoaxes, Impostures, Ruses, and Frauds*, ed. Alexander Klein. *Christian Living*, April, 35.

Review of *Creative Intuition in Art and Poetry*, by Jacques Maritain. *Christian Living*, April, 35.

Review of *Judaism for the Modern Age*, by Robert Gordis. *Christian Living*, May, 35.

Review of *Man and His Tragic Life, Based on Dostoevsky*, by László Vatai. *Christian Living*, May, 35.

Review of *Religion in Prison*, by J. Arthur Hoyles. *Christian Living*, May, 35.

Review of *This World and the Church: Studies in Secularism*, by Howard V. Hong. *Christian Living*, May, 35.

Review of *Introduction to Philosophy*, by Max Rosenberg. *Christian Living*, June, 35.

Review of *The Great Story of Whales*, by Georges Blond. *Christian Living*, June, 35.

Review of *Exploring the Small Community*, by Otto G. Hoiberg. *Christian Living*, June, 35.

Review of *The Art of Happy Christian Living*, by Leslie Parrott. *Christian Living*, June, 35.

Review of *Teaching for Results*, by Findley B. Edge. *Christian Living*, July, 35.

Review of *Principles of Mental Health for Christian Living*, by C. B. Eavey. *Christian Living*, July, 35.

Review of *Reinhold Niebuhr: His Religious, Social, and Political Thought*, ed. Charles W. Kegley and Robert W. Bretall. *Christian Living*, July, 35.

Review of *Ethics*, by Dietrich Bonhoeffer, ed. Eberhard Bethge. *Christian Living*, July, 35.

Review of *What Should We Expect of Education?* by Homer T. Rosenberger. *Christian Living*, September, 35.

"A Mennonite Encyclopedia." *Dutchman* 7, no. 3:30–31.

Review of *In Search of Utopia: The Mennonites in Manitoba*, by Emerich K. Francis. *Rural Sociology* 21:331–32.

1957   "A Surprise Publication." Review of *The Recovery of the Anabaptist Vision*, ed. Guy F. Hershberger. *Gospel Herald*, 23 July, 665.

Review of *The Amish Year*, by Charles S. Rice and Rollin C. Steinmetz. *Pennsylvania Magazine of History and Biography* 81:334–35.

1958   Review of *The Amish People: Seventeenth-Century Tradition in Modern America*, by Elmer Lewis Smith. *Gospel Herald*, 13 May, 455.

1959   Review of *Christian Maturity*, by Richard C. Halverson. *Gospel Herald*, 24 March, 268.

Review of *Village Life in Northern India*, by Oscar Lewis. *Christian Living*, May, 33.

Review of *Understanding and Preventing Juvenile Delinquency*, by Haskell M. Miller. Christian Living, June, 33.

Review of *A Pillar of Cloud: The Story of Hesston College, 1909–1959*, by Mary Miller. *Christian Living*, November, 33.

Review of *The Anabaptist View of the Church: A Study of the Origins of Sectarian Protestantism*, by Franklin H. Littell. *Religion in Life* 28:614–15.

Review of *The Free Church*, by Franklin H. Littell. *Religion in Life* 28:614–15.

1961   Review of *They Came to Emmaus: A History*, by Preston A. Barba. *Pennsylvania Magazine of History and Biography* 85:340–41.

Review of *Even Unto Death: The Heroic Witness of the Sixteenth-Century Anabaptists*, by John C. Wenger. *Budget*, 14 December, 7.

1962   Review of *The Mennonites in Indiana and Michigan*, by John C. Wenger. *Gospel Herald*, 30 January, 109.

Review of *Our Amish Neighbors*, by William I. Schreiber. *Mennonite Quarterly Review* 37:139–41.

1965   Review of *Two Paths to Utopia: The Hutterites and the Llano Colony*, by Paul K. Conkin. *Mennonite Quarterly Review* 39:324–25.

1970   Review of *Hutterian Brethren: The Agricultural Economy and Social Organization of a Communal People*, by John W. Bennett. *Mennonite Quarterly Review* 44:128–29.

Review of *Gemeinschaftssiedlungen auf religiöser und weltanschaulicher Grundlage*, by Hermann Schempp. *Mennonite Quarterly Review* 44:133–34.

1987   Review of *Shaker Village Views*, by Robert P. Emlen. *Journal of Historical Geography* 15:335–36.

Contributors

SIMON J. BRONNER is Distinguished University Professor of American Studies and Folklore and Director of the Center for Pennsylvania Culture Studies at The Pennsylvania State University, Harrisburg. He is series editor of the Pennsylvania German History and Culture Series for Penn State Press, and is also editor of the multivolume *Encyclopedia of American Folklife*. Bronner's recent publications include *Folk Nation: Folklore in the Creation of American Tradition* (2002), *Lafcadio Hearn's America* (2002), *Following Tradition: Folklore in the Discourse of American Culture* (1998), and *Popularizing Pennsylvania* (1996).

ANN HOSTETLER is Associate Professor of English at Goshen College, where she teaches literature and creative writing. She is author of a collection of poetry, *Empty Room with Light* (2002), and is editor of *A Cappella: Mennonite Voices in Poetry* (2003). Her essays have appeared in *PMLA*, *Mennonite Quarterly Review*, and other publications. Her poems have been published in many magazines and journals, including *American Scholar* and *Cream City Review*.

DONALD B. KRAYBILL is Distinguished College Professor and Senior Fellow at the Young Center for Anabaptist and Pietist Studies at Elizabethtown College in Elizabethtown, Pennsylvania. He has published numerous articles and books on Anabaptist communities, including *The Riddle of Amish Culture* (rev. ed., 2001) and *On the Backroad to Heaven: Old Order Hutterites, Mennonites, Amish, and Brethren* (2001).

SUSAN FISHER MILLER received her Ph.D. in English from Northwestern University in 1986. She has since taught at a variety of institutions, and currently teaches in the English Department at Wheaton College in Wheaton,

Illinois. Fisher Miller is author of *Culture for Service* (1994), a scholarly history of Goshen College published to mark the college's centennial, and her articles have appeared in *Mennonite Quarterly Review*, *Éire-Ireland*, and other publications. Her ongoing research focuses on Irish literature, Mennonite literature, and American Mennonite history.

DAVID L. WEAVER-ZERCHER is Associate Professor of American Religious History and Chair of the Department of Biblical and Religious Studies at Messiah College, Grantham, Pennsylvania. He has published articles in *Church History* and *Mennonite Quarterly Review*, and is editor of *Minding the Church: Scholarship in the Anabaptist Tradition* (2002). His book, *The Amish in the American Imagination* (2001), explores popular conceptions of the Amish in twentieth-century America.

Index

Unless otherwise noted, all places are in Pennsylvania and all publications are by John A. Hostetler. Page numbers in *italics* refer to illustrations.